TRAVELS IN CENTRAL ASIA

BY ARMINIUS VÁMBÉRY

PREFACE.

I was born in Hungary in 1832, in the small town of Duna Szerdahely, situated on one of the largest islands in the Danube. Impelled by a particular inclination to linguistic science, I had in early youth occupied myself with several languages of Europe and Asia. The various stores of Oriental and Western literature were in the first instance the object of my eager study. At a later period I began to interest myself in the reciprocal relations of the languages themselves; and here it is not surprising if I, in applying the proverb 'nosce teipsum,' directed my principal attention to the affinities and to the origin of my own mother-tongue.

That the Hungarian language belongs to the stock called Altaic is well known, but whether it is to be referred to the Finnish or the Tartaric branch is a question that still awaits decision. This enquiry, interesting [Footnote 1] to us Hungarians both in a scientific and {viii} a national point of view, was the principal and the moving cause of my journey to the East. I was desirous of ascertaining, by the practical study of the living languages, the positive degree of affinity which had at once struck me as existing between the Hungarian and the Turco-Tartaric dialects when contemplating them by the feeble light which theory supplied. I went first to Constantinople. Several years' residence in Turkish houses, and frequent visits to Islamite schools and libraries, soon transformed me into a Turk--nay, into an Efendi. The progress of my linguistic researches impelled me further towards the remote East; and when I proposed to carry out my views by actually undertaking a journey to Central Asia, I found it advisable to retain this character of Efendi, and to visit the East as an Oriental.

[Footnote 1: The opinion consequently that we Hungarians go to Asia to seek there those of our race who were left behind, is erroneous. Such an object, the carrying out of which, both from ethnographical as well as philological reasons, would be an impossibility, would render a man amenable to the charge of gross ignorance. We are desirous of knowing the etymological construction of our language, and therefore seek exact information from cognate idioms.]

The foregoing observations will explain the object which I proposed to myself in my wanderings from the Bosphorus to Samarcand. Geological or astronomical researches were out of my province, and had even become an impossibility from my assumption of the character of a Dervish. My attention was for the most part directed to the races inhabiting Central Asia, of whose social and political relations, character, usages, and customs I have striven, however imperfectly, to give a sketch in the following {ix} pages. Although, as far as circumstances and my previous avocations permitted, I allowed nothing that concerned geography and statistics to escape me, still I must regard the results of my philological researches as the principal fruits of my journey. These I am desirous, after maturer preparation, to lay before the scientific world. These researches, and not the facts recorded in the present pages, must ever be regarded by me as the real reward of a journey in which I wandered about for months and months with only a few rags as my covering, without necessary food, and in constant peril of perishing by a death of cruelty, if not of torture. I may be reproached with too much limiting my views, but where a certain object is proposed we should not lose sight of the principle, 'non omnia possumus omnes.'

A stranger on the field to which the publication of this narrative has introduced me, I feel my task doubly difficult in a land like England, where literature is so rich in books of travels. My design was to record plainly and simply what I heard and saw, whilst the impression still remained fresh on my mind. I doubt much whether I have succeeded, and beg the kind indulgence of the public. Readers and critics may find many errors, and the light that I may throw upon particular points may be accounted too small a compensation for the hardships I actually encountered; but I entreat them not to forget that I return from a country where to hear is regarded as impudence, to ask as crime, and to take notes as a deadly sin. {x}

So much for the grounds and purposes of my journey. With respect to the arrangement of these pages, in order that there may be no interruption, I have divided the book into two parts; the first containing the description of my journey from Teheran to Samarcand and back, the second devoted to notices concerning the geography, statistics, politics, and social relations of Central Asia. I hope that both will prove of equal interest to the reader; for whilst on the one hand I pursued routes hitherto untrodden by any European, my notices relate to subjects hitherto scarcely, if at all, touched on by writers upon Central Asia. And now let me perform the more pleasing task of expressing my warm acknowledgments to all those whose kind reception of me when I arrived in London has been a great furtherance and encouragement to the publication of the following narrative. Before all let me mention the names of SIR JUSTIN and LADY SHEIL. In their house I found English open-heartedness associated with Oriental hospitality; their kindness will never be forgotten by me. Nor are my obligations less to the Nestor of geological science, the President of the Royal Geographical Society, SIR RODERICK MURCHISON; to that great Oriental scholar, VISCOUNT STRANGFORD; and to MR. LAYARD, M.P., Under-Secretary of State. In Central Asia I bestowed blessing for kindness received; here I have but words, they are sincere and come from the heart.

A. VÁMBÉRY.

London: September 28, 1864.

Je marchais, et mes compagnons flottaient comme des branches par l'effet du sommeil.--Victor Hugo, from Omaïah ben Aiëdz.

[Travelling in Persia]

Whoever has travelled through Persia in the middle of July will sympathise with me when I say how glad I felt at having got through the district that extends from Tabris to Teheran. It is a distance of only fifteen, or perhaps we may rather say of only thirteen karavan stations: still, it is fearfully fatiguing, when circumstances compel one to toil slowly from station to station under a scorching sun, mounted upon a laden mule, and condemned to see nothing but such drought and barrenness as characterise almost the whole of Persia. How bitter the disappointment to him who has studied Persia only in Saadi, Khakani, and Hafiz; {2} or, still worse, who has received his dreamy impressions of the East from the beautiful imaginings of Goethe's 'Ost-Westlicher Divan,' or Victor Hugo's 'Orientales,' or the magnificent picturings of Tom Moore!

[Sleep on Horseback; Teheran]

It was not until we were about two stations from Teheran, that the idea struck our Djilodar [Footnote 2] to change our march by day into night marches. But even this expedient had its inconveniences: for the coolness of the night in Persia is a great disposer to slumber; the slow pace of the animals has a composing effect, and one must really firmly cling to them, or sometimes even suffer oneself to be bound on by cords, to avoid being precipitated during one's sleep down upon the sharp flint stones below. The Oriental, habituated to this constant torment, sleeps sweetly enough, whatever may be the kind of saddle, whether it be upon horse, camel, mule, or ass; and it gave me many a moment of merry enjoyment, as I contemplated the tall, lanky, long-robed Persians, lying outstretched with their feet nearly touching the ground, and their heads supported upon the necks of the patient beasts. In this position the Persians take their nap quite tranquilly, whilst they unconsciously pass many stations. But, at that time, Necessity, the mother of invention, had not yet imparted to me the necessary experience; and whilst the greater part of my travelling companions near me, in spite of their soft slumbers, were still riding on, I was left undisturbed to the studious contemplation of the Kervankusch and Pervins (Pleïades); and I looked with inexpressible longing to that quarter where the Suheil (Canopus){3} and the Sitarei Subh (morning star) emerging, should announce the dawn of day, the proximity of the station, and the end of our torments. What wonder that I was somewhat in the condition of a half-boiled fish, when on the 13th July, 1862, I approached the capital of Persia? We stopped at a distance of a couple of English miles on the banks of a stream, to let our beasts drink. The halt awakened my companions, who, still sleepily rubbing their eyes, pointed out to me how Teheran was there lying before us to the north-east. I looked about me, and perceived in that direction a blue smoke rising and lengthening in long columns upwards, permitting me, however, here and there to distinguish the outline of a glittering dome, till at last, the vaporous veil having gradually disappeared, I had the enjoyment, as Persians express themselves, of beholding before me, in all her naked wretchedness, the Darül Khilafe, or Seat of Sovereignty.

[Footnote 2: The same as Kervanbashi; one who hires the camels, mules, asses, etc.]

I made my entry through the Dervaze (gate) No, and shall certainly not soon forget the obstacles amidst which I had to force my way. Asses, camels, and mules laden with barley straw, and bales of Persian or European merchandise, were all pressing on in the most fearful confusion, at the very entrance of the gate. Drawing up my legs under me upon the saddle, and screaming out as lustily as my neighbours, 'Khaberdar, Khaberdar' (Take care), I at last succeeded in getting into the city, though with no little trouble. I traversed the bazaar, and finally reached the palace of the Turkish Embassy, without having received any serious wound either by squeeze, blow, or cut.

{4}

[Reception at the Turkish Embassy]

A native of Hungary, sent by the Hungarian Academy upon a scientific mission to Central Asia, what had I to do at the Turkish Embassy? This will appear from the Preface, to which I respectfully request my readers' attention, in spite of the prejudice condemning such introductions as tiresome and unnecessary.

With Haydar Efendi, who then represented the Porte at the Persian Court, I had been already acquainted at Constantinople. He had previously filled similar functions at St. Petersburg and at Paris. But, notwithstanding my being personally known to him, I was bearer also of letters from his most esteemed friends; and, counting upon the oft-proved hospitality of the Turks, I felt sure of meeting with a good reception. I consequently regarded the residence of the Turkish Embassy as my future abode; and as these gentlemen had resorted already to their yailar or summer seat at Djizer (eight English miles from Teheran), I only changed my clothes, and after indulging in a few hours' repose to atone for my recent sleepless nights, I mounted an ass, hired for an excursion into the country, and in two hours found myself in the presence of the Efendis, who, in a magnificent tent of silk, were just about to commence a dinner possessing in my eyes still superior magnificence and attraction.

My reception, both by the ambassador and the secretaries, was of the most friendly description: room was soon found for me at the table, and in a few moments we were in deep conversation, respecting Stamboul and her beautiful views, the Sultan and his mode of government. Ah! how refreshing in Teheran is the recollection of the Bosphorus!

{5}

[Turkey and Persia]

What wonder if, in the course of the conversation, frequent comparisons were instituted between the Persian and the Turkish manner of living?

If one too hastily gives way to first impressions, Iran, the theme of so much poetic enthusiasm, is, after all, nothing but a frightful waste; whereas Turkey is really an earthly paradise. I accord to the Persian all the politeness of manners, and all the readiness and vivacity of wit, that are wanting to the Osmanli; but in the latter the absence of these qualities is more than compensated by an integrity and an honourable frankness not possessed by his rival. The Persian can boast a poetic organisation and an ancient civilisation. The superiority of the Osmanli results from the attention he is paying to the languages of Europe, and his disposition gradually to acquaint himself with the progress that European savans have made in chemistry, physics, and history.

Our conversation was prolonged far into night. The following days were devoted to my presentation at the other European embassies. I found Count Gobineau, the Imperial ambassador, under a small tent in a garden like a caldron, where the heat was awful. Mr. Alison was more comfortably quartered in his garden at Gulahek, purchased for him by his Government. He was very friendly. I had often the opportunity, at his hospitable table, of studying the question why the English envoys everywhere distinguish themselves amongst their diplomatic brethren, by the comfortableness as well as the splendour of their establishments. In addition to the diplomatic corps of Europe, I found at that time at Teheran many officers, French or Italian; an Austrian officer, too, of the engineers, R. von Gasteiger; all of them in the service of the Shah, with liberal allowances. {6} These gentlemen, as I heard, were disposed to render themselves very serviceable, possessing all the requisite qualifications; but any benefit that might have resulted was entirely neutralised by the systematic want of system that existed in Persia, and by the low intrigues of the Persians.

[Ferrukh Khan's Visit to Europe]

The object of Ferrukh Khan's diplomatic journeys in Europe was in reality to show our cabinets how much Iran had it at heart to obtain admittance into the comity of States. He begged aid everywhere, that his country might have the wondrous elixir of civilisation imparted to it as rapidly as possible. All Europe thought that Persia was really upon the point of adopting every European custom and principle. As Ferrukh Khan has a long beard, wears long robes and a high hat, which give him a very earnest look, our ministers were kind enough to attach to him unlimited credit. Wishing to honour a regular Government in Persia, troops of officers, artists, and artisans flocked to him. They went still further, and hastened to return the visits of the Envoy Extraordinary of the Shah. In consequence we saw Belgium, at no small expense, forwarding an ambassador to Persia to study commercial relations, to make treaties of commerce, and to give effect to numberless other strokes of policy. He arrived, and I can scarcely imagine that his first report home could have begun with 'Veni, vidi, vici,' or that he could have felt the slightest desire to pay a second visit to 'la belle Perse.' Next to Belgium came Prussia. The learned diplomatist Baron von Minutoli, to whom the mission was entrusted, devoted his life to it. His thirst after science impelled him to proceed to South Persia; and at only two days' journey from 'heavenly Shiraz,' as the Persians call it, he fell a sacrifice to the pestilential air, and now {7} reposes in the place last mentioned, a few paces from Hafiz, and behind the Baghi Takht.

A few days after I came, the embassy of the new kingdom of Italy arrived also, consisting of twenty persons, divided into diplomatic, military, and scientific sections. The object they had in view has remained always a mystery to me. I have much to recount respecting their reception, but prefer to keep these details for a better occasion, and to busy myself more especially with the preparations I then made for my own journey.

[War between Dost Mohammed Khan and Sultan Ahmed Khan; Excursion to Shiraz]

By the kind offices of my friends at the Turkish Embassy, I was in a condition very little suited to the character of a mendicant Dervish which I was about to assume: the comforts I was enjoying were heartily distasteful to me, and I should have preferred, after my ten days' repose at Teheran, to proceed at once to Meshed and Herat, had not obstacles, long dreaded, interfered with my design. Even before the date of my leaving Constantinople, I had heard, by the daily press, of the war declared by Dost Mohammed Khan against his son-in-law and former vassal at Herat, Sultan Ahmed Khan, because the latter had broken his fealty to him, and had placed himself under the suzerainty of the Shah of Persia. Our European papers seemed to me to exaggerate the whole matter, and the story failed to excite in me the apprehensions it really ought to have done. I regarded the difficulties as unreal, and began my journey. Nevertheless, here in Teheran, at a distance of only thirty-two days' journey from the seat of war, I learnt from undeniable sources, to my very great regret, that the war in those parts had really broken off all communications, and that since the siege had begun, no karavan, still less any solitary {8} traveller, could pass either from or to Herat. Persians themselves dared not venture their wares or their lives; but there would have been far more cause for apprehension in the case of a European whose foreign lineaments would, in those savage Asiatic districts, even in periods of peace, be regarded by an Oriental with mistrust, and must singularly displease him in time of war. The chances, indeed, seemed to be, if I ventured thither, that I should be unceremoniously massacred by the Afghans. I began to realise my actual position, and convinced myself of the impossibility, for the moment, of prosecuting my journey under such circumstances; and in order not to reach, during the wintry season, Bokhara, in the wastes of Central Asia, I immediately determined to postpone my journey till next March, when I should have the finest season of the year before me; and, perhaps, in the meantime the existing political relations, which barricaded Herat, the gate of Central Asia, from all approach, might have ceased. It was not till the beginning of September that I became reconciled to this necessity. It will be readily understood how unpleasant it was for me to have to spend five or six months in a country possessing for me only secondary interest, and respecting which so many excellent accounts have already appeared. Not, then, with any serious intention of studying Persia, but rather to withdraw myself from a state of inactivity calculated to be prejudicial to my future purposes, I quitted, in a semi-dervish character, my hospitable Turkish friends, and proceeded at once by Ispahan to Shiraz, and so obtained the enjoyment of visiting the oft-described monuments of ancient Iran civilisation.

{9}

CHAPTER II.

RETURN TO TEHERAN

RELIEF OF SUNNITES, DERVISHES, AND HADJIS AT THE TURKISH EMBASSY

AUTHOR BECOMES ACQUAINTED WITH A KARAVAN OF TARTAR HADJIS RETURNING FROM MECCA

THE DIFFERENT ROUTES

THE AUTHOR DETERMINES TO JOIN THE HADJIS

HADJI BILAL

INTRODUCTION OF AUTHOR TO HIS FUTURE TRAVELLING COMPANIONS

ROUTE THROUGH THE YOMUTS AND THE GREAT DESERT DECIDED UPON.

The Parthians held it as a maxim to accord no passage over their territory to any stranger.--Heeren, **Manual of Ancient History**.

[Return to Teheran; Relief of Sunnites, Dervishes, and Hadjis at the Turkish Embassy]

Towards the middle of January 1863, I found myself back in Teheran, and again sharing the hospitality of my Turkish benefactors. A change came over me; my hesitation was at an end, my decision was made, my preparations hastened. I resolved, even at the greatest sacrifice, to carry out my design. It is an old custom of the Turkish Embassy to accord a small subsidy to the Hadjis and Dervishes, who every year are in the habit of passing in considerable numbers through Persia towards the Turkish Empire. This is a real act of benevolence for the poor Sunnitish mendicants in Persia, who do not obtain a farthing from the Shiitish Persians. The consequence was, that the Hotel of the Embassy received guests from the most remote parts of Turkestan. I felt the greatest pleasure whenever I saw these ragged wild Tartars enter my apartment. They had it in their power to give {10} much real information respecting their country, and their conversations were of extreme importance for my philological studies. They, on their part, were astonished at my affability, having naturally no idea of the objects which I had in view. The report was soon circulated in the karavanserai, to which they resorted in their passage through, that Haydar Efendi, the ambassador of the Sultan, has a generous heart; that Reshid Efendi (this was the name I had assumed) treats the Dervishes as his brethren; that he is probably himself a Dervish in disguise. As people entertained those notions, it was no matter of surprise to me that the Dervishes who reached Teheran came first to me, and then to the minister; for access to the latter was not always attainable, and now, through me, they found a ready means of obtaining their obolus, or the satisfaction of their other wishes.

It was thus that in the morning of the 20th March four Hadjis came to me with the request that I would present them to the Sultan's envoy, as they wished to prefer a complaint against the Persians who, on their return from Mecca, at Hamadan, had exacted from them the Sunni tribute--an exaction not only displeasing to the Shah of Persia, but long since forbidden by the Sultan. For here it must be remarked, that the good Tartars think that the whole world ought to obey the chief of their religion, the Sultan. [Footnote 3]

[Footnote 3: In the eyes of all the Sunnites, the lawful khalife (successor) of Mahomet is he who is in possession of the precious heritage, which comprises--1st, all the relics preserved in Stamboul, in the Hirkai Seadet, e.g. the cloak, beard, and teeth of the Prophet, lost by him in a combat; articles of clothing, Korans, and weapons which belonged to the first four khalifs, 2ndly, the possession of Mecca and Medina, Jerusalem, and other places of pilgrimage resorted to by the Islamite.]

{11}

[Author becomes acquainted with a Karavan of Tartar Hadjis returning from Mecca; The different Routes]

'We desire,' they say, 'from his excellency the ambassador, no money: we pray only, that for the future our Sunnitish brethren may visit the holy places without molestation.' Words so unselfish proceeding from the mouth of an Oriental much surprised me. I scrutinised the wild features of my guests, and must avow that, barbarous as they seemed, wretched as was their clothing, I was yet able to discover in them a something of nobility, and from the first moment was prepossessed in their favour. I had a long conversation with them, to inform myself more fully respecting their companions, and the route which they had selected to go to Mecca, and the one which they thought of taking after leaving Teheran. The spokesman of the party was, for the most part, a Hadji from Chinese Tartary (called also Little Bokhara), who had concealed his ragged dress under a new green Djubbe (over-dress), and wore on his head a colossal white turban, and, by his fiery glance and quick eye, showed his superiority over the whole body of his associates. After having represented himself as the Court Imam of the Vang (Chinese Governor) of Aksu (a province in Chinese Tartary), who had twice visited the Holy Sepulchre--hence being twofold a Hadji--he made me acquainted with his friend seated near him, and gave me to understand that the persons present were to be regarded as the chiefs of the small Hadji karavan, amounting to twenty-four in all. 'Our company,' said their orator, 'consists of young and old, rich and poor, men of piety, learned men and laity; still we live together with the greatest simplicity, since we are all from Khokand and Kashgar, and have amongst us no Bokhariot, no viper of that race.' The hostility of the Özbeg (Tartar) tribes of Central {12} Asia to the Tadjiks (the ancient Persian inhabitants) had been long previously known to me: I listened, therefore, without making any comment, and preferred informing myself of the plan of their journey onwards. 'From Teheran to our homes,' the Tartars explained, 'we have four roads: viz., first, by Astrakhan, Orenburg, and Bokhara; secondly, by Meshed, Herat, and Bokhara; thirdly, by Meshed, Merv, and Bokhara; fourthly, through the Turkoman wilderness, Khiva, and Bokhara. The first two are too costly, and the war at Herat is also a great obstacle; the last two, it is true, are very dangerous routes. We must, nevertheless, select one of these, and we wish, therefore, to ask your friendly counsel.'

[The Author determines to join the Hadjis]

We had now been nearly an hour in conversation. It was impossible not to like their frankness, and in spite of the singular lineaments marking their foreign origin, their wretched clothing, and the numerous traces left behind by their long and fatiguing journeys--all which lent a something forbidding to their appearance--I could not refrain from the thought. What if I journeyed with these pilgrims into Central Asia? As natives, they might prove my best Mentors: besides, they already know me as the Dervish Reshid Efendi, and have seen me playing that part at the Turkish Embassy, and are themselves on the best understanding with Bokhara, the only city in Central Asia that I really feared from having learnt the unhappy lot of the travellers who had preceded me thither. Without much hesitation, my resolution was formed. I knew I should be questioned as to the motives that actuated me in undertaking such a journey. I knew that to an Oriental 'pure sang' it was impossible to assign a scientific {13} object. They would have considered it ridiculous, perhaps even suspicious, for an Efendi--that is, for a gentleman with a mere abstract object in view--to expose himself to so many dangers and annoyances. The Oriental does not understand the thirst for knowledge, and does not believe much in its existence. It would have been the height of impolicy to shock these fanatical Musselmans in their ideas. The necessity of my position, therefore, obliged me to resort to a measure of policy, of deception, which I should otherwise have scrupled to adopt. It was at once flattering to my companions, and calculated to promote the design I had in view. I told them, for instance, that I had long silently, but earnestly, desired to visit Turkestan (Central Asia), not merely to see the only source of Islamite virtue that still remained undefiled, but to behold the saints of Khiva, Bokhara, and Samarcand. It was this idea, I assured them, that had brought me hither out of Roum (Turkey). I had now been waiting a year in Persia, and I thanked God for having at last granted me fellow-travellers, such as they were (and I here pointed to the Tartars), with whom I might proceed on my way and accomplish my wish.'

[Hadji Bilal]

When I had finished my speech, the good Tartars seemed really surprised, but they soon recovered from their amazement, and remarked that they were now perfectly certain of what they before only suspected, my being a Dervish. It gave them, they said, infinite pleasure that I should regard them as worthy of the friendship that the undertaking so distant and perilous a journey in their company implied. 'We are all ready not only to become your friends, but your servants,' said Hadji Bilal (such was the name of their {14} orator above mentioned); 'but we must still draw your attention to the fact that the routes in Turkestan are not as commodious nor as safe as those in Persia and in Turkey. On that which we shall take, travellers meet often for weeks with no house, no bread, not even a drop of water to drink; they incur, besides, the risk of being killed, or taken prisoners and sold, or of being buried alive under storms of sand. Ponder well, Efendi, the step! You may have occasion later to rue it, and we would by no means wish to be regarded as the cause of your misfortune. Before all things, you must not forget that our countrymen at home are far behind us in experience and worldly knowledge, and that, in spite of all their hospitality, they invariably regard strangers from afar with suspicion: and how, besides, will you be able without us and alone to perform that great return journey?' That these words produced a great impression it is easy to imagine, but they did not shake me in my purpose. I made light of the apprehensions of my friends, recounted to them how I had borne former fatigues, how I felt averse to all earthly comforts, and particularly to those Frankish articles of attire of which we would have to make a sacrifice. 'I know,' I said, 'that this world on earth resembles an hotel, [Footnote 4] in which we merely take up our quarters for a few days, and whence we soon move away to make room for others, and I laugh at the Musselmans of the present time who take heed not merely for the moment but for ten years of onward existence. Yes, dear friend, take me with you; I must hasten away from this horrid kingdom of Error, for I am too weary of it.'

[Footnote 4: Mihmankhanei pendjruzi, 'a five days' hostelry,' is the name employed by the philosophers of the East to signify this earthly abode.]

{15}
My entreaties prevailed; they could not resist me: I was consequently immediately chosen by the chiefs of the Dervish karavan as a fellow-traveller: we embraced and kissed. In performing this ceremony, I had, it is true, some feeling of aversion to struggle against. I did not like such close contact with those clothes and bodies impregnated with all kinds of odours. Still, my affair was settled. It only now remained for me to see my benefactor, Haydar Efendi, to communicate to him my intentions, ask him for his recommendation to the Hadjis, whom I proposed immediately to present to him.

I counted, of course, at first upon meeting with great opposition, and accordingly I was styled a lunatic who wanted to journey to a place from which few who had preceded me had returned; nor was I, they said, content with that, but I must take for my guides men who for the smallest coin would destroy me. Then they drew me the most terrifying pictures; but, seeing that all efforts to divert me from my plans were fruitless, they began to counsel me, and in earnest to consider how they could be of service in my enterprise. Haydar Efendi received the Hadjis, spoke to them of my design in the same style as I had used, and recommended me to their hospitality, with the remark that they might look for a return for any service rendered by them to an Efendi, a servant of the Sultan, now entrusted to their charge. At this interview I was not present, but I was informed that they promised the faithful performance of their engagement.

{16}
The reader will see how well my worthy friends kept their promise, and how the protection of the excellent Envoy of Turkey was the means of saving my life so often threatened, and that it was always the good faith of my pilgrim companions that rescued me from the most critical positions. In the course of conversation, I was told that Haydar Efendi, when Bokhara came under discussion, expressed his disapprobation of the policy of the Emir. [Footnote 5] He afterwards demanded the entire list of all the poor travellers, to whom he gave about fifteen ducats--a magnificent donation to these people, who sought no greater luxury in the world than bread and water.

[Footnote 5: Emir is a title given to the sovereign of Bokhara, whereas the princes of Khiva and Khokand are styled Khans.]

[Introduction of Author to his future Travelling Companions]

It was fixed that we should begin our journey a week later. In the interval, Hadji Bilal alone visited me, which he did very frequently, presenting to me his countrymen from Aksu Yarkend and Kashgar. They looked to me, indeed, rather like adventurers, dreadfully disfigured, than pious pilgrims. He expressed especial interest in his adopted son, Abdul Kadér, a bumpkin of the age of twenty-five years, whom he recommended to me as 'famulus.' 'He is,' said Hadji Bilal, 'a faithful fellow: although awkward, he may learn much from you; make use of him during your journey; he will bake bread and make tea for you, occupations that he very well understands.' Hadji Bilal's real object, however, was not merely that he should bake my bread, but help me to eat it; for he had with him a second adopted son on the journey, and the two, with appetites sharpened by their wanderings on foot, were too heavy a burthen upon the resources of my friend. I promised to accede to their request, and they were accordingly delighted. To {17} say the truth, the frequent visits of Hadji Bilal had made me a little suspicious: for I readily thought this man supposes that in me he has had a good catch, he takes a great deal of trouble to get me with him; he dreads my not carrying out my intentions. But no, I dare not, I will not think ill of him; and so to convince him of my unbounded confidence, I showed the little sum of money that I was taking with me for the expenses of the journey, and begged him to instruct me as to what mien, dress, and manners I ought to assume to make myself as much as possible like my travelling companions, in order that by doing so I might escape unceasing observation. This request of mine was very agreeable to him, and it is easy to conceive how singular a schooling I then received.

Before all things he counselled me to shave my head, and exchange my then Turkish-European costume for one of Bokhara; as far as possible to dispense with bedclothes, linen, and all such articles of luxury. I followed exactly his direction, and my equipment, being of a very modest nature, was very soon made; and three days before the appointed day I stood ready prepared for my great adventure.

In the meantime I went one day to the karavanserai, where my travelling companions were quartered, to return their visit. They occupied two little cells; in one were fourteen, in the other ten persons. They seemed to me done filled with filth and misery. That impression will never leave me. Few had adequate means to proceed with their journey, for the majority their beggar's staff was the sole resource. I found them engaged in an occupation of the toilette which I will not offend the reader by recording, although {18} the necessity of the case obliged me myself later to resort to it.

[Route through the Yomuts and the Great Desert decided upon.]

They gave me the heartiest reception, offered me green tea, and I had to go through the torture of drinking without sugar a large Bokhariot bowl of the greenish water. Worse still, they wished to insist upon my swallowing a second; but I begged to be excused. I was now permitted even to embrace my new associates; by each I was saluted as a brother; and after having broken bread with them individually, we sat down in a circle in order to take counsel as to the route to be chosen. As I before remarked, we had the choice between two; both perilous, and traversing the desert home of the Turkomans, the only difference being that of the tribes through which they pass. The way by Meshed, Merv, and Bokhara was the shortest, but would entail the necessity of proceeding through the midst of the Tekke tribes, the most savage of all the Turkomans, who spare no man, and who would not hesitate to sell into slavery the Prophet himself, did he fall into their hands. On the other route are the Yomut Turkomans, an honest, hospitable people. Still that would necessitate a passage of forty stations through the desert, without a single spring of sweet drinking water. After some observations had been made, the route through the Yomuts, the Great Desert, Khiva, and Bokhara was selected. 'It is better, my friends, to battle against the wickedness of the elements than against that of men. God is gracious, we are on His way; He will certainly not abandon us.' To seal their determination, Hadji Bilal invoked a blessing, and whilst he was speaking we all raised our hands in the air, and when he came to an end every one seized his beard and said aloud, 'Amen!' We rose from {19} our seats, and they told me to make my appearance there two days after, early in the morning, to take our departure together. I returned home, and during these two days I had a severe and a violent struggle with myself. I thought of the dangers that encircled my way, of the fruits that my travels might produce. I sought to probe the motives that actuated me, and to judge whether they justified my daring; but I was like one bewitched and incapable of reflection. In vain did men try to persuade me that the mask they bore alone prevented me from perceiving the real depravity of my new associates; in vain did they seek to deter me by the unfortunate fate of Conolly, Stoddart, and Moorcroft, with the more recent mishaps of Blôcqueville, who fell into the hands of the Turkomans, and who was only redeemed from slavery by the payment of 10,000 ducats: their cases I only regarded as accidental, and they inspired me with little apprehension. I had only one misgiving, whether I had enough physical strength to endure the hardships arising from the elements, unaccustomed food, bad clothing, without the shelter of a roof, and without any change of attire by night; and how then should I with my lameness be able to journey on foot, I, who was liable to be tired so soon? and here for me was the chief hazard and risk of my adventure. Need I say which side in this mental struggle gained the victory?

The evening previous I bade adieu to my friends at the Turkish Embassy; the secret of the journey was entrusted but to two; and whereas the European residents believed I was going to Meshed, I left Teheran to continue my course in the direction of Astrabad and the Caspian Sea.

{20}

CHAPTER III.

DEPARTURE FROM TEHERAN IN NORTH-EASTERLY DIRECTION

THE COMPONENT MEMBERS OF KARAVAN DESCRIBED

ILL-FEELING OF SHIITES TOWARDS THE SUNNITISH HADJIS

MAZENDRAN

ZIRAB

HEFTEN

TIGERS AND JACKALS

SARI

KARATEPE.

Beyond the Caspian's iron gates. --Moore.

[Departure from Teheran in North-easterly Direction]

On the morning of the 28th March, 1863, at an early hour, I proceeded to our appointed rendezvous, the karavanserai. Those of my friends whose means permitted them to hire a mule or an ass as far as the Persian frontiers were ready booted and spurred for their journey; those who had to toil forwards on foot had on already their jaruk (a covering for the feet appropriate for infantry), and seemed, with their date-wood staves in their hands, to await with great impatience the signal for departure. To my great amazement, I saw that the wretched clothing which they wore at Teheran was really their city, that is, their best holiday costume. This they did not use on ordinary occasions; every one had now substituted his real travelling dress, consisting of a thousand rags fastened round the loins by a cord. Yesterday I regarded myself in my clothing as a beggar; to-day, in the midst of them, I was a king in his royal robes. At last Hadji Bilal raised his hand for the parting benediction; {21} and hardly had every one seized his beard to say 'Amen,' when the pedestrians rushed out of the gate, hastening with rapid strides to get the start of us who were mounted. Our march was directed towards the north-east from Teheran to Sari, which we were to reach in eight stations. We turned therefore towards Djadjerud and Firuzkuh, leaving Taushantepe, the little hunting-seat of the king, on our left; and were, in an hour, at the entrance of the mountainous pass where one loses sight of the plain and city of Teheran. By an irresistible impulse I turned round. The sun was already, to use an Oriental expression, a lance high; and its beams illuminated, not Teheran alone, but the distant gilded dome of Shah Abdul Azim. At this season of the year, Nature in Teheran already assumes all her green luxuriance; and I must confess that the city, which the year before had made so disagreeable an impression upon me, appeared to me now dazzlingly beautiful. This glance of mine was an adieu to the last outpost of European civilisation. I had now to confront the extremes of savageness and barbarism. I felt deeply moved; and that my companions might not remark my emotion, I turned my horse aside into the mountainous defile.

In the meantime my companions were beginning to recite aloud passages from the Koran, and to chant telkins (hymns), as is seemly for genuine pilgrims to do. They excused me from taking part in these, as they knew that the Roumis (Osmanli) were not so strictly and religiously educated as the people in Turkestan; and they besides hoped that I should receive the necessary inspiration by contact with their society. I followed them at a slow pace, and will {22} now endeavour to give a description of them, for the double motive that we are to travel so long together and that they are in reality the most honest people I shall ever meet with in those parts. There were, then,

[The Component Members of Karavan described]

1. *Hadji Bilal*, from Aksu (Chinese Tartary), and Court Iman of the Chinese Musselman Governor of the same province: with him were his adopted sons,

2. *Hadji Isa*, a lad in his sixteenth year; and

3. *Hadji Abdul Kader*, before mentioned, in the company, and so to say under the protection, of Hadji Bilal. There were besides,

4. *Hadji Yusuf*, a rich Chinese Tartar peasant; with his nephew,

5. *Hadji Ali*, a lad in his tenth year, with little, diminutive, Kirghish eyes. The last two had eighty ducats for their travelling expenses, and, therefore, were styled rich; still this was kept a secret: they hired a horse for joint use, and when one was riding the other walked.

6. *Hadji Amed*, a poor Mollah, who performed his pilgrimage leaning upon his beggar's staff. Similar in character and position was

7. *Hadji Hasan*, whose father had died on the journey, and who was returning home an orphan;

8. *Hadji Yakoub*, a mendicant by profession, a profession inherited by him from his father;

9. *Hadji Kurban* (senior), a peasant by birth, who as a knife-grinder had traversed the whole of Asia, had been as far as Constantinople and Mecca, had visited upon occasions Thibet and Calcutta, and twice the Kirghish Steppes, to Orenburg and Taganrok;

9

10. ***Hadji Kurban***, who also had lost his father and brother on the journey;
{23}
11. ***Hadji Said***; and
12. ***Hadji Abdur Rahman***, an infirm lad of the age of fourteen years, whose feet were badly frozen in the snow of Hamadan, and who suffered fearfully the whole way to Samarcand.

The above-named pilgrims were from Khokand, Yarkend, and Aksu, two adjacent districts; consequently they were Chinese Tartars, belonging to the suite of Hadji Bilal, who was besides upon friendly terms with

13. ***Hadji Sheikh Sultan Mahmoud*** from Kashgar, a young enthusiastic Tartar, belonging to the family of a renowned saint, Hazreti Afak, whose tomb is in Kashgar. The father of my friend Sheikh Sultan Mahmoud was a poet; Mecca was in imagination his child: after the sufferings of long years he reached the holy city, where he died. His son had consequently a double object in his pilgrimage: he proceeded as pilgrim alike to the tombs of his prophet and his father. With him were

14. ***Hadji Husein***, his relative; and
15. ***Hadji Ahmed***, formerly a Chinese soldier belonging to the regiment Shiiva that bears muskets and consists of Musselmans.

From the Khanat Khokand were

16. ***Hadji Salih Khalifed***, candidate for the Ishan, which signifies the title of Sheikh, consequently belonging to a semi-religious order; an excellent man of whom we shall have often occasion to speak. He was attended by his son,

17. ***Hadji Abdul Baki***, and his brother
18. ***Hadji Abdul Kader*** the ***Medjzub***, which means, 'impelled by the love of God,' and who, whenever he has shouted two thousand times 'Allah,' foams at the mouth and falls into a state of ecstatic blessedness (Europeans name this state epilepsy).

{24}
19. ***Hadji Kari Messud*** (Kari has the same signification in Turkey as Hafiz, one who knows the whole Koran by heart). He was with his son,

20. ***Hadji Gayaseddin***;
21. ***Hadji Mirza Ali***; and
22. ***Hadji Ahrarkuli***; the bags of the two last-named pilgrims still contained some of their travelling provision in money, and they had a beast hired between them.

23. ***Hadji Nur Mohammed***, a merchant who had been twice to Mecca; but not on his own account, only as representing another.

[Ill-feeling of Shiites towards the Sunnite Hadjis]

We advanced up the slopes of the chain of the Elburs mountains, which rose higher and higher. The depression of spirits in which I was, was remarked by my friends, who did all in their power to comfort me. It was, however, particularly Hadji Salih who encouraged me with the assurance that 'they would all feel for me the love of brothers, and the hope that, by the aid of God, we should soon be at liberty beyond the limits of the Shiite heretics, and be able to live comfortably in lands subject to the Sunnite Turkomans, who are followers of the same faith.' A pleasant prospect certainly, thought I; and I rode more quickly on in order to mix with the poor travellers who were preceding us on foot. Half an hour later I came up with them. I noticed how cheerfully they wended their way; men who had journeyed on foot from the remotest Turkestan to Mecca, and back again on foot. Whilst many were singing merry songs, which had great resemblance to those of Hungary, others were recounting the adventures they had gone through in the course of their wanderings; a conversation which occasioned {25} me great pleasure, as it served to make me acquainted with the modes of thought of those distant tribes, so that at the very moment of my departure from Teheran I found myself, so to say, in the midst of Central Asiatic life.

During the daytime it was tolerably warm, but it froze hard in the early morning hours, particularly in the mountainous districts. I could not support the cold in my thin clothing on horseback, so I was forced to dismount to warm myself. I handed my horse over to one of the pedestrian pilgrims. He gave me his stick in exchange, and so I accompanied them a long way on foot, hearing the most animated descriptions of their homes; and when their enthusiasm had been sufficiently stimulated by reminiscences of the gardens of Mergolan, Namengan, and Khokand, they all began with one accord to sing a telkin (hymn), in which I myself took part by screaming out as loud as I was able, 'Allah, ya Allah!'

Every such approximation to their sentiments and actions on my part was recounted by the young travellers to the older pilgrims, to the great delight of the latter, who never ceased repeating 'Hadji Reshid (my name amongst my companions) is a genuine Dervish; one can make anything out of him.'

[Mazendran]

After a rather long day's march, on the fourth day we reached Firuzkuh, which lies rather high, and is approached by a very bad road. The city is at the foot of a mountain, which is crowned by an ancient fortification, now in ruins; a city of some importance from the fact that there the province Arak Adjemi ends, and Mazendran begins. The next morning our way passed in quite a northerly direction, and we had scarcely proceeded three or four hours when we {26} reached the mouth of the great defile, properly called Mazendran, which extends as far as the shores of the Caspian. Scarcely does the traveller move a few steps forwards from the karavanserai on the top of the mountain, when the bare dry district changes, as by enchantment, into a country of extraordinary richness and luxuriance. One forgets that one is in Persia, on seeing around everywhere the splendour of those primaeval forests and that magnificent green. But why linger over Mazendran and all its beauties, rendered so familiar to us by the masterly sketches of Frazer, Conolly, and Burnes?

On our passage Mazendran was in its gala attire of spring. Its witchery made the last spark of trouble disappear from my thoughts. I reflected no more on the perils of my undertaking, but allowed imagination to dwell only upon sweet dreams of the regions through which lay my onward path, visions of the various races of men, customs, and usages which I was now to see. I must expect to behold, it is true, scenes a perfect contrast to these; I must anticipate immense and fearful deserts--plains whose limits are not distinguishable to the human eye, and where I should have for days long to suffer from want of water. The enjoyment of that spot was doubly agreeable, as I was so soon to bid adieu to all sylvan scenes.

Mazendran had its charms even for my companions. Their feelings found expression in regrets that this lovely Djennet (paradise) should have become the possession of the heretical Shiites. 'How singular,' said Hadji Bilal, 'that all the beautiful spots in nature should have fallen into the hands of the unbelievers! The Prophet had reason to say, "This world is the prison of the believers, and the paradise of the unbelievers."' [Footnote 6]

[Footnote 6: 'Ed dünya sidjn ül mumenin, ve djennet ül kafirin.']

{27}

In proof, he cited Hindoostan, where the 'Inghiliz' reign, the beauties of Russia which he had seen, and Frenghistan, that had been described to him as an earthly paradise. Hadji Sultan sought to console the company by a reference to the mountainous districts that lie between Oosh (boundaries of Khokand) and Kashgar. He represented that place to me as far more lovely than Mazendran, but I can hardly believe it.

[Zirab; Heften; Tigers and Jackals]

At the station Zirab we came to the northern extremity of the mountainous pass of Mazendran. Here the immense woods begin, which mark the limits of the shore of the Caspian Sea. We pass along a causeway made by Shah Abbas, but which is fast decaying. Our night quarters--we reached them betimes--was Heften, in the middle of a beautiful forest of boxwood. Our young people started off in quest of a good spring of water for our tea; but all at once we heard a fearful cry of distress. They came flying back, and recounted to us that they had seen animals at the source, which sprang away with long bounds when they approached them. At first I thought they must be lions, and I seized a rusty sword, and found, in the direction they had described, but at a good distance off, two splendid tigers, whose beautifully-striped forms made themselves visible occasionally from the thickets. In this forest the peasants told me that there were numbers of wild beasts, but they very rarely attacked human beings. At all events, we were not molested by the jackals, who even dread a stick, but which are here so numerous that we cannot drive them away. There are jackals throughout {28} all Persia; they are not uncommon even in Teheran, where their howling is heard in the evenings. But still, they did not there approach men, as they did here. They disturbed me the whole night long. I was obliged, in self-defence, to use both hands and feet to prevent their making off with bread-sack or a shoe.

[Sari]

The next day we had to reach Sari, the capital of Mazendran. Not far from the wayside lies Sheikh Tabersi, a place long defended by the Babis (religious enthusiasts who denied Mohammed and preached socialism). They made themselves the terror of the neighbourhood. Here also are beautiful gardens, producing in exuberance crops of oranges and lemons. Their fruit, tinted with yellow and red, presented an enchanting contrast with the green of the trees. Sari itself has no beauty to recommend it, but is said to carry on an important trade. As we traversed the bazaar of this last Persian city, we received also the last flood of every possible imprecation and abuse; nor did I leave their insolence without rebuke, although I judged it better not to repeat my threatening movements of stick or sword in the centre of a bazaar and amid hundreds of Shiites.

[Karatepe]

We only remained in Sari long enough to find horses to hire for a day's journey to the seashore. The road passes through many marshes and morasses. It is impossible to perform the journey here on foot. From this point there are many ways by which we can reach the shore of the Caspian, e. g. by Ferahabad (Parabad, as it is called by the Turkomans), Gez, and Karatepe. We preferred, however, the last route, because it would lead us to a Sunnite colony, where we were certain of a hospitable reception, having already had opportunities of becoming acquainted with many of these colonists at Sari, and having found them good people.

{29}

After a rest of two days in Sari we started for Karatepe. It was not until evening, after a laborious journey of nine hours, that we arrived. Here it is that the Turkomans first become objects of terror. Piratical hordes of them hide their vessels along the coast, whence extending their expeditions to a distance of a few leagues into the interior, they often return to the shore, dragging a Persian or so in bonds.

{30}

CHAPTER IV.

KAEATEPE

AUTHOR ENTERTAINED BY AN AFGHAN, NUR-ULLAH

SUSPICIONS AS TO HIS DERVISH CHARACTER

HADJIS PROVISION THEMSELVES FOR JOURNEY THROUGH DESERT

AFGHAN COLONY

NADIR SHAH

FIRST VIEW OF THE CASPIAN

YACOUB THE TURKOMAN BOATMAN

LOVE TALISMAN

EMBARKATION FOR ASHODRADA

VOYAGE ON THE CASPIAN

RUSSIAN PART OF ASHOURADA

RUSSIAN WAR STEAMERS IN THE CASPIAN

TURKOMAN CHIEF, IN THE SERVICE OF RUSSIA

APPREHENSION OF DISCOVERY ON THE AUTHOR'S PART

ARRIVAL AT GÖMÜSHTEPE AND AT THE MOUTH OF THE GORGHEN.

</p>

Ultra Caspium sinum quidnam esset, ambiguum aliquamcliu fuit. --Pomponius Mela, *De Situ Orbis*.

[Karatepe; Author entertained by an Afghan, Nur-Ullah]

Nur-Ullah, an Afghan of distinction, whose acquaintance I had already formed at Sari, conducted me to his house on my arrival at Karatepe; and as I objected to be separated from all my friends, he included Hadji Bilal also in his invitation, and did not rest until I had accepted his hospitality. At first I could not divine the motive of his extraordinary kindness, but I observed a little later that he had heard of the footing upon which I stood at the Turkish Embassy in Teheran, and he wished me to repay his kindness by a letter of recommendation, which I promised, and very willingly gave him before we parted.

{31}

[Suspicions as to his Dervish Character]

I had hardly taken possession of my new abode when the room filled with visitors, who squatted down in a row all round against the walls, first staring at me with their eyes wide open, then communicating to each other the results of their observations, and then uttering aloud their judgment upon the object of my travelling. 'A Dervish,' said the majority, 'he is not, his appearance is anything but that of a Dervish; for the wretchedness of his dress contrasts too plainly with his features and his complexion. As the Hadjis told us, he must be a relative of the ambassador, who represents our Sultan at Teheran,' and here all stood up. 'Allah only knows what a man who issues from so high an origin has to do amongst the Turkomans in Khiva and Bokhara.'

This impudence amazed me not a little. At the first glance they wanted to tear the mask from my face; in the meantime I was acting the genuine part of an Oriental, sat seemingly buried in thought, with the air of one who heard nothing. As I took no part in the conversation, they turned to Hadji Bilal, who told them I was really an Efendi, a functionary of the Sultan, but had withdrawn myself, in pursuance of a Divine inspiration, from the deceptions of the world, and was now engaged with Ziaret (a pilgrimage to the tombs of the saints); whereupon many shook their heads, nor could this subject any more be broached. The true Musselman must never express a doubt when he is told of Divine inspiration (Ilham); and however speaker or listener may be convinced that there is imposture, they are still bound to express their admiration by a 'Mashallah! Mashallah!' This first scene had, however, clearly unfolded to me that, although still on Persian soil, I had nevertheless at last gained the frontiers of Central Asia; for on hearing the distrustful enquiries of these few Sunnites-- enquiries never made in any part of Persia--I could {32} easily picture to myself the splendid future in store for me further on in the very nest of this people. It was not until two hours had elapsed, spent in chattering and questioning, that these visitors retired and we prepared tea, and then betook ourselves to repose. I was trying to sleep when a man in a Turkoman dress, whom I regarded as a member of the family, came near me, and began to tell me, in strict confidence, that he had travelled the last fifteen years on business matters to and from Khiva; that he was born at Khandahar; but that he had a perfect knowledge of the country of Özbeg and Bokhara; and then proposed that we should be friends, and make the journey together through the Great Desert. I replied, 'All believers are brethren,' [Footnote 7] and thanked him for his friendliness, with the observation that as a Dervish I was very much attached to my travelling companions. He seemed desirous to continue the conversation; but as I let him perceive how inclined I was to sleep, he left me to my slumbers.

[Footnote 7: 'Kulli mumenin ihvetun.']

[Hadjis provision themselves for Journey through Desert; Afghan Colony; Nadir Shah]

Next morning Nur-Ullah informed me that this man was a Tiryaki (opium-eater), a scapegrace, whom I should, as much as possible, avoid. At the same time he warned me that Karatepe was the only place for procuring our stock of flour for a journey of two months, as even the Turkomans themselves got their provisions in this place; and that at all events we must furnish ourselves with bread to last as far as Khiva. I left this to Hadji Bilal to manage for me, and ascended in the meantime the black hill which is situated in the village, and from which it derives its name, Karatepe. One side is peopled by Persians, {33} the other by 125 or 150 Afghan families. It is said that this Afghan colony was at the beginning of this century of far more importance than at present, and was founded by the last great conqueror of the Asiatic world, Nadir Shah, who, as is well known, accomplished his most heroic actions at the head of the Afghans and Turkomans. Here also was pointed out to me the spot on the hill where he sat when he passed in review the thousands of wild horsemen who flocked from the farthest recesses of the desert, with their good horses and thirsty swords, under his banners. On these occasions Nadir is described as always having been in a good humour; so Karatepe had its holidays. The precise object of the transplantation of this Sunnite colony is unknown to me, but its existence has been found to be of the greatest service, as the Afghans serve as negotiators between Turkomans and Persians, and without them many a Persian would languish for months in Turkoman bonds, without any medium existing by which his ransom could be effected. On the east of Persia similar services are rendered by the Sunnites of Khaf, Djam, and Bakhyrz, but these have to deal with the Tekke, a far more dangerous tribe than the Yomuts.

[First View of the Caspian; Yacoub the Turkoman Boatman; Love Talisman]
From the summit of the black hill I was able to gain a view of the Caspian Sea. It is not the main sea which is here visible, but rather that portion of it shut in by the tongue of land which ends at Ashourada: it is termed the Dead Sea. This tongue of land looks at a distance like a thin strip on the water, whence shoots up a single line of trees, which the eye can follow a long, long way. The sight of this, with its bleak solitary beach, was anything but inspiriting. I burnt with desire to behold its eastern shore, and I {34} hurried back to my abode to ascertain how far our preparations were in a forward state for my embarkation in quest of the Turkoman coast. Nur-Ullah had taken upon himself to make all necessary preparations. The evening before we had been told that for a kran (franc) per head we might be taken to Ashourada by an Afghan vessel employed in supplying the Russians with provisions, and that thence we might, with the aid of Turkomans, reach Gömüshtepe in a few hours. 'In Ashourada itself,' they said, 'there is Khidr Khan, a Turkoman chieftain in the service of Russia, who gives assistance to poor Hadjis, and whom we may also visit.' We were all delighted to learn this, and greeted the intelligence with acclamation. How great then was my astonishment when I learnt that this Afghan was ready for the voyage, that he would allow the Hadjis to accompany him, but that he objected to my highness, whom he regarded as a secret emissary of the sultan; fearing lest he might lose his means of subsistence from the Russians should he venture to take such an individual on board his vessel. His resolution surprised me not a little. I was glad to hear my companions declare that if he did not take me they would not go, but would prefer to wait another occasion. So I heard, in an accent of peculiar emphasis, from the opium-smoker, Emir Mehemmed. Later, however, came the Afghan himself (his name was Anakhan), expressing his regret, promising secresy, and begging me to give him a letter of recommendation to Haydar Efendi. I considered it good policy not to say a syllable calculated to quiet his apprehensions, laughed heartily at his ideas, and promised to leave for him with Nur-Ullah some lines for Teheran, a promise {35} which I did not forget. I felt it quite necessary to leave my real character enveloped in a veil of doubt or mystery. The Oriental, and particularly the Islamite, bred up in lies and treachery, always believes the very contrary of what a man shows particular earnestness in convincing him of, and the slightest protestation on my part would have served to confirm their suspicions. No further allusion was made to the subject, and that very evening we heard that a Turkoman who plies to Gömüshtepe was prepared, from feelings of mere piety, without remuneration, to take all the Hadjis with him; that we had but to station ourselves early in the morning on the seashore, to profit by a tolerably favourable wind. Hadji Bilal, Hadji Salih, and myself, the recognised triumvirate of the mendicant karavan, immediately paid a visit to the Turkoman, whose name was Yakoub; he was a young man, with an uncommonly bold look; he embraced each of us, and did not object to wait a day that we might complete our provisioning. He received beforehand his benediction from Hadji Bilal and Hadji Salih. We had already risen to go, when he called me aside, and tried to get me to tarry a few moments with him. I remained behind. He then, with a certain timidity, told me that he had long entertained an unhappy unreturned affection for a girl of his own race, and that a Jew, an accomplished magician, who for the moment was staying in Karatepe, had promised to prepare an efficacious Nuskha (talisman) if he would but procure thirty drops of attar of roses fresh from Mecca, as this could not be dispensed with in the formula.

'We know,' said Yakoub, 'that the Hadjis bring back with them out of the holy city essences of roses {36} and other sweet perfumes; and as you are the youngest of their chiefs, I apply to you, and hope you will listen to my entreaty.'

The superstition of this son of the desert did not so much astonish me as the trust he had reposed in the words of the cunning Israelite, and as my travelling friends had really brought with them such attar of roses his wish was soon gratified. The joy that he displayed was almost childish. The second day afterwards, early in the morning, we all assembled on the sea-shore, each furnished, besides his mendicant equipment, with a sack of flour. We lost considerable time before the boat (called Teïmil), which was formed out of a hollow tree, set us alongside the little vessel, or skiff, called by Turks 'mauna.' This, on account of the shallowness of the water near the

14

shore, was lying out at sea at a distance of about an English mile. Never shall I forget the mode in which we embarked. The small tree, in the hollow of which passengers were stowed away, together with flour and other effects, in the most diversified confusion, threatened each instant to go to the bottom. We had to bless our good fortune that we arrived on board all dry. The Turkomans have three kinds of vessels--

(1) Keseboy, furnished with a mast and two sails, one large and one small, principally for carrying cargoes;

(2) Kayuk, with a simple sail, generally used on their predatory expeditions; and

(3) The Teïmil, or skiff, already mentioned.

{37}

[Embarkation for Ashourada; Voyage on the Caspian]

The vessel provided for our use by Yakoub was a keseboy, that had conveyed a cargo of naphtha, pitch, and salt to the Persian coast from the island Tchereken, and was now homeward-bound with corn on board.

As the vessel had no deck, and consequently had no distinction of place, every one suited himself, and sat down where he wished as he entered. Yakoub, however, observing that this would disturb the trim and management of the vessel, we each seized our bundle and our provisions, and were closely packed in two rows near each other like salted herrings, so that the centre of the boat remained free for the crew to pass backwards and forwards. Our position then was none of the most agreeable. During the daytime it was supportable, but at night it was awful, when sleep threw the sitters from their perpendicular position to the right and left, and I was forced to submit for hours to the sweet burthen of a snoring Hadji. Frequently a sleeper on my right and another on my left fell one over the other upon me: I dared not wake them, for that would have been a heinous sin, to be atoned by never-ending suffering.

It was mid-day on the 10th April, 1863, when a favourable wind distended our sails, driving the little vessel before it like an arrow. On the left side we had the small tongue of land; on the right, thickly covered with wood, extending down to the very sea, stood the mountain upon which rose the Palace Eshref, built by Shah Abbas, the greatest of the Persian kings. The charm of our Argonautic expedition was augmented by the beautiful spring weather; and in spite of the small space within which I was pent up, I was in very good spirits. The thought might have suggested itself to me that I had to-day left the Persian coast; that at last I had reached a point from which there was no drawing back, and {38} where regrets were useless. But no! at that moment no such idea occurred to me. I was firmly convinced that my travelling friends, whose wild appearance had at first rendered them objects of alarm, were really faithful to me, and that under their guidance I might face the greatest dangers.

Towards evening there was a calm; we cast anchor near the shore, and were allowed in turn to make our tea on the little hearth of the vessel. Having stored away some pieces of sugar in my girdle, I invited Yakoub and honoured him with a bowl of tea. Hadji Salih and Sultan Mahmoud were of the party; the young Turkoman was the great talker, and began to recount stories of the Alaman (as the Turkomans name their marauding expeditions), a favourite topic with this people. His eye, always fiery, now vied with the stars of his own heaven, for his vein was stimulated by the desire to win golden opinions from the Sunnite Mollahs (we passed for such) by details of the conflicts in which he had engaged with the Shiite heretics, and of the numbers of the heretics that he had made prisoners. My friends soon began to slumber around me; still I did not tire of listening to him, and it was not until midnight that he thought of retiring. Before he withdrew he told me that Nur-Ullah had directed him to take me as a guest to the tent of Khandjan, a Turkoman chieftain; and he added that Nur-Ullah was right, for I was not like the rest of the Hadjis, and deserved better treatment. 'Khandjan,' said Yakoub, 'is the Aksakal (chief) of a mighty race, and even in the time of his father, no Dervish, Hadji, or other stranger ever dared to pass through Gömüshtepe without having tasted his bread and drunk his water. He will, as you come out of {39} foreign Roum (Turkey), certainly give you a good reception, and you will be grateful to me.'

[Russian War Steamers in the Caspian]

The following morning, the weather being unfavourable, we could only move slowly; it was already evening when we reached Ashourada, the most southerly point of the Russian possessions in Asia. It fell definitively into the hands of the Czar twenty-five years ago: perhaps it would be better to express ourselves thus, that it became subject to Russia from the time when, with their steamers, they began to strike the necessary degree of terror into the daring Alaman cruisers of the Turkoman pirates. The name Ashourada is of Turkoman origin; it was inhabited, but served them rather as a station for their then frequent and unchecked piratical expeditions. The Ashourada of the present day produces upon the traveller arriving from Persia an agreeable impression. Small, it is true, is the number of houses built at the east end of the tongue of land; but the European fashion of the buildings, as well as the church that the eye encounters, were not indifferent objects for me. The war steamers more particularly reminded me of European modes of existence; and I cannot say how inspiriting it was to see towards evening a steamer from Gez (a place that serves as the port for Astrabad) gliding proudly by. The Russians here maintain three war steamers (two large and one small), without the protection of which neither the Russian settlers nor the sailing vessels proceeding from Astrakhan would be safe from the attacks of the Turkomans. So long indeed as the merchantman remains out at sea, it has no cause for alarm; and it rarely ventures to approach the coast without being in the escort of a steamer, whose {40} protection is also necessary for the voyage back. The Russian Government makes, naturally, the greatest exertions, and at the greatest cost, to paralyse the predatory habits of the Turkomans. This plague has, in effect, somewhat diminished; still to establish security is an impossibility, and many unhappy Persians, and even occasionally Russian, sailors are hurried away in chains to Gömüshtepe. The Russian ships cruise incessantly day and night in the Turkoman waters; and every Turkoman vessel that is about to proceed from the east coast to the Persian shore on the south, must be provided with a pass, for which the owner has to pay yearly 8, 10, or 15 ducats. This pass is renewable at the end of each year, and must be exhibited every time the vessel passes Ashourada, when it is visited by the Russian functionaries to ascertain if it has on board prisoners, arms, or other contraband merchandise. The consequence of this salutary regulation is that a great part of the Turkoman merchant shipping has been overhauled and registered, and the rest mostly navigate in indirect courses, and if encountered by the Russian cruisers are taken, or, in case of resistance, sunk. Whilst thus on the one side steps of necessary vigour have been taken, on the other a policy has been adopted of establishing friendly relations with one tribe so as to make use of it against another.

[Turkoman Chief, in the Service of Russia]

At the time when I passed by Ashourada, Khidr Khan, sprung from the race of the Gazili Kör, had already borne the title of Derya bêghi (admiral) thirty years in the Russian service, and had a salary of about forty ducats per month, out of which he gave ten to his Mirza or writer. Khidr Khan still continued to live in a tent in the middle of the semi-European {41} colony; his functions consisted in using his influence with the Turkomans generally to prevent their piracies, or at least in conveying to the Russians intelligence of any intended expedition, for his clansmen, as eye-witnesses, were well able to perform the duty of spies. But this he could not effect. This Khidr Khan, though once so good a Musselman, had formed at an early date acquaintance with the generous vodki (Russian brandy): the consequence was that, day and night, he was intoxicated; and his sons, who were to be his successors, had come to an understanding with the Karaktchi (robbers), and were very careful not to give intelligence to the Russians of any projected marauding expedition.

[Apprehension of Discovery on the Author's part]

Our friend Yakoub was bound to produce his pass, and our little vessel could not proceed without having been first searched. As night had commenced when we neared Ashourada, we found that the visit of the authorities was postponed till an early hour in the morning. We cast anchor a short distance from land. My friends seemed greatly to regret their being prevented from waiting upon Khidr Khan, the ill-famed Maecenas of Dervishes and Hadjis. The circumstance was, however, to me a cause of unmingled satisfaction; for I could not have remained behind, and Khidr's experience in European countenances would have easily detected me; or, at all events, would have left me ill at ease. I was, however, somewhat disturbed by the reflection that, as an examination of the vessel must ensue in the morning, my European features, in strange contrast with those of my companions, and my complexion not yet brought to an Asiatic hue, might still play me false, and make the Russians alive to the real facts of the case. Far from {42} apprehending any inhumane treatment at their hands, my principal dread was their discovering me, and endeavouring to dissuade me from persisting in my adventure; and besides I feared still more that the affair might be noised abroad, and that the Turkomans might get wind of my incognito. I thought of how much more ransom I should have to pay than Blôcqueville, to rescue me from such cruel slavery! These ideas occasioned me the deepest anxiety, and I felt so troubled that I could not gaze with pleasure upon this last picture reflected from Western life.

Next morning I awoke in the greatest agitation; the sound of a bell was heard from Ashourada; my fellow-travellers said that this was Sunday, the holiday of the Unbelievers. I knew not which Sunday [Footnote 8] it was. We were close to a ship of war that had all its colours flying; suddenly we saw sailors in full uniform in a boat approach the shore with regular measured strokes of their oars; an officer in full dress then stepped in, and was soon taken on board the ship of war. Ten minutes had hardly elapsed when they called to us to approach, and I then saw on their deck near the gangway several fair-haired officers standing together. My heart began to beat violently; we approached nearer and nearer; all my effort now was to maintain such an attitude as might least attract attention, and avoid as far as possible the dreaded ***tête-à-tête***. As fortune willed, our vessel on approaching the Russians presented to it first that side upon which I was seated, so that the assembled officers were only able to see my neck.

[Footnote 8: During my journey I often lost sight of dates, and it was only later that I learned that this was Easter Sunday (Russian style).]

{43}

On account of the day, the examination was but slight and formal. The Dollmetsh exchanged a few words with Yakoub; our mendicant company fixed the attention of the officers. Amongst other things I heard one say, 'See how white this Hadji is.' [Footnote 9]

[Footnote 9: 'Smotrite kakoi bieloï etot Hadji.']

This allusion was probably made to me, whose complexion had not yet assumed the hue of uncivilised life. If so, it was the only observation they made upon me; for they had soon done with Yakoub, and in a moment we were far away from the side of the Russian vessel.

I now raised myself from my stooping and half-sleeping position, and took a long breath, for my anxiety was at an end. Soon afterwards the wind began to blow strongly from the west. Now was the time to get up our sails and make all haste for Gömüshtepe, which was but three leagues off; but Yakoub kept his eye fixed on a white point in the distance, and held a council with his crew: nor was it until this dreaded object had entirely vanished, that our large sail was unfurled, and we darted with the swiftness of an arrow towards the east.

At about half a league distance from Ashourada, we passed several sea-marks, consisting of long painted poles. I was told by Yakoub that they had been placed there by the 'Inghiliz.' to mark the limits of the Russian waters, the other side belonging to the Turkomans, whom the 'Inghiliz 'would always protect against the attack of the Russians. It was always a riddle to me to discover who had instilled into these wild sons of the desert such far-reaching ideas of policy. It is not for me to discriminate these {44} sea-marks; still less to weigh the amount of sympathy felt by England for the Turkomans.

[Arrival at Gömüshtepe and at the Mouth of the Gorghen.]

In less than an hour the Turkoman coast lay well defined before us, appearing as a long tract of land with elevated ground here and there. We followed the direction indicated by other craft which were running in before us: the sails were soon lowered, for we had reached the end of the navigable waters, and lay off about a mile and a half from the mouth of the Görghen. On both of its banks we saw the encampment of Gömüshtepe, in form like a hundred beehives lying close together.

As it had been at Karatepe, so was it also here, on account of the shallowness: even boats that draw little water cannot approach the shore, or run into the river Görghen, which is itself tolerably deep and never wants water. We were therefore obliged to wait at a considerable distance off shore until Yakoub should have disembarked, reported his arrival, and sent back to us several Teïmils to aid us in our disembarkation. After some delay, three of these very original transports came; they were to perform their little voyages as often as our numbers rendered it necessary, until all should be landed.

Hadji Bilal and I were the last to land, and I was really delighted when, on touching shore, I heard that Khandjan, informed of my arrival by my honest friend Yakoub, had hastened down to receive me. There I found him on landing, a few paces behind, in the attitude necessitated by the repetition of the afternoon prayer (Aszr-Namazi).

Reception by Turkoman Chief of the Caspian Shore.

{45}

CHAPTER V.

ARRIVAL AT GÖMÜSHTEPE, HOSPITABLE RECEPTION OF THE HADJIS

KHANDJAN

ANCIENT GREEK WALL

INFLUENCE OF THE ULEMAS

FIRST BRICK MOSQUE OF THE NOMADS

TARTAR RAIDS

PERSIAN SLAVES

EXCURSION TO THE NORTH-EAST OF GÖMÜSHTEPE

TARTAR FIANCÉE AND BANQUET, ETC.

PREPARATION OF THE KHAN OF KHIVA'S
KERVANBASHI FOR THE JOURNEY THROUGH THE DESERT

LINE OF CAMELS

ILIAS BEG, THE HIRER OF CAMELS

ARRANGEMENTS WITH KHULKHAN

TURKOMAN EXPEDITION TO STEAL HORSES IN PERSIA

ITS RETURN.

Ad introeuntium dextram Scythae nomades, freti litoribus, insident.-- Pompon. Mela,*De Situ Orbis*, 1. iii. c. v.

[Arrival at Gömüshtepe, hospitable Reception of the Hadjis; Khandjan]

After his prayer was ended, Khandjan arose, and as I perceived him standing before me, he was a handsome, tall, and slender man, about forty years of age, dressed in extremely modest attire, with a long beard descending to his breast. He at once approached me, hastily embraced, and gave me a hearty welcome; in doing so he greeted me by my name. He received the Hadjis Bilal and Salih in a similar manner; and after the karavan had stowed away their sacks, and was once more afoot, we closed the procession, all taking the road towards the tents. The report of our arrival had spread everywhere: our numbers were exaggerated: women, children, and dogs all hastened in strange confusion out of the tents, to gaze upon the approaching pilgrims, and by an embrace (as the {46}Mollahs pretend) to acquire, in obedience to the Divine command respecting pilgrimage, a participation in the merit and rewards of pilgrims. This first picture of Central Asiatic life had so taken me by surprise, that I was puzzled whether I should pause first to admire the singular construction of the tents, formed of felt, and the women with their silk shifts extending to the ankles, or at once gratify the wish implied by their outstretched hands and arms. Strange! young and old, without distinction of sex or family, all wished to touch the Hadjis on whom the holy dust of Mecca and Medina still rested. Judge, too, of my amazement when women of the greatest beauty, some girls even, hurried up to embrace me. We were tired, worn out by these demonstrations of respect arising from blended feelings of religion and hospitality, when we arrived before the tent of the chief Ishan (priest), where our little karavan was concentrated: then began one of the most interesting spectacles that my eyes have ever witnessed. Here were to begin the arrangements for quartering the guests that had just arrived. The passion and warmth with which all disputed the honour and right of harbouring one or more of these poor strangers astounded me. I had heard, it is true, the hospitality of the nomads spoken of, but never dreamed that it could have risen to such a point.

Khandjan quieted the quarrels which had commenced among the women; he restored order, and assigned the different guests to each, retaining as his own peculiar guests Hadji Bilal and myself, with all that belonged to us: he took us with him to his Ova (tent). [Footnote 10]

[Footnote 10: Ova, properly translated *tent*, is used here by the Turkomans to indicate a house and court.]

As he lived quite at the extremity of Gömüshtepe, we had to pass through the whole encampment, which extended on both banks of the Gorghen, [Footnote 11] and consisted of tents standing close together. It was near sunset when, quite worn out, we reached his dwelling, in the fond hope of being able at last to find some repose; but a sad disappointment awaited us. Our new abode consisted, it is true, of a separate tent, pitched two paces from the river; but we had hardly taken possession of it, with the customary ceremonials (twice performing its circuit and peeping in the four corners), when it was filled with visitors, who lingered till a late hour at night, and so wearied us by their thousands of questions, that even Hadji Bilal, the Oriental *par excellence*, began gradually to lose patience. In the evening supper was served by Baba Djan, [Footnote 12] the son of Khandjan, a lad twelve years old. It consisted of boiled fish and sour milk, and was served up in a large wooden dish. This, a Persian slave, heavily laden with chains, in the first instance brought near to us, when it was received by Baba Djan, who, after having set it before us, went and took his seat close to his father, at a little distance from us; and then both looked on with visible pleasure as they saw us attacking the provisions with the appetites of giants. Supper at an end, the prayer was said, Hadji Bilal raising his hands, in which gesture he was imitated by all present, as he was again when, in conclusion, after saying 'Bismillah, Allah Ekber,' every one stroked his beard, and offered their felicitations to Khandjan upon his guests.

[Footnote 11: This river, whose remotest springs rise in the mountains of Khurdistan, traverses the greater part of the district peopled by the Yomuts, in an extent of nearly thirty German geographical miles (120 miles). A man on horseback can ford it to a point far below Pisarak; and even below the Atabegs its depth is not considerable until it comes within eight geographical miles of Gömüshtepe, where its two banks are mere morasses. It is everywhere narrow. It is fabulously rich in fish at about four or five geographical miles from its mouth, so that its waters appeared almost coloured by them, and are in summer hardly drinkable. After I had only twice used it for washing, my hands and face acquired a strong fishy smell.]

[Footnote 12: Baba Djan, *father's soul*, is merely a term of endearment given by the Turkomans to their eldest sons.]

13th April.--I awoke for the first time in a Turkoman tent, which among the Yomuts receives the appellation of Tchatma, but amongst other tribes is called Aladja. The sweet sleep that I had enjoyed, and the light construction in which I found myself, had made me feel fresh and light of heart: the charm of novelty transported me, and my delight was without bounds. This did not escape the notice of Hadji Bilal, who invited me to take a short walk with him, and when we had got to a short distance from the Tchatma, he observed to me that it was now high time to lay aside entirely my Efendi character, and become body and soul a Dervish. 'You must have already remarked,' said my good friend, 'that both I and my associates bestow upon the public Fatiha (blessings): this you must do also. I know that this is not the custom in Roum, but people here will expect and demand it. It will occasion great surprise, if, representing yourself to be a Dervish, you do not carry out the character to its full extent. You know the form of benediction: assume, therefore, a serious face, and distribute your Fatiha (blessings); you can also give the Nefes (holy breath) when you are summoned to the sick, only never forget to extend your hand at the same time, for it is a matter of notoriety that Dervishes subsist by such acts of piety, and they are always ready with some little present or other.' Hadji Bilal apologised for presuming to school me; still, he said that it was for my benefit, and that I must have heard of the story of the traveller who, when he reached the land of the one-eyed nation, to put himself upon an equality with them, kept one of his eyes closed. After I had warmly thanked him for his counsel, he told me also that Khandjan, and many other Turkomans, had made particular enquiries respecting me, and that it had cost him much trouble and strong protestations to convince them that my journey had not in the slightest degree an official character. The Turkomans naturally inclined to the idea that I had been sent by the Sultan to Khiva and Bokhara on some anti-Russian mission; that he was not disposed to disturb their belief, as they had the greatest respect for the Sultan. The result of all was that I should never for a moment throw aside my Dervish character, for that enigmas and ambiguities were what best suited this people. Having said this, we returned to our quarters, where our host was waiting for us, with many of his friends and relatives. First he presented his wife and aged mother, whom he commended to our powerful intercession and blessings; then we were made acquainted with other near members of his family. After we had rendered to all the expected services, Khandjan remarked that it was the custom of the Turkomans to regard a guest as the dearest member of the family, that we might without obstacle move about, not only amongst his own clan, but amongst the whole tribe of the

Yomuts, and should anyone dare to touch a hair of his guest's head, the Kelte (that was the name of his clan) would {50} exact satisfaction. 'You will have to remain here, and wait at least two weeks till a caravan is ready to start for Khiva; repose a little, and then pay a visit to the more distant Ovas. The Turkoman never permits the Dervish to proceed empty-handed from his tent. It will do you no harm to fill your bread-sack--you have a long way before you ere you can get any supply--since it is your purpose to go as far as Khiva and Bokhara.'

As I wished so much to move about at my ease, the reader may judge how these words delighted me. It was my desire to remain in Gömüshtepe only so long as was necessary to extend my acquaintance a little with the people, and to acquire greater fluency in their dialect. During the first few days I accompanied Khandjan, his brother, or other intimate friend of his family, in their round of visits. A little later I attended the Hadji Bilal in his tour of religious benedictions, or went with Hadji Salih, who was actively engaged in his medical capacity. Upon the latter occasions, whilst he was administering the medicine, I repeated aloud the blessing: this finished, I received a present of a little mat of felt, or a dried fish, or some other trifle. Whether it was owing to good luck attending our joint treatment, or a motive of mere curiosity with respect to the Turkish Hadji (Hadji Roumi)--that was my title amongst them--I was never able to unriddle; but my friends were much amazed that, after having only been five days in Gömüshtepe, I had a numerous levée of sick persons, or at least of men who pretended to be such, to whom I administered blessings and 'breath,' or for whom I wrote little sentences to serve as talismans, but never did this take place without my receiving {51} afterwards the proper 'honorarium.' Now and then I fell in with a stiff-necked politician, who, regarding me as a mere political emissary, questioned my Dervish character. This, however, troubled me but little, for at least the original mask that I had assumed remained unsuspected: no one thought of discovering me to be an European. Judge, then, how pleased I was to think that I could now undisturbedly move about on a soil hitherto so little known to Europeans.

[Influence of the Ulemas]

The number of my acquaintances increased rapidly. I soon counted amongst them the most powerful and influential. I found particular advantage in the friendship of Kizil Akhond (his proper name was Molla Murad), a Turkoman 'savant' of high distinction, with whom I was upon the best footing, and whose recommendation procured access for me everywhere. Kizil Akhond had in his time, when studying in Bokhara, fallen upon a work in the Osmanli Turkish language, a sort of comment or explanation of sentences and expressions in the Koran. This he did not exactly understand. I possessed the necessary key. My cooperation consequently gave him the greatest delight: he spoke everywhere in the highest terms of my acquaintance with the literature of Islam. I entered into friendly relations with Satlig Akhond also, who was a highly-esteemed priest and a man of no little learning. When I first met him, he returned formal thanks to Providence for permitting him to behold, face to face, a Musselman from Roum, from that pure source of faith; and some one in the company having made a remark respecting my white complexion, he said that that was the true light of Islam (nur ül Islam) that {52} beamed from my countenance, of which Divine blessing only the believers of the West could boast. I was also in the habit of sedulously cultivating the acquaintance of Molla Durdis, who was invested with the rank of a Kazi Kelan (superior judge); for I had soon acquired the conviction that it was only the class of the Ulemas that would exercise any influence upon these wild people, and that the ascendency of the (Aksakal) grey beards, regarded in Europe as predominant, was really of very little moment.

[First Brick Mosque of the Nomads]

The increasing confidence evinced for me by the Turkomans showed me that the line of conduct I had adopted was a prudent one; and when the intention was entertained of building a mosque with the bricks from the old Grecian ruins which have given name to Gömüshtepe, it was I who was requested to indicate the Mihrab (altar), as Kizil Akhond had pointed me out as the best informed and most experienced Dervish for the purpose.

[Ancient Greek Wall]

In the whole district of Gömüshtepe there had never been till now, with the exception of the construction in its vicinity attributed to the Greeks, which was now in ruins, anything in the shape of a wall; and certainly it is to be regarded as some indication of a progress in civilisation that the idea of erecting an edifice for divine worship in this spot, which is regarded as the principal seat of the Yomuts, had been even broached. Each pious Turkoman had imposed it upon himself as a duty to bring to the same place a few hundreds of the beautiful square bricks from the fortified works built by Alexander; and as the materials were now regarded as sufficient, a Turkoman was expressly engaged as architect. His business had often carried him to {53} Astrakhan, and he passed for a man of experience in such matters. He was entrusted with the execution of the entire building. After I had, by means of my compass, indicated to them the direction in which Mecca lies, they began to build the walls without laying any foundations: a forgetfulness affording very little guarantee for the solidity of the whole construction, and yet so much the better for them, perhaps; for, should it last long enough, the Russians may, possibly, some day or other, make use of it as the advanced works of a fort, and the vast designs of the great Macedonian may be turned to account by the rival ambition of a Romanoff.

I had hardly spent a week in Gömüshtepe when, through the protection above mentioned, I had made acquaintances everywhere. I was now able to penetrate the secrets of their social relations, to learn the numerous ramifications and families into which the tribe is divided, and, if possible, form an idea concerning the bond that holds together elements apparently so discordant and confused. The task was somewhat more difficult than I had supposed. I had only to touch upon a question relating to ordinary life, or to show a curiosity for some matter or other, to make men wonderingly ask what a Dervish, whose proper business was only God and religion, had to do with the affairs of this transitory world. My enquiries, therefore, on these heads cost me great trouble, for direct questions I never dared to put. Most fortunately, however, the Turkomans, who pass all their lives, with the exception of that part devoted to marauding expeditions, in the greatest indolence, are prone to indulge for hours and hours in conversations on political matters, to which I only listened in {54} silence; and sitting there thus dreamily, with my beads in my hands, it has been permitted to me to study the history of their raids (alaman), of their relations with Vilayet (Persia), with the Khan of Khiva, and with other nomad nations.

[Excursion to the North-east of Gömüshtepe]

During that time I had an opportunity, under the conduct of Kizil Akhond, of making an excursion to the Atabeg, the tribe of the Yomuts which dwells furthest to the east, and the Göklen Turkomans--an excursion to me of the highest interest, as it gave me an opportunity of seeing a great part of the wall built by Alexander to serve as a bulwark against the much-dreaded tribe that peopled the wilderness.

The object of Kizil Akhond's journey was connected with the administration of justice: he had to make investigation in a lawsuit. We consequently made halts in several places, and took four days for a tour which might have been accomplished in two. The direction in which we journeyed was easterly; but we were frequently obliged to take circuitous ways to avoid morasses covered with reeds, and to keep clear of the hundreds of wild boars which were roaming about.

The morasses are caused by the inundations of the Görghen, which swells in spring, and often overflows its banks for miles and miles. This must also have been the case in ancient times, for it was considered advisable to build the great wall before mentioned, as a defence, at a distance of from four to six English miles from the north bank of the river; and as this was always on one of the highest parts which could be found in the plain, the parts adjoining the wall, now in ruins, constitute at the present day the safest route in all seasons of the year. And for a like reason we find {55} in the same vicinity the majority of the tents: we had seldom to walk an hour without falling in with these in either greater or smaller groups. I did not see the west end of this ancient construction, and am not, therefore, inclined to accord any credit to the fabulous accounts with which I was favoured. On the east end I think I really discovered where the wall began in two points; one to the north-east of Gömüshtepe, where larger accumulations of ruins, close upon the sea-shore, mark the commencement; and the second about twenty English miles to the south of the river Etrek, also near to the sea, which two lines unite a little higher above the Altin Tokmak. As for the line that takes its departure from Gömüshtepe, I was able to follow it up during two days to a distance of ten geographical miles from the west to the north-east. It is easy to distinguish it by its elevation of two or three feet above the surface of the surrounding earth. In its entirety the work presents rather the appearance of a long line of intrenchments, from the midst of which, at intervals of a thousand paces, rise the ruins of ancient towers; the dimensions of these seem to have been alike throughout.

In the direction of these walls, there are also visible other great mounds, the investigation of which I would rather leave to others, not feeling myself competent to give any satisfactory explanation or even reasonable surmise about them. Some of the smaller ones have been opened by the Turkomans, and, as I was told, there was found in the interior of a four-sided building a colossal pot, of the thinness of paper, containing blue-coloured ashes, a few gold coins, and other precious objects. Hence the wall is styled, throughout the whole country, the **gold receiver** (Kizil Alan). {56} The mounds of which I here speak must, however, be distinguished from the Toska elevations, raised by the Turkomans in commemoration of great departed ones of their nation whom they so wish to honour. My learned guide, Kizil Akhond, was amazed at my showing so much interest in the wall of Alexander (Seddi Iskender). [Footnote 13]

[Footnote 13: The history of the great Macedonian is invested by the Orientals with all the characteristics of a religious myth, and although some of their writers are anxious to distinguish Iskender Zul Karnein (the two-horned Alexander), the hero of their fable, from Iskenderi Roumi (the Greek Alexander), I have yet everywhere found that these two persons were regarded as one and the same.]

According to Khizil, the wall had been erected by the genii (Djins), at the command of the mighty sovereign Alexander. 'Alexander,' he said, 'was a more pious Musselman than we are, and therefore all subterranean spirits, whether they would or no, owed him allegiance.' He was about to proceed with the well-known fable of Alexander's descent into the realms of darkness, when he became dumb on seeing that I was absorbed in the occupation of forcibly detaching one of the bricks: and really these bright red bricks do seem as it were fused together into one material, for it is easier to break them into two than to separate them from the entire mass.

The whole neighbourhood cannot fail to be of the highest interest to archaeologists, as there are to be found in it, not only many remains of the Greek domination, but also hidden monuments of ancient Iran civilisation; for the Arabian historians relate much to us concerning the importance of the lower Görghen, the existing ruins of Shehri Djordjan. Even the Kumbezi-Kaus (the dome of Khaus), a ruin which I only heard spoken of without actually seeing it, would also, in all probability, merit more attention than rapidly-travelling Englishmen have hitherto been able to devote to it.

{57}

I was very much surprised to see that Kizil Akhond, whom I had regarded merely as a 'savant' and not as a rich man, possessed in different spots tents, wives, and children, the different component parts of a family, the issue of three marriages. It was not until I had thus, in different places, had the honour of being introduced to fresh wives and children, that I began to understand that his little tour might possibly have other ends in view than those of a simple juridical circuit. Nor was the difference great between the manner in which he was received in his own tents and in those of strangers; the Mollah, as he was styled *par excellence*, was in the tents of the Turkomans everywhere at home, everywhere master. Even in the settlements of hostile tribes, he was not only treated with honourable distinction, but laden with presents: nor was I, who was here playing the part of his disciple, forgotten in the award of favour, but was presented with Namdzdjï (mats for kneeling upon when at prayer), made of felt, a Turkoman over-cloak, and a large felt cap, the ordinary headdress of these nomad tribes. Setting this upon my head, and winding around it the scarf to form the light turban, behold me now for the moment metamorphosed into a Turkoman Mollah!

When I returned to Gömüshtepe I found my fellow-hadjis, who had not approved of my excursion, very anxious on account of my prolonged absence. I enquired respecting the health of each of them. I learnt that Hadji Salih had carried on a brilliant trade with his physic; that a theft had been committed upon Hadji Kari Meszud in a mosque, that is, in a {58} tent that served as such, in which he had taken up his quarters. After a long search in every direction, as no discovery was made, the Ishan (priest) declared that he would at once utter his malediction upon the thief, should he not restore the stolen property. Before twenty-four hours had expired, the conscience-stricken criminal came forward, bringing with him not only the stolen property, but a present as atonement. I venture to recommend this practice to the London detectives, as a substitute for their present system.

[Tartar Raids; Persian Slaves]

I now learnt, also, satisfactory intelligence respecting a karavan proceeding to Khiva. My friends told me that the Khan of Khiva, who had been recommended to the physicians the use of the milk of the buffalo for his health, had sent express to Gömüshtepe his Kervanbashi [Footnote 14] to purchase for him two pair of these animals, which were not to be met with in his own country. This official had proceeded to Astrabad, and on his return the journey was to be at once made with every guarantee of success, as it would be under the immediate guidance of a man whose experience of the desert was unrivalled. I was astonished to find how many of my fellow-travellers, the poorest of the poor, in spite of the noble hospitality of which they had been partakers, were already weary of the Turkomans; for it would be, they said, impossible for men having the least sentiment of humanity to be eye-witnesses any longer of the cruel treatment to which the wretched Persian slaves had to submit. {59} 'True, the Persians are heretics, and they tormented us terribly in our journey through their country; but what the poor wretches here suffer is really too much.' The compassion evinced by my fellow-travellers, in whose own country the slave-trade is not carried on, and the imprecations they used against the Karaktchi (robbers) for their inhumanity, convey the best impression of the sufferings to which the poor captives are exposed. Let us only picture to ourselves the feelings of a Persian, even admitting that he is the poorest of his race, who is surprised by a night attack, hurried away from his family, and brought hither a prisoner, and often wounded. He has to exchange his dress for old Turkoman rags that only scantily cover parts of his body, and is heavily laden with chains that gall his ancles, and occasion him great and unceasing pain every step he takes; he is forced upon the poorest diet to linger the first days, often weeks of his captivity. That he may make no attempt at flight, he has also during the night a Karabogra (iron ring) attached to his neck and fastened to a peg, so that the rattle betrays even his slightest movements. No other termination to his sufferings than the payment of a ransom by his friends; and, failing this, he is liable to be sold, and perhaps hurried off to Khiva and Bokhara!

[Footnote 14: Kervanbashi, leader or chief of karavans. He receives his appointment from the Khan, and is generally a person of great experience in the different routes. Each karavan route has its own Kervanbashi, who is distinguished by the name of his particular route.]

To the rattle of those chains I could never habituate my ears; it is heard in the tent of every Turkoman who has any pretensions to respectability or position. Even our friend Khandjan had two slaves, lads, only in their eighteenth and twentieth year; and to behold these unfortunates, in the bloom of their youth, in fetters made me feel indescribable emotion, repeated every day. In addition, I was forced to {60} listen in silence to the abuse and curses with which these poor wretches were loaded. The smallest demonstration of compassion would have awakened suspicions, as, on account of my knowledge of Persian, I was most frequently addressed by them. The youngest of our domestic slaves, a handsome black-haired Irani, begged of me to be so good as to write a letter for him to his relatives, praying them for God's sake to sell sheep and house in order to ransom him, which letter I accordingly wrote. Upon one occasion I thought, without being perceived, I might give him a cup of tea, but unluckily at the moment when he extended his hand to receive it some one entered the tent. I pretended to be only beckoning to him, and, instead of presenting him the tea, I felt constrained to give him a few slight blows. During my stay in Gömüshtepe no night passed without a shot echoing from the sea-shore to announce the arrival of some piratical vessel laden with booty. The next morning I went to demand from the heroes the tithes due to the Dervishes, or rather, let me say, to behold the poor Persians in the first moments of their misfortune. My heart bled at the horrid sight; and so I had to harden myself to these most striking contrasts of virtue and vice, of humanity and tyranny, of scrupulous honesty and the very scum of knavery.

I had stayed only a fortnight when, like my companions, I began to weary of the place, my eyes feeding with inexpressible longing upon the frontiers of Persia. Only a few leagues separate the two countries, and yet the manners, customs, and modes of thinking amongst the Turkomans are just as different as if the two nations were a thousand miles asunder. How wonderful the influence of religion {61} and of historical tradition upon mankind! I cannot refrain from laughing when I think that these Turkomans, in some particulars so cruel and so inhuman, were at this very time constantly giving entertainments, 'Lillah' (for pious ends), at which it was necessary that our entire company of pilgrims should be present. These invitations were repeated several times during the day. It was only the first and second that I was disposed to accept; from the third I showed by my manner that I wished to be excused; but my would-be host forced me by many pushes in the ribs to leave my tent. According to the rule of Turkoman etiquette, 'the harder the push, the more hearty the invitation.' On such festal occasions the Amphytrion threw down before the tent some pieces of felt--or, if it were his humour to be sumptuous, a carpet--whereupon the guests seated themselves in groups of five or six in a circle, and each group received a large wooden dish proportioned in size and contents to the number and ages of those who were to share it. Into the dish every guest plunged his half-open fist, until emptied to the very bottom. The quality and dressing of the meats which were served to us are not calculated to interest much our 'gastronomes.' I merely remark, therefore, in passing, that horse-flesh and camel-flesh were the order of the day: what other dishes represented our venison, I must decline mentioning.

[Tartar Fiancée and Banquet, etc.]

During my sojourn with Khandjan, he affianced his son (twelve years old, as before mentioned) to a maiden in her tenth year. This event was accompanied by a festival, from which, as his guests, we could not absent ourselves. On entering the tent of the 'fiancee,' we found her completely occupied with {62} working a shawl. Her maimer was that of one unconscious of the presence of others; and during our stay, which lasted two hours, I only once remarked from her furtive glance that she took any interest in our company. During the banquet, which, in my honour, consisted of rice boiled in milk, Khandjan observed that this festival had been fixed for the next autumn; but he had wished to turn to account the occasion of our presence, that the event might take place under our auspices and benedictions.

Let me not here forget to mention that we were entertained also on this occasion by a Karaktchi, who had, alone on foot, not only made three Persians prisoners, but had also by himself driven them before him into captivity for a distance of eight miles. He gave us the tithes of the spoil due to the Church, consisting of a small sum of two krans, and how happy he was when we with one voice intoned a Fatiha to bless him!

23

[Preparation of the Khan of Khiva's Kervanbashi for the Journey through the Desert; Line of Camels; Ilias Beg, the Hirer of Camels]

After having lingered, very much against my will, three weeks in Gömüshtepe, the hospitable Khandjan at last showed a disposition to aid our preparations for departure. We considered that the purchase of camels would entail too much expense; we consequently determined to hire one for every two of us to carry our water and our flour. This might have been very difficult, had we not been so fortunate as to possess in our cattle-dealer, Ilias Beg, a proper adviser for the purpose. He was not, perhaps, a religious person, nor had he much reverence for our Hadji character; but he only showed the more exactitude to fulfil the law of hospitality, and the more disposition to make the greatest sacrifices to give us satisfaction. Ilias is properly a Turkoman from Khiva, and {63} of the tribe of the Yomuts; he makes a journey of business every year through the desert to Gömüshtepe, and during his stay is under the protection of Khandjan, without which his position is as insecure as that of any other stranger. He comes generally in autumn, and returns in spring, with twenty or thirty camels loaded with his own merchandise, or that of strangers. Having been induced this year to take back with him some extra camels, the small additional sum for hire of these camels was, as it were, a God-send. Khandjan had recommended us in the warmest manner, and the words, 'Ilias, you will answer with your life,' had clearly shown him in what degree of estimation we stood with our host. Ilias cast his eyes down to the ground, as the nomads are in the habit of doing when they appear most in earnest; and his answer, in a low tone, which seemed to issue from him without any movement of the lips, was, 'You surely do not know me.' The singular *sang-froid* of the two Turkomans, as they dealt together, began to irritate my still half-European character, and forgetting that Hadji Bilal and my other companions were also present, and yet remained motionless, I made some remarks; but I soon had occasion to regret it, for even after having addressed them several times, my words remained without notice. Without, therefore, venturing to mix in the negotiation, it was determined that we should hire a camel for two ducats to go as far as Khiva; and as for our flour and water, Ilias declared that he would take it with him without compensation.

The small sum of money belonging to me, which I had sewn and hidden in different parts of my mendicant attire, together with the tolerably rich harvest of my Hadji dealings amongst the Turkomans, had {64} abundantly provided for me, so that I was in a position to hire a camel for myself alone; but I was dissuaded by Hadji Bilal and Sultan Mahmoud, who remarked that an appearance of wretchedness calculated to excite compassion was the best guarantee for safety amongst these nomads; while their covetousness was sure to be excited by the slightest sign of affluence. A suspicion of wealth might convert the best friend into a foe. They named several of the Hadjis who were well provided with means, and who, nevertheless, for the sake of prudence, were obliged to wander on in rags and on foot. I admitted the necessity, and secured a joint share in a camel, only stipulating for permission to make use of a kedjeve (pair of wooden baskets, hanging down from the two sides of the camel), as I should find it very fatiguing, with my lame foot and without cessation, to ride day and night forty stations, squeezed with another into the same wooden saddle. At first, Ilias objected, because, according to him (and he was indeed right), the kedjeve in the desert would have been a double burden for the poor beast. Khandjan, however, at last persuaded him, and he consented. On the journey to Khiva, which we were to perform in twenty days, and of which everyone spoke in a manner to make us feel fearful misgivings, I should at least have the consolation of being able now and then to sleep a little; but what pleased me most in the whole arrangement was, that I should have for my *vis-à-vis* and 'equipoise,' as the two kedjeve were termed, my bosom friend Hadji Bilal, whose society began by degrees to become indispensable for me. After the dialogue was over, we paid, as is the custom, the hire beforehand. Hadji Bilal said a Fatiha; and after Ilias {65} had passed his fingers through his beard, consisting, it is true, of only a few straggling hairs, we had no occasion to take any other steps, and we but begged that the departure might be hastened as much as possible. This, however, he could not promise, as it depended upon the Kervanbashi of the Khan, who, with his buffaloes, was to place himself at the head of our karavan. In a few days we were ready to start for Etrek, our rendezvous. After the preparations had been completed I burnt with twofold ardour to quit Gömüshtepe: for, first, we had lost time here, and I perceived that the hot season was more and more advancing, and we feared that the rain-water, still to be found in the desert, would become scarcer; and secondly, I began to grow uneasy at the ridiculous reports which were in circulation respecting me. Whilst many saw in me merely a pious Dervish, others could not rid themselves of the idea that I was a man of influence, an envoy of the Sultan, in correspondence with the Turkish Ambassador in Teheran, who was bringing a thousand muskets with him, and was engaged in a plot against Russia and Persia. Had this come to the ears of the Russians in Ashourada, they would have certainly laughed at it, but still it might have led to enquiries respecting the singular stranger; and the discovery of my disguise might have involved a cruel, perhaps a life-long captivity. I therefore begged Hadji Bilal repeatedly at least to leave Gömüshtepe, but his previous impatience had given way to absolute indifference as soon as Ilias had engaged with us; on my urging him, he even answered how ridiculously childish it was for me to seek to anticipate the decrees of destiny. 'Thy haste,' said he to me, 'is all thrown away; thou must perforce {66} remain on the Görghen's banks until the Nasib (fate) has decreed that thou shouldst drink water in another place; and no one knows whether this will occur at an early or a late period.' Only imagine what effect an answer so oriental was calculated to produce upon a mind that had just cause to feel impatience! I saw, however, but too well, the impossibility of escape, and so submitted to my fate.

About this time, it happened that some Karaktchi had, by treachery, in one of their depredatory expeditions, seized upon five Persians. One of these was a man of property. The robbers had sailed in a vessel up beyond Karatepe, under the pretence of purchasing a cargo from the village of the Persians. The bargain was soon made; and scarcely had the unsuspicious Persians appeared with their goods upon the sea-shore, than they were seized, bound hand and foot, buried up to their necks in their own wheat, and forcibly carried off to Gömüshtepe. I was present when these unfortunates were unpacked, so to say. One of them was also dangerously wounded; and I heard the Turkomans themselves characterise the act as a deed of shame. Even the Russians in Ashourada interested themselves in the affair, and threatened a landing if the prisoners were not immediately set at liberty. As the robbers resolutely refused to let their prize go, I thought that now the rest of the Turkomans, who run common risk from the Russians, would compel their countrymen to give way. Not at all; they ran up and down, distributing arms, in order, should the Russians land, to give them a warm reception. It may be interesting to know that I was also appointed to shoulder a musket, and great was my embarrassment when I reflected upon whom I should be expected to fire. {67} Happily, no attempt was made to carry out the threat. [Footnote 15]

[Footnote 15: Let not the reader be surprised by the equivocal attitude of the Russian authorities. Persia regards every landing of the Russian forces on the coasts as a hostile invasion of its own soil, and prefers to endure the depredations of the Turkomans rather than avail itself of the Russian arms, which might, it is true, in particular cases, be of service to them, but would not fail, on the whole, to be most detrimental.]

[Arrangements with Khulkhan; Turkoman Expedition to steal Horses in Persia; Its Return.]

Next morning a Russian steamer came quite close to the shore, but the matter was disposed of by a political manoeuvre; that is to say, the Turkomans gave hostages for the future, but the Persians remained in chains. The wealthy prisoner paid a ransom of 100 ducats; another, who was crippled in both hands and feet, and was not worth the sum of four ducats, was set free in honour of the Russians; but the three others--strong men--were loaded with still heavier chains, and led away to the usual place of torture for the slaves, at Etrek. The name of Etrek, which is given both to a river and the inhabited district in its vicinity, is a word of terror and a curse for the unfortunate inhabitants of Mazendran and Taberistan. The Persian must be very incensed when he allows the words 'Etrek biufti!' (May you be driven to Etrek!) to escape his lips. As it was fixed for the rendezvous of our karavan, I was soon to have the opportunity of seeing closely into this nest of horror. Khandjan had also had the goodness to recommend me as guest to Kulkhan the Pir (grey-beard) of the Karaktchi. He came to us very opportunely. The old sinner had a sombre repulsive physiognomy. He did not by any means meet me in a friendly manner when I was transferred to his hospitality. He examined my {68} features a long time, occasionally whispering something in the ear of Khandjan, and seemed determined to discover in me more than other people had seen. The cause of this distrust I soon detected. Kulkhan had in his youth travelled through the southern parts of Russia, in company with Khidr Khan, who was in the service of the Czar. He had also long lived at Tiflis, and was pretty familiar with our European modes of existence. He remarked that he had seen many nations, but never the Osmanlis. He had heard it said of them that they had sprung from a tribe of Turkomans, whom besides they resembled in every respect; and that his astonishment was great to distinguish in me quite opposite characteristics. Hadji Bilal remarked that his own information upon the subject was not good, and that he had actually lived several years in Roum, without having occasion to make any similar observation; whereupon Kulkhan told us he would return two days afterwards, early in the morning, to his Ova in Etrek, recommended us to make ourselves ready for our journey, inasmuch as without his conduct we should be unable to travel hence to Etrek, although only a distance of twelve miles; and, in short, that he was only waiting the return of his son

Kolman [Footnote 16] from the Alaman (predatory expedition) to the Persian frontiers, in quest of some fine mares.

[Footnote 16: Properly Kulumali.]

The return of his son from this piratical adventure was awaited by Kulkhan with almost the same feelings as those with which a father amongst us would expect his son coming home from an heroic expedition, or other honourable enterprise. He also informed us that we might walk forwards a little way down the banks of the Görghen, for his son {69} was to return about this time, and we should then see something worth seeing. As I had nothing at that moment else to do, I was not displeased to comply with the invitation. I mixed with the crowd which was looking, with the greatest impatience, for the first sight of the party. At last eight mounted Turkomans appeared on the opposite bank, bringing ten led horses with them. I thought that now the expectant multitude would give vent to their enthusiasm in hurrahs, but they uttered no sound; all measured with greedy eyes and speechless admiration those who were approaching. The latter dashed into the Görghen, across which in an instant they swam to the bank on our side, where, dismounting, they extended their hands with indescribable earnestness to their relatives. Whilst the seniors were passing the spoil in review with the greatest attention, the young heroes were occupied in arranging their dress. Lifting their heavy fur caps, they wiped the sweat from head and forehead.

The whole spectacle was splendid. Whatever my contempt for the robbers and their abominable doings, my eye fell still with particular pleasure upon these young men, who, in their short riding dresses, with their bold looks, and hair falling to their breasts in curly locks as they laid aside their weapons, were the admiration of all. Even the gloomy Kulkhan seemed cheerful: he introduced his son to us, and after Hadji Bilal had bestowed his benediction upon him, we separated. The next morning we were to proceed from Gömüshtepe, accompanied by Kulkhan, his son, and stolen horses, to Etrek.

{70}

CHAPTER VI.

DEPARTURE FROM GÖMÜSHTEPE

CHARACTER OF OUR LATE HOST

TURKOMAN MOUNDS OR TOMBS

DISAGREEABLE ADVENTURE WITH WILD BOARS

PLATEAU TO THE NORTH OF GÖMÜSHTEPE

NOMAD HABITS

TURKOMAN HOSPITALITY

THE LAST GOAT

PERSIAN SLAVE

COMMENCEMENT OF THE DESERT

A TURKOMAN WIFE AND SLAVE

ETREK

PERSIAN SLAVES

RUSSIAN SAILOR SLAVE

PROPOSED ALLIANCE BETWEEN YOMUTS AND TEKKE

RENDEZVOUS WITH THE KERVANBASHI

TRIBE KEM

ADIEU TO ETREK

AFGHAN MAKES MISCHIEF

DESCRIPTION OF KARAVAN.

Gens confinis Hyrcaniae, cultu vitae aspera et latrociniis assueta.-- Q. Curtii Ruf. lib. vi. cap. 5.

[Departure from Gömüshtepe; Character of our late Host]
At noon the following day I left Gömüshtepe with my most intimate fellow-travellers, accompanied for some time by Khandjan and all my other friends. Kandjan went on foot with us nearly a league on our way, as is the custom amongst the nomads in the case of very esteemed guests. I entreated him several times to return, but fruitlessly; he insisted upon punctually fulfilling all the rules of ancient Turkoman hospitality, that I might never afterwards have any ground of complaint against him. To say the truth, my heart was very heavy when I extricated myself from his last embrace, for I had known in him one of the most honourable of men. Without any interested motive, he had not only for a long time entertained me and five other pilgrims in his own {71} house, but had given me every explanation that I had required. I feel even now pained that I cannot make him any return for his kindness, but still more that I was forced to deceive so sincere a friend by any mystery.

[Turkoman Mounds or Tombs; Disagreeable Adventure with Wild Boars]
Our path was north-easterly, departing more and more from the sea-shore, in the direction of the two great mounds, of which one bears the name of Köresofi, the other that of Altin Tokmak. Besides these mounds, one discovers here and there numerous Joszka (Turkoman barrows); with these exceptions, the district is one boundless flat. Scarcely a quarter of a league from Gömüshtepe, we found ourselves proceeding through splendid meadows, where the grass was as high as the knee, and of a delicious odour. It all withers away without being of service to any one, for the inhabitants of Gömüshtepe are Tchomru (that is, not cattle-breeders). What lovely villages might flourish in this well-watered district; what animated life might here reign, instead of the stillness of death! Our small karavan, consisting of the camels belonging to Ilias and of six horses, kept close together, for Kulkhan affirmed that there were hereabouts Karaktchis who were not under his orders, and who would assail him if they felt themselves strong enough to do so. Ilias, this once, was pleased to spare me my ride upon the camel; he took from Kulkhan one of the stolen horses, upon which I was to ride as far as Etrek. Unfortunately, as it happened, Emir Mehemmed, the Afghan opium-eater from Karatepe, who had already fastened himself upon our karavan, had remained on foot, and whenever we had to traverse any puddle or other wet ground, I could not refuse to take him on my saddle, and then he grasped my clothes so tightly that I often {72} thought I should be thrown down. This partnership ride made me run much risk when we were obliged to cut our way through the great marshes, covered with reeds, which swarmed with herds of wild boars, numerous beyond conception. Kulkhan and Ilias rode before, to find a circuitous way, to enable us to avoid hundreds of these animals, whose proximity we perceived, not only by their incessant grunting, but more especially by the cracking sound caused by their movements amongst the reeds. Whilst I was riding on with attentive ear, my horse suddenly shied and took a great bound sideways. I had hardly time to look round to ascertain the cause, when I and my comrade lay stretched upon the ground. The loud laughter of my companions, who were a few paces from us, mingled with a strange howling, I turned myself

round, and found that I had been thrown upon two wild boars of tender age; it was their mother that had caused our horse to shy, but now, rendered savage by the cry of her young ones, she stood showing her tusks at no great distance from us, and would most certainly have charged us, had not Shirdjan, the cousin of Ilias, come to our aid, and barred the way with his extended lance. Whether it was owing to the bravery of the young Turkoman, or the silence of the young pigs-- now liberated from their constrained position--I cannot say, but the incensed mother beat a retreat, and, with her face still to the foe, hastened back to her lair, which we had not been slow to abandon. Kulkhan's son had in the meantime secured our horse, that had escaped. He restored him to me with the remark that 'I might regard myself as lucky, for that a death by the wound of a wild boar would send even the most pious Musselman nedjis (unclean) {73} into the next world, where a hundred years' burning in purgatorial fire would not purge away his uncleanness.'

Intruding upon the Haunts of the wild Boar.

[Plateau to the North of Gömüshtepe; Nomad Habits]
After having continued our way for about four hours in the above-named direction, amidst marshes and meadows, I noticed that we had gained the sloping sides of the plateau that extends north from Gömüshtepe, for not only the elevations, but the Persian mountains on the frontiers themselves, began gradually to disappear; only a few groups of tents, in the vicinity of which camels were grazing, were visible at a great distance, and although, on all the four sides, the most lovely verdure enchanted the eye, the eastern district which I had visited before with Kizil Akhond, is far more thickly peopled. There being no river like the Görghen, the well-water, of which the people make use, is exhausted by the time the rich meadows have sufficiently fattened their sheep. Tents, consequently, are only to be seen here in May and in June. One of these groups of tents, peopled by the dependents of Kulkhan, was to give us shelter this night, as Etrek was still six miles [Footnote 17] distant--a whole day's journey for our heavily-laden camels. Due notice had been given of our approach, and my hungry fellow-travellers soon saw in the rising smoke the prospect of a good supper. Although Gömüshtepe is only four miles distant from this spot, the journey took us nearly eight hours, and this first ride had tolerably wearied both man and beast.

[Footnote 17: The reader is requested to understand, here and elsewhere, German miles.]

[Turkoman Hospitality; The last Goat]
The young nephew of Kulkhan advanced ten paces before the tents to welcome us; and, whilst Ilias and the Afghan were the special guests of Kulkhan, I was quartered with the Hadjis in the small tent of Allah Nazr. {74} This old Turkoman was beside himself from joy that heaven had sent him guests; the recollection of that scene will never pass from my mind. In spite of our protestations to the contrary, he killed a goat, the only one which he possessed, to contribute to our entertainment. At a second meal, which we partook with him next day, he found means to procure bread also, an article that had not been seen for weeks in his dwelling. Whilst we attacked the dish of meat, he seated himself opposite to us, and wept, in the exactest sense of the expression, tears of joy. Allah Nazr would not retain any part of the goat he had killed in honour of us. The horns and hoofs, which were burned to ashes, and were to be employed for the galled places on the camels, he gave to Ilias; but the skin, stripped off in one piece, he destined to serve as my water-vessel, and after having well rubbed it with salt, and dried it in the sun, he handed it over to me.

[Persian Slave]
The arrival of a slave, one of the five of whom I spoke in the last chapter, who had fallen into the snare so treacherously laid for them, detained Kulkhan and our party a day. This poor Persian was transferred, for chastisement, to Kulkhan, who had the peculiar reputation of being able most easily to ascertain from a captive whether he possessed sufficient means to enable his relatives to ransom him, or whether, being without relatives or property, he ought to be sent on to Khiva for sale.

The former alternative is much the more agreeable one to the Turkomans, as they may demand any sum they please. The Persian, who is cunning even in his misfortune, always contrives to conceal his real position; he is therefore subjected to much ill-treatment, {75} until by the lamentations which he forwards to his home his captors have squeezed from his friends the highest possible ransom, and it is only when that arrives that his torment ceases. The other alternative is worse for both parties; the robber, after much expenditure, only gets at last the current price in the slave-market, and the unfortunate Persian is removed to a distance of some hundreds of miles from his country, which he very rarely sees again. Kulkhan has, as before mentioned, great experience in this department; his latest victim arrived before evening, and the next day the journey was continued, after I had been warmly embraced by Allah Nazr, who was just as much a Turkoman as Kulkhan.

[Commencement of the Desert]

This day I took my seat for the first time in my wooden basket on the camel, having, however, some sacks of flour for my equipoise, as Hadji Bilal wished on this occasion to deprive himself of the pleasure. Our route was always in a northerly direction, and we had scarcely advanced two leagues, when the verdure ceased, and for the first time we found ourselves in the dismal strong-smelling salt ground of the wilderness. What our eyes encountered here was a good specimen; a low foreland called Kara Sengher (black wall) elevated itself at a distance of about eight miles to the north of Gömüshtepe. The nearer we approached this hill, the looser the soil became; near to its foot we fell upon a real morass, and our march was attended by increasing difficulties in the slippery mud, in which the camels, with their spongy feet, slid at each step--indeed, mine threatened to upset both myself and my basket into the dirt. I preferred dismounting *proprio motu*, and after tramping an hour and a half through the mud, arrived at last at {76} Kara Sengher, whence we soon reached the Ova of Kulkhan.

On arriving, I was greatly surprised by Kulkhan's immediately leading me into his tent, and charging me earnestly not to quit it, until he should call me. I began to suspect something wrong, when I heard how he was cursing his women, accusing them of always mislaying the chains, and ordering them to bring them to him immediately. Searching gloomily for them he returned frequently to the tent without addressing a word to me: moreover Hadji Bilal did not show himself--he who so seldom left me to myself. Sunk in the most anxious reflections, I at last heard the rattling sound of fetters approaching, and saw the Persian who had come with us enter the tent dragging with his wounded feet the heavy chains after him; for he was the party on whose account Kulkhan was making these preparations. He was not long in making his appearance. He ordered tea to be prepared, and after we had partaken of it, he directed me to rise, and led me to a tent which had been in the meantime set up; he wished it to be a surprise for me. Such was the object he had in view in his whole conduct. Notwithstanding this, I could never feel any attachment to him, for how great the difference between him and Khandjan clearly appeared from this, that during the ten days I was his guest, this tea was the only repast Kulkhan's hospitality accorded me. I was afterwards informed of his treacherous plans, to which he would most certainly have given effect, had not Kizil Akhond, whom he particularly dreaded, charged him to treat me with every possible respect.

{77}

[A Turkoman Wife and Slave]

The tent which I now occupied, in company with ten of my travelling companions, did not belong to Kulkhan, but was the property of another Turkoman who, with his wife--formerly his slave, sprung from the tribe of the Karakalpak--joined our party for Khiva. I learnt that their object in proceeding to Khiva was that this woman, who had been carried off in a surprise by night and brought hither, might ascertain whether her former husband, whom she had left severely wounded, had afterwards perished; who had purchased her children, and where they now were; and--which she was particularly anxious to know--what had become of her daughter, a girl in her twelfth year, whose beauty she described to me with tears in her eyes. The poor woman, by extraordinary fidelity and laboriousness, had so enchained her new master, that he consented to accompany her on her sorrowful journey of enquiry. I was always asking him what he would do if her former husband were forthcoming, but his mind on that point was made up--the law guaranteed him his possession. 'The Nassib (fate),' said he, 'intended to bestow on me Heidgul' (properly Eidgul, 'rose of the festival'), 'and none can withstand Nassib.' There was besides, amongst the other travellers freshly arrived, who were to journey with Ilias, a Dervish named Hadji Siddik, a consummate hypocrite, who went about half naked, and acted as groom to the camels in the desert; it was not until after we had arrived in Bokhara that we learnt that he had sixty ducats sewn up in his rags.

[Etrek; Persian Slaves]

The whole company inhabited the tents in common, expecting that the Khan's Kervanbashi would come up as soon as possible, and that we should commence our journey through the desert. The delay was painful to us all. I became alarmed on account {78} of the decrease of my stock of flour, and I began at once to diminish my daily allowance by two handfuls. I also baked it without leaven in the hot ashes; for the produce is greater, it remains longer on the stomach, and hunger torments one less. Fortunately we could make short mendicant excursions; nor had we the least reason to complain of any lack of charity on the part of the Turkomans of Etrek, who are notwithstanding the most notorious robbers. We passed,

29

indeed, very few of their tents without seeing in them two or three Persians heavily laden with chains.

[Russian Sailor Slave]

It was also here in Etrek, in the tent of a distinguished Turkoman named Kotchak Khan, that I encountered a Russian, formerly a sailor in the naval station at Ashourada. We entered the above-named chief's abode, to take our mid-day repose; and scarcely had I been presented to him as a Roumi (Osmanli), when our host remarked; 'Now I will give thee a treat. We know the relation in which the Osmanlis stand with the Russians: thou shalt behold one of thy arch-enemies in chains.' I was forced to behave as if I was highly delighted. The poor Russian was led in, heavily chained: his countenance was sickly, and very sorrowful. I felt deeply moved, but was careful not to betray my feelings by any expression. 'What would you do with this Efendi,' said Kotchak Khan, 'if you encountered him in Russia? Go and kiss his feet.' The unfortunate Russian was about to approach me, but I forbade, making at the same time the observation, I had only to-day begun my Gusl (great purification), and that I did not want to render myself unclean by my contact with this unbeliever; that it would even be more agreeable to me if he disappeared immediately from before my eyes, for that ***this*** nation {79} was my greatest aversion. They motioned him to withdraw, which he accordingly did, throwing at me a sharp look. As I learnt later, he was one of two sailors from the new station at Ashourada; the other had died in captivity about a year before. They had fallen into the hands of the Karaktchis some years previously, in one of their night expeditions. Their government offered to ransom them, but the Turkomans demanded an exorbitant sum (five hundred ducats for one); and as during the negotiation Tcherkes Bay, the brother of Kotshak Khan, was sent by the Russians to Siberia, where he died, the liberation of the unfortunate Christians became matter of still greater difficulty; and now the survivor will soon succumb under the hardships of his captivity, as his comrade has done before him. [Footnote 18]

[Footnote 18: When I afterwards drew the attention of the Russians to the occurrence, they laboured to excuse themselves, saying that they did not desire to accustom the Turkomans to such large ransoms, for that with any encouragement these bold robbers would devote themselves night and day to their profitable depredations.]

Such are the ever-fluctuating impressions of hospitable virtues and unheard-of barbarisms produced by these nomads upon the minds of travellers! Sated and overflowing with their kindness and charity, I often returned to our abode, when Kulkhan's Persian slave, already mentioned, would perhaps implore me for a drop of water, as, according to his tale, they had for two entire days given him dried salt fish instead of bread, and although he had been forced to work the whole day in the melon fields, they had denied him even a drop of water. Luckily I was alone in the tent; the sight of the bearded man bathed in tears made me forget all risks: I handed him my water-skin, and he {80} satisfied his thirst whilst I kept watch at the door. Then thanking me warmly, he hastened away. This unfortunate man, maltreated by every one, was especially tormented by Kulkhan's second wife, herself once a Persian slave, who was desirous of showing how zealous a convert she had become.

Even in Gömüshtepe these cruel scenes were loathsome to me: judge, then, how my feelings must have revolted when I learnt to regard the last-named place as the extreme of humanity and civilisation! Tents and dwellers therein became objects of loathing to me.

[Proposed Alliance between Yomuts and Tekke]

Still no news came of the arrival of the Kervanbashi, although all who had desired to join our karavan were already assembled. New friends were greeted and reciprocal acquaintances formed; and very often did I hear the question mooted as to the route likely to be selected by the Kervanbashi. We were engaged in one of these conversations, when one of the Etrekites brought us the cheering intelligence that the Tekke, whose hostility is the dread of the karavans during the greatest part of their journey to Khiva, had sent a peaceful embassy to the Yomuts, proposing, at length, a reconciliation, and an attack with combined forces, upon their common enemy, the Persians.

As I propose to touch upon this political transaction in the next chapter, suffice it here to say, that the occurrence was incidentally of the greatest advantage to us. They explained to me that there were from Etrek to Khiva three different ways, the choice between them being determined by considerations as to the numbers forming the karavan.

{81}

[Rendezvous with the Kervanbashi]

The routes are as follows:--

1. The first, close along the shore of the Caspian, behind the greater Balkan, which direction it follows for a two days' journey towards the north from these mountains, and then,

after proceeding ten days, the traveller has to turn to the east, in which quarter Khiva lies. This way is only accessible for the smaller karavans, as it affords but little water, but presents as little danger from attacks, except in times of extraordinary revolutions, when the Kasaks (Kirghis) or the Karakalpaks send hither their Alaman.

2. The middle route, which follows a northerly direction only as far as the original ancient channel of the Oxus, and then, passing between the Great and the Little Balkhan, turns to the north-east towards Khiva.

3. The third is the straight route and the shortest; for while we require twenty-four days for the first, and twenty for the second, this one may be performed in fourteen. Immediately on leaving Etrek one takes a north-easterly direction, through the Göklen and Tekke Turkomans. At every station wells of sweet drinkable water occur. Of course a karavan must be on good terms with the tribes above named, and must count from two to three thousand men, otherwise the passage is impossible. How great then was my joy, when one evening a messenger from Ata-bay brought us the intelligence that the Kervanbashi would leave his encampment early the following morning, and would give us rendezvous the day after at noon, on the opposite bank of the Etrek, whence we were to proceed all together upon our great journey through the desert! Ilias issued orders for us all to complete our preparations as speedily as possible. We therefore that very same evening got our bread ready; we once more salted our large pieces of camel-flesh, which we had received from the nomads in payment for the benedictions we had lavished on them. Who then was {82} happier than I, when the next day I mounted the kedjeve with Hadji Bilal, and in my creaking seat slowly left Etrek, borne forwards by the wave-like pace of the camel?

For the sake of security, Kulkhan was pleased to regard it as necessary to give us his escort for this day; for although we numbered from fifteen to twenty muskets, it was yet very possible that we might have to encounter a superior force of robbers, in which case the presence of Kulkhan might prove of the most important service, as the greater part of the Etrek bandits were under his spiritual guidance, and followed his orders blindfold. I had almost forgotten to mention that our Kulkhan was renowned, not only as the grey-beard of the Karaktchi, but also as Sofi (ascetic), a title he bore upon his seal: of the pious appellation he was not a little proud. I had indeed before my eyes one of the best-defined pictures of hypocrisy when I saw Kulkhan, the author of so many cruelties, sitting there amongst his spiritual disciples: he who had ruined the happiness of so many families, expounding what was prescribed respecting the holy purifications, and the ordinances directing the close cutting of the moustache! Teacher and scholar seemed alike inspired. In the confident assurances of their own piety, how many of these robbers were already dreaming of their sweet rewards in Paradise!

[Tribe Kem]

To avoid the marshes formed by the overflowing of the Etrek, our route turned now to the north-west, now to the north-east, for the most part over a sandy district on which very few tents were visible; on the edge of the desert we observed about 150 tents of the Turkoman clan Kem. I was told that this race had time out of mind separated itself from the
Yomut {83} Turkomans, to whom they properly belonged, and had inhabited the edge of the desert; their great propensity to thieving is the cause why all the other tribes make war upon them and treat them as enemies, so that their numbers never increase. Near their resorts we came upon many stragglers from our karavan, who did not dare to pass on without our company; and according to all appearances the Kemites would have assailed us, had they not seen at our head Kulkhan, the mighty scarecrow.

A quarter of an hour's journey from their encampment farther to the north, we crossed a little arm of the Etrek, whose waters had already begun to have a very salt taste, a sign that its bed would soon be dry. The interval between its farther bank and a second and still smaller arm of the same river is alternately a salt bottom and a fine meadow, thickly overgrown with monstrous fennel, which took us a whole hour to traverse. This deep stream was like a ditch, and on account of its stiff loamy bank presented considerable impediments to our progress; several camels fell with their loads into the water: it was shallow, but still the wetting they received rendered the packs heavier and added greatly to our labour in reaching the hill on the opposite side, named Delili Burun. By two o'clock in the afternoon we had only advanced four miles on our way, notwithstanding our early start in the morning; nevertheless the resolution was taken to make a halt here, as it was only the next morning at mid-day that we were to meet the Kervanbashi on the other side of the Etrek.

{84}
The hill above named, which is but a sort of promontory jutting out from a long chain of inconsiderable hills stretching to the south-east, affords an extensive and fine view. To the west we discover the Caspian Sea like a range of blue clouds, the mountains of Persia are also distinguishable: but the greatest interest attaches to the mountain plain to our south, whose limit

31

the eye cannot discern, on which the scattered groups of tents in many places have the appearance of mole-hills. Almost the whole of Etrek, with the river flowing through it, lies before us, and the places where the river spreads over both banks produce upon the eye the effect of lakes. As we were near the encampment of the Kem, we were counselled by Kulkhan, who thought proper to tarry with us this one more night, to keep a sharp look-out; and evening had not closed in before we posted watches, which, relieved from time to time, observed every movement around us.

Understanding that this station formed the last outpost towards the Great Desert, I profited by the opportunity which the return of our escort afforded, and spent the afternoon in writing letters whilst my companions were sleeping. Besides the small pieces of paper concealed in the wool of my Bokhariot dress for the purpose of notes, I had two sheets of blank paper in the Koran which was suspended from my neck in a little bag: upon these I wrote two letters, one to Haydar Effendi, addressed to Teheran, and the second to Khandjan, requesting him to forward the former. [Footnote 19]

[Footnote 19: Upon my return I found at the Turkish Embassy this letter, acquainting my friends with my being about to commence my journey in the desert, as well as other communications which I had sent on from Gömüshtepe. My good friend Khandjan had forwarded them with the greatest zeal and exactitude.]

{85}

The next morning a four hours' march brought us to the banks of the Etrek, properly so called. A good deal of time was devoted to finding the shallowest points where the river could be most readily forded, a task by no means easy, for although the usual breadth of the river is only from twelve to fifteen paces, this was now doubled by the water having overflowed its banks, and the softened loamy ground caused a real martyrdom to the poor camels, so that our Turkomans were justified in their long hesitation. The current, indeed, was not very strong, still the water came up to the bellies of the camels; and the uncertain wavering steps of our labouring, wading animals dipped our kedjeve now on the right side, now on the left, into the troubled waters of the Etrek: one false step and I should have been plunged into mud and dirt, and at no small risk have had to make my way by swimming to the opposite bank. Happily all crossed in good order, and scarcely had we come to a halt when the anxiously-expected karavan of the Kervanbashi came in sight, having in its van three buffaloes (two cows and a bull), to whose health-promising advent the sick Lord of Khiva could hardly look forward with greater impatience than we had done.

The reader will remember that Hadji Bilal, Yusuf, some foot travellers and myself, had been obliged to separate from the main body of our Dervish karavan, because the others had found greater difficulties than myself in finding camels to hire. As we had heard no tidings of them in Etrek, we began to be anxious lest these poor people might have no opportunity of following us. We were, therefore, greatly rejoiced to see them all coming up in good condition in the karavan that now joined us. We kissed and hugged one another with the heartiness of brethren who meet {86} after a long separation. My emotion was great when I once more saw around me the Hadji Salih and Sultan Mahmoud, and all the others too; yes, all my mendicant companions; for, although I regarded Hadji Bilal as my dearest friend, I was compelled to avow to myself my warm attachment to them all, without distinction.

[Adieu to Etrek]

As the river Etrek afforded us the last opportunity of sweet water until, after twenty days' journey, we should refresh ourselves on the banks of the Oxus, I counselled my companions not to let the opportunity slip, but at least, this last time, to drink our fill of tea. We therefore brought forward the tea-vessels, I proffered my fresh-baked bread, and long afterwards did we remember the luxury and abundance of this festival held in honour of our meeting.

[Afghan makes Mischief]

In the meantime also arrived the Kervanbashi who was to be our leader and protector in the desert. As I attached great importance to being presented to him under good auspices, I went amongst the others accompanied by Hadji Salih and Messud, who had mentioned me to him on the way. Let the reader then picture to himself my wonder and alarm when Amandurdi (such was his name), a corpulent and good-tempered Turkoman, although he greeted my friends with great distinction, received me with striking coldness; and the more Hadji Salih was disposed to turn the conversation upon me, the more indifferent he became: he confined himself to saying, 'I know this Hadji already.' I made an effort not to betray my embarrassment. I was about to withdraw, when I noticed the angry glances that Ilias, who was present, darted at the Emir Mehemmed, the crazy opium-eater, whom he thus signalised as the cause of what had just occurred.

{87}

We withdrew, and hardly had the occurrence been recounted to Hadji Bilal, when he grew angry and exclaimed, 'This wretched sot of an Afghan has already expressed himself in Etrek to the effect that our Hadji Reshid, who was able to give him instructions in the Koran and in Arabic, was only a Frenghi in disguise' (thereupon adding, three different times, the phrase Estag farullah! 'God pardon me my sins'); 'and in spite of my assuring him that we had received him from the hands of the ambassador of our great Sultan, and that he had with him a pass sealed with the seal of the Khalife, [Footnote 20] he still refuses to believe and persists in his defamation. As I remark, he has gained the ear of the Kervanbashi, but he shall repent it on our arrival in Khiva, where there are Kadis and Ulemas; we shall teach him there what the consequence is of representing a pious Musselman as an unbeliever.'

[Footnote 20: Follower of Mahomed, that is, the Sultan of Constantinople.]

I now began to understand the whole mystery. Emir Mehemmed, born at Kandahar, had, after the occupation of his native city by the English, been compelled to fly on account of some crime he had committed. He had had frequent opportunities of seeing Europeans, and had recognised me as a European by my features. Consequently, from the very first moment he regarded me as a secret emissary travelling with hidden treasures under my mendicant disguise, one whom he might succeed in plundering at any time he wished, as he would always have at his service a formidable menace, namely, 'denunciation.' Often had he counselled me to separate from those mendicants, and to join his own society; but I never omitted replying that Dervish and merchant were elements too {88} heterogeneous to offer any prospect of a suitable partnership; that it would be impossible to speak of sincere friendship until he had given up his vicious habit of opium-eating, and devoted himself to pious purifications and prayers. The resolute stand I took--and indeed I had no other course--made him furious; and as from his impiety he was the object of the Hadjis' aversion, I can only regard his notorious enmity as a particular instance of good fortune.

[Description of Karavan.]

About two hours after this occurrence, the Kervanbashi, who now assumed the command over the whole karavan, pointed out to us that everyone ought to fill his water-skin with water, as we should not come to another well for three days. I therefore took my goat-skin and went with the rest to the stream. Never having hitherto suffered much from the torment of thirst, I was filling it carelessly, when my colleagues repaired my error with the remark that in the desert every drop of water had life in it, and that this fount of existence should be kept by everyone as the 'apple of his eye.' The preparations completed, the camels were packed, the Kervanbashi had them counted, and we found that we possessed eighty camels, that we were forty travellers in all, amongst whom twenty-six were Hadjis without weapons, and the rest tolerably armed Turkomans of the tribe Yomut, with one Özbeg and one Afghan. Consequently we formed one of those small karavans, that set out on their way in right Oriental fashion, leaving everything to fate.

When we had all seated ourselves, we had still to take leave of our Turkoman escort, who had led us to the margin of the desert. The Fatiha of the farewell was intoned on the one side by Hadji Bilal, and on the other by Kulkhan.

{89}

After the last Amen had been said, and had been followed by the inseparable stroking of the beard, the two parties divided in contrary directions; and when our late escort had recrossed the Etrek and lost sight of us, they sent a few shots after us as a farewell. From this point we proceeded in a straight direction towards the north. For further information on the political and social relations of the Turkomans, I beg to refer the reader to the Second Part of this volume.

{90}

CHAPTER VII.

KERVANBASHI INSISTS THAT AUTHOR SHOULD TAKE NO NOTES

EID MEHEMMED AND HIS BROTHER'S NOBLE CONDUCT

GUIDE LOSES HIS WAY

KÖRENTAGHI, ANCIENT RUINS, PROBABLY GREEK

LITTLE AND GREAT BALKAN

ANCIENT BED OF THE OXUS

VENDETTA

SUFFERINGS FROM THIRST.

C'était une obscurité vaste comme la mer, au sein de laquelle le guide s'égarait . . . où périt le voyageur effrayé .--Victor Hugo, from ***Omaiah ben Aiedz***.

[Kervanbashi insists that Author should take no Notes]
Without being able to discover the slightest trace of a path indicated by foot of camel or hoof of other animal, our karavan proceeded towards the north, directing its course in the day by the sun, and at night by the pole star. The latter is called by the Turkomans, from its immovability, Temir kazik (the iron peg). The camels were attached to one another in a long row, and led by a man on foot; and, although there was no positive place of honour, it was regarded as a certain sort of distinction to be placed near the Kervanbashi. The districts on the further side of Etrek, which form the foreground of the Great Desert, are indicated by the name of Bogdayla. We proceeded for two hours after sunset over a sandy bottom, which was not however particularly loose, and which presented an undulating, wavy surface, in no place of much elevation. By degrees the sand disappeared, and about midnight we had so firm a clayey soil under us, {91} that the regulated tread of the distant camels echoed as if some one was beating time in the still night. The Turkomans name such spots Takir; and as the one on which we were had a reddish colour, it bore the name Kizil-takir. We marched uninterruptedly till it was nearly dawn of day; altogether we had hardly advanced six miles, as they did not wish at the outset to distress the camels, but especially because the greatest personages in our company of travellers were unquestionably the buffaloes, of which one was in an interesting situation, and could not with her unwieldy body keep up even with the ordinary step of the camel,--consequently there was a halt for repose until eight o'clock in the morning; and whilst the camels were eating their fill of thistles and other plants of the desert, we had time to take our breakfast, which had not yet ceased to be luxurious, as our skins were still richly stored with fresh water, and so our heavy unleavened bread slipped down aided by its sweet draughts. As we had encamped close together, I remarked that the Kervanbashi, Ilias, and the chiefs of my companions, were conversing, and, as they did so, kept casting glances at me. It was easy for me to divine the subject of their conversation. I pretended, however, to pay no attention; and after having for some time fervently turned over the leaves of the Koran, I made a movement as if I had proposed to take part in the conversation. When I had approached a few steps, I was met by honest Ilias and Hadji Salih, who called me aside and told me that the Kervanbashi was making many objections to my joining him on the journey to Khiva, my appearance seeming suspicious to him; and he particularly feared the anger of the Khan, as he had some years before {92} conducted a Frenghi envoy to Khiva, who, in that single journey, took off a faithful copy of the whole route, and with his diabolical art had not forgotten to delineate any well or any hill on the paper. This had very much incensed the Khan; he had had two men executed who had betrayed information, and the Kervanbashi himself had only escaped with his life owing to the intercession of influential persons. 'After many objections,' said my friends, 'that we could not leave thee here behind in the desert, we have so far prevailed with him that he will take thee with him on the condition that thou wilt, first, permit thyself to be searched to see if thou hast any drawings or wooden pens (lead pencils), as the Frenghis generally have; and secondly that thou promise to take away with thee no secret notes respecting the hills and routes, for in the contrary case thou must remain behind, were we even in the midst of the desert.'

I heard all with the greatest patience, and, when they had finished, I played the part of one very angry, turned round to Hadji Salih, and, speaking so loud that the Kervanbashi could not fail to hear, said: 'Hadji, thou sawest me in Teheran and knowest who I am; tell Amandurdi (the name of the chief of our karavan) that it was by no means becoming in him as an honest man to lend ear to a drunken Binamaz (one who does not repeat his prayers) like the Afghan. We must not jest with religion, and he shall never again have an opportunity to assail one in so dangerous a particular; for he shall learn in Khiva to know with whom he has to deal.' The last words uttered with great violence, so as to be heard through the whole karavan, caused my colleagues, particularly the poorer ones, to grow very warm, and had I {93} not restrained them they would have assailed Emir Mehemmed, the malicious Afghan. The person most surprised by this zeal of theirs was the Kervanbashi himself; and I heard how he always contrived to repeat, in answer to the very different representations that were made to him, the same words, 'Khudaïm bilir!' (God knows!) He was an extremely honest, good-humoured man, an Oriental however, disposed, not so much out of malice as fondness for mysteries, to discover in me, any how and at all events, a stranger in disguise; and this, although he allowed himself on the one side to receive instruction from me in many a point of religion, and even in Gömüshtepe had heard that I was acquainted with many books. My artful manoeuvre had, as I have said, diminished my danger; but I still saw to my great regret that the injurious suspicion increased with every step, and that I should have the greatest difficulty in talking even the shortest notes of my journey. I was very much annoyed at not daring to put any questions as to the names of the different stations; for however immense the desert, the nomads inhabiting the various oases have affixed a specific designation to every place, every hill, and every valley, so that if exactly informed I might have marked each place on the map of Central Asia. Cunning has to be employed against cunning, and the scanty notices which I have been able to collect respecting the route is the fruit of an artifice with which I will not weary the reader. What bitter disappointment, what annoyance, must not the traveller feel who, after having through long struggles and great perils reached at length the fountain he longs for, cannot even then slake his thirst!

{94}

[Eid Mehemmed and his Brother's noble Conduct]

After the lapse of eight hours, we again set out; but our march, after having proceeded without interruption for two hours, gradually slackened. Some of the Turkomans dismounted, and occupied themselves busily to the right and to the left in carefully examining the smaller hills. As I learnt afterwards, one of our travelling companions, Eid Mehemmed, was desirous of discovering the tomb of his brother, who had fallen here in a combat the previous year. He had also brought a coffin with him to transport the corpse to Khiva. It may have been about two o'clock in the afternoon when we stopped. They found the grave, and applied themselves to the task of opening it. After having laid the half-putrid body in the coffin and packed it in felt, accompanying the operation with recitations of the usual prayers and citations from the Koran, in which I also had to take my part, we were treated with the details of the combat by an eye-witness. The intention of this man was to do honour to the departed, for praise such as he bestowed none but the noblest of men could deserve. 'We had in our karavan,' said the speaker, 'several Persians, journeying from Khiva to Astrabad, and amongst them there was a very wealthy merchant, named Mollah Kaszim, from the city last named. He had for years been engaged in the traffic carried on between Persia and Khiva, and, having constant occasion to visit the latter country, was the guest of the deceased, and consequently under the safeguard of his hospitality, both in Khiva and in the desert. It so happened that last year he was returning home with a large sum of money, and although dressed as a Turkoman, and perfectly familiar with our language, his presence amongst us was detected by the Haramzadeh (bastards) of Etrek. They hastened to meet {95} and assail us. In number they were superior, but in spite of that we maintained a combat that lasted eight hours. After we had killed two of their number, they called to us to surrender the fat Persian dog, thereby meaning Mollah Kaszim, and that the fight would be at an end, for that they wanted nothing from us. That no one of us, still less the departed one, was disposed to consent to this, may readily be imagined; and although the Persian himself, who feared the balls hissing about in all directions, begged that the fighting might be put an end to, and was desirous of surrendering himself as a prisoner, the battle had to be fought out. Soon afterwards *he*' (and he pointed to the corpse) 'was pierced by a bullet. He fell from his horse, and the few words that he was able to utter were to the effect that he commended his guest, the Persian, who was sobbing all the time like a child with terror, to his brother Eid Mehemmed. Under the leadership of the latter we continued the contest till the morning, when the robbers retreated, with loss. After having buried the deceased here, we travelled on, and three days afterwards the Persian was conducted to Astrabad.'

[Guide loses his Way]

In commemoration of the sad event, Eid Mehemmed had bread baked here also, which he shared amongst us. We then started, keeping to the north, and proceeding through a great sterile plain. To make up for our loss of time we were obliged to journey the whole night without interruption. The weather was lovely, and, cowering in my basket, I long amused myself with the beautiful starry heavens, more beautiful and more sublime in the desert than anywhere else. I was at last overcome by sleep. Perhaps I had scarcely reposed an hour, when I was harshly roused {96} from my slumber, and heard on all sides the cry, 'Hadji, look to thy Kiblenuma (compass), we seem to have lost our way.' I awoke, and saw by the light of a piece of burning

35

tinder that we were going in an easterly direction, instead of a northerly. The Kervanbashi, alarmed, fearing our vicinity to the dangerous marshes, issued the command that we should not stir from the spot till the dawn of day. Luckily we had only swerved from the right course about half-an-hour previously, at a moment when the sky was overcast. In despite of the delay we reached the appointed station, and our wearied beasts were let loose to make their meal upon the thorns and thistles. In the spot where we were encamped I saw with astonishment that my companions collected a great number of carrots, half a foot long, of the thickness of the thumb, and particularly well-flavoured and sweet. The inner part, however, was as hard as wood, and was uneatable, as was also the wild garlic, which we found here in large quantities. I seized the opportunity of giving myself a feast, boiling a good portion of carrots for my breakfast, and storing away a quantity in my girdle.

To-day (May 15) our way passed through a wild district cut up with ditches. I heard it said that each journey it assumes a different form, and presents different difficulties from the numerous steep places.

The poor camels, some of them laden with very heavy burdens, suffered exceedingly--the dry sand giving way under their feet; so that having continually to mount and descend, they could hardly get a firm footing. It is remarkable that it is the custom here to fasten their annuals with a cord, one end of which is attached to the tail of the creature that precedes, the other to the {97} perforated nose of the one that follows; and it is very painful to see how, as they are all so bound together, if one of the beasts in the line stands still a moment, the line in front continues to move on till the cord is torn away from the animal behind, who suffers thereby dreadful torture. To spare the poor animals we all dismounted where the route was bad, as to-day; and although my sufferings were great in the deep sand, I was forced to walk on foot four hours, although slowly, still without a halt. Plodding on thus, I several times came in contact with the Kervanbashi, who, after my last spirited conduct, loaded me with politeness; his nephew, a young frank-hearted Turkoman from Khiva, seemed to be particularly fond of my society. He had not seen his young wife since the year before, and his conversation always turned upon his Ova (tent), as the rules of Islamite politeness obliged him to name the object of his affections. [Footnote 21] Khali Mollah (this was his name) reposed the fullest confidence in my character as a Dervish. I was very much surprised when he requested me to search in my Koran a Fal or prognostic regarding his family. I made the usual hocus pocus, shut my eyes, and fortunately opened the book at a place where women are spoken of (for the passages Mumenin and Mumenat frequently recur), in which my explanation of the Arabian text--for here is the whole art--enchanted the young Turkoman. He thanked me, and I was delighted to find that I had won his friendship.

[Footnote 21: According to the precepts of Islam, it is very unbecoming to speak of one's wife, metaphors are used to express the idea, where the whole is taken to designate the part (*totum pro parte*). Accordingly, the Turk in society names his wife Harem, **Familia**; Tcholuk Tschodjuck; the Persian terms her Khane or Ayal ü avlad, the former expression meaning house, the latter wife's child; the Turkoman, Ova; the central Asiatic, Balachaka, meaning children.]

{98}

Up to the present moment it was not clear which of the three ways the karavan would follow. The concealment of plan is in this country especially necessary, as one is never a single moment safe from surprise; and although nothing was said, it was still plain to all that the middle way would be chosen, for our water supply was running short, and necessity would force us, on the morrow at latest, to make for a well, which is only accessible provided peaceable relations permit the Yomut shepherd to penetrate thither from Ataboz. Our evening march was a successful one; the camel-chain was not often rent asunder, or if any such accident occurred it was observed before the lapse of many minutes, and men were sent back to look up the missing animals. The karavan continued its march; and in order that the individual sent out in the dark night might not lose his way, one of the followers of the karavan had the particular duty assigned to him of holding with the other a dialogue at a distance, so that the words, which echoed sadly in the gloomy night, served as a guide; and yet woe to the wretch in case a contrary wind renders the sound inaudible!

[Körentaghi, Ancient Ruins, probably Greek.]

The next morning (May 16) we discovered, in a north-easterly direction, the mountainous chain called the Körentaghi. The buffalo-cow, near her time, compelled us all to adopt a slow pace, and it was afternoon before we approached close enough to be able to distinguish the outline of the lower part of the mountain. When in Etrek, we had heard that this was the spot where, on account of the prevailing sentiments in favour of peace, we should meet Yomuts; still they {99} were not perfectly assured, and the greatest anxiety existed to know whether the news of a peace would be confirmed, or whether, in case the mountains were abandoned, we might not be surprised by some hostile horde. A courageous Turkoman was sent on to ascertain how matters stood, and his progress was watched by all with anxious eyes. Fortunately, as we approached, the different tents were distinguished, the alarm was dissipated, and the only desire was, to learn to what tribe the encampment belonged. Whilst my fellow-travellers amused themselves with the view of the Körentaghi and its green valleys, my heart beat within me for joy, as I believed that I was approaching ruins, probably of Greek origin, which extended in a westerly direction from the above-named mountain. At the moment when the latter became visible, I had remarked to the south-west a single pillar, which from the distance produced upon the eye the effect of an animated colossal figure. As we mounted the plateau higher and higher I discerned, in the same direction, a second column, somewhat thicker than the former, but not so elevated, and now close to the mountain. I had the ruins, known as the Meshedi Misriyan, so near to me on the left that I was able even to distinguish the particular parts with precision. As none but Yomuts were encamped here, it was resolved to make it a rest-day, and to employ it for the purchase of some camels. This accorded fully with my own wish, as it afforded me the opportunity of beholding the ruins from a closer proximity.

The next morning (May 17) I started, accompanied by Ilias and some of the pilgrims. I was obliged to use many pretexts to induce the latter to visit a spot which they would have preferred avoiding{100} as the abode of Djins (genii). It was distant about half a league from our encampment, although the high walls of the square building, as well as the two entire and the two half-ruined towers in form of domes, seemed to be nearer to us. Around these, and encircling the high wall, from six to eight feet broad and from forty to fifty high, there is a lower one, on the south side, quite in ruins, which must have served as an outwork to the fort, still erect; I regard the entire construction, as it rises amongst the other heaps of dilapidation, as a fortress of ancient date; and I think, to complete its system of defence, its builders must have formed the aqueduct, which runs in a south-westerly direction as far as the Persian chain of mountains, whence it brought hither to the fortress water, for drinking purposes, a distance of 150 English miles.

My acquaintance with archaeology and architecture being limited, I admit my incompetency to form any precise judgment respecting ruins, certainly of high interest, except that I believe myself justified in affirming them to be of Greek origin, because I have found the square bricks which compose them to resemble exactly, in quality, size, and colour, those of Gömüshtepe, and the Kizil Alan (Alexander's wall). [Footnote 22]

[Footnote 22: The Turkomans recounted, with respect to the ruins, that God, from especial love to the brave Turkomans, had placed the Kaaba first here instead of transporting it to Arabia, but that a green devil, who was at the same time lame, named Gökleng (green hobbler) from whom the Göklens were descended, had destroyed it. 'The insolent act of their ancestor is the reason,' added the savage etymologist, 'why we live in hostility with that tribe.']

{101}

Besides these, I remarked a group of other ruins on the north summit of the Körentaghi. We passed them by night, and as far as I could distinguish in the obscurity, there are six separate dome-like chapels still standing.

To-day our karavan was visited by crowds of the nomads dwelling on the spot. Some business was transacted, and bargains struck between the merchants and cattle-dealers of our karavan, and upon credit, too. They applied to me to draw up in writing their cheques. I was surprised to find that the debtor, instead of handing over his signature to tranquillise his creditor, put it into his own pocket; and this was the Turkoman way of arranging the whole business. When I questioned the creditor as to this remarkable manner of procedure, his answer was, 'What have I to do with the writing? The debtor must keep it by him as a reminder of his debt.'

In the evening, when we were ready to start, an event took place, for Madame Buffalo did us the honour of increasing our number by the addition of a healthy little calf, a subject of supreme delight to the Kervanbashi; and not until we were actually on the route, did it occur to him that the poor little calf was not strong enough to accompany our march on foot, and that he must search for a more commodious place for it on one of the camels. As the only kedjeve was the one occupied by Hadji Bilal and myself, all eyes were directed to us. We were asked to cede our place to the new-born calf. My friend was cunning enough at once to evince his readiness to be of service, with the observation that he would, out of friendship to me, whose lameness rendered me less easy to accommodate with a seat, vacate his own, and content himself with any exchange. Hardly had he surrendered his place to the young calf, than the extremely disagreeable smell of my new *vis-à-vis* betrayed to me the real{102} motive of my friend. By night it was endurable, as my slumbers were only disturbed by the frequent bleating of the calf; but in the daytime, particularly when the heat was very great, my situation became intolerable. Happily my torments did not last long, for the calf succumbed the second day of its ride through the desert.

[Little and Great Balkan]

From this day (May 18) we reckoned two days to the Great Balkan, and thence twelve days to Khiva (altogether fourteen days). During the whole time we should come to only four wells of bitter salt water, and should not encounter a single living human being.

As we were still in the middle of May, our leader hoped to find in the lone places some rain-water (called kák). We had filled our skins with dirty water from the miserable cistern at Körentaghi. The jolting on the backs of the camels had changed it into something very like mud, having a most nauseous taste, and yet we were obliged to make a very sparing use of it, for there was no hope of finding kák until we reached a station on the other side of the Great Balkan.

Our march, as we were now every day more inured to its hardships, began to assume great regularity. We made usually every day three halts, each of an hour and a half or two hours: the first before sunrise, when we made our bread for the whole day; the second at noon, to give man and beast the indulgence of a little repose from the scorching heat; and the third before sunset, to devour our scanty supper, consisting of the oft-mentioned bread and water, every drop of which we had to count. My friends, as well as the Turkomans, had with them supplies of sheep-fat. This they ate with their bread, and offered to me, but I was {103} careful not to partake of it, from the conviction that nothing but the greatest moderation could diminish the torments of thirst, and harden one to endure fatigue. The district we were now traversing consisted of a firm clay bottom, only producing here and there a few wretched plants, and forming for the most part barren ground, in which crevices, like veins, extended beyond the reach of the eye, and offered the most variegated picture. And yet how this eternal sadness of plain, from which every trace of life is banished, wearies the traveller; and what an agreeable change he finds when, arriving at the station, he is permitted to rest a few minutes from the wave-like movements of the camel!

The next morning (May 19) we discovered something like a dark blue cloud towards the north. It was the Little Balkan, which we were to reach the next day, of the height, beauty, and mineral wealth of which the Turkomans gave me such long accounts. Unfortunately, this very night, our generally so wakeful Kervanbashi was overtaken with sleep, and the guide at the head of the line of camels brought us into a position of such jeopardy that it nearly cost us all our lives. For it is necessary to mention that at the foot of the Little Balkan there are many of those dangerous salt morasses, covered with a thick white crust, which are not distinguishable from the firm ground in their vicinity, as all is covered in the same proportion with layers of salt of the thickness of a finger. We had advanced in that direction until the camels, by their footing giving way under them, in spite of all encouragement, were brought to a standstill. We sprang down, and judge of my alarm when I felt, although standing upon the earth, as if I were {104} in a moving boat. The consternation was general. The Kervanbashi shouted out that every one should stop where he was, for it was idle to think of extricating ourselves until daybreak. The strong smell of soda was insupportable; and we were forced to wait three hours, till the first beams of the 'aurora liberatrix' should shine forth. The movement in the backward direction was attended with many difficulties; but we were all glad, for Heaven had been gracious to us, as, had we only advanced a little farther, we might have reached a place where the earth had no consistence, and might have swallowed up a part or perhaps the whole karavan. Such, at all events, was the expressed opinion of the Turkomans.

It was ten o'clock on the morning of the 20th of May when we reached the Little Balkan. It stretched from the south-west to the north-east. We discovered also the feebly-defined promontory belonging to the Great Balkan, running parallel with the former range. The Little Balkan, at the foot of which we encamped, forms an almost uninterrupted chain of mountains of equal elevation, for a distance of about twelve miles. It is not perhaps so barren and naked as those in Persia, it yields grass in some places, and in the rest has a bluish-green colour. Its height, measured by the eye, seems about 3,000 feet.

Our route this day and the next morning (May 21) continued to pass along its side; about evening we reached the foot of the promontory of the Great Balkan. Although I could only see a part of this close, I yet perceived the propriety of the appellation that distinguished it; for on an average, as far as the eye can reach, it has greater circumference and greater height. We found ourselves on a branch stretching {105} in an easterly direction. The Great Balkan, properly so called, runs towards the shore of the Caspian, having nearly a north-easterly direction. According to what I heard in Khiva and amongst the Turkomans, it must be rich in precious minerals; but the fact cannot be relied upon without the opinion of competent judges.

Taken altogether, the spot where we encamped this evening was not without its charms; for, as the setting sun projected its rays upon the lovely valleys of the Little Balkan, one could almost fancy oneself actually in a mountainous district. The view might even be characterised as beautiful; but then the idea of a fearful desolation, the immense abandonment, which covers the whole, as it were, with a veil of mourning! We turn fearfully to see whether the next moment our eye may not encounter some strange human face that will oblige us to grasp our weapon, for every human being encountered in the desert must be met with ready arms.

An hour after sunset the start was determined upon. The Kervanbashi pointed out to us that from this point the true desert began; that, although we had all the appearance of being experienced travellers, still he considered it not unprofitable to remark that, as far as possible, we should avoid speaking loudly, or uttering any cry by day or night; and that henceforth we should each bake his bread before sunset, as no one here ought to light a fire by night for fear of betraying his position to an enemy; and finally that we should, in our prayers, constantly implore Amandjilik for security, and in the hour of danger we should not behave like women.

{106}

Some swords, a lance, and two guns were divided amongst us; and as I was regarded as one having most heart, I received fire-arms and a tolerable provision of powder and ball. I must openly avow that all these preparations did not seem to me calculated to inspire much confidence.

[Ancient Bed of the Oxus]

After leaving the Balkan my compass permitted me no longer to doubt, in spite of all attempts at concealment, our having taken the middle route. In Körentaghi we had received intelligence that fifty Karaktchi, of the tribe of Tekke, were prowling about in the vicinity of the mountains; but the Kervanbashi seemed only so far influenced by the information as to give a wide berth to the wells and station called Djenak kuyusu, the water of which is besides very salt, so that no camel would touch it unless it had been without water for three days. It may have been about midnight--we had gone about two miles, and had reached a steep declivity--when the word was given that we should all dismount, for we were in the Döden (as the nomads of the district name the ancient bed of the Oxus), and the storms and the rains of the last winter had now entirely washed away all traces of the route which had been tolerably well defined the year before. We cut across the ancient channel of the river in a crooked line, in order to find a way out on to the opposite bank, the steeper one; it was not till break of day that we contrived, with great fatigue, to reach the high plateau. The nomads in their fables seek to connect the ancient bed of the Oxus with the ruins of Meshedi Misriyan, and declare that the Oxus formerly flowed near the walls of the edifice designed for the Kaaba, and that, at a later period, incensed at the sins of the Göklens, the river turned to the north.

{107}

The more the Balkan disappeared in the blue clouds in our rear, the greater and more awful became the majesty of the boundless desert. I had before been of opinion that the desert can only impress the mind with an idea of sublimity where both fancy and enthusiasm concur to give colouring and definiteness to the picture. But I was wrong. I have seen in the lowlands of my own beloved country a miniature picture of the desert; a sketch of it, too, on a larger scale, later, when I traversed, in Persia, a part of the salt desert (Deschti Kuvir): but how different the feelings which I here experienced! No; it is not the imagination, as men falsely suppose, it is nature itself, that lights the torch of inspiration. I often tried to brighten the dark hues of the wilderness by picturing, in its immediate vicinity, cities and stirring life, but in vain; the interminable hills of sand, the dreadful stillness of death, the yellowish-red hue of the sun at rising and setting, yes, everything tells us that we are here in a great, perhaps in the greatest, desert on the surface of our globe!

About mid-day (May 22) we encamped near Yeti Siri, so named from the seven wells formerly existing here; from three of these a very salt bad-smelling water can still be obtained, but the other four are entirely dried up. As the Kervanbashi expressed a hope of our finding this evening some rain-water--although what remained in my skin was more like mud, I would not exchange it for the bitter, nauseous fluid of these wells, out of which the camels were made to drink and some of my fellow-travellers made their provisions. I was astonished to see how the latter vied with their four-footed brethren in drinking; they laughed at my counsels to be abstemious, but had later occasion to rue their having slighted them.

{108}

[Vendetta]

After a short halt we again started, passing by a hill higher than the rest of the sand-hills, upon the former we saw two empty kedjeve. I was told that the travellers who had been seated therein had perished in the desert, and that everything that had held men was respected amongst the Turkomans, and its destruction regarded as a sin. Singular superstition! Men sold to slavery and lands laid waste regarded as acts of virtue, and a wooden basket held in honour because men have once been seated in it! The desert and its inhabitants are really singular and extraordinary. The reader will be still more surprised when I relate to him what we witnessed this same evening.

39

When it became cooler I dismounted with the Kervanbashi and some other Turkomans, in search of some rain-water that we hoped to find. We were all armed, and each went in a different direction. I followed the Kervanbashi; and we had advanced perhaps forty steps, when the latter observed some traces in the sand, and in great astonishment exclaimed, 'Here there must be men.' We got our muskets ready, and, guided by the track, that became clearer and clearer, we at last reached the mouth of a cave. As from the prints in the sand we could infer that there was but a single man, we soon penetrated into the place, and I saw, with indescribable horror, a man--half a savage, with long hair and beard, clad in the skin of a gazelle--who, no less astonished, sprang up and with levelled lance rushed upon us. Whilst I was contemplating the whole scene with the greatest impatience, the features of my guide showed the most imperturbable composure. When he distinguished the half-savage man, he dropped the end of his weapon, and murmuring in a low voice, 'Amanbol' (peace be unto thee!) he {109} quitted the horrible place. 'Kanli dir, he is one who has blood upon his head,' exclaimed the Kervanbashi, without my having ventured to question him. It was not till later that I learnt that this unhappy man, fleeing from a righteous ***vendetta***, had been for years and years, summer and winter, wandering round the desert; man's face he must not, he dares not, behold! [Footnote 23]

[Footnote 23: The 'vendetta' is here even tolerated by religion! and I was eye-witness in Etrek to an occurrence where a son, in the presence of his mother, avenged the death of his father, that had taken place eight years before, by shooting his step-father, who had married her, and who it appeared had been an accomplice. It was very characteristic that the people who were present at his interment condoled with the mother, and at the same time felicitated the son on the act of piety which he had accomplished.]

Wild man in the desert.

[Sufferings from Thirst.]

Troubled at the sight of this poor sinner, I sighed to think that, in the search after sweet water, we had discovered only traces of blood. My companions returned also without having been successful, and the thought made me shudder that this evening I should swallow the last dregs of the 'sweet slime.' Oh! (thought I) water, dearest of all elements, why did I not earlier appreciate thy worth? Man uses thy blessing like a spendthrift! Yes, in my country man fears thee even; and now what would I give could I only obtain thirty or twenty drops of thy divine moisture!

I ate only a few bits of bread, which I moistened in hot water, for I heard that in boiling it loses its bitter flavour. I was prepared to endure all until we could meet with a little rain-water--I was terrified by the condition of my companions all suffering from violent diarrhoea. Some Turkomans, especially the Kervanbashi, were much suspected of having concealed some of the necessary liquid; but who dared to speak out his thought when every design upon his {110} water-skin would be considered as a design upon the life of its owner, and when a man would have been regarded as out of his senses who should have asked another for a loan of water or present of water? This evening my appetite left me. I had not the slightest craving even for the smallest piece of bread: my sensations were those of extreme debility; the heat of the day was indescribable. My strength was gone, and I was lying there extended, when I perceived that all were pressing round the Kervanbashi; they made a sign to me also to approach. The words 'Water, water,' gave me fresh vigour. I sprang up; how overjoyed and how surprised I was when I saw the Kervanbashi dealing out to each member of the karavan about two glasses of the precious liquid. The honest Turkoman told us that for years it had been his practice in the desert to keep concealed a considerable quantity, and this he doled out when he knew that it would be most acceptable; that this would be a great Sevab (act of piety), for a Turkoman proverb says, 'That a drop of water to the man thirsty in the wilderness washes away a hundred years' sins.'

It is as impossible to measure the degree of the benefit as to describe the enjoyment of such a draught! I felt myself fully satisfied, and imagined that I could again hold out three days! The water had been replenished, but not my bread. Debility and want of appetite had rendered me somewhat careless, and I thought that I could employ for firing, not the wood which was at a little distance, but the camels' dung. I had not collected enough. I placed the dough in the hot ashes, and it was not till after half an hour that I discovered the insufficiency of the heat. I hastened {111} to fetch wood, which I set on fire; it was now dark, and the Kervanbashi called out to me, demanding, 'if I wanted to betray the karavan to the robbers.' So I was obliged to extinguish the fire, and to remove my bread, which was not only not leavened, but was only half baked.

The next morning, May 23, our station was Koymat Ata. It had formerly a well, now dried up; no great loss, for the water, like that from all the other wells in the district, was undrinkable. Unfortunately the heat, particularly in the forenoon, was really unendurable. The rays of the sun often warm the dry sand to the depth of a foot, and the ground becomes so hot, that even the wildest inhabitant of Central Asia, whose habits make him scorn all covering for the feet, is forced to bind a piece of leather under his soles, in the form of a sandal. What wonder if my refreshing draught of yesterday was forgotten, and I saw myself again a prey to the most fearful torments of thirst! At mid-day the Kervanbashi informed us that we were now near the renowned place of pilgrimage and station named Kahriman Ata, and that to fulfil our pious duty we should dismount and walk on foot a quarter of an hour to the tomb of the saint. Let the reader picture to himself my sufferings. Weak and enfeebled from heat and thirst, I was forced to quit my seat, and join the procession of pilgrims, to march to a tomb situated on an elevation, at a distance of fifteen minutes' walk, where, with parched throat, I was expected to bellow forth telkin and passages from the Koran, like one possessed. 'Oh! (thought I) thou cruel saint, couldst thou not have got thyself interred elsewhere, to spare me the terrible martyrdom of this pilgrimage?' Quite out of {112} breath, I fell down before the tomb, which was thirty feet long, and ornamented with rams' horns, the signs of supremacy in Central Asia. The Kervanbashi recounted to us that the saint who therein reposed was a giant as tall as his grave was long; [Footnote 24] that he had for countless years past defended the wells around from the attacks of evil spirits that sought to fill them up with stones. In the vicinity, several small graves are visible, the last resting-places of poor travellers, who in different parts of the desert have perished from the hands of robbers or from the fury of the elements. The news of wells under the protection of the saint overjoyed me. I hoped to find water that I could drink. I hastened so much that I really was the first to reach the place indicated. I soon perceived the well, which was like a brown puddle. I filled my hands; it was as if I had laid hold of ice. I raised the moisture to my lips. Oh! what a martyrdom! not a drop could I swallow--so bitter, so salt, so stinking, was the ice-cold draught. My despair knew no bounds: it was the first time that I really felt anxiety for the result.

[Footnote 24: The Orientals love to dignify their saints also with the attribute of bodily size. In Persia I have remarked several giant graves; and even in Constantinople, on the Asiatic shore of the Bosphorus, on the so-called Mount of Joshua, exists a long tomb which the Turks venerate as that of the Joshua of the Bible, but the Greeks as that of Hercules.]

{113}

CHAPTER VIII.

THUNDER

GAZELLES AND WILD ASSES

ARRIVAL AT THE PLATEAU KAFTANKIR

ANCIENT BED OF OXUS

FRIENDLY ENCAMPMENT

APPROACH OF HORSEMEN

GAZAVAT

ENTRY INTO KHIVA

MALICIOUS CHARGE BY AFGHAN

INTERVIEW WITH KHAN

AUTHOR REQUIRED TO GIVE SPECIMEN OF TURKISH PENMANSHIP

ROBES OF HONOUR ESTIMATED BY HUMAN HEADS

HORRIBLE EXECUTION OF PRISONERS

PECULIAR EXECUTION OF WOMEN

KUNGRAT

AUTHOR'S LAST BENEDICTION OF THE KHAN.

On n'y verra jamais que l'heroisme et la servitude.--Montesq., *Esprit des Lois*, 1. xvii. c. 6.

Chiefs of the Uzbek race Waving their heron crests with martial grace.
Moore, *Veiled Prophet*.

[Thunder; Gazelles and Wild Asses]

Thunder, heard for hours at a distance, not coming near to us till midnight, and then only bringing a few heavy drops of rain, was the herald that announced to us the end of our torments. Towards the morning of the 24th May we had reached the extreme boundary of the sand through which we had toiled during three days; we were now certain to find this day rain-water wherever we should meet a sub-soil of clay. The Kervanbashi had found a confirmation of this hope in the traces of numbers of gazelles and wild asses; he did not betray his thoughts but hastened on, and was in effect the first happy one to discover with his ferret eyes, and to point out to the karavan, a little lake of rain-water. 'Su! Su!' (water, water) shouted all {114} for joy; and the mere sight, without wetting the lips, satisfied the craving and quieted our uneasiness. At noon we reached the spot. We afterwards found, in addition to our previous discovery, other pits filled with the sweetest water. I was one of the first to hurry thither with my skin and vessels--not to drink, but rather to collect the water before it was disturbed and converted into mire by the crowd. In half-an-hour everybody in a rapture was seated at his breakfast; it is quite impossible to convey an idea of the general delight. From this station, called Deli Ata, all the way to Khiva our skins were constantly full, and henceforth our journey in the desert may be styled, if not an agreeable, at least free from uneasiness. In the evening we reached a spot where spring reigned in all its glory. We encamped in the midst of countless little lakes, surrounded as it were by garlands of meadows; it seemed a dream when I compared it with our encampment of the previous day. To complete our delight, we were here informed that all fear of a surprise, that we most dreaded, was at an end, but it was recommended that for this night we should still abstain from lighting fires. It must not be omitted that the sons of the desert ascribed the unexpected abundance of water solely to our pious Hadji character. We filled our skins and started again in excellent spirits.

[Arrival at the Plateau Kaftankir]

This evening we reached the trench for which we had so longed. On the further side of it is the plateau Kaflankir (tiger field). It marks the commencement of the territory forming the Khanat of Khiva.

{115}

[Ancient Bed of Oxus]

A wearisome task for man and beast was the ascent, nearly 300 feet long, that led up to the plateau. I was told that its north side had an approach equally steep and high. The whole presents an extraordinary spectacle; the land on which we stand, as far as the eye can reach, seems to raise itself like an island out of the sea of sand. One cannot discern the limit either of the deep trench here or of that on the north-east; and if we can credit the assertion of the Turkomans, both are *old channels of the Oxus*, and Kaflankir itself was formerly an island surrounded on all sides by these cuttings. Certain, however, it is that the entire district is very distinguishable from the rest of the desert by its soil and vegetation, and the number of animals with which it abounds. We had before occasionally met with gazelles and wild asses, single and separate, but how astounded I was to find them here by hundreds and grazing in large herds. I think it was during the second day passed by us on the Kaflankir, that we perceived, about noon, an immense cloud of dust rising toward the north. The Kervanbashi and the Turkomans all grasped their arms; the nearer it approached, the greater grew our anxiety. At last we could distinguish the whole moving mass; it seemed like a rank or column of squadrons on the point of charging. Our guides lowered the points of their weapons. I strove to remain faithful to my Oriental character and not to betray my curiosity, but my impatience knew no bounds; the cloud came nearer and nearer: at a distance of about fifty paces we heard a clatter as if a thousand practised horsemen had halted at the word of command. We saw a countless number of wild asses, animals in good condition and full of life, standing still, ranged in a well-formed line. They gazed intently at us a few moments, and then, probably discovering of how heterogeneous a character we were, they again betook themselves to their flight, hurrying with the swiftness of arrows towards the west.

{116}
Observed from the side towards Khiva, the elevated ground of the Kaflankir has the appearance of a regular wall; its margin is parallel with the horizon, and as level as if it were only yesterday that the water had retired. From this point a day's march brought us, on the morning of May 28, to a lake named Shor Göl (salt sea), which forms a rectangle, and is twelve English miles in circumference. It was resolved that we should here make a halt of six hours to complete the Gusl [Footnote 25] prescribed to Mahommedans, especially as this day was the festival of Eidi Kurban, one of the most famous holidays of Islam. My companions loosed their knapsacks: each had his fresh shirt to put on; I alone was unprovided. Hadji Bilal wanted to lend me one, but I declined the proffered kindness, being firmly convinced that the greater my apparent poverty the less risk I should run. I could not refrain from laughing when for the first time I gazed upon myself in a glass, and contemplated my face covered with a thick crust of dirt and sand. True, I might have washed in many places in the desert, but I had purposely forborne in order that the coating might defend me from the burning sun; but the expedient had not altogether produced the desired effect, and many marks I shall retain all my life long to remind me of my sufferings. Not I alone, but all {117} my comrades were disfigured by the Teyemmün, [Footnote 26] for believers are required to wash themselves with dust and sand, and so render themselves dirtier. After I had completed my toilette, I observed that my friends in comparison with me looked really like gentlemen. They compassionated me, and insisted upon lending me some articles of attire; thanking them I declined with the remark, that I should wait until the Khan of Khiva himself should dress me.

[Footnote 25: Gusl is the ablution of the whole body, only in exceptional cases necessary. The ordinary washings before each of the five prayers of the day are called Abdest in Turkish, Vudhu in Arabic, and Teharet in Central Asia.]

[Footnote 26: A substitute Abdest prescribed by the Prophet for use in the dry desert when no water can be obtained.]

We passed now for four hours through a little thicket, called here Yilghin, where we met an Özbeg coming from Khiva, who informed us as to the actual position of affairs there. However agreeable a surprise the sight of this horseman to us all, it was as nothing compared with the feeling experienced in beholding in the afternoon a few abandoned mud houses; for since quitting Karatepe, on the frontiers of Persia, I had not seen so much as a wall or other indication of a house. These had been inhabited a few years before, and were reckoned a portion of Medemin, a village which stretches off in an easterly direction. This district had never been put under cultivation until Mehemmed Emin took it in hand fifteen years ago; on which account it bears its present designation, an abbreviation of his name. Since the last war this village had lain waste and desolate, as we shall observe to be the case with many others in Turkestan.

This morning (29th May) it seemed to me that instead of following the direction to the north-east, in which Khiva lies, we had changed our course directly to the north. I made enquiries and found that we {118} were taking a circuitous way for the sake of security. The Özbeg, met yesterday, had warned us to be on our guard, for that the Tchaudors were in open rebellion against the Khan, and that their Alamans were often making forays on these frontiers.

[Friendly Encampment]
This evening we continued our onward march, not without caution, and who happier than I when we next morning saw on our right hand and on our left groups of tents, and everywhere as we passed we were greeted with the most friendly cry of 'Aman geldingiz' (welcome)! Our comrade Ilias, having friends amongst those encamped here, proceeded at once to fetch some warm bread and other Kurban presents (holiday dainties). He came back richly laden, and shared amongst us flesh, bread, and Kimis (a sharp acid drink made with mare's milk). Although we only

43

passed here one brief hour of repose, many God-fearing nomads approached us to realise by the pressure of our hands their holy aspirations. In return for four or five formulae I received a quantity of bread and several pieces of flesh of camel, horse, and sheep.

[Approach of Horsemen]

We crossed many Yap (artificial trenches for irrigation), and arrived by midday at a deserted citadel named Khanabad, whose high square walls had been visible at a distance of three miles. We passed there the afternoon and evening. The sun was glowing hot. How refreshing was it to slumber under the shade of the wall, although the bare earth was my bed, and a stone my pillow! We left Khanabad, which is distant twenty-five miles from Khiva, before daybreak, and were surprised during the whole day's march that we did not perceive a single tent. We even found ourselves in the evening below large hills of sand, and I fancied myself once more transported to the desert. {119} We were occupied taking our tea, when the camels sent to pasture began to run wildly about; we suspected some one was chasing them, when five horsemen came in sight, who proceeded immediately at a gallop towards our encampment. To exchange the tea-things for muskets, and to present a line of fire, was the work of an instant; the horsemen in the meantime approached slowly, and we discerned by the pace of the horses that fortunately we had mistaken, and that instead of having to deal with enemies we should have a friendly escort to accompany us as far as Khiva.

The next morning (30th May) we reached an Özbeg village, belonging to Akyap. And here the desert between Gömüshtepe and Khiva terminated entirely. The inhabitants of this village were the first Ozbegs that I had an opportunity of seeing; we found them excellent people. In accordance with the practice of the country we visited their houses and reaped a rich harvest with our Fatihas. I now again saw, after a long interval, some articles coming from the beloved west, and my heart leapt within me for joy. We might still have reached this day the habitation of Ilias, for here begins a village [Footnote 27] peopled by Khivan Yomuts, and called Akyap, but our friend the cattle-dealer was a little indolent, or did not wish us to arrive unexpected guests; we consequently passed the night two leagues from his house at his uncle's, Allahnazr Bay, [Footnote 28] who was a man in opulent circumstances, and gave {120} us a most hospitable and distinguished reception. This afforded an opportunity for Ilias to inform his wife of our arrival. We made our formal entry next morning (1st June), a countless host of members of his family and relatives having first hastened to meet and welcome us. He offered me a neat tent for my habitation, but I preferred his garden, for there were trees, and for shade my soul pined! Long was it since I had seen any!

[Footnote 27: Village is here called Aul or Oram; it does not correspond with our idea of a number of continuous houses, but a district where the people belonging to one Aul encamp and dwell in a scattered manner about their meadows and lands.]

[Footnote 28: Bay or Bi; in Turkey, Bey means a personage of distinction.]

During my two days' sojourn amongst the half-civilised Turkomans--by which I mean those who were only half settled, half fixed in their abodes--what most surprised me was the aversion these nomads have to everything in the form either of house or government. Although they have dwelt now several centuries side by side with the Ozbegs, they detest the manners and customs of the latter, avoid their company, and, although of kindred origin and tongue, an Özbeg is as much a stranger in their eyes as a Hottentot is in ours.

[Gazavat; Entry into Khiva]

After we had taken a little repose, the karavan proceeded on its way to the capital. We traversed Gazavat, where the weekly market was being held, and had a first glimpse at the Khivan mode of living. We passed the night in a meadow, before Sheikhlar Kalesi. Here I encountered a species of gnat, larger and more impudent than any I ever met with. We were plagued to death, both man and beast, the whole night long, and I was not therefore in the best of spirits when I was forced again to mount my camel in the morning without having for so many hours closed an eye. Happily, we soon forgot what we had suffered from sleeplessness in the impression derived from the magnificent productions of spring. The vegetation {121} became more and more luxuriant and abundant the nearer we approached Khiva. I, at first, thought that the only reason why Khiva seemed so very beautiful was the contrast it presented with the desert, of which the terrible form still floated before my eyes. But, ah! the environs of Khiva with its small havlis, [Footnote 29] in the form of strongholds shaded by lofty poplars, with its fine meadows and rich fields, seem to me still, after I have visited the most charming countries of Europe, as beautiful as ever. Had the Eastern poets tuned their lyres here, they would have found a more worthy theme than in the horrid wastes of Persia!

[Footnote 29: Havli means literally radius, but here taken in the sense of our word court. It contains the tents, the stalls, store-room for produce, and such like things which pertain to the homestead of an Özbeg countryman.]

Even its capital, Khiva, as it rises in the midst of these gardens, with its domes and minarets, makes a tolerably favourable impression when seen at a distance. A prominent feature is the projection of a tongue of barren earth belonging to the sandy desert of Merv: it stretches to within a league of the city, as if to mark completely here, too, the sharply-defined contrast between life and death. This tongue of earth is known under the name of Töyesitchti, and we were already before the gate of the city, and yet those sand-hills were still in sight.

The reader will easily imagine in what a state my spirits were when I found myself before the walls of Khiva, if he reflects on the risks to which any suspicion of my disguise would expose me, as soon as a first introduction should discover my European features. I was well aware that the Khan of Khiva, whose cruelty was displeasing to the Tartars {122} themselves, would, in case he felt any distrust, become far severer to me than the other Turkomans. I had heard that the Khan was in the habit of at once making slaves of all strangers of doubtful character; that he had, not long before, so treated a Hindustani, who claimed to be of princely origin, and who was now, like the other slaves, employed in dragging along the artillery carriages. My nerves were all strung to the highest point, but I was not intimidated. I had, from constant risk, become inured to it. Death, the least serious result of my enterprise, had now been floating continually before my eyes for three months, and instead of trembling I considered how, on any pressing emergency, I might by some expedient get the better of the watchfulness of the superstitious tyrant. On the journey I had acquired exact information respecting all the distinguished Khivites who had been in Constantinople. They named to me oftenest a certain Shükrullah Bay, who had been in residence ten years at the Court of the Sultan. Of his person I had a half recollection, for I had seen him several times at the house of Ali Pasha, the present minister of Foreign Affairs. This Shükrullah Bay, thought I, only knows Stamboul and its language, its manners and its great personages: whether he will or not, I must compel him to admit a previous knowledge of me, and as I can deceive, personating the Stambouli, the Stambouli himself, the ex-ambassador of the Khan of Khiva, will never be able to disavow me, and must serve my purpose.

[Malicious Charge by Afghan]

At the very entrance of the gate we were met by several pious Khivites, who handed up to us bread and dried fruits as we sat upon our camels. For years so numerous a troop of Hadjis had not arrived{123} in Khiva. All stared at us in astonishment, and the exclamations 'Aman eszen geldin ghiz' (welcome)! 'Ha Shah bazim! Ha Arszlanim!' (ah, my falcon, my lion!) resounded on all sides in our ears. On entering the bazaar, Hadji Bilal intoned a telkin. My voice was heard above them all, and I felt real emotion when the people impressed their kisses upon my hands and feet-- yes, upon the very rags which hung from me. In accordance with the custom of the country we dismounted at the karavanserai. This served also as a custom-house, where the new arrivals of men and merchandise are subjected to severe examination. The testimony of the chiefs of the karavans have, as is natural, the greatest weight in the balance. The functions of chief of the customs are filled in Khiva by the principal Mehrem (a sort of chamberlain and confidant of the Khan). Scarcely had this official addressed the ordinary questions to our Kervanbashi, when the Afghan pressed forward and called out aloud, 'We have brought to Khiva three interesting quadrupeds and a no less interesting biped.' The first part of this pleasantry was, of course, applied to the buffaloes, animals not before seen in Khiva; but as the second part was pointed at me, it was no wonder that many eyes were immediately turned upon me, and amidst the whispering it was not difficult to distinguish the words 'Djansiz' [Footnote 30] (spy), 'Frenghi,' and 'Urus' (Russian).

[Footnote 30: From the Arabic word djasus (spy).]

I made an effort to prevent the blood rising to my cheeks, and was upon the point of withdrawing when the Mehrem ordered me to remain. He applied himself to my case, using exceedingly uncivil expressions. I was about to reply, when Hadji Salih, whose exterior {124} inspired respect, came in, and, entirely ignorant of what had passed, represented me in the most flattering colours to my inquisitor, who, surprised, told me, smiling as he did so, to take a seat by his side. Hadji Salih made a sign to me to accept the invitation, but, assuming the air of one highly offended, and throwing an angry look upon the Mehrem, I retired. My first step was to go to Shükrullah Bay, who, without filling any functions, occupied a cell at that time in the Medresse of Mehemmed Emin-Khan, the finest edifice in Khiva. I announced myself to him as an Efendi arrived from Stamboul, with the observation that I had made his acquaintance there, and had wished, in passing, to wait upon him. The arrival of an Efendi in Khiva, an occurrence so unprecedented, occasioned the old man some surprise. He came forward himself to meet me, and his wonder increased when he saw a mendicant, terribly disfigured and in rags, standing before him: not that this prevented him from admitting me. I had only interchanged a few words with him, in the dialect of Stamboul, when, with ever-increasing eagerness, he put question upon question concerning his numerous friends in the Turkish capital, and the recent doings and position of the Ottoman empire since the accession of the present Sultan. As I before said, I was fully confident in the part I was playing. On his side, Shükrullah Bay could not contain himself for joy when I gave him news of his acquaintances there in detail. Still he felt not the less astonishment. 'In God's name, Efendi, what induced you to come to this fearful country, and to come to us too from that paradise on earth, from Stamboul?' Sighing, I exclaimed, 'Ah, Pir!' (spiritual chief), laid one hand on my {125} eyes, a sign of obedience, and the excellent old man, a Musselman of tolerably good education, could not misapprehend my meaning, i.e. that I belonged to some order of Dervishes, and had been sent by my Pir (chief of my order) upon a journey, which is a duty that every Murid (disciple of an order of Dervishes) must fulfil at the hazard of his life. My explanation rejoiced him; he but asked the name of the order. On my mentioning the Nakishbendi, he at once understood that Bokhara was the aim of my journey. He wished immediately to obtain for me quarters in the Medresse before named, but I mentioned at the same time my situation with respect to my companions. I then almost immediately withdrew, with the promise soon to repeat my visit.

On returning to the karavanserai, I was told that my fellow-travellers had already found lodgings in a tekkie, a sort of convent where travelling Dervishes put up, called Töshebaz. [Footnote 31] I proceeded thither, and found that they had also reserved and got ready a cell for me. Scarcely was I again in their midst when they questioned me as to the cause of my delaying to rejoin them; all expressed their regret at my not having been present when the wretched Afghan, who had wished so to compromise me, had been obliged to beat a retreat, loaded with curses and reproaches, not only by them, but by the Khivites. 'Very good,' thought I, 'the popular suspicion removed, it will be easy enough to deal with the Khan, for he will be immediately informed of my arrival by Shükrullah Bay; and as the rulers of Khiva have ever evinced the {126} greatest respect for the Sultan, the present sovereign will certainly venture a step towards an Efendi; nay, it is not impossible that the first man from Constantinople who has come to Kharezm (the political name of Khiva) may even be treated with particular distinction.

[Footnote 31: So called from Tört Shahbaz, which means the four falcons or heroes, as the four kings are designated whose tomb is here, and who gave rise to the pious establishment.]

My anticipations did not deceive me. The next day there came a Yasaul (officer of the court), bringing to me a small present from the Khan, with the order that I should in the evening go to the Ark (palace), 'as the Hazret' (a title of sovereignty in Central Asia, corresponding with our expression, Majesty) 'attached great importance to receiving the blessing from a Dervish born in the Holy Land.' I promised compliance, betook myself an hour previously to Shükrullah Bay; and as he was desirous of being himself present at the interview, he accompanied me to the palace of the King, which was in his immediate vicinity, giving me, on the way, counsel as to the ceremonies to be observed in my interview. He also told me of the bad footing in which he himself stood with the Mehter (a sort of Minister of the Home Department), who feared him as a rival, and neglected nothing to do him an injury, and who, owing to my being introduced by him, would not perhaps give me the most friendly reception. As the Kushbeghi and the elder brother of the King were commanding in the field against the Tchaudors, the Mehter was provisionally the first official minister of the Khan. Both usage and necessity forced me to begin by paying him my respects, for his office was in a hall in a forecourt at the very gate that leads directly to the Khan's apartments.

{127}

[Interview with Khan]

As at this hour there was almost every day an Arz (public audience), the principal entrance, as well as all the other chambers of the royal residence traversed by us, were crowded with petitioners of every class, sex, and age. They were attired in their ordinary dresses, and many women had even children in their arms, waiting to obtain a hearing; for no one is required to inscribe his name, and he who has managed to force his way first is first admitted. The crowd, however, gave way for us on all sides; and it was a source of great satisfaction to hear the women, whilst pointing to me, saying to one another, 'Behold the Dervish from Constantinople, who is to give his blessing to our Khan. May God give ear to his words!'

I found the Mehter, as I had been told, in a hall surrounded by his officers, who accompanied every word of their lord with approving smiles. It was easy to distinguish, by his brown complexion and his long thick beard falling down to his breast, that he was Sart (of Persian origin). His clumsy dress and his great fur cap especially suited his rough features admirably. As he saw me approach he spoke a few words laughingly to those around him. I went

46

straight up, saluted him with a serious expression of countenance, and assumed at once the place of honour in the company, belonging of right to the Dervishes. I uttered the usual prayers, and after all had added the Amen with the ordinary stroking of the beard, the customary civilities were interchanged with the Mehter. The minister was desirous of showing his wit, and remarked that even Dervishes in Constantinople were well educated, and spoke Arabic (although I had only made use of the Stambouli dialect). He proceeded to say that the Hazret (his majesty)--and here every {128} one rose from his seat--desired to see me, and that 'he would be glad to hear that I had brought with me a few lines from the Sultan or his ambassador in Teheran.' Whereupon I observed that my journey had no secular object, that I wanted nothing from any one; but that for my personal security I had with me a Firman, bearing at the top the Tugra (seal of the Sultan). I then handed to him my printed pass. On receiving this sign of paramount sovereignty, he kissed it reverently, rubbed it on his forehead, rose to place it in the hands of the Khan, and, returning almost immediately, told me to step into the hall of audience.

I was preceded by Shükrullah, and was constrained to wait a few moments until the necessary preparations had been made; for although I was announced as a Dervish, my introducer had not neglected to draw attention to the fact that I was acquainted with all the Pashas of distinction in Constantinople, and that it was desirable to leave upon me as imposing an impression as possible. After the lapse of a few moments my arms were held with every demonstration of respect by two Yasaul. The curtain was rolled up, and I saw before me Seid Mehemmed Khan, Padishahi Kharezm, or, as he would be styled in ordinary prose, the Khan of Khiva, on a sort of elevation, or dais, with his left arm supported upon a round silk velvet pillow, and his right holding a short golden sceptre.

According to the ceremonial prescribed, I raised my hands, being imitated in the act by the Khan and the others present, recited a short Sura from the Koran; then two Allahumu Sella, and a usual prayer beginning with the words 'Allahumu Rabbena,' and concluding with a loud Amen and stroking of the beard. Whilst the Khan was still stroking his beard, each of {129} the rest exclaimed, 'Kabul bolgay!' (May thy prayer be heard). I approached the sovereign, who extended his hands to me, and after we had duly executed our Musafeha, [Footnote 32] I retired a few paces and the ceremonial was at an end. The Khan now began to question me respecting the object of my journey, and the impression made upon me by the desert, the Turkomans, and Khiva. I replied that I had suffered much, but that my sufferings were now richly rewarded by the sight of the Hazrets Djemal (beauty of his majesty). 'I thank Allah,' I said, 'that I have been allowed to partake this high happiness, and discern in this special favour of Kismet (fate) a good prognostic for my journey to come.' Although I laboured to make use of the Özbeg dialect instead of that of Stamboul, which was not understood here, the King was, nevertheless, obliged to have much translated for him. He asked me how long I proposed to stay, and if I was provided with the necessary journey expenses. I replied that I wished first to visit the Sunnite saints who repose in the soil of the Khanat, and that I should then prepare for my journey further on. With respect to my means, I said, 'We Dervishes do not trouble ourselves with such trifles. The holy Nefes (breath) which my Pir (chief of my order) had imparted to me for my journey can support me four or five days without any nourishment,' and that I had no other wish than that God would permit his majesty to live a hundred and twenty years!

[Footnote 32: Musafeha is the greeting prescribed by the Koran, accompanied by the reciprocal extension of the open hands.]

{130}

My words seemed to have given satisfaction, for his royal highness was pleased to order that I should be presented with twenty ducats and a stout ass. I declined the ducats with the remark that for a Dervish it was a sin to keep money; thanked him, however, warmly for the second part of his most gracious favour, but begged permission to draw his attention to the holy commandment which prescribed a white ass for pilgrimages, and entreated him therefore to vouchsafe me such a one. I was on the point of withdrawing when the Khan desired that, at least during my short stay in the capital, I should be his guest, and consent to take for my daily board two Tenghe (about one franc and fifty centimes) from his Haznadar. I thanked him heartily, concluded by giving my blessing, and withdrew. I hurried home through the waving crowds in the forecourt and the bazaar, whilst all encountered me with the respectful 'Selam Aleïkum.' When I found myself again alone within the four walls of my cell I drew a long breath, not a little pleased to find that the Khan, who in appearance was so fearfully dissolute, and who presents in every feature of his countenance the real picture of an enervated, imbecile, and savage tyrant, had behaved to me in a manner so unexceptionable; and that, so long as my time permitted, I could now traverse the Khanat in all directions unmolested. During the whole evening I had floating before me the picture of the Khan with his deep-set eyes, with his chin thinly covered with hair, his white lips, and trembling voice. 'What a happy fatality,' I repeated to myself, 'that gloomy superstition often imposes limits to the might and blood-thirstiness of such tyrants!'

As I proposed making extensive excursions into the interior, I was desirous as far as possible to shorten my stay in the capital. What was most worth seeing {131} might quickly be despatched, had not repeated invitations of the Khan, of the officials, and of the most distinguished of the mercantile community, robbed me of so much time. After it was known that I shared the favour of royalty, everybody wanted to have me as guest, and with me all the other Hadjis. What a torture this to me, to have daily to accept six, seven, or eight invitations, and to comply with the usage by taking something in every house. My hair stands on end at the recollection how often I was forced to seat myself, between three and four o'clock in the morning, before sunrise, opposite a colossal dish of rice swimming in the fat of the sheep tail, which I was to assail as if my stomach was empty. How, upon such occasions, I again longed for the dry unleavened bread of the desert, and how willingly I would have exchanged this deadly luxury for wholesome poverty!

In Central Asia it is the practice, even on the occasion of an ordinary visit, to set before you the Desturkhan (a napkin of coarse linen and of a variety of colours, for the most part dirty). In this enough bread is generally placed for two persons, and the guest is to eat some pieces of this. 'To be able to eat no more,' is an expression regarded by the Central Asiatic as incredible, or, at least, as indicating low breeding. My pilgrim brethren always gave brilliant proofs of their ***bon ton***. My only wonder is that they could support the heavy pilow, for upon one occasion I reckoned that each of them had devoured one pound of fat from the tail of the sheep, two pounds of rice, without taking any account of bread, carrots, turnips, and radishes; and all this washed down, without any exaggeration, by from fifteen to twenty large soup plates full of green tea. In such heroic feats I {132} was naturally a coward; and it was the astonishment of every one that I, so well versed in books, should have acquired only a half acquaintance with the requisites of polite breeding!

Another source of torment to me not less considerable was that of the ***beaux-esprits*** of the Ulemas of the city of Khiva. These gentlemen, who give the preference to Turkey and Constantinople beyond all other places, were desirous of receiving from me, the standard of Turkish Islamite learning, an explanation of many Mesele (religious questions). Oh! how warm those thick-headed Ozbegs made me, with their colossal turbans, when they opened a conversation concerning the prescriptions as to the mode of washing hands, feet, face, and occiput; and how a man should, in obedience to his holy religion, sit, walk, lie, and sleep, etc. The Sultan (a recognised successor of Mohammed) and his grandees are accounted in Khiva the practical examples of all these important laws. His Majesty the Emperor of Turkey is here designated as a Musselman, whose turban is at least 50 ells in length, whose beard extends below his breast, and whose robe to his toes. A man might place his life in jeopardy who should assert the fact that the Sultan has head and beard shaved ***à la*** Fiesko, and clothes made for him at Paris by Dusetoye. I was often really sorry to be unable to give to these people, often persons very amiable, the satisfactory explanation they seemed to require; and how, indeed, could I have ventured upon such explanation, standing, as we do, in such direct contrast and opposition!

The Töshebaz or convent that gave us shelter, from the great reservoir of water and mosque which it encloses, was looked upon in the light of a public place: {133} the court consequently swarmed always with visitors of both sexes. The Özbeg in his high round fur hat, great thick boots of leather, walks about merely in a long shirt, in summer a favourite undress. This I myself adopted afterwards, as I found it was not regarded as indecent, so long as the shirt retained its whiteness, even to appear with it in the bazaar. The women wear lofty globular turbans, consisting of from fifteen to twenty Russian kerchiefs. They are forced, striding along, in spite of all the overpowering heat, muffled in large gowns, and with their coarse boots, to drag to their houses heavy pitchers full of water. Ah, I see them now! Many a time one remains standing at my door, entreating for a little Khaki Shifa (health dust [Footnote 33]), or a Nefes (holy breath) for the real or feigned ill of which she complains. I have it not in my heart to refuse these poor creatures, many of whom bear a striking resemblance to the daughters of Germany. She cowers before my door: I touch, moving my lips at the same time as if in prayer, the suffering part of the body; and after having thrice breathed hard upon her, a deep sigh is uttered, and my part is done. Many in these cases persist that they perceive an instantaneous alleviation of their malady!

[Footnote 33: This the pilgrims bring back with them from a house in Medina, affirmed to have been the Prophet's. It is used by the believers of the true faith as a medicine for many different maladies.]

What in Europe idlers seek in coffee-houses they find in Khiva in the courts of the mosques. These have in most cases a reservoir of water, and are shaded by the finest palms and elm-trees. Although at the beginning of June the heat was here unusually oppressive, {134} I was nevertheless forced to keep my cell, although it was without windows, for immediately I issued forth and betook myself to the inviting shade, I was surrounded by a crowd, and plagued to death with the most stupid enquiries. One wanted religious instruction; another asked if the world offered elsewhere places as beautiful as Khiva; a third wished, once for all, to receive authentic information whether the Great Sultan really had his each day's dinner and supper forwarded to him from Mecca, and whether they passed to his palace from the Kaaba in one minute. Ah! if the good Ozbegs only knew how much Chateau Lafitte and Margot garnished the sovereign's table in the reign of Abdul Medjid!

Amongst the acquaintance made by me here, under the elm trees, an interesting one resulted from my meeting with Hadji Ismael, represented to me as a Stambouli; and, indeed, so like one in speech, demeanour, and dress, that I was obliged to accept and tenderly embrace him as my countryman! Hadji Ismael had, it seems, passed twenty-five years in the Turkish capital, was intimate in many good houses, and asserted that he had seen me in such and such a house, and at such and such a time. He even insisted that it was no effort for him to remember my father, who was a Mollah, he said, in Topkhane. [Footnote 34] Far from charging him with impudent mendacity, I assured him, on the contrary, that he had himself left a good name behind him in Stamboul, and that every one awaited his return with impatience. According to his account, Hadji Ismael had carried on, on the shore of the Bosphorus, the business of tutor, proprietor of baths, leather-cutter, caligraphist, chemist, and, {135} consequently, also of conjuror. In his native city, they had a high opinion of him, particularly with reference to his last-named capacity; he had in his house several little apparatuses for distillation, and as he was in the habit of pressing out the oil from leaves, fruits, and other similar substances, it is easy to conceive that his countrymen applied to him for a variety of elixirs. The Maadjun (decoctions) used in case of 'impuissance,' and favourite remedies in Turkey and Persia, are here in the highest consideration. Hadji Ismael had long placed his art at the disposal of the Khan, but his Majesty had neglected the requisite diet, for the simple reason that he was too weak to resist the darts of the boy god. Debility and gout naturally ensued. The Khan grew angry with the court physician, gave him his dismissal, and named in his place a matron renowned for her marvellous success with her patients.

[Footnote 34: One of the quarters of Constantinople.]

The good woman had the happy idea to prescribe to the sick Khan five hundred doses of that medicine said to have worked such beneficial effect upon the renowned poet-monarch of ancient history. The making up of such a prescription would not be found so easy in Europe, but the provisions of the Khivan Constitution afforded facilities, and the poor patient, after having taken from fifty to sixty of these pills, began to observe that they produced a directly contrary effect. The evil counsel cost the counsellor her head. This had occurred not long before our arrival. The last medical prescription had been the buffalo milk already mentioned. During my stay in Khiva, the Khan wanted to reinstate Hadji Ismael in his functions of conjuror, doctor, and powder-maker; the latter, however, declined to resume them, an audacity {136} which he would have certainly paid for with his life, had the superstitious monarch been courageous enough to go near his wonder-working subject.

In Khiva, in the meantime, my Hadji business throve, both with me and my colleagues. In this place alone I collected fifteen ducats. The Khivan Özbeg, although but rough-hewn, is the finest character of Central Asia, and I may style my sojourn amongst his race here as most agreeable, were it not that the rivalry between the Mehter and Shükrullah made me incur some danger, the former being always disposed, from hostility to my introducer, to do me harm; and as he could no longer question the genuineness of my Turkish character, he began to insinuate to the Khan that I was only a sham Dervish, probably sent upon some secret mission by the Sultan to Bokhara.

[Author required to give Specimen of Turkish Penmanship.]

Informed of the progress of this intrigue, I was not at all astonished, soon after my first audience with the Khan, to receive a second invitation. The weather was intensely hot. I did not like to be disturbed in my hour of repose, but what I liked least of all was to be obliged to cross the square of the castle, whither the prisoners taken in the campaign against the Tchaudors had been sent, and where they were to be executed. The Khan, who was numerously attended, told me that he had heard I was also versed in worldly sciences, and possessed a beautiful florid Insha (style); he added that I must write him a few lines in Stambouli fashion, which he would like much to see. Knowing that this had been suggested by the Mehter, who enjoyed himself the reputation of being a caligraphist, and had elicited the fact of my accomplishment from the Hadjis, I took the proffered writing materials and wrote the following lines:--

{137}

Literally translated.

Most Majestic, Mighty, Dread King and Sovereign!

Immersed in thy royal favour, the poorest and humblest of thy servants keeping before his eyes (the Arabian proverb) [Footnote 35] that 'all beautiful penmen are fools,' has until this day very little devoted himself to the study of caligraphy, and only because he calls to mind (a Persian proverb), that 'every failing which pleases the king is a virtue,' does he venture to hand to him most submissively these lines.

[Footnote 35: Doctores male pingunt.]

The extravagant sublimity of the titles, which are, however, still in use in Constantinople, delighted the Khan. The Mehter was too stupid to understand my sarcasm. I was ordered to take a seat, and after having been offered tea and bread, the Khan invited me to converse with him. The subject to-day was exclusively political. To remain true to my Dervish character, I forced them to press every word out of me. The Mehter watched each expression, wishing to see the confirmation of his suspicions. All his trouble was fruitless. The Khan, after graciously dismissing me, ordered me to take the money for my daily support from the treasurer.

[Horrible Execution of Prisoners]

On my saying that I did not know where he dwelt, they then gave me a Yasaul for escort, who had also other commissions to execute; and terrible indeed is the recollection of the scenes to which I was witness in his presence. In the last court I found about three hundred Tchaudors, prisoners of war, covered with rags; they were so tormented by the dread of their approaching fate, and by the hunger which they had endured several days, that they looked as if they {138} had just risen from their graves. They were separated into two divisions, namely, such as had not yet reached their fortieth year, and were to be sold as slaves, or to be made use of as presents, and such as from their rank or age were regarded as Aksakals (grey beards) or leaders, and who were to suffer the punishment imposed by the Khan. The former, chained together by their iron collars in numbers of ten to fifteen, were led away; the latter submissively awaited the punishment awarded. They looked like lambs in the hands of their executioners. Whilst several were led to the gallows or the block, I saw how, at a sign from the executioner, eight aged men placed themselves down on their backs upon the earth. They were then bound hand and foot, and the executioner gouged out their eyes in turn, kneeling to do so on the breast of each poor wretch; and after every operation he wiped his knife, dripping with blood, upon the white beard of the hoary unfortunate.

Ah! cruel spectacle! As each fearful act was completed, the victim liberated from his bonds, groping around with his hands, sought to gain his feet! Some fell against each other, head against head; others sank powerless to the earth again, uttering low groans, the memory of which will make me shudder as long as I live.

However dreadful these details may seem to the reader, they must still be told that this cruelty was only a retaliation for a no less barbarous act committed by the Tchaudors last winter upon an Özbeg karavan. It was a rich one, composed of two thousand camels, which, on its way from Orenburg to Khiva, was surprised and entirely plundered. The Turkomans, {139} greedy of booty, although they had taken possession of stores of Russian merchandise, despoiled the travellers (for the most part Khivan Ozbegs) of their victuals and clothes, so that they died in the middle of the desert, some of hunger and others of cold; only eight out of sixty contrived to save their lives.

[Peculiar Execution of Women]

A treatment of prisoners such as I have described is indeed horrible; but it is not to be regarded as an exceptional case. In Khiva, as well as in the whole of Central Asia, wanton cruelty is unknown; the whole proceeding is regarded as perfectly natural, and usage, law, and religion all accord in sanctioning it. The present Khan of Khiva wanted to signalise himself as a protector of religion, and believed he should succeed by punishing with the greatest severity all offences against it. To have cast a look upon a thickly-veiled lady, sufficed for the offender to be executed by the Redjm according as religion directs. The man is hung, and the woman is buried up to the breast in the earth near the gallows, and there stoned to death. As in Khiva there are no stones, they use Kesek (hard balls of earth). At the third discharge, the poor victim is completely covered with dust, and the body, dripping with blood, is horribly disfigured, and the death which ensues alone puts an end to her torture.

The Khan has affixed the punishment of death, not only to adultery, but to other offences against religion, so that in the first years of his reign, the Ulemas were even obliged to cool his religious zeal; still no day passes, but some one is led away from an audience with the Khan, hearing first the fatal words pronounced, which are his doom, 'Alib barin' (away with him).

[Robes of Honour estimated by Human Heads]

I had almost forgotten to mention that the Yasaul led me to the treasurer to receive the sum for my daily board. My claim was soon settled; but this personage was engaged in so singular an occupation that I must not omit to particularise it. He was assorting the Khilat (robes of honour) which were to be sent to the camp, to reward those who had distinguished themselves. They consisted of about four kinds of silken coats with staring colours, and large flowers worked in them in gold. I heard them styled four-headed, twelve-headed, twenty-headed, and forty-headed coats. As I could see upon them no heads at all in painting or embroidery, I demanded the reason of the appellation, and I was told that the most simple coats were a reward for having cut off four heads of enemies, and the most beautiful a recompense for forty heads, and that they were now being forwarded to the camp. Some one proceeded to tell me 'that if this was not an usage in Roum, I ought to go next morning to the principal square, where I should be a witness of this distribution.' Accordingly, the next morning I did really see about a hundred horsemen arrive from the camp covered with dust. Each of them brought at least one prisoner with him, and amongst the number, children and women, also bound either to the tail of the horse or to the pommel of the saddle; besides all which, he had buckled behind him a large sack containing the heads of his enemies, the evidence of his heroic exploits. On coming up he handed over the prisoners as presents to the Khan, or some other great personage, then loosened his sack, seized it by the two lower corners, as if he were about to empty potatoes, and there rolled the bearded or beardless heads before the accountant, who kicked them together with his feet until a large heap was composed, consisting of several hundreds. Each hero had a receipt given to him for the number of heads delivered, and a few days later came the day of payment.

Receiving payment for Human Heads--Khiva.

In spite of these barbarous usages, in spite of these startling scenes, it was in Khiva and its dependent provinces that I passed, in my incognito as a Dervish, the most agreeable days of my whole journey. If the Hadjis were met by the inhabitants in a friendly manner, to me they were exceedingly kind. I had only to appear in public when passers by, without any begging on my part, absolutely pelted me with many articles of attire and other presents. I took care never to accept considerable sums. I shared these articles of attire amongst my less fortunate brethren, always yielding to them what was best and handsomest, and reserving for myself, as became a Dervish, what was poorest and least pretending. Notwithstanding this, a great change had taken place in my position, and, to avow it openly, I saw with joy that I was now well furnished with a strong ass, with money, clothing, and provisions, and that I was perfectly equipped for my journey.

[Kungrat]

What happened to me in my excursions, which extended as far as Kungrat, would afford ample matter to swell my book with two additional chapters.

In four days and a half going down the Oxus [Footnote 36] I reached Kungrat, and the return journey by land took us twice the time. The two banks, with the exception of that part of the left one where, opposite to Kanli, rises the mountain Oveis Karayne, is flat, and on an average well cultivated and peopled. Between Kanli and Kungrat there is a desert, lasting three days' journey; the opposite bank, on the contrary, particularly where the Karakalpak dwell, is covered by primaeval forests. On my return to Khiva I found my friends tired of waiting; they urged me to quit Khiva the very next day, as the heat, which was increasing in intensity, inspired just apprehensions for our journey to Bokhara. I went to take my leave of Shükrullah Bay, to whom during my stay in Khiva I had been under so much obligation. I was really deeply moved to see how the excellent old man tried to dissuade me from my purpose, sketching to me the most horrible picture of Bokhara Sherif (noble Bokhara). He pictured to me the policy of the Emir as suspicious and treacherous--a policy not only hostile to Englishmen but to all foreigners,--and then he told me as a great secret, that a few years before even an Osmanli, sent by the late Reshid Pasha to Bokhara as a military instructor, had been treacherously murdered by order of the Emir, when he was desirous, after a stay of two years, to return to Stamboul.

[Footnote 36: The upward navigation of the Oxus from Kungrat to Khiva takes 18 days.]

This warm dissuasion of Shükrullah Bay, who at first had the most confident belief in my Dervish character, surprised me extremely. I began to think, 'this man, if he is not sure of my identity, still having seen more of me, has penetrated my incognito, and now perhaps has some widely different idea and suspicion.' The excellent old man had in his younger days been sent in

1839 to Herat to Major Todd, and had also been several times to St. Petersburg. He had often, as he told me, frequented in Constantinople the society of the Frenghi, a source of great pleasure to him. What if, entertaining some idea of our real way of thinking--of our efforts in a scientific direction-- {143} he had from some peculiar feeling of benevolence taken me under his protection? When I bade him farewell I saw a tear in his eye--a tear, who knows by what feeling dictated?

[Author's last Benediction of the Khan.]

To the Khan also I gave a final blessing. He enjoined me to return by Khiva, for he wanted to send an envoy with me to Constantinople, to receive at the hands of the new Sultan the usual investiture of his Khanat. My reply was 'Kismet,' which means that it was a sin to think of the future. We shall see what fate had in store. Bidding farewell to all my friends and acquaintances, I left Khiva, after having sojourned there nearly a month.

{144}

CHAPTER IX.

FROM KHIVA TO BOKHARA.

DEPARTURE FROM KHIVA FOR BOKHARA

FERRY ACROSS THE OXUS

GREAT HEAT

SHURAKHAN

MARKET

SINGULAR DIALOGUE WITH KIRGHIS WOMAN ON NOMADIC LIFE

TÜNÜKLÜ

ALAMAN OF THE TEKKE

KARAVAN ALARMED RETURNS TO TÜNÜKLÜ

FORCED TO THROW ITSELF INTO THE DESERT, 'DESTROYER OF LIFE'

THIRST DEATH OF CAMELS

DEATH OF A HADJI

STORMY WIND

PRECARIOUS STATE OF AUTHOR

HOSPITABLE RECEPTION AMONGST PERSIAN SLAVES

FIRST IMPRESSION OF BOKHARA THE NOBLE.

Et nous marchions à l'heure de midi traversant les souffles brûlants et empestés qui mettent en fusion les fibres du cerveau...

Je m'enfonce dans une plaine poussièreuse dont le sable agité ressemble à un vêtement rayé.-
-Victor Hugo, from **Omaïah ben Aiëdz**.

[Departure from Khiva for Bokhara]

At last, having got all ready for our journey, we gradually assembled in the well-shaded court of Töshebaz. I was able that day for the first time fully to appreciate the influence that the pious charity of the Khivites had exercised upon our mendicant karavan. It was only in the case of the more stingy that we could discern any traces of their former rags: in the place of the torn felt caps, worn amongst the Yomuts, my friends had donned the snow-white turban; all the knapsacks were better filled; and what was most pleasing to see was, that even the poorest of the pilgrims had now his small ass to ride upon. My {145} position was greatly changed, for I had the use of an ass, and half a share in a camel too; the former I was to ride, the latter I was to employ for the transport of my travelling bag containing my clothes (in the strict plural sense), a few MSS. I had purchased, and my provisions. I no longer carried, as I had done in the desert, merely black flour; but white Pogatcha (small cakes baked in the fat of mutton), rice, butter, and even sugar. I still preferred retaining the same dress. True I had come into possession of a shirt, but I took care not to put it on; it might have rendered me effeminate, and it was too soon to indulge in any such luxury.

From Khiva to Bokhara we had the option between three routes, (a) by Hezaresp and Fitnek, crossing the Oxus at Kükurtli; (b) by Khanka and Shurakhan on its right bank, with two days of desert from the Oxus to Karaköl; and (c) up the river by water, and then, disembarking at Eltchig, proceeding through the desert to Karaköl.

As we had decided to go by land, our Kervanbashi's Tadjik from Bokhara, named Aymed, left it to us to choose between the first two ways. We had, in company with a dealer in clothes from Khiva, hired the camels from Aymed, and the latter had recommended us the route by Khanka as, at this period of the year, the safest and easiest.

It was on a Monday late in the afternoon when we suspended the functions of conferrers of blessings, and extricated ourselves from the embraces that seemed as if they never would end, and quitted Khiva by the Ürgendj gate. Many, whose zeal was transcendental, ran for half a league after us; their feeling of devotion forced tears from their eyes, and full of {146} despair we heard them exclaim, 'Who knows when Khiva will again have the great good fortune to harbour in her walls so many pious men!' My colleagues, seated up aloft on their camels, were not again disturbed; but I, on my ass below, was repeatedly visited with active evidence of their friendship, until even my steed could no longer endure it, and, to my great delight, galloped of with me: and it was not until I was far beyond their reach that I thought it proper to recommend him greater steadiness. I was obliged, however, to tug a long time at the reins before I could induce my long-eared hippogriff to change his headlong career into a more sober yet still somewhat rapid trot; when I sought to moderate this still further, he began to show temper, and, for the first time, emitted a distracting cry, the richness, pliancy, and fulness of which I should have preferred criticising at a little farther distance.

We passed the first night in Godje, distant two miles from Khiva. In spite of its insignificance it possesses a Kalenterkhane (quarters for Dervishes); we meet with such in Khiva and Khokand, even in the smallest hamlets. Hence to Khanka we traversed a country uninterruptedly under cultivation; along the whole way we saw excellent mulberry trees; and as my ass continued of good courage, and kept his place in advance of the karavan, I had time in passing to regale myself with berries as large and as thick as my thumb.

Still keeping the lead, I was the first to reach Khanka; it was the weekly market. I dismounted at the Kalenterkhane at the furthermost end of the town, situated upon the bank of a rivulet, and, as usual, well shaded by poplar and elm trees.

{147}

I found here two half-naked Dervishes on the point of swallowing down their noonday dose of opium; they offered me a little portion also, and were astonished to find me decline. They then prepared tea for me, and whilst I drank it, they took their own poisonous opiate, and in half an hour were in the happy realms, then, although I saw in the features of one slumberer traces of internal gladness, I detected in those of the other convulsive movements picturing the agony of death.

I should have liked to remain, to hear from their own lips on awaking an account of their dreams; but our karavan was just then passing, and I was obliged to join it, for as it takes hardly an hour to reach the bank of the Oxus from here, time was important if, as we intended, we were to cross the same day. Unluckily for us, this part of the way was very bad; we did not get out of

53

the mud and marshy ground until evening was drawing in; and we consequently determined to pass the night in the open air on the bank of the river.

The breadth of the Oxus was here so great that both banks were hardly distinguishable at the same time; this was probably owing to the season, for its waters were swollen, and covered a greater surface from the abundant supplies it had received in the spring. Its yellow waves and tolerably rapid current presented a spectacle not without interest to my eye. The nearer bank is crowned far away to the horizon with trees, and with farms. One discovers on the further side also of the river, far in the interior, marks of cultivation, and towards the north the Oveïs Karaayne mountain appears like a cloud suspended perpendicularly from heaven. The water of the {148} Oxus in its proper bed is not so drinkable as in the canals and cuttings, where by its long passage the sand has had time to settle. In this place the water grits under the teeth, just as if you had taken a bite of a sand cake, and it must be allowed to stand some moments before it can be used. As for its quality of sweetness and good flavour, the inhabitants of Turkestan are of opinion that there is no river on the earth comparable to it, not even the Nile, Mubarek (the blessed). At first I thought that this good flavour proceeded rather from fancy wrought up to a fit of enthusiasm on reaching its banks after having traversed the thirsty waterless desert. But no, the idea is founded on error; and I must admit myself that, as far as my experience of water extends, I have never found river or source that yielded any so precious as that of the Oxus.

[Ferry across the Oxus]

Early next morning we found the ferry. Here at Görlen Hezaresp, and other places, the fords are the private property of the Government, and are let to private individuals. The latter dare to transport to the opposite bank only such strangers as have from the Khan a Petek [Footnote 37] (passport), which is obtained on payment of a small tax. The Hadjis had one joint passport, but I had procured an extra one, which was to the following effect:--

Literal Translation.

'It is notified to the watchers of the frontiers and the toll-collectors, that permission has been given to the Hadji Mollah Abdur Reshid Efendi, and that no one is to trouble him.'

[Footnote 37: Literally, a writing.]

{149}

The Ferry Across The Oxus.

[Great Heat]

No objections had been made to us on the part of the police. The document merely had this effect--that we, as Hadjis, were to pay nothing for being ferried over in a boat belonging to the Khan. The ferryman at first would not understand it so, but at last he consented, finding himself obliged, whether he had the feeling or not, to act upon the principle of charity, and to transport us, with our baggage and asses, to the further bank. We began to cross at ten o'clock in the morning, and did not reach before sunset a lofty bank that leads on the right to the Shurakhan canal. The great river, properly so called, took us half-an-hour to pass; but we were carried by the stream far down the current, and before we reached the desired point through the armlets, now up, now down, the whole day passed away, and under such a broiling heat as I rarely before had experienced. In the main stream it was well enough, but in the armlets at the side we settled every ten paces on the sand, when men and asses were forced to quit the boat until it was got afloat; and when the water sufficed to bear it we again embarked. Be it said, that the landing and re-embarkation of the asses was a terrible labour, and particularly with respect to some of the obstinate ones; these had to be carried out and in like helpless babes; and I laugh, even now, when I think how my long-legged friend, Hadji Yakoub, took his little ass upon his back, held it firmly by the fore-feet that hung down upon his chest, whilst the poor little brute, all in a tremor, strove to hide his head in the neck of the mendicant.

[Shurakhan; Market]

We were obliged to wait a day on the bank at Shurakhan, until the camels were brought over; we then set out, proceeding through the district called Yapkenary (bank of canal), which was cut up everywhere by canals. Yapkenary forms an oasis, eight miles {150} long and five or six broad. It is tolerably well cultivated. After it begins the desert, whose edge, called Akkamish, has good pasturage and is peopled by Kirghis. At Akkamish the karavan began slowly to wind along its way. The Kervanbashi, with myself and two others who could depend upon the pace of our asses, went out of our way to make an excursion to Shurakhan, and to complete our store of provisions at the weekly market there, or, to speak more plainly, to divert ourselves.

Shurakhan, which is surrounded by a good wall of earth, boasts only a few houses for dwellings, but consists of 300 shops. These are opened twice a week, and visited by the nomads and settlers of the country round. It is the property of the Emir-ül-Umera, or elder brother of the Khan, who has a fine garden here. Leaving my companions to make their purchases, I went back to the Kalenterkhane, that stands before the gate of the town. I found here several Dervishes, who had become as thin as skeletons by the fatal indulgence in that opium called Beng (prepared from flax) and the Djers, and were lying about dreadfully disfigured upon the damp ground in their dark cells.

When I introduced myself they bade me welcome, and had bread and fruit laid before me. I offered money, but they laughed at that, and they told me that several of them had not, for twenty years, had any money in their hands. The district maintains its Dervishes; and I saw, indeed, in the course of the day, many a stately Özbeg horseman arrive, bringing with him some contribution, but receiving in return a pipe, out of which he extracted his darling poison. In Khiva, beng is the favourite narcotic; and many are {151} addicted to this vice, because indulgence in wine and spirituous liquors is forbidden by the Koran, and any infringement is a sin punished by the government with death.

As it grew late I proceeded to the market to look for my friends, and it cost me much labour to make my way through the waving crowd. All were on horseback, sellers as well as buyers; and it was extremely droll to see how the Kirghis women, with their great leathern vessels full of Kimis, [Footnote 38] sitting on the horses, hold the opening of the skin above the mouth of the customer. There is adroitness in both parties, for very seldom do any drops fall aside.

[Footnote 38: A very acid drink, made of the milk of the mare or camel, for the preparation of which the Kirghis are famous. The nomads of Central Asia use it as an intoxicating beverage, and it has the peculiar property of fattening. I tried it very often, but never could take more than a few drops, because the sharp acid affected my mouth and set my teeth on edge.]

[Singular Dialogue with Kirghis Woman on Nomadic Life]

I found my fellow-travellers, and we proceeded together to rejoin the karavan, now five leagues distant. The day was intensely hot; but, happily, here and there we came, in spite of the sandiness of the land, upon Kirghis' tents, and I had only to approach one of them for the women to make their appearance with their skins, when a regular squabble arose amongst them if I did not accept a drink from everyone. To quicken thus a thirsty traveller in the heat of summer, is regarded as the supreme degree of hospitality, and you confer a kindness upon a Kirghis when you give him an occasion to carry out its laws. The karavan was waiting our arrival with the greatest impatience: they were upon the point of starting, as henceforth we began to march only by night, a great solace both {152} for us and for the cattle. Immediately upon our coming up the move began, and bewitching was the view by the clear moonlight of the karavan winding onwards, the Oxus rolling with a dull sound on our right, and the fearful desert of Tartary on our left. The next morning we encamped on an elevated bank of the same river. The district there bears the name of Töyeboyun (camel's neck), probably from the curves described by the bank: it is inhabited in certain months of the year by Kirghis. In an interval of ten hours I saw in our neighbourhood three families of them, who in turn remained near us, but at most only three hours, when they moved on further. Nothing could give me a more vivid picture of nomadic life; and when I afterwards questioned a Kirghis woman respecting this unsettled mode of existence, she answered, laughingly, 'We shall, I am certain, never be so indolent as you Mollahs, and remain sitting days and days in one place! Man must keep moving; for, behold, sun, moon, stars, water, beast, bird, fish, all are in movement; it is but the dead and the earth that remain in their place!' I was upon the point of making many objections to the philosophy of this nomadic lady, when a cry was heard from a distance, in which I could distinguish the word Büri! Büri! (the wolf, the wolf). She hurried like lightning to the herd that was grazing afar off, and her shouting had such an effect that this time the wolf contented himself with the fat tail of a sheep, and with it took to his heels. I felt very disposed to ask her, as she returned, what advantages resulted from the wolf keeping 'moving,' but she was too much troubled by the loss she had sustained, and I returned to the karavan.

{153}

Before sunset we started again, and marched without stopping in the vicinity of the river. Its deep banks are almost everywhere overgrown with willows, gigantic grass, and rushes. Although the way between Khiva and Bokhara had been described to me as a frequented one, we had as yet, with the exception of the frontier watchers and the nomads who were roaming about, not met a single traveller. What, then, was our astonishment when, about midnight, we saw five horsemen approaching at full speed! These were Khivan merchants, who had come hither from Bokhara, by Karaköl, in four days. They communicated to us the pleasing intelligence that the routes were quite safe, and told us, at the same time, that we should meet, the day after the next, their karavan, which they had left behind them.

We had heard on starting from Khiva that the Tekke Turkomans, profiting by the absence from Bokhara of the Emir and his army, were infesting the approaches to the latter city, and our Kervanbashi felt secretly anxious on that account; but what we now heard set his mind at ease. We were in hopes of reaching the end of our journey in six or eight days, of which we should have to pass only two without arriving at water, that is to say, in the desert between the Oxus and Karaköl.

The next morning we encamped at Tünüklü, the ruins of an ancient fortress on a little hill, at the foot of which flows the Oxus, and which is itself covered with the most beautiful verdure. From this point there is a way lying in a north-easterly direction, through the sandy desert of Khalata Tchöli, otherwise designated Djan Batirdigan [Footnote 39] (life destroyer), but {154} which is only frequented in winter, after heavy falls of snow, at times when the Karaköl route is infested by the Turkomans, who at that period of the year, owing to the freezing of the Oxus, circulate in every direction without obstacle.

[Footnote 39: More correctly Batirdurgan, present participle of the verb batirmak (destroy).]

In the meantime the heat became more and more intense, but it did not much affect us, as we reposed every day on the banks of a mighty river, full of sweet water; and what feelings of grateful gladness were ours when we recollected Kahriman Ata, and other places in the great desert between Khiva and Gömüshtepe. Unhappily we were soon disturbed in our agreeable reflections, and placed, by the freaks of some Turkoman adventurers, in a position of danger such as might have brought us all to a terrible end, had we not been preserved by an accident or fatality.

[Alaman of the Tekke; Karavan alarmed returns to Tünüklü]

It was just about daybreak when we met on our march two half-naked men, who from a distance shouted out to our karavan. On coming up to us they sank upon the ground, uttering the words, 'A morsel of bread, a morsel of bread!' I was one of the first to tender them bread and mutton fat. After eating a little, they began to tell us that they were boatmen from Hezaresp, and that they had been robbed by a Tekke Alaman of boat, clothes, and bread, and had been dismissed with life alone; that the robbers were 150 in number, and contemplated a *razzia* upon the herds of the Kirghis round about. 'For God's sake,' said one of them, 'fly or conceal yourselves, or in a few hours you will encounter them, and in spite of your all being pious pilgrims, they will leave you behind in the desert, without beasts or food, for the Kair, disbelieving Tekke, are capable of anything.' Our Kervanbashi, who had {155} been already twice robbed, and had had great difficulty in escaping with his life, needed not the counsel; scarcely had he heard the words 'Tekke' and 'Alaman,' when he in all haste gave the command to face about, and began the retreat with as much rapidity as the poor heavily-laden camels permitted. To attempt to fly with these animals from Turkomans mounted on horses, would of course have been the height of folly; still, according to our calculation, 150 horsemen could not be transported over the river till the morning, and whilst the robbers were cautiously proceeding on the route, we might again reach Tünüklü, and having refilled our water-skins, throw ourselves into the Khalata (desert), where our destruction might not be so certain. After the most excessive exertions, our poor brutes arrived quite exhausted before Tünüklü. Here we were obliged to accord them a little pasture and repose, otherwise it would have been impossible to reach even the first station in the sand. We tarried on the spot therefore perforce, tremblingly, three hours, until we had had time to fill our skins, and to make preparations for the terrible journey.

The dealer in clothes from Khiva, who had himself been once already robbed by the Turkomans, had, in the meantime, persuaded several of the Hadjis--those I mean who had well-filled sacks, but no courage --rather to hide themselves with him in the underwood on the river's bank, than during the Saratan (dog-days) to throw themselves into the desert, where they would be menaced not only with death from thirst, but with destruction from the Tebbad (hot-wind from the east).

{156}

He painted the perils in such lively terms that many separated themselves from our party; and as just at that moment an empty skiff appeared on the river, and the boatmen, approaching the bank where we were, offered to take us to Hezaresp, every one began to waver, and soon there remained only fourteen faithful to the original plan of the Kervanbashi. That, indeed, was the most critical moment of my whole journey! To return to Khiva might, I reflected, disturb the whole design of my journey. 'My life, indeed, is threatened everywhere--is everywhere in danger; forward, then, forward! better to perish by the fury of the elements than by the racks of tyrants!'

I remained with the Kervanbashi, as did also Hadji Salih and Hadji Bilal. It was a painful scene, that parting from our cowardly fellow-travellers; and behold, as the skiff was upon the point of putting off, our friends already on board proposed a Fal. [Footnote 40]

[Footnote 40: Fal (prognostic) is where one opens either the Koran or any other religious book at random, and seeks on the page before him a passage appropriate to his wish.]

The pebbles, indicating the number of verses to be read, were shared amongst us, and hardly had Hadji Salih, with the eye of experience, ascertained the result, when nearly all the Hadjis, abandoning the skiff, came back to us, and as everything was at hand, to prevent further hesitation and wavering, the impulse was at once obeyed, and we started. The sun had not yet set when we found ourselves already on the way to the Khalata, diverging sideways from the ruins of Tünüklü.

[Forced to throw itself into the Desert, 'Destroyer of Life']

It is easy to imagine what mood we were in, I and my companions, already so well acquainted with the terrors of the desert! From Gömüshtepe to Khiva we had been in the month of May; we were now in July. {157} Then we had had rain-water; but here there was not a single source that could be turned to account. With unutterable regret our eyes rested on the Oxus, that became more and more remote, and shone doubly beautiful in the last beams of the departing sun. Even the camels, who before we started had drunk abundantly, kept their eyes so full of expression for a long, long time turned in the same direction!

A few stars began to gleam in the heavens when we reached the sandy desert. We maintained the stillness of death during our march, in order that we might escape the notice of the Turkomans probably then in our vicinity. They might perhaps not see us on account of the darkness of the night, the moon not rising till later. We wished also that no sound might betray our position to them. On the soft ground the tread of the camels produced no echo. We feared, however, that some freak of braying might occur to our asses, for their voices would echo far and wide in the still night. Towards midnight we reached a place where we were all obliged to dismount, as both asses and camels were sinking down to their knees in the fine sand. This, indeed, formed there an uninterrupted chain of little hills. In the cool night march I could just manage to tramp on through this endless sand; but towards morning I felt my hand beginning to swell from continually resting upon my staff. I consequently placed my baggage on the ass, and took its place upon the camel; which, although breathing hard, was still more in his element in the sand than I with my lame leg.

[Thirst]

Our morning station bore the charming appellation of Adamkyrylgan (which means 'the place where men perish'), and one needed only to cast a look at the {158} horizon to convince himself how appropriate is that name. Let the reader picture to himself a sea of sand, extending as far as eye can reach, on one side formed into high hills, like waves, lashed into that position by the furious storm; on the other side, again, like the smooth waters of a still lake, merely rippled by the west wind. Not a bird visible in the air, not a worm or beetle upon the earth; traces of nothing but departed life, in the bleaching bones of man or beast that has perished, collected by every passer-by in a heap, to serve to guide the march of future travellers! Why add that we moved on unnoticed by the Turkomans? The man does not exist on earth that could make a station here on horseback; but whether the elements would not oppose our progress was a point the consideration of which shook even the *sang froid* of the Oriental, and the sombre looks of my fellow-travellers during the whole way best betrayed their anxiety. According to what the Kervanbashi told us, we should have had altogether on this way, from Tünüklü to Bokhara, only six days' journey, half through sand, the rest over firm and even ground, where here and there grass is met with and shepherds resort. Consequently, after the examination of our skins, we calculated that we should only have to apprehend a deficiency of water during one day and a half; but the very first day I remarked that the Oxus water did not bear out our calculations; that that most precious liquid, although we made a most sparing use of it, diminished every moment, either from the heat of the sun, its own evaporation, or some such cause. This discovery made me watch my stores with double carefulness; in this I was imitated by the others, and, in spite of our anxiety, it was even comical to see how {159} the slumberers slept, firmly embracing their water vessels.

[Death of Camels]

Notwithstanding the scorching heat, we were obliged to make, during the day also, marches of from five to six hours' duration, for the sooner we emerged from the region of sand, the less occasion we had to dread the dangerous wind Tebbad, [Footnote 41] for on the firm plain it can but bring with it the torture of fever, whereas in the region of sand it can in a moment bury everything. The strength of the poor camels was taxed too far; they entered the desert wearied by their nocturnal journey; it was not, therefore, surprising that some fell ill through the torments of the sand and the heat, and that two died even at this day's station. It bears the name of Shorkutuk. This word signifies salt fountain, and one, in fact, is said to exist here, adequate for the refreshment of beasts, but it was entirely choked up by the stormy wind, and a day's labour would have been necessary to render it again serviceable.

[Footnote 41: Tebbad, a Persian word signifying *fever wind*.]

[Death of a Hadji]

But let alone the Tebbad, the oppressive heat by day had already left us without strength, and two of our poorer companions, forced to tramp on foot by the side of their feeble beasts, having exhausted all their water, fell so sick that we were forced to bind them at full length upon the camels, as they were perfectly incapable of riding or sitting. We covered them, and as long as they were able to articulate they kept exclaiming, 'Water! water!' the only words that escaped their lips. Alas! even their best friends denied them the life-dispensing draught; and when we, on the fourth day, reached Medemin Bulag one {160} of them was freed by death from the dreadful torments of thirst. It was one of the three brothers who had lost their father at Mecca. I was present when the unfortunate man drew his last breath. His tongue was quite black, the roof of his mouth of a greyish white; in other respects his features were not much disfigured, except that his lips were shrivelled, the teeth exposed, and the mouth open. I doubt much whether, in these extreme sufferings, water would have been of service; but who was there to give it to him?

It is a horrible sight to see the father hide his store of water from the son, and brother from brother; each drop is life, and when men feel the torture of thirst, there is not, as in the other dangers of life, any spirit of self-sacrifice, or any feeling of generosity.

[Stormy Wind]

We passed three days in the sandy parts of the desert. We had now to gain the firm plain, and come in sight of the Khalata mountain, that stretches away toward the north. Unhappily, disappointment again awaited us. Our beasts were incapable of further exertion, and we passed a fourth day in the sand. I had still left about six glasses of water in my leathern bottle. These I drank drop by drop, suffering, of course, terribly from thirst. Greatly alarmed to find that my tongue began to turn a little black in the centre, I immediately drank off at a draught half of my remaining store, thinking so to save my life; but, oh! the burning sensation, followed by headache, became more violent towards the morning of the fifth day, and when we could just distinguish, about mid-day, the Khalata mountains from the clouds that surrounded them, I felt my strength gradually abandon me. {161} The nearer we approached the mountains, the thinner the sand became, and all eyes looked eagerly to discover a drove of cattle or shepherd's hut, when the Kervanbashi and his people drew our attention to a cloud of dust that was approaching, and told us to lose no time in dismounting from the camels. These poor brutes knew well enough that it was the Tebbad that was hurrying on; uttering a loud cry, they fell on their knees, stretched their long necks along the ground, and strove to bury their heads in the sand. We entrenched ourselves behind them, lying there as behind a wall (*see Plate*); and scarcely had we, in our turn, knelt under their cover, than the wind rushed over us with a dull, clattering sound, leaving us, in its passage, covered with a crust of sand two fingers thick. The first particles that touched me seemed to burn like a rain of flakes of fire. Had we encountered it when we were six miles deeper in the desert, we should all have perished. I had not time to make observations upon the disposition to fever and vomiting caused by the wind itself, but the air became heavier and more oppressive than before.

Tebbad--Sand Storm in the Desert.

Where the sand comes entirely to an end, three different ways are visible: the first (22 miles long) passes by Karaköl; the second (18 miles), through the plain to the immediate vicinity of Bokhara; the third (20 miles) traverses the mountains where water is to be met with, but it is inaccessible to camels on account of its occasional steepness. We took, as it had been previously determined, the middle route, the shortest, particularly as we were animated by the hope of finding water amongst those who tended their flocks there. Towards evening we reached fountains that had not yet been visited this year by the {162} shepherds; the water, undrinkable by man, still refreshed our beasts. We were ourselves all very ill, like men half dead, without any animation but that which proceeded from the now well-grounded hope that we should all be saved!

[Precarious State of Author; Hospitable Reception amongst Persian Slaves]

I was no longer able to dismount without assistance; they laid me upon the ground; a fearful fire seemed to burn my entrails; my headache reduced me almost to a state of stupefaction. My pen is too feeble to furnish even a slight sketch of the martyrdom that thirst occasions; I think that no death can be more painful. Although I have found myself able to nerve myself to face all other perils, here I felt quite broken. I thought, indeed, that I had reached the end of my life. Towards midnight we started, I fell asleep, and on awaking in the morning found myself in a mud hut, surrounded by people with long beards; in these I immediately recognised children of 'Iran.' They said to me: 'Shuma ki Hadji nistid' (You, certainly, are no Hadji). I had no strength to reply. They at first gave me something warm to drink, and a little afterwards some sour milk, mixed with water and salt, called here 'Airan:' that gave me strength and set me up again.

I now first became aware that I and my other fellow-travellers were the guests of several Persian slaves, who had been sent hither in the middle of the wilderness, at a distance of ten miles from Bokhara, to tend sheep; they had received from their owners only a scanty supply of bread and water, so that they might find it impossible to make such a provision as should help them to flee away through the wilderness. And yet these unfortunate exiles had had the magnanimity to share their store of water with their arch-enemies, {163} the Sunnite Mollahs! To me they showed peculiar kindness, as I addressed them in their mother tongue. Persian, it is true, is spoken also in Bokhara, but the Persian of the Irani is different from the former.

I was much touched to see amongst them a child five years old, also a slave, of great intelligence. He had been, two years before, captured and sold with his father. When I questioned him about the latter, he answered me confidingly. 'Yes; my father has bought himself (meaning paid his own ransom); at longest I shall only be a slave two years, for by that time my father will have spared the necessary money.' The poor child had on him hardly anything but a few little rags, to cover his weak little body; his skin was of the hardness and colour of leather. I gave him one of my own articles of attire, and he promised me to have a dress made out of it for himself.

The unhappy Persians gave us besides a little water to take with us. I left them with a mixed feeling of gratitude and compassion. We started with the intention of making our next station at Khodja Oban, a place to which pilgrims resort to visit the grave of a saint of the same name: it was, indeed, out of our road, lying a little to the north, still, as Hadjis, we were bound to proceed thither. To the great regret of my companions we lost our way at night between the hills of sand that are on the margin of the desert, and out of the middle of which Khodja Oban projects like an oasis; and when, after a long search, the day broke we found ourselves on the bank of a lake full of sweet water. Here terminated the desert, and with it the fear of a death from thirst, robbers, wind, or other hardships. We had now come positively to the frontiers of Bokhara, properly so called; and when, {164} after two leagues' journey, we reached Khakemir (the village where the Kervanbashi resided), we found ourselves already in the middle of a country tolerably well cultivated. The whole district is watered by canals connected with the river Zereshan.

In Khakemir there are but 200 houses. It is only two leagues distant from Bokhara. We were obliged to pass the night here, that the tax-collector (Badjghir) and reporter (Vakanüvisz), informed of our arrival in accordance with the law, might be in a position to complete their report of search and examination outside the city.

The very same day a messenger went express, and the following one, very early in the morning, arrived three of the Emir's officers, with faces full of official dignity and importance, to levy upon us the imposts and duties, but more especially to learn tidings concerning the adjoining countries. They first began to overhaul our baggage. The Hadjis had, for the most part, in their knapsacks holy beads from Mecca, dates from Medina, combs from Persia, and knives, scissors, thimbles, and small looking-glasses from Frenghistan. And although my friends declared that the Emir, 'God grant him to live 120 years,' would never take any customs from Hadjis, the collector did not in the slightest degree allow himself to be diverted from his functions, but wrote down each article separately. I remained, with two other mendicants, to the last. When the official looked at my face he laughed, told me to show my trunk, 'for that *we*' (meaning, probably, Europeans, as he took me for one) 'had always fine things with us.' I happened to be in excellent humour, and had on my Dervish or fool's cap. I interrupted the cunning Bokhariot, saying, 'that I had, {165} in effect, some beautiful things, which he would see himself when he came to examine my property, movable and immovable.' As he insisted upon seeing everything, I ran into the court, fetched my ass, and led it to him up the stairs and over the carpets into the room; and after having introduced it, amid the loud laughter of my companions, I lost no time in opening my knapsack, and then showed him the few rags and old books which I had collected in Khiva. The disappointed Bokhariot looked round him in astonishment, demanding if I really had

59

nothing more. Whereupon Hadji Salih gave him explanations as to my rank, my character, as well as the object I had in view, in my journey; all of which he noted down carefully, accompanying the act with a look at me and a shake of the head full of meaning. When the collector had finished with us, the functions of the Vakanüvisz (writer of events) began. He first took down the name of each traveller with a detailed description of his person, and then whatever information or news each might have it in his power to give. What a ridiculous proceeding--a long string of questions respecting Khiva, a land of kindred language, origin, and religion with Bokhara; their frontiers having been for centuries and centuries coterminous, and their capitals lying only a few days' journey distant from each other.

[First Impression of Bokhara the Noble.]

Everything was in order, only some difference of opinion arose as to the quarter in the capital where we should first put up. The collector proposed the custom-house, hoping, at least, there to be able to squeeze something out of us, or to subject me to a stricter examination. Hadji Salih (for the latter, possessing much influence in Bokhara, now took the lead in the {166} karavan) declared, on the contrary, his purpose to put up in the Tekkie; and we started at once from Khakemir, and had only proceeded half-an-hour through a country resplendent with gardens and cultivated fields, when Bokhara Sherif (the noble, as the Central Asiatics designate it) appeared in view, with, amongst some other buildings, its clumsy towers, crowned, almost without exception, by nests of storks. [Footnote 42]

[Footnote 42: In Khiva nightingales abound, but there are no storks; the reverse is the case at Bokhara, in which there is not a single tower or other elevated building where we do not see birds of the last-named description, sitting, like single-legged sentinels, upon the roofs. The Khivite mocks the Bokhariot upon this subject, saying, 'Thy nightingale song is the bill-clapping of the stork.']

At the distance of about a league and a half from the city we crossed the Zerefshan. It flows in a southerly direction, and, although its current is tolerably strong, is fordable by camels and horses. On the opposite side was still visible the *tête du pont* of a once handsomely-built stone bridge. Close to it stood the ruins of a palace, also of stone. I was told that it was the work of the renowned Abdullah Khan Sheibani. Taken altogether, there are, in the immediate environs of the capital of Central Asia, few remains of her former grandeur.

{167}

CHAPTER X.

BOKHARA

RECEPTION AT THE TEKKIE, THE CHIEF NEST OF ISLAMISM

RAHMET BI

BAZAARS

BAHA-ED-DIN, GREAT SAINT OF TURKESTAN

SPIES SET UPON AUTHOR

FATE OF RECENT TRAVELLERS IN BOKHARA

BOOK BAZAAR

THE WORM (RISHTE)

WATER SUPPLY

LATE AND PRESENT EMIRS

HAREM, GOVERNMENT, FAMILY OF REIGNING EMIR

SLAVE DEPOT AND TRADE

DEPARTURE FROM BOKHARA, AND VISIT TO THE TOMB OF BAHA-ED-DIN.

> *Within earth's wide domains   Are markets for men's lives;   Their necks are galled with chains,   Their wrists are cramped with gyves.   Dead bodies, that the kite In deserts makes its prey;   Murders that with affright   Scare school-boys from their play!*   --Longfellow.

[Bokhara; Reception at the Tekkie, the Chief Nest of Islamism]

The road led us to the Dervaze Imam, situated to the west, but we did not pass through it, because, as our Tekkie lay to the north-east, we should have been forced to make our way through all the throngs in the bazaar. We preferred, therefore, to take a circuitous route along the city wall. This we found, in many places, in a ruinous state. Entering by the gate called Dervaze Mezar, we speedily reached the spacious Tekkie. It was planted with fine trees, formed a regular square, and had forty-eight cells on the ground floor. {168} The present Khalfa (principal) is grandson of Khalfa Hüsein, renowned for his sanctity, and the Tekkie itself is named after him. The estimation in which his family stands is shown by the fact that his relative, above mentioned, is Imam and Khatib (court priest) of the Emir, an official position which made me not a little proud of my host. Hadji Salih, who was a Mürid (disciple) of the saint, and was consequently regarded as a member of the family, presented me. The respectable 'Abbot,' a man of gentle demeanour and agreeable exterior, whom his snow-white turban and summer dress of fine silk well became, received me in the warmest manner, and, as I maintained for half-an-hour a conversation couched in tumid and far-fetched language, the good man was overjoyed, and regretted that the Badewlet [Footnote 43] (his Majesty the Emir) was not in Bokhara, that he might immediately present me.

[Footnote 43: Badewlet means properly 'the prosperous one.']

[Rahmet Bi]

He assigned me a cell to myself in the place of honour, that is where I had, as neighbours, on one side a very learned Mollah, and on the other Hadji Salih: this establishment was filled with personages of celebrity. I had fallen, without having remarked it, upon the chief nest of Islamite fanaticism in Bokhara. The locality itself, if I could but accommodate myself to its spirit, might turn out the best and safest guarantee against all suspicions, and save me all disagreeable scenes with the civil authorities. The reporter had returned my arrival as an event of importance; the first officer of the Emir, Rahmet Bi, who during his master's campaign in Khokand commanded in Bokhara, had directed that the Hadjis should, that very day, be questioned concerning me; {169} but in the Tekkie the Emir's orders were inoperative, and so little respect was entertained for the investigation, that no communication at all was made to me on the subject. My good friends replied in the following manner to the doubts of laymen:--'Hadji Reshid is not only a good Musselman, but at the same time a learned Mollah; to have any suspicion of him is a mortal sin.' But, in the meantime, they advised me how I was to act, and it is solely to their counsels and invaluable suggestions that I can ascribe my having entirely escaped mishap in Bokhara; for, not to mention the sad ends of those travellers who preceded me to this city, I have found it a most perilous place, not only for all Europeans, but for every stranger, because the Government has carried the system of espionage to just as high a pitch of perfection as the population has attained pre-eminence in every kind of profligacy and wickedness.

[Bazaars]

I went next morning, accompanied by Hadji Salih and four others of our friends, to view the city and the bazaars; and although the wretchedness of the streets and houses far exceeded that of the meanest habitations in Persian cities, and the dust, a foot deep, gave but an ignoble idea of the 'noble Bokhara,' I was nevertheless astonished when I found myself for the first time in the bazaar, and in the middle of its waving crowd.

These establishments in Bokhara are indeed far from splendid and magnificent, like those of Teheran, Tabris, and Isfahan; but still, by the strange and diversified intermixture of races, dresses, and customs, they present a very striking spectacle to the eye of a stranger. In the moving multitude most bear the type of Iran, and have their heads surmounted by {170} a turban, white or blue--the former colour being distinctive of the gentleman or the Mollah, the latter the appropriate ornament of the merchant, handi-craftsman, and servant. After the Persian it is the Tartar physiognomy that predominates. We meet it in all its degrees, from the Özbeg, amongst whom we find a great intermixture of blood, to the Kirghis, who have preserved all the wildness of their origin. No need to look the latter in the face; his heavy, firm tread suffices alone to distinguish him from the Turani and the Irani. Then imagine that you see in the midst of the throng of the two principal races of Asia some Indians (Multani, as they are here called) and Jews. Both wear a Polish cap, for the sake of distinction, [Footnote 44] and a cord round their loins; the former, with his red mark on his forehead, and his yellow repulsive face, might well serve to scare away crows from rice fields; the latter, with his noble, pre-eminently-handsome features, and his splendid eye, might sit to any of our artists for a model of manly beauty. There were also Turkomans distinguished from all by the superior boldness and fire of their glance, thinking, perhaps, what a rich harvest the scene before them would yield to one of their Alamans. Of Afghans but few are seen. The meaner sort, with their long dirty shirts, and still dirtier hair streaming down, throw a cloth, in Roman fashion, round their shoulders; but this does not prevent their looking like persons who rush for safety from their beds into the streets, when their houses are on fire.

[Footnote 44: Elameti Tefrikie, which according to the provisions of the Koran, every subject, not a Musselman, must wear in order that the salutation 'Selam Aleïkum' (Peace be with you!) may not be thrown away upon him.]

{171}

This diversified chaos of Bokhariots, Khivites, Khokandi, Kirghis, Kiptchak, Turkomans, Indians, Jews, and Afghans, is represented in all the principal bazaars; and although everything is in unceasing movement up and down, I am yet unable to detect any trace of the bustling life so strikingly characteristic of the bazaars in Persia.

I kept close to my companions, casting as I passed glances at the booths, which contain, with a few articles from the other countries in Europe, fancy goods and merchandise, more especially of Russian manufacture. These have no particular intrinsic attractions in themselves for a European traveller to this remote city; but they interest him nevertheless, for each piece of calico, each ticket attached to it, identifying the origin with the name of the manufacturer, makes him feel as if he has met a countryman. How my heart beat when I read the words 'Manchester' and 'Birmingham,' and how apprehensive I was of betraying myself by an imprudent exclamation! There are very few large warehouses or wholesale dealers; and in spite of cotton, calico, and fine muslin being sold, not only in the Restei Tchit Furushi (the place where cotton is exposed for sale), which has 284 shops, but also in many other places in the city, I might boldly affirm that my friends 'Hanhart and Company,' in Tabris, dispose alone of as much of the articles above named as the whole city of Bokhara, in spite of the latter being denominated the capital of Central Asia. That department in its bazaar has more interest for the stranger, where he sees spread out before him the products of Asiatic soil and native industry; such, for instance, as that cotton stuff named Aladja, which {172} has narrow stripes of two colours, and a fine texture; different sorts of silken manufactures, from the fine handkerchief of the consistence of the spider's web, to the heavy Atres; but particularly manufactures in leather. These play, indeed, a preeminent part; in this department the skill of the leather-cutter, and still more, that of the shoemaker, deserves commendation. Boots, both for male and female wear, are tolerably well made: the former have high heels, terminating in points about the size of a nail's head; the latter are somewhat thick, but often ornamented with the finest silk.

I had almost forgotten the bazaar and booths where clothes are exposed to tempt the eyes of purchasers. They consist of articles of attire of brilliant bright colours.

The Oriental, only here to be met with in his original purity and peculiarity, is fond of the Tchakhtchukh or rustling tone of the dress. It was always an object of great delight to me to see the seller parading up and down a few paces in the new Tchapan (dress), to ascertain whether it gave out the orthodox tone. All is the produce of home manufacture, and very cheap; consequently it is in the clothes' market of Bokhara that 'believers,' even from remote parts of Tartary, provide themselves with fashionable attire. Even the Kirghis, Kiptchak, and Kalmuks are in the habit of making excursions hither from the desert; and the wild Tartar, with his eyes oblique and chin prominent, laughs for joy when he exchanges his clothes, made of the undressed horse-skins, for a light Yektey (a sort of summer dress), for it is here that he sees his highest ideal of civilisation. Bokhara is his Paris or his London.

{173}

After having strolled around for about three hours, I begged my guide and excellent friend, Hadji Salih, to lead me to a place of refreshment, where I might be allowed a little repose. He complied, and conducted me through the Timtche Tchay Furushi (Tea Bazaar) to the renowned place Lebi Hauz Divanbeghi (bank of the reservoir of the Divanbeghi). For Bokhara, I found this a most attractive spot. It is almost a perfect square, having in the centre a deep reservoir, 100 feet long and 80 broad; the sides are of square stones, with eight steps leading down to the surface of the water. About the margin stand a few fine elm trees, and in their shade the inevitable tea booth, and the Samovars (tea-kettle), looking like a colossal cask of beer. It is manufactured in Russia expressly for Bokhara, and invites every one to a cup of green tea. On the other three sides, bread, fruit, confectionery, and meats warm and cold, are exposed for sale on stands shaded by cane mats. The hundreds of shops improvised for the occasion, around which crowds of longing mouths or hungry customers hum like bees, present us with a very characteristic spectacle. On the fourth side, that to the west, which is in the form of a terrace, we find the mosque Mesdjidi Divanbeghi. At its front there are also a few trees, where Dervishes and Meddah (public reciters) recount in verse and prose, and actors represent simultaneously, the heroic actions of famous warriors and prophets; to which performances there are never wanting crowds of curious listeners and spectators. When I entered this place, as fate would have it, still further to enhance the interest of the exhibition, there were passing by, in their weekly procession, Dervishes of the order of the Nakishbendi, of whom this city is {174} the place of origin and the principal abode. Never shall I forget that scene when those fellows, with their wild enthusiasm and their high conical caps, fluttering hair, and long staves, danced round like men possessed, bellowing out at the same time a hymn, each strophe of which was first sung for them by their grey-bearded chief. With eye and ear so occupied, I soon forgot my fatigue. My friend was obliged positively to force me to enter a booth, and, after the precious Shivin (a kind of tea) was poured out, wishing to profit by the ecstatic feeling in which he found me, he asked me, chucklingly, 'Now, then, what do you say to Bokhara Sherif (the noble)?' 'It pleases me much,' I replied; and the Central Asiatic, although from Khokand, and an alien enemy, as his nation was at that moment at war with Bokhara, was nevertheless delighted to find that the capital of Turkestan had made such a conquest of me, and gave me his word that he would show me its finest features in the course of the following days.

[Baha-ed-din, Great Saint of Turkestan]

In spite of the costume, strictly Bokhariot, which I had this day assumed, and of my being so tanned by the sun that even my mother would have had a difficulty in recognising me, I was surrounded, wherever I appeared, by a crowd of inquisitive persons. Ah! how they shook me by the hands, and how they embraced me; how they wearied me to death! An immense turban [Footnote 45] crowned my head, a large Koran hung suspended from my neck;

[Footnote 45: The turban, it is well known, represents the pall that every pious Musselman must bear on his head as a continual memento of death. The Koran only enjoins a pall (Kefen) having a length of 7 ells. But zealots often exceed the measure, and carry about on their heads 4 to 6 such palls, thus making altogether from 28 to 42 ells of fine muslin.]

{175}

I had thus assumed the exterior of an Ishan or Sheikh, and was obliged to submit to the ***corvée*** which I had so provoked. Still, I had reason to be contented, for the sanctity of my character had protected me from secular interrogations, and I heard how the people about questioned my friends, or whispered their criticisms to each other. 'What extreme piety,' said one, 'to come all the way from Constantinople to Bokhara alone, in order to visit our Baha-ed-din!' [Footnote 46] 'Yes,' said a second, 'and we, too, we go to Mecca, the holiest place of all, to be sure, with no little trouble.' But these people (and he pointed to me) having nothing else to do, their whole life is prayer, piety, and pilgrimage.' 'Bravo! you have guessed it,' I said to myself, delighted that my disguise was becoming so pregnant of consequence. And really I was, during my whole stay in the capital of Turkestan, not once an object of doubt or suspicion to the people, in other respects cunning and malicious enough. They came to me for my blessing; they listened to me when, on the public places, I read to them the history of the great Sheikh of Bagdad, Abdul Kadr Ghilani. They praised me, but not a farthing did I ever get from them; and the semblance of sanctity in this nation presented a singular contrast with the genuine piety and benevolence of the Khivan Ozbegs.

[Footnote 46: Baha-ed-din,--or according to Bokhariot pronunciation, Baveddin--is an ascetic and saint renowned throughout all Islam, the founder of the Nakishbendi order; members of it are to be met with in India, China, Persia, Arabia, and Turkey. He died in 1388, and the convent, as well as the mosque, and space walled in for his grave in the village of Baveddin, were erected by direction of Abdul Aziz Khan in the year 1490.]

[Spies set upon Author; Fate of recent Travellers in Bokhara]

But in playing my part it was not so easy to deceive the Government as the people. Rahmet Bi, whom I before spoke of, not being able to come at me openly, set spies incessantly at work. These, in conversing with me, took care to embrace a variety of subjects, but always came to the subject of Frenghistan, hoping, probably, that I should betray myself by some unguarded expression or other. Perceiving that the twig which they had so limed did not catch its bird, they began to speak of the great pleasure which the Frenghis experience in the 'noble' Bokhara, and how already many of their spies, but particularly the Englishmen, Conolly and Stoddart, had been punished. [Footnote 47] Or they recounted to me the story of the Frenghis who had arrived only a few days before, and had been imprisoned (referring to the unfortunate Italians); how they had brought with them several chests of tea sprinkled with diamond dust, to poison all the inhabitants of the holy city; how they converted day into night, and brought about other infernal strokes of art. [Footnote 48]

[Footnote 47: The sad fate of these two martyrs has continued to remain, as I remarked, a secret even in Bokhara; the most contradictory reports are up to the present day in circulation upon this subject. The reader will readily understand that without betraying my real identity it was impossible for me to put the necessary questions to elicit any fresh information; and the sad event having been so frequently and so fully entered into by Wolff, Ferrier, T. W. Kaye, and others who have written officially and unofficially upon the subject, any notices collected by myself in my journey through Bokhara seem entirely useless and uncalled for.]

[Footnote 48: They, it appears, have recently been liberated.]

[Book Bazaar]

These bloodhounds were for the most part Hadjis who had long dwelt in Constantinople, and whose design was to test at once my knowledge of its language, and my acquaintance with its mode of living. After listening to them a long time with patience, it was my habit to put on an air of disgust, and to beg them to spare me any further conversation about the Frenghis. 'I quitted Constantinople,' I said, 'to get away from these Frenghis, who seem indebted to the devil for their understanding. Thank God I am now in the "noble" Bokhara, and do not wish to embitter the time I spend here by any recollections.' Similar language I employed also with the crafty Mollah Sherefeddin, the Aksakal of the booksellers, who showed me a list of books which a Russian ambassador, a few years ago, had left behind him. I threw my eye carelessly over them and observed, 'Allah be praised, my memory is not yet corrupted by the science and books of the Frenghis, as unhappily is too often the case with the Turks of Constantinople!' [Footnote 49]

[Footnote 49: One day, a servant of the Vizir brought to me a little shrivelled individual, that I might examine him to see whether he was, as he pretended, really an Arab from Damascus. When he first entered, his features struck me much, they appeared to me European: when he opened his mouth, my astonishment and perplexity increased, for I found his pronunciation anything rather than that of an Arab. He told me that he had undertaken a pilgrimage to the tomb of Djafen Ben Sadik at Khoten in China, and wanted to proceed on his journey that very day. His features during our conversation betrayed a visible embarrassment, and it was a subject of great regret to me that I had not an occasion to see him a second time, for I am strongly disposed to think that he was playing a part similar to my own!]

When Rhamet Bi saw that he could not, by his emissaries, found any accusation, he summoned me to attend him. Of course, this was in the form of a public invitation to a Pilow, which was also attended by a circle composed of Bokhariot Ulemas. At my very entry I found that I had a hard nut to crack, for the whole interview was a sort of examination, in which my incognito had to stand a running fire. I saw, however, while it was yet time, the danger to which I was exposed; and, to escape being surprised by some sudden question or other, I assumed the part of one himself curious of information, frequently interrogating these gentlemen as to the difference of religious principles in the Farz, Sünnet, Vadjib, and Mustahab. [Footnote 50]

[Footnote 50: These are the four grades expressing the importance of the commandments of Islam. Farz means the duty enjoined by God through the Prophet; Sünnet, the tradition emanating from the Prophet himself without Divine inspiration. The latter two words, Vadjib and Mustahab, signify ordinances originating with more recent interpreters of the Koran; the former being obligatory, the latter discretionary.]

My earnestness met with favour; and soon a very warm dispute arose upon several points in Hidayet, Sherkhi Vekaye, and other books treating of similar subjects; in this I was careful to take part, praising loudly the Bokhariot Mollahs, and admitting their great superiority, not only over me, but over all the Ulemas of Constantinople. Suffice it to say that I got safe through this ordeal also. My brethren, the Mollahs, gave Rahmet Bi to understand, both by their signs and words, that his reporter had made a great mistake, and that, even supposing me not to be a Mollah of distinction, I was still one on the high road to receive worthily the lightning-flash of true knowledge.

After this scene they left me to live a quiet life in Bokhara. It was my practice first of all to fulfil at home the different duties imposed upon me by my character of Dervish. I then proceeded to the book bazaar, which contains twenty-six shops. A printed {179} book is here a rarity. In this place, and in the houses of the booksellers (for there is the great depot), many are the treasures that I have seen, which would be of incalculable value to our Oriental historians and philologists. Their acquisition was, in my case, out of the question, for in the first place I had not the adequate means, and in the second, any appearance of worldly knowledge might have prejudiced my disguise. The few manuscripts that I brought back with me from Bokhara and Samarcand cost me much trouble to acquire, and my heart bled when I found that I was obliged to leave behind me works that might have filled many an important history in our Oriental studies. From the book market I was in the habit of resorting to the Righistan (public place); it lay rather remote. Although larger and more bustling than the Lebi Hauz, which I before described, it is far from being so agreeable; we find here also a reservoir surrounded by booths for tea; from the bank we can discern the Ark (castle or palace) of the Emir, which is on the opposite side, situate upon high ground. The portal was crowned by a clock; it had a gloomy appearance. I shuddered when I passed by this nest of tyranny, the place where, perhaps, many who preceded me had been murdered, and where, even at that moment, three wretched Europeans were languishing so far from their country and every possibility of succour. Near the gate lay fourteen pieces of brass cannon, the long barrels of which were highly ornamented. The Emir had sent them home from Khokand as trophies of the victories gained in his campaign. Above, to the right of the palace, is Mesdjidi Kelan, the largest mosque in Bokhara; it was built by Abdullah Khan Sheibani.

{180}

After leaving the Righistan, I entered the tea-booth of a Chinese from Komul, [Footnote 51] a man perfectly acquainted with the Turko-Tartar language, and who passed here for a Musselman. This good man was very friendly to me, and yet how far were our homes asunder! He recounted to me much concerning the beautiful locality, much of the customs, and the excellent dishes, too, of his fatherland! But his experience was particularly great in matters connected with teas. How enthusiastically he spoke when treating of the tea-shrub, which displayed upon a single stem leaves of such a variety of flavours! He had in his shop sixteen different kinds, which he could distinguish by the touch. [Footnote 52]

[Footnote 51: Komul is distant 40 stations from Kashgar and 60 from Bokhara.]

[Footnote 52: The teas were of the following kinds:--
(1) Kyrkma.
(2) Akhbar.
(3) Ak Kuyruk.
These kinds, rarely seen in Central Asia and in China, are more used in Russia, Persia, and Europe.
(4) Kara Tchaj.
(5) Sepet Tchaj.
These two, sold like Chinese Kynaster, pressed into the form of a brick, are drunk only in the morning with cream and salt, and are very stimulating.
(6) Shibaglu.
(7) Gore Shibaglu.
(8) Shivin.
(9) It Kellesi.
(10) Dönge.
(11) Poshun.
(12) Pu-Tchay.
(13) Tun tey.
(14) Gülbuy.
(15) Mishk-göz.
(16) Lonka.

These are all green teas, none others are in favour in the north of China and in Central Asia. The last-named (Lonka) is regarded as the most precious, a single leaf suffices for a cup which equals two of ours.

The purchaser first forms a judgment of his tea by tasting a leaf that has been already boiled: when the tea is good the leaf is extremely fine and soft.]

{181}

I had, during my journey from Teheran to Bokhara, heard the latter city so often described by my companions, that after a sojourn of eight days I was quite at home. First of all Hadji Salih led me everywhere, and then I continued my investigations alone, through the city, its bazaars, and its colleges (Medresse), only accompanying my friends when we received joint invitations to the house of a Chinese Tartar who had settled there. We were on these occasions usually treated to national dishes, to which my friends (I mean Hadji Bilal and his party) had long been strangers. There is one which I will impart in confidence to my European readers, for I can recommend it as a dainty. It is called Mantuy, a sort of pudding filled with hashed meat mixed with fat and spices. This they boil in a singular manner. They place upon the fire a kettle of water, which is covered in at the top, with the exception of an opening of about the size of one's closed hand. Upon this opening are placed three or four strainers or sieves, which close firmly, the under one being made fast with dough to the kettle itself. As soon as the water begins to boil, and a sufficient quantity of steam passes into the strainers, the Mantuy is at first laid in the upper, and then in the lowest strainer; here it is suffered to remain until done. It seems singular that the Chinese should employ steam in the preparation of their meats! The Mantuys, after having been boiled, are then often broiled in fat, when they receive the name Zenbusi (lady's kiss). My friends from Kashgar and Yarkend have many more dishes peculiarly their own, but these receipts would only suit a Tartar cookery book.

{182}

[The Worm (Rishte)]

During the whole time of my stay in Bokhara, the weather was insupportably hot; but another circumstance doubled my sufferings--the apprehension of the Rishte (filaria Medinensis), by which, during the season, one person in every ten is attacked. This obliged me to be continually drinking warm water or tea. This affection is quite usual, and is treated with as much indifference by those residing in Bokhara during the summer season, as colds are with us. One feels, at first, on the foot or on some other part of the body, a tickling sensation, then a spot becomes visible whence issues a worm like a thread. This is often an ell long, and it ought some days after to be carefully wound off on a reel. This is the common treatment, and occasions no extraordinary pain; but if the worm is broken off, an inflammation ensues, and instead of one, from six to ten make their appearance, which forces the patient to keep his bed a week, subjecting him to intense suffering. The more courageous have the Rishte cut out at the very beginning. The barbers in Bokhara are tolerably expert in this operation. The part where the tickling sensation takes place is in an instant removed, the worm extracted, and the wound itself soon heals. Sometimes this malady, which is also common in Bender Abbasi (Persia), recurs in the following summer, and that too, even when the patient is in a different climate. It happened so with Dr. Wolff, the well-known traveller, who dragged with him all the way from Bokhara one of these long memorials of his journey. It did not show itself till he came to England, when it was extracted, in Eastern fashion, {183} by the late Sir Benjamin Brodie. Besides this affliction, the Bokhariots exhibit many malignant sores, occasioned by their bad climate and still worse water. It is more especially remarked that the women, who would otherwise pass for not unattractive brunettes, are thus quite disfigured with scars, perhaps to be remotely referred to their sedentary habits.

[Water Supply]

Bokhara derives its water from the Zerefshan (distributor of gold), whose course is north-easterly. Its channel is lower than the city itself, and even in summer affords but a scanty supply. The water flows through a canal, deep enough, but not maintained in a state of cleanliness. It is permitted to enter the city at the gate Dervaze Mezar once in intervals of from every eight to fourteen days, according as the height of the river may allow. The appearance of the water, tolerably dirty even when it first enters, is always a joyful occurrence for the inhabitants. Then first the inhabitants, young and old, precipitate themselves into the canals and reservoirs to make their ablutions; afterwards the horses, cows, and asses come to take their baths; and when the dogs finally have cooled themselves there a little, all entrance is forbidden, the water is left to settle, become clear and pure. It has, it is true, absorbed thousands of elements of miasma and filthiness! Such is the attention that Bokhara, the noble, pays to this indispensable necessary of life--Bokhara, whither flock thousands of scholars to learn the principles of a religion that consecrates the principle that 'Cleanliness is derived from Religion.' [Footnote 53]

[Footnote 53: 'El nezafet min el iman.']

{184}

[Late and present Emirs; Harem, Government, Family of Reigning Emir.]

It is impossible for me to forget Bokhara, were it only on account of the efforts with respect to religion which I have noticed there both on the part of Government and people. I often heard it affirmed that 'Bokhara is the true support of Islam.' [Footnote 54] The title is too weak; it should be rather termed the 'Rome of Islam,' since Mecca and Medina are its Jerusalem. Bokhara is aware of her superiority, and plumes herself upon it in the face of all the other nations of Islam; yes, even before the Sultan himself, who is yet acknowledged as the official chief of religion; but he is not so readily pardoned for having suffered so much to be corrupted in his territories by the influence of the Frenghis. In my supposed character of Osmanli, I was called upon to explain fully:

[Footnote 54: 'Bokhara kuvveti islam ü din est.']

First. Why the Sultan does not put to death all the Frenghis who live in his dominions, and yet pay no Djizie (tribute); why he does not every year undertake a Djihad (religious war), as he has unbelievers on all his frontiers.

Secondly. Why the Osmanlis, who are Sunnites, and belong to the sect of the Ebuhanife, do not wear the turban, nor the long garments prescribed by the law and reaching to the ancles; why they have not a long beard and short moustachios, like 'the glory of all mundane creatures,' as the Prophet is styled.

Thirdly, why the Sunnites, both in Constantinople and Mecca, sing the Ezan (call to prayer) when they utter it, which is a frightful sin; why they are not all Hadjis there, as they dwell so nigh the holy places; &c. &c.

I did my utmost to save the religious honour of the honest Osmanlis, and if I was obliged occasionally to pronounce, with a blush on my cheek, the 'Pater, {185} peccavi,' I could not but internally felicitate the Turks on retaining, in spite of their being under the influence of a corrupt Islamism, many good qualities and fine traits of character, whereas their fellow-religionists, who boast that they are refreshing themselves at the very fountain of the pure faith, delight in nothing but the blackest mendacity, in hypocrisy, and in impositions. How often was I forced to witness one of the Khalka (circle) which devotees form by squatting down close to each other in a ring, to devote themselves to the Tevedjüh (contemplation), or, as the western Mahomedans call it, the Murakebe of the greatness of God, the glory of the Prophet, and the futility of our mortal existence! If you, a stranger, behold these people, with their immense turbans, and their arms hanging down folded upon their laps, sitting in their cramped position, you could not help believing them to be beings of a purer, loftier nature, who seek to cast from them the burden of clay, and adopt the full spirit of the Arabian saying--

'The world is an abomination, and those who toil about it are dogs.' [Footnote 55]

[Footnote 55: 'Ed dünya djitetun ve talıbeha kılab.']

Look only more attentively, and you will not fail to perceive that many have, from deep reflection, fallen into deeper slumber; and although they begin to snore, like hounds after a hard day's hunting, beware how you breathe any reproach, or the Bokhariot will soon set you right with the observation, 'These men have made such progress, that even whilst they snore they are thinking of God and of immortality!' In Bokhara only the external form of the thing is required. {186} Each city has its Reïs, [Footnote 56] who, with a cat-o'-four-tails in his hand, traverses the streets and public places, examines each passer by in the principles of Islamism, and sends the ignorant, even if they be grey-bearded men of threescore years, for periods varying from eight to fourteen days, to the boys' school; or he drives them into the mosques at the hour of prayer. But whether, in the former case, they learn anything in school, or go to sleep there-- whether, in the latter, they pray in the mosque, or are thinking how their daily occupations have been cut short,--all this is the affair of nobody whatever. The Government insists upon nothing but the external appearance; what lies within is known to God alone.

[Footnote 56: Guardian of religion.]

What need to insist that the spirit in which religion is administered has a powerful influence upon both Government and society? The Iranian blood of the inhabitants (for two-thirds of the inhabitants of the city of Bokhara are Persians, Mervi, and Tadjiks), gives a little semblance of vitality to the bazaars and public places; but what dreariness and monotony in the private houses! Every trace of gladness and cheerfulness is banished from those circles where the influence of religion and the system of surveillance are so tyrannically felt. The Emir's spies force their way even into the sanctuaries of families, and woe to the man who permits himself to offend against the forms of religion or the authority of the sovereign. Ages of oppression have now so intimidated the people that husband and wife, even with no third person present, do not dare to pronounce the Emir's name without adding the words, 'God grant him to live 120 years!' It must be also admitted that the poor people feel no sentiment of hatred for their ruler, because tyrannical caprice does not seem to them as a {187} thing to be wondered at, but is rather looked upon in the light of an inevitable attribute of princely dignity. Emir Nasr Ullah, the father of the present ruler of Bokhara, was, in the last years of his life, a cruel profligate, who visited with capital punishment immorality in others, and yet himself violated, in the most shameless manner, the honour of his subjects. Few were the families who escaped unscathed; and still no one permitted even a breath of blame to escape his lips. The reigning Emir, Mozaffar-ed-din Khan, happily, is a well-disposed man; and although he enforces with severity the laws respecting religion and morals, he cannot be charged himself with any crime; hence the unceasing praises and glorifications of which he is the object on the part of his people.

I saw the Emir afterwards in Samarcand; he is in the forty-second year of his age, of middle stature, somewhat corpulent. He has a very pleasing countenance, fine black eyes, and a thin beard. In his youth he acted as governor one year in Karshi, and eighteen in Kermineh, and was always distinguished for the gentleness and affability of his manners. He carries out strictly the political principles of his father, and in his capacity as Mollah and pious Musselman is the declared enemy of every innovation even when he may be convinced of its utility. On his accession he had impressed upon his signet the device

'Government by justice,' [Footnote 57]

and up to the present moment has most scrupulously observed it. Many reports in circulation respecting him confirm the remark. True, according to our view of things, there seems great exaggeration in{188} a system of justice which led the Emir to send his Mehter, the second in rank of his officers, to execution, for having (for it was in this form that the report reached Khokand) thrown a dubious glance at one of the royal slaves; nor should a prince, whose device is 'justice,' have conducted himself as the Emir did in Khokand. But all these faults are very pardonable in a Khan of Bokhara. Towards his grandees, who for the most part well merit the treatment they meet with, he is very severe, for although punishing with death even trivial offences in these, he spares the poorer classes. Hence the expression applied to him by the people, and which does him honour, for they say of him that he is 'killer of elephants and protector of mice.' [Footnote 58]

[Footnote 57: 'El Hükm bil Adl.']

[Footnote 58: Filkush and Mushperver.]

It is singular what pains the Emir takes to throw obstacles in the way of his subjects whenever they seek to depart from the simplicity and modesty of their present, in his opinion, happy condition. The introduction of articles of luxury, or other expensive merchandise, is forbidden, as also the employment of sumptuousness in house or dress: in offences of this description there is no respect of persons. His Serdari Kul (commandant-in-chief), Shahrukh Khan, sprung from a collateral branch of the royal family of Persia (Kadjar), having fled hither from Astrabad, where he had been governor, had been long held here in high honour and distinction; but, desirous of living in the Persian manner, he ordered, at great expense, a house to be erected one story high, like those in Teheran; in this, besides other articles of luxury, glass windows were inserted; it is said to have cost altogether 15,000 Tilla, regarded {189} in Bokhara an enormous sum; it was of a description calculated to throw into the shade even the Ark (palace) itself. The Emir had been informed of this from the very beginning, but he waited until the whole was quite finished, and then suddenly Shahrukh Khan was accused of an offence against religion, thrown into confinement, and then exiled. The house was confiscated and reverted to the Emir: an offer was made to purchase it, and at a sum exceeding the cost price, but no! he directed it to be demolished, the ruins themselves, however, appearing too ornamental, he ordered them to be entirely destroyed, with the sole reservation of the timber, which was sold to a baker for 200 Tilla, in scorn and mockery of all who should venture to give way to a taste for luxuries. Even in his domestic arrangements the Emir is widely different from his father; and it did not appear to me that there could have been more than half the retinue of servants which M. de Khanikoff saw at the Court of Nasr Ullah, and of which, as of so many other particulars concerning Bokhara, the Russian traveller gives so careful, so exact and circumstantial an account.

Mozaffar-ed-din Khan has (for it is a custom of his religion) four legitimate wives and about twenty others, the former natives of Bokhara, the latter slaves, and, as I was told seriously, only employed to tend upon the children, of whom there are sixteen, ten girls (but I beg pardon, princesses), and six boys (Tore). The two eldest princesses are married to the governors of Serepool and Aktche; only, as these two cities have fallen into the hands of the Afghan, his two sons-in-law live as the Emir's guests, like kings *sans portefeuilles*. The harem is presided over by the sovereign's mother, formerly a{190} Persian slave (born at Kademgihah, near Meshed), and by his grandmother, Hakim Ayim. It bears a high character for chastity and orderly training. It is forbidden to the laity on pain of death to enter, or even to throw a glance or direct a thought thither: this is permitted alone to pious Sheikhs or Mollahs, whose Nefes (breath) is of notorious sanctity; and it was by this title that our friend Hadji Salih was summoned to administer a dose of the Khaki Shifa (health powder from Medina). The cost of the harem, as far as dress, board, and other necessaries are concerned, is very small. The ladies make not only their own clothes, but often even the garments of the Emir, who is known to be a strict economist, and to exercise severe control over everything. The daily kitchen expenses of the palace are said to be from sixteen to twenty Tenghe (rather more than from nine to ten shillings), which is very likely, as his table rarely offers any confectionery, and consists merely of pilow boiled with mutton fat. The expression 'princely table' is inapplicable to Bokhara, where one and the same dish satisfies prince, official, merchant, mechanic, and peasant.

The man that has wandered about through the deserts of Central Asia will still find in Bokhara, in spite of all its wretchedness, something of the nature of a metropolis. My fare now consisted of good bread, tea, fruit, and boiled meats. I had two shirts made, and the comforts of civilised life became to me so agreeable that I was really sorry when I received notice from my friends to prepare for the journey, as they wished to gain their remote Eastern homes before the winter set in. My intention was to keep them company provisionally as far as
Samarcand, {191} as I somewhat dreaded my interview with the Emir, and their society in many respects would be of great service to me. I was to decide in the last-named city whether to proceed to Khokand and Kashgar, or to return alone by Kerki, Karshi, and Herat. My excellent friends, Hadji Bilal and Hadji Salih, did not wish to influence me, but to provide for the case of a possible return. Desirous as far as they could to aid me, they had introduced me to a Kervanbashi from Herat, who was staying in Bokhara, and thought of finally returning in three weeks to the former city. His name was Mollah Zeman: he had been formerly known to my friends. They recommended me to his care, as if I had been their own brother, and it was determined, if I returned from Samarcand, that we should meet three weeks afterwards in Kerki, on the farther bank of the Oxus. This, the first step suggestive of a final separation, was very affecting to us all. Hitherto I had found consolation in the very uncertainty of my purpose; for to my fancy an extension of my travels to Kashgar, Aksu, and Khoten, rich in musk--countries to which no European before me had penetrated--had infinite charm and poetical attraction.

[Slave Depot and Trade]

But my thoughts have been so engaged by the memory of this visit to Mollah Zeman, that I was about to forget to describe the spot where I found him. It was in a karavanserai appropriated to the trade in slaves. Of this I cannot forbear to give the reader a slight sketch. The building, which formed a square, contained, it may be, from thirty to thirty-five cells. Three wholesale dealers in this abominable traffic had hired these buildings as a depôt for the poor wretches, who were partly their own goods and {192} chattels, and partly entrusted to them as commission brokers for the Turkomans. As is well known, the Karaktchi, unable to wait long, are accustomed to sell their slaves to some Turkoman who has more means at his disposal. The latter brings them to Bokhara, and is the chief gainer by these transactions, as he buys immediately from the producer. In the very first days of his arrival in the capital, he sells all those for whom he can find customers; the remainder he leaves behind him in the hands of the Dellal (broker), who is more especially the wholesale dealer. Human beings are sold in Bokhara and Khiva from the age of three to that of sixty, unless they possess such defects as cause them to be regarded as cripples. According to the precepts of their religion, unbelievers alone can be sold as slaves; but Bokhara, that has nothing more than the semblance of sanctity, evades without scruple such provisions, and makes slaves not only of the Shiite Persians, who were declared 'unbelievers' so long ago as 1500 by the Mollah Schemseddin, but also many professors of the Sunnite tenets themselves, after they have, by blows and maltreatment, been compelled to style themselves Shiites. It is only the Jew, whom they pronounce to be incapable, that is unworthy of becoming a slave, a mode of showing their aversion, of course, anything but disagreeable to the children of Israel, for although the Turkoman will make booty of his property, and strip him of everything, he will not touch his body. At an earlier period, the Hindoos also formed an exception. More recently, as they flocked by Herat into Bokhara, the Tekke or Sarik began to lay down new rules for their procedure. The unfortunate worshipper of Vishnoo is now first metamorphosed {193} into a Musselman, then made a Shiite; and not until this double conversion has taken place is the honour conferred upon him of being plundered of all his property, and being reduced to the condition of a slave.

The slave exposed to sale is, when a male, made the subject of public examination: the seller is obliged to guarantee that he has none of those moral or bodily defects, which constitute to his knowledge latent unsoundness: that is to say, where, though they are not discernible to the eye, they exist in a rudimentary state.

To the slave himself, the happiest hour is when he passes out of the hand of the slave-dealer; for no treatment, however hard, which awaits him with his eventual master can be so oppressive and painful as that which he has to pass through whilst he remains an article of commerce exposed for sale in the shop.

The price varies with the political circumstances of the Turkomans, according as they find (for upon such does the production of the article depend) greater or less facility for their Alaman in the adjoining district. For instance: at the present day the highest price of a man in the maturity of his strength is from 40 to 50 Tilla (about from £21-£36); after a victory, when 18,000 Persian soldiers had been made prisoners at one time, a man was to be had for a sum of 3 or 4 Tillas.

[Departure from Bokhara, and Visit to the Tomb of Baha-ed-din.]

After having stayed twenty-two days in Bokhara I found it impossible any longer to delay my friends, and it was arranged that we should at once start for Samarcand. Our living in Bokhara, as no one here, however liberal with his shakings of the hand, gave us a single farthing, had very much impaired our {194} finances. What we had been able to make in Khiva was all exhausted, and, like many of my companions, I had been forced to dispose of my ass, and henceforth our journey was to be continued in a hired two-wheeled cart. Particular members of our karavan, who belonged to Khokand or Khodjend, had already parted from us, and gone their own several ways alone. Those who had hitherto remained together were natives of Endighan or Chinese Tartars. These, however, in proceeding to Samarcand, selected different routes. Hadji Salih, Hadji Bilal's party, and myself determined upon following the straight road; the others, who were on foot, were anxious to undertake a pilgrimage, by way of Gidjdovan, to the tomb of the Saint Abdul Khalik. [Footnote 59]

[Footnote 59: Khodja Abdul Khalik (named Gidjovani, died 1601) was contemporary with the famous Payende Zamini, and stands in high repute for learning, asceticism, and sanctity.]

Many Bokhariots, on my return, intimated a wish to accompany me to Mecca. I, therefore, was obliged to employ much delicate diplomacy, for certainly their company would have been a source of great embarrassment in either case, whether we found ourselves before the Kaaba or on the banks of the Thames!

I took leave of all my friends and acquaintances. Rahmet Bi gave me letters of introduction for Samarcand, and I promised to wait upon the Emir there. The Khokand vehicle, which we had hired to convey us as far as Samarcand, had been previously sent on to wait for us at the village Baveddin, to which place of pilgrimage we had now, according to the custom of the country, to pay our second visit--our visit of adieu. This village is distant two leagues from Bokhara, and is, as before said, the place of {195} interment of the renowned Baha-ed-din Nakishbend, founder of the order bearing the same name, and the chief fountain of all those extravagances of religion which distinguish Eastern from Western Islamism. Without entering into more details, suffice it to mention, that Baha-ed-din is venerated as the national saint of Turkestan, as a second Mohammed; and the Bokhariot is firmly persuaded that the cry alone of a 'Baha-ed-din belagerdan' [Footnote 60] is sufficient to save from all misfortune. Pilgrimages are made to this place even from the most remote parts of China. It is the practice in Bokhara to come hither every week, and the intercourse is maintained with the metropolis by means of about 300 asses that ply for hire. These stand before the Dervaze Mezar, and may be had for a few Pul (small copper coins). Although the road, in many places, passes over deep sand, these animals run with indescribable speed on their journey to the village; but, what is considered very surprising, they cannot, without repeated blows, be induced to return. The Bokhariot ascribes this circumstance to the feeling of devotion that the saint inspires even in brutes; for do they not run to his tomb, and evince the greatest indisposition to quit it?

[Footnote 60: 'O Baha-ed-din, thou avevter of evil!']

The tomb is in a small garden. On one side is a mosque. This may be approached through a court filled with blind or crippled mendicants, the perseverance of whose applications would put to shame those of the same profession in Rome or Naples. In the front of the tomb is the famous Senghi murad (stone of desire), which has been tolerably ground away and made smooth by the numerous foreheads of pious pilgrims that have been rubbed upon it. Over {196} the tomb are placed several rams' horns and a banner, also a broom that served a long time to sweep out the sanctuary in Mecca. Attempts have also been made upon several occasions to cover the whole with a dome, but Baha-ed-din, like many other saints in Turkestan, has a preference for the open air, and every edifice has been thrown down after a lapse of three days from its first erection. Such is the tale told by the Sheikhs, descendants of the saint, who keep watch in turn before the tomb, and recount, with impudence enough, to the pilgrims that their ancestor was particularly fond of the number seven. In the seventh month he came into the world, in his seventh year he knew the Koran by heart, and in his seventieth he died. Hence also the contributions and gifts laid upon his grave are to have the peculiarity that they must not be anything else than multiples of seven or the number seven itself.

A quarter of a league from the tomb of Baha-ed-din, in an open field, is that of Miri Kulah, the master and spiritual chief of the former. But the master is far from enjoying the same honour and repute as the disciple.

{197}

CHAPTER XI.

BOKHARA TO SAMARCAND

LITTLE DESERT OF CHÖL MELIK

ANIMATION OF ROAD OWING TO WAR

FIRST VIEW OF SAMARCAND

HASZRETI SHAH ZINDE

MOSQUE OF TIMOUR

CITADEL (ARK)

RECEPTION HALL OF TIMOR

KÖKTASH OR TIMOUR'S THRONE

SINGULAR FOOTSTOOL

TIMOUR'S SEPULCHER AND THAT OF HIS PRECEPTOR

AUTHOR VISITS THE ACTUAL TOMB OF TIMOUR IN THE SOUTERRAIN

FOLIO KORAN ASCRIBED TO OSMAN, MOHAMMED'S SECRETARY

COLLEGES

ANCIENT OBSERVATORY

GREEK ARMENIAN LIBRARY NOT, AS PRETENDED, CARRIED OFF BY TIMOR

ARCHITECTURE OF PUBLIC BUILDINGS NOT CHINESE BUT PERSIAN

MODERN SAMARCAND

ITS POPULATION

DEHBID

AUTHOR DECIDES TO RETURN

ARRIVAL OF EMIR

AUTHOR'S INTERVIEW WITH HIM

PARTING FROM THE HADJIS, AND DEPARTURE FROM SAMARCAND.

Hinc quarto die ad Maracanda perventum est . . . Scythiae confinis est regio, habitaturque pluribus ac frequentibits vicis, quia ubertas terra non indigenas modo detinet, sed etiam advenas invitat.--Q. Curtii Rufi libb. vii. et viii.

[Bokhara to Samarcand]

Our whole karavan had now, on starting from Bokhara for Samarcand, dwindled down to two carts. In one of these sat Hadji Salih and myself; in the other, Hadji Bilal and his party. Sheltered from the sun by a matting awning, I should have been glad to settle myself quietly on my carpet, but this was impossible, owing to the violent motion of our very primitive vehicle; it disposed of us 'at its own sweet will,' shaking us, now here, now there; our heads were continually cannoning each other like balls {198} on a billiard table. During the first few hours I felt quite sea-sick, having suffered much more than I had done when on the camels, the shiplike movements of which I had formerly so much dreaded. The poor horse, harnessed to the broad heavy cart, besides having to make the clumsy wheels--far from perfect circles--revolve laboriously through the deep sand or mud, was obliged also to convey the driver and his provision sack. The Turkoman is right in doubting whether the Bokhariot will ever be able to justify in another world his maltreatment of the horse--the noblest of the brute creation.

As it was night when we started from Baha-ed-din, the driver (a native of Khokand), not sufficiently familiar with the road, mistook the way, so that, instead of midnight, it was morning before we reached the little town of Mezar. It is distant from Bokhara five Tash (fersakh), and is regarded as the first station on the road to Samarcand. We halted here but a short time, and about noon arrived at sheikh Kasim, where we encountered some of our brother pilgrims. They were taking the road by Gidjdovan. We consequently indulged ourselves by remaining there quietly together until late at night.

[Little Desert of Chöl Melik]

I had heard many wonderful accounts of the flourishing cultivation of the country between Bokhara and Samarcand, but thus far I had seen nothing astonishing during our day's journey, nothing at all corresponding to my high-wrought expectations. We perceived, indeed, everywhere, and on both sides of the road, with rare exceptions, the land under cultivation; the following day, however, a real surprise awaited me. We had passed the little desert of Chöl Melik (six leagues in length by four in {199} breadth), where there are a karavanserai and water reservoir, and at last reached the district of Kermineh, which constitutes the third day's station. We now passed every hour, sometimes every half-hour, a small Bazarli Djay (market-place), where there were several inns and houses for the sale of provisions, and where gigantic Russian teakettles, ever on the boil, are held to be the *ne plus ultra* of refinement and of comfort. These villages have quite a different character from those in Persia and Turkey, the farm-yards are better filled with earth's blessings; and were there only more trees, we might say that all the way from the Pontos Mountains this is the only country resembling our own in the far West. About mid-day we halted at Kermineh, in a lovely garden, on the side of a reservoir, where we found abundant shade. My friends seemed to endear themselves to me more and more the nearer the moment of our separation approached; it appeared impossible that I was to journey alone that long way back from Samarcand to Europe! We started from Kermineh about sunset, considering that the freshness of the night would lighten, in some respects, the torments of our overtasked horse; at midnight we halted again for two hours, as we hoped to reach our station the next morning, before the heat of the day commenced. I remarked in many places along the road square mile-stones, some entire, others broken, [Footnote 61] which owe their erection to Timour; nor need this surprise us, for Marco Polo, in the time of Oktai, found regular post-roads in Central Asia. The whole way from Bokhara to Kashgar is said, indeed, {200} still to bear marks of an ancient civilisation which, although with frequent intervals, is nevertheless traceable far into China. The present Emir, also wishing to distinguish himself, has caused in several places small terraces to be raised for purposes of prayer, these serving as a sort of occasional mosques, and mementos to passers-by to fulfil their religious duties. So each age has its own peculiar objects in view!

[Footnote 61: The Turkish word for stone is Tash, which is also used to denote mile. So the Persian word Fersang (in modern Persian fersakh) is compounded of fer (high) and seng (stone).]

[Animation of Road owing to War]

The evening we passed at the village Mir, taking up our quarters there in the mosque. This rises from the centre of a pretty flower garden. I lay down to sleep near a reservoir, but was startled out of my slumber by a troop of quarrelsome Turkomans. They were the Tekke horsemen who had served the Emir as auxiliaries in his campaign against Khokand, and were now returning to Merv with the booty they had taken from the Kirghis. The Emir, in his anxiety to civilise them, had presented many with a white turban, and hoped that they would throw aside altogether their wild fur caps. They wore them as long as they were under the eye of the Emir, but I heard that they had subsequently sold them all.

From Mir we proceeded to the Kette Kurgan ('great fortress'). It is the seat of a Government, and has the most famous shoemakers in the whole Khanat. This fortress is defended by a strong wall and deep fosse. By night no one is permitted either to pass in or out; we therefore remained in a karavanserai, on the road outside the fort. There were wagons everywhere; the roads, indeed, in all directions presented a bustling and singularly animated appearance: this was to be ascribed to the war, that employs all conveyances between Bokhara and Khokand. From Kette Kurgan a distinct way leads through the desert {201} to Karshi, and is said to be four leagues shorter than the usual one thither from Samarcand; but travellers are obliged to take their water with them, as there are very few wells that human beings can use, although there are several fit for cattle. I found the drivers and peasants discussing political subjects before the tea-shops, the prohibitions here not being enforced as in Bokhara. The poor people are enchanted when they hear of the heroic acts of their Emir; they recount that he has already forced his way from Khokand into China, and after he has there in the East reduced all under his sceptre, he will, they insist, proceed to take possession of Iran, Afghanistan, India, and Frenghistan (these they consider as adjoining counties), as far as Roum: the whole world, in fact, is, according to them, to be divided between the Sultan and the Emir!

After having left behind me Karasu, which is a place of some importance, we reached Daul, the fifth station, and the last before coming to Samarcand itself. Our road passed over some hills from which we could perceive extensive woods stretching away on our left. I was told that they reach half-way to Bokhara, and serve as retreats to the Özbeg tribes, Khitai and Kiptchak, which are often at enmity with the Emir. Being familiar with all the secret corners and recesses of their own forests, they are not easily assailable.

[First View of Samarcand]

What I heard in Bokhara had very much diminished in my eyes the historical importance of Samarcand. I cannot, however, describe my feeling of curiosity when they pointed out to me, on the east, Mount Chobanata, at whose foot was situate, I was told, the Mecca I so longed to see. I therefore gazed intently in the direction indicated, and at last, on toiling up {202} a hill, I beheld the city of Timour in the middle of a fine country. I must confess that the first impression produced by the domes and minarets, with their various colours, all bathed in the beams of the morning sun—the peculiarity, in short, of the whole scene—was very pleasing.

As Samarcand, both by the charm of its past and its remoteness, is regarded in Europe as something extraordinary, we will, as we cannot make use of the pencil, endeavour to draw a view of the city with the pen. I must beg the reader to take a seat in the cart by my side; he will then see to the east the mountain I before mentioned. Its dome-like summit is crowned by a small edifice, in which rests Chobanata (the holy patron of shepherds). Below lies the city. Although it equals Teheran in circumference, its houses do not lie so close together; still the prominent buildings and ruins offer a far more magnificent prospect. The eye is most struck by four lofty edifices, in the form of half domes, the fore-fronts or frontispieces of the Medresse (Pishtak). They seemed all to be near together; but some, in fact, are in the background. As we advance we perceive first a small neat dome, and further on to the south a larger and more imposing one; the former is the tomb, the latter the mosque, of Timour. Quite facing us, on the south-westerly limit of the city, on a hill, rises the citadel (Ark), round which other buildings, partly mosques and partly tombs, are grouped. If we then suppose the whole intermixed with closely planted gardens, we shall have a faint idea of Samarcand--a faint one; for I say with the Persian proverb--

'When will hearing be like seeing?' [Footnote 62]

[Footnote 62: 'Shuniden keï buved manendi diden.']

{203}

But, alas! why need I add that the impression produced by its exterior was weakened as we approached, and entirely dissipated by our entry into the place itself? Bitter indeed the disappointment in the case of a city like Samarcand, so difficult of access, and a knowledge of which has to be so dearly acquired; and when we drove in through the Dervaze Bokhara, and had to pass through the greater part of the cemetery to reach the inhabited part of the town, I thought of the Persian verse--

'Samarcand is the focus of the whole globe.' [Footnote 63]

[Footnote 63: 'Samarkand seïkeli rui zemin est.']

In spite of all my enthusiasm, I burst out into a loud fit of laughter. We first proceeded to a karavanserai, on the side of the bazaar, where Hadjis have quarters awarded to them gratuitously; but the very same evening we were invited to a private house situate beyond the bazaar, near the tomb of Timour, and what was my joy and surprise when I learnt that our host fortunately was an officer of the Emir, and entrusted with the surveillance of the palace in Samarcand!

As the return of the Emir from Khokand, where he had just terminated a victorious campaign, was announced to take place in a few days, my companions decided to wait in Samarcand, on my account, till I had seen the Emir, and until I found other Hadjis passing whose company I could join on my return journey. In the interval I passed my time visiting all that was worth seeing in the city; for in spite of its miserable appearance, it is in this respect the richest in all Central Asia.

{204}

In my character as Hadji I naturally began with the saints; but as all, even what is historically interesting, is intimately blended with some holy legend, I felt it a very agreeable duty to see everything.

[Haszreti Shah Zinde]

They enumerate here several hundred places of pilgrimage; but we will only particularise the more remarkable:--

Hazreti Shah Zinde (Summer Palace of Timour).

The proper name is Kasim bin Abbas. He is said to have been a Koreïshite, and consequently stands here in the highest repute, as the chief of those Arabs who introduced Islamism into Samarcand. His sepulchre lies without the city, to the north-west, near the wall and the edifice that served the great Timour as a summer residence. The latter has retained even to the present day much of its ancient splendour and luxury. All these structures are situate upon elevated ground, and are approached by an ascent of forty tolerably broad marble steps. On reaching the summit, one is conducted to a building lying at the end of a small garden. Here several little corridors lead to a large apartment, from which, by a small gloomy path, you arrive at the equally gloomy tomb of the saint. Besides the room above mentioned, there are others whose coloured bricks and mosaic pavement produce as brilliant an effect as if they were the work of yesterday.

Each different room that we entered had to be saluted with two Rikaat Namaz. My knees began to ache, when they led me on into a room paved with marble. Three flags, an old sword, and breastplate, were presented to be kissed as relics of the renowned {205} Emir. This act of homage I did not decline any more than my companions, although I entertained great doubt whether the objects themselves are authentic. I heard also of a sword, breastplate, Koran, and other relics of the saint, but I could not get sight of them. Opposite to this edifice, the reigning Emir has erected a small Medresse, which looks like the stable of a palace.

[Mosque of Timour]

Mesdjidi Timour (The Mosque of Timour).

This mosque is situate on the south side of the city: in size, and painted brick decorations, it has much resemblance to the Mesdjidi Shah, in Ispahan, which was built by order of Abbas II. The dome differs, however; it is in the form of a melon, which is never the case in Persia. The inscriptions from the Koran, in gold Sulus lettering, next to those at the ruins of Sultanieh, are the finest I ever saw.

[Citadel (Ark)]

Ark (Citadel--Reception Hall of Timour).

The ascent to the Ark is tolerably steep; it is divided into two parts, of which the outer is composed of private dwellings, whereas the other is only used for the reception of the Emir.

[Reception Hall of Timour; Köktash or Timour's Throne Singular Footstool.]

The palace had been described to me as extremely curious; it is, however, a very ordinary edifice, and is scarcely a century old, and I confess I found nothing remarkable in it. First they showed me the apartments of the Emir: amongst these the Aynekhane, which is a room composed of fragments of looking-glass, passing for a wonder of the world; but to me it had far less interest than the place designated Talari Timour, or 'reception-hall of Timour.' This is a {206} long narrow court, having round it a covered foot-pavement or cloister. The side that fronts you contains the celebrated Köktash (green stone), upon which Timour caused his throne to be placed: to it flocked vassals from all parts of the world to do homage, and were ranged there according to their rank; whilst in the central space, that resembled an arena, three heralds sat ready mounted to convey, on the instant, the words of the conqueror of the world to the farthest end of the hall. As the green stone is four feet and a half high, some prisoner of illustrious birth was always forced to serve as a footstool. It is singular that, according to the tradition, this colossal stone (ten feet long, four broad, and four and a half high) was transported hither from Broussa. Fixed in the wall to the right of this stone is a prominent oval piece of iron, like half a cocoa-nut; upon it there is an inscription in Arabic, engraved in Kufish letters. It is said to have been brought from the treasury of the Sultan, Bayazid Yildirin, and to have served one of the Khalifs as an amulet. I saw, high above the stone on the wall, two firmans, written in golden Divani letters, one from Sultan Mahmoud, the other from Sultan Abdul Medjid. They were sent to Emir Saïd, and Emir Nasrullah, from Constantinople, and contained both the Rukhsati-Namaz (official permission for the prayer), [Footnote 64] and the investiture in the functions of a Reïs (guardian of religion) which the Emirs formerly made it a point of etiquette to receive. The Emirs, now-a-days, content themselves on their accession with doing homage at the Köktash; and the stone is no longer used but for this purpose, and as a {207} place of pilgrimage for pious Hadjis who say three Fatihas, and rub their heads with peculiar unction upon that monument whence, once, every word uttered by their glorious monarch echoed as a command to the remotest parts of Asia. Timour is spoken of in Samarcand as if the news of his death had only just arrived from Otrar; and the question was put to me, as Osmanli, what my feelings were on approaching the tomb of a sovereign who had inflicted upon 'our' Sultan so terrible a defeat.

[Footnote 64: The Friday prayer, which no Sunnite could or can pronounce until the Khalif or his successor has first done so.]

[Timour's Sepulchre and that of his Preceptor; Author visits the actual Tomb of Timour in the Souterrain]

Turbeti Timour (Timour's Sepulchre) .

This monument lies to the south-west, and consists of a neat chapel, crowned with a splendid dome, and encircled by a wall; in the latter there is a high arched gate, and on both sides are two small domes, miniature representations of the large one first mentioned. The space between the wall and the chapel is filled with trees, and should represent a garden, but great neglect is now apparent there. The entrance into the chapel is on the west, and its front, according to the law, is towards the south (Kible). On entering, one finds oneself in a sort of vestibule, which leads directly into the chapel itself. This is octagonal, and ten short paces in diameter. In the middle, under the dome, that is to say, in the place of honour, there are two tombs, placed lengthwise, with the head in the direction of Mecca. One is covered with a very fine stone of a dark green colour, two and a half spans broad and ten long, and about the thickness of six fingers. It is laid flat, in two pieces, [Footnote 65] over the grave of Timour; the other has a {208} black stone, of about the same length, but somewhat broader. This is the tomb of Mir Seid Berke, the teacher and spiritual chief of Timour, at whose side the mighty Emir gratefully desired to be buried. Round about lie other tombstones, great and small, those of wives, grandsons, and great grandsons of the Emir; but, if I do not err, their bodies were brought thither at a subsequent period from different parts of the city. The inscriptions upon the tombs are in Persian and Arabic, no enumeration of titles is there, and even that of the Emir is very simple. The family name, Köreghen, is never omitted.

[Footnote 65: Different reasons are assigned for this. Some say that the victorious Nadir Shah ordered it to be sent to him, and that it was broken on the journey. Others affirm that it was originally in two pieces, and the present of a Chinese (Mongol) princess.]

[Folio Koran ascribed to Osman, Mohammed's Secretary]

As for the interior of the chapel, arabesques in alabaster, whose gildings are in rich contrast with a lovely azure, bear evidence of taste truly artistic, and produce an effect surprisingly beautiful. It reminds us, but can give only a faint idea, of the inside of the sepulchre of Meesume Fatma in Kom (Persia). [Footnote 66] Whilst the latter is too much filled, the former is simply and modestly beautiful. At the head of the graves are two Rahle (table with two leaves, upon which, in the East, are laid sacred volumes), where the Mollahs day and night read in turn the Koran, and contrive to extract from the Vakf (pious foundation) of the Turbe a good salary. They, as well as the Mutevali (stewards), are taken from the Nogai Tartars, because the Emir expressed in his will the {209} desire that the watch over him should be entrusted to this race, which had always been particularly well disposed towards him. I paid my visit to the inspector, and was forced to remain his guest the whole day. As a mark of his peculiar favour he permitted me to view the actual grave, an honour which, he assured me, was rarely accorded even to natives. We descended by a small long staircase behind the entrance. It leads directly into a room below the chapel, not only of the same size, but resembling it closely in all its arabesque decorations. The tombs here are also in the same order as those above, but not so numerous. It is said that Timour's grave contains great treasures; but this cannot be true, as it would be an infraction of the law. Here again is a Rahle, with a Koran lying upon it in folio, written upon the skin of a gazelle. I was informed in many quarters, and upon good authority, that this was the same copy that Osman, Mohammed's secretary, and the second Khalif, wrote, and that this relic Timour had brought with him out of the treasury of the Sultan Bajazet, from Broussa, and that it is here concealed as a precious deposit, inasmuch as Bokhara, if publicly known to possess it, would be certainly regarded with ill-will by the other Musselman potentates.

[Footnote 66: A sister of the Imam Riza, who after having long implored, at last obtained, permission from Meemun Khalife to visit her brother who was living as an exile in Tus (Meshed). On the journey thither she died at Kom, and her tomb is a highly venerated place of pilgrimage in Persia.]

On the front of the Turbe, in the very place to strike the eyes of all, we read the inscription, written in white letters upon a blue ground:--

'This is the work of poor Abdullah, the son of Mahmoud of Ispahan.' I could not ascertain the date. About a hundred paces from the building {210} which I have described, is another dome of simple architecture, but considerable antiquity, where reposes one of Timour's favourite wives, also venerated as a saint. Quite above, on the side of the dome, hangs a sort of skein, said to contain Muy Seadet (hair from the beard of the Prophet), and which has for many long years--although the dome has crevices in all its sides--protected it from further decay, *s'il vous plait.*

[**Colleges; Ancient Observatory**]
Medresses.
Some of those are still peopled; others abandoned, and likely soon to become perfect ruins. To those in the best state of repair belong the Medresse Shirudar and Tillakari; but these were built long subsequently to the time of Timour. The one last named, Tillakari (worked in gold), was built 1028 (1618), by a rich Kalmuk named Yelenktosh, who was a convert to Islamism; and really that portion called Khanka, is so rich that it is only surpassed by the interior of the mosque of Iman Riza. Opposite to these we see the Medresse Mirza Ulug, built in 828 (1434) by Timour, grandson of the same name who was passionately fond of astrology; but which even in 1115 (1701) were in so ruinous a condition that, to borrow the expression employed by its historian, 'owls housed, instead of students, in its cells, and the doors were hung with spiders' webs instead of silk curtains.' In this building stood the observatory famous throughout the world, which was commenced in 832 (1440), under the direction of the ***savants*** Gayas-ed-dir Djemshid, Muayin Kashani, and of the learned Israelite Silah-ed-din Bagdadi, but was{211} completed under Ali Kushtchi. This was the second and last observatory erected in Central Asia. The first had been constructed at Maraga, under Helagu, by the learned Nedjm-ed-din. The place where it had stood was pointed out to me, but I could only discern a slight trace.

These three Medresse form the principal open space, the Righistan of Samarcand; which is smaller, indeed, than the Righistan at Bokhara, but still filled with booths and ever frequented with buzzing crowds.

At a distance from those, and near the Dervaze Bokhara, are the extensive ruins of the once really magnificent Medresse Hanym, which a Chinese princess, wife of Timour, erected out of her private purse. It is said at one time to have accommodated a thousand students, each of whom received from the Vakf (foundation) the annual sum of a hundred Tilla. The sum may be regarded as an Oriental one; an evidence, nevertheless, of bygone splendour appears in its ruins, of which three walls and the fore-front or frontispiece (Pishtak) still exist; the latter with its towers and portal, that might serve for a model, has its pavement completely covered with mosaic made of earth, the composition and colouring of which are of incomparable beauty, and so firmly cemented that it occasioned me indescribable trouble to cut away the calyx of a flower; and even of this I could only remove in a perfect state the innermost part, with three leaves folded together. Although the work of destruction is eagerly proceeded with, we can still perceive in the interior where at present the hired carriages that ply to Khokand and Karshi take up their quarters--the mosque, with the wonder-working gigantic Rahle; and many a century must the people of Samarcand {212} continue to tear away and cut down before this work of annihilation is complete.

[Greek Armenian Library not, as pretended, carried off by Timour.]

Besides these edifices, there are some other towers and dome-shaped buildings, the work of bygone days. After having made every possible investigation, in spite of all exertions, I have not been able to discover any trace of that once famous Armenian Greek library, which, according to a universally accredited tradition, the victorious Timour swept away to Samarcand to ornament his capital. This fable, so I must at once pronounce it, originated from the over-strained patriotism of an Armenian priest, named Hadjator, who insists that he came from Caboul to Samarcand, and discovered in the latter city large folios with heavy chains (*à la* Faust) in those towers, into which no Musselman, from fear of Djins (Genii), would dare to venture. The story was later, if I mistake not, made use of by a French *savant*, in his 'History of the Armenians;' and as we Europeans are just as fond as the Orientals of amusing ourselves with subjects that lie half in light and half in darkness, it was actually believed by some (that is, by those who busied themselves with antiquities) that the mighty Asiatic conqueror had sent back to his capital, a distance of a hundred stations, some hundred mules laden with Armenian Greek manuscripts, in order that his Tartars might also familiarise themselves with foreign languages and history!

[Architecture of Public Buildings not Chinese but Persian; Modern Samarcand; Its Population]

I disbelieve altogether the story that any such library ever existed; my opinion is as strong also upon another subject, for I entirely differ from those who ascribe a Chinese character to the monuments of Samarcand. The political frontiers of China are, it is true, at a distance of only ten days' journey, but China proper can {213} only be reached in sixty days, and those who have even a faint idea of the rigorous line of demarcation that guards the Celestial Empire, will not very easily believe that the Chinese can have any idea in common with the genuine Mahommedans, who are also themselves separatists. The inscription upon the façade of the sepulchre of Timour, to which all the other edifices in Samarcand have more or less resemblance in point of style and decoration, shows clearly enough that the artists were Persians, and one needs only to compare the monuments of this city with those of Herat, Meshed, and Ispahan, to be convinced that the architecture is Persian.

So much of the ancient and historical city of Samarcand. The new city, whose actual walls are at the distance of a full league from the ruins of the old walls, [Footnote 67] has six gates and a few bazaars that have still survived from the ancient times; in these are offered at low prices, manufactures in leather of high repute, and wooden saddles, the enamel of which might even do honour to European artisans. During my stay in the city of Timour the bazaars and other public places and streets were continually thronged, because every spot was occupied by the troops returning from their campaign; still the regular residents can hardly exceed from 15,000 to 20,000, of whom two-thirds are Özbegs, and one-third Tadjiks. The Emir, whose usual residence is Bokhara, {214} is in the habit of passing two or three of the summer months in Samarcand, because the situation is more elevated, and the city has certain advantages of climate. In Bokhara the heat is insupportable, but I found the temperature here very agreeable; only the water recommended as Abi-Hayat (ambrosia) tasted to me very detestable.

[Footnote 67: It is possible that the ruins only mark the boundary of a suburb, for E. G. de Clavijo, who in 1403 formed part of an embassy at the Court of Timour, informs us (see the translation of that account by C. E. Markham, page 172), that the citadel lies at one end of the town, where in fact it still is. The space between the ruins and the modern wall may have been inhabited and yet not have belonged to the city.]

[Dehbid]

I may mention Dehbid (the ten willows) as singularly beautiful; it forms at once a place of pilgrimage and of recreation, a league distant from Samarcand, on the other side of the Zerefshan, and peopled by the descendants of Mahkdum Aázam, who died in 949 (1542), and is here interred. The inhabitants have a fine Tchanka (convent), and receive pilgrims with the greatest hospitality. Dehbid lies actually higher than Samarcand; still, to my surprise, I met here with mulberries in the middle of the month of August. I found it cool even at mid-day in the great 'Alley,' which was planted in 1632, by order of Nezr Divabeghi, in honour of the saint above mentioned. On the road to Dehbid, I was shown the spot where stood the famous Baghi-Chinaran (poplar garden). Ruins only now mark the site of the palace; of the trees nothing is visible.

Although we cannot go so far as the inhabitant of Central Asia--who applies to these ruins, even at the present day, the expression,

'Samarcand resembles Paradise' [Footnote 68]--

we must still be just, and characterise the ancient capital of Central Asia, from its site and the luxuriant vegetation in the midst of which it stands, as the most beautiful in Turkestan. Khokand and Namengan, {215} according to native appreciation, rank still higher, but a stranger may be pardoned if he withholds the palm, so long as it has been denied to him with his own eyes to see the superiority.

[Footnote 68: 'Samarkand firdousi manend.']

[Author decides to return]

After having remained eight days in Samarcand, I formed, at last, my final resolution, and determined to return to the West by the route before mentioned. Hadji Bilal was desirous of taking me with him to Aksu, and promised to try to get me forwards to Mecca, either by way of Yerkend, Thibet, and Cashmere, or, if fortune were favourable, by way of Komul to Bidjing (Pekin); but Hadji Salih did not approve of the plan, both on account of the great distance to be traversed, and the small capital at my disposal. 'You might, indeed, pass as far as Aksu, perhaps even as Komul, for so far you would meet with Musselmans and brethren, all disposed to show you great honour as a Dervish from Roum, but from that point onwards you would find black unbelievers everywhere, who, although they might throw no obstacle in your way, would give you nothing. By the way of Thibet you may find fellow-travellers going from Kashgar and Yerkend, but I cannot charge myself with the responsibility of taking you with me at this time to Khokand, where everything, owing to the recent war, is in the greatest disorder. But Khokand you must see; come, then, when things are tranquil: for the present it is better to return by Herat to Teheran, with the friends whom we have found for you.'

Although these words of my excellent friend were sensible enough, still I had for hours a long struggle with myself. A journey, I thought, by land to Pekin, across the ancient homes of the Tartars, Kirghis, Kalmuks, Mongols, and Chinese--a way by which {216} Marco Polo himself would not have ventured--is really grand! But moderation whispered in my ear, 'Enough for the moment!' I made a retrospect of what I had done, of what countries I had traversed, what distances I had travelled over, and by ways, too, by which no one had preceded me; would it not, I thought, be a pity if I sacrificed the experience which I had acquired, however trifling, in a hazardous and uncertain enterprise? I am but thirty-one years old; what has not happened may still occur; better, perhaps, now, that I should return. Hadji Bilal jested with me upon my cowardice, and the European reader may agree with him; but local experience has taught me that, at least here, one need not scorn the Turkish proverb, that says:--

'To-day's egg is better than to-morrow's fowl.'

[Arrival of Emir]

I was in the midst of the preparations for my departure, when the Emir made his triumphal entry, which, as it had been announced three days previously, great crowds assembled in the Righistan to witness. No particular pomp, however, distinguished it. The procession was opened by about 200 Serbaz, who had thrown leather accoutrements over their clumsy Bokhariot dress, and that was supposed to entitle them to the name of regular troops. Far in their rear, there followed troops in ranks with standards and kettle-drums. The Emir Mozaffar-ed-din, and all his escort of higher functionaries, looked, with their snow-white turbans and their wide silk garments of all the colours of the rainbow, more like the chorus of women in the opera of Nebuchadnezzar than a troop of Tartar warriors. So also it may be said with respect to other officers of the court, of whom some bore white staves {217} and others halberds, that there was in the whole procession nothing to remind one of Turkestan, except in the followers, of whom many were Kiptchaks, and attracted attention by their most original Mongol features, and by the arms which they bore, consisting of bows, arrows, and shields.

ENTRY OF THE EMIR INTO SAMARCAND.
The Buildings after a sketch by Mr. Lehman.

The day of his entry the Emir made, by public notice, a national holiday. Several of their kettles of monstrous size were put in requisition, and brought forward in the Righistan, for boiling the 'princely Pilow,' which consisted of the following ingredients in each kettle:--a sack of rice, three sheep chopped to pieces, a large pan of sheep's fat (enough to make, with us, five pounds of candles), a small sack of carrots; all these were allowed to boil, or perhaps we had better call it *ferment*, together, and, as tea was also served out at discretion, the eating and drinking proceeded bravely.

[Author's Interview with him]

The day following it was announced that an Arz (public audience) would take place. I took advantage of the opportunity to present myself to the Emir under the conduct of my friends, but to my surprise, on entering, our party was stopped by a Mehrem, who informed us that his Majesty wished to see me apart from my companions. This was a blow, for we all now suspected that something was going wrong. I followed the Mehrem, and, after being kept an hour waiting, I was introduced into a room which I had on a previous occasion visited, and there I now saw the Emir sitting on a mattress or ottoman of red cloth, surrounded by writings and books. With great presence of mind, I recited a short Sura, with the usual prayer for the welfare of the Sovereign, and after the Amen, to which he himself responded, I {218} took my seat, without permission, quite close to his royal person. The boldness of my proceeding--quite, however, in accordance with the character which I assumed--seemed not displeasing to him. I had long forgotten the art of blushing, and so was able to sustain the look which he now directed full in my face, with the intention, probably, of disconcerting me. 'Hadji, thou comest, I hear, from Roum, to visit the tombs of Baha-ed-din, and the saints of Turkestan.'

'Yes, Takhsir (sire [Footnote 69]); but also to quicken myself by the contemplation of thy sacred beauty' (Djemali mubarek), according to the forms of conversation usual on these occasions.

[Footnote 69: Takhsir signifies Sir, and is employed not only in conversing with Princes, but all other personages.]

'Strange! and thou hadst then no other motive in coming hither from so distant a land?'

'No, Takhsir (sire), it had always been my warmest desire to behold the noble Bokhara, and the enchanting Samarcand, upon whose sacred soil, as was remarked by Sheikh Djelal, one should rather walk on one's head than on one's feet. But I have, besides, no other business in life, and have long been moving about everywhere as a Djihangeshte' (world pilgrim).

'What, thou, with thy lame foot, a Djihangeshte! That is really astonishing.'

'I would be thy victim!' (an expression equivalent to 'pardon me.') 'Sire, thy glorious ancestor (peace be with him!) had certainly the same infirmity, and he was even Djihanghir' (conqueror of the world). [Footnote 70]

[Footnote 70: Timour, whom these Emirs of Bokhara erroneously claim as their ancestor, was, it is well known, lame; hence, his enemies called him Timur 'Lenk' (Tamerlane, *the lame Timour*) .]

{219}

This reply was agreeable to the Emir, who put questions to me respecting my journey, and the impression made upon me by Bokhara and Samarcand. My observations, which I incessantly strove to ornament with Persian sentences and verses from the Koran, produced a good effect upon him, for he is himself a Mollah, and tolerably well acquainted with Arabic. He directed that I should be presented with a Serpay (dress) [Footnote 71] and thirty Tenghe, and dismissed me with the command that I should visit him a second time in Bokhara.

[Footnote 71: This word means Ser ta pay (from head to foot); it is a complete dress, consisting of turban, over-dress, girdle, and boots.]

When I had received the princely present, I hurried, like a man possessed by a devil, back to my friends, who were delighted at my good fortune. I heard (and there is no improbability in the account) that Rahmet Bi had drawn up his report concerning me in ambiguous terms, and that the Emir had consequently conceived suspicions. My triumph was entirely owing to the flexibility of my tongue (which is really impudent enough). In fact, I had every reason on this occasion to appreciate, the truth of the Latin proverb, 'Quot linguas cales tot homines vales.'

After this scene, I was advised by my friends to quit Samarcand in all speed, not to make any stay even in Karshi, but to gain as rapidly as possible the further bank of the Oxus, where, amongst the hospitable Ersari Turkomans, I might await the arrival of the karavan for Herat.

[Parting from the Hadjis, and Departure from Samarcand.]

The hour of departure was at hand. My pen is too feeble to convey any adequate idea of the distressing scene that took place between us; on both sides we were really equally moved. For six long months we {220} had shared the great dangers of deserts, of robbers, and inclement weather. What wonder if all difference of position, age, and nationality had been lost sight of, and

79

if we regarded each other as all members of a single family? Separation was, in our case, equivalent to death. How could it be otherwise in these countries, where there was positively not even a hope of seeing each other again? My heart seemed as if it would burst, when I thought that I was not permitted to communicate the secret of my disguise to these, my best friends in the world, that I must deceive those to whom I owed even my life. I tried to imagine a way--I wished to make trial of them; but religious fanaticism, to be found sometimes even in civilised Europe, has a fearful influence upon the Oriental, and particularly so upon the Islamite.

My confession, in itself a capital offence [Footnote 72] by the law of Mohammed, might not perhaps, for the moment, have severed all ties of friendship; but how bitterly, how dreadfully would my friend Hadji Salih, who was so sincere in his religious opinions, have felt the deception! No, I determined to spare him this sorrow, and to save myself from any reproach of ingratitude. He must, I thought, be left in the fond delusion.

[Footnote 72: A Murtad (renegade) is directed to be stoned to death.]

After having commended me to some pilgrims, whom I was to accompany to Mecca, as their very brother, son in fact, as one whom they most valued, they accompanied me after sunset to the outside of the city gate, where the cart that my new companions had hired for the journey to Karshi was waiting for us. I wept like a child when, tearing myself from their embraces, I took my seat in the vehicle. My {221} friends were all bathed in tears, and long did I see them--and I see them now--standing there in the same place, with their hands raised to heaven, imploring Allah's blessing upon my far journey. I turned round many times to look back. At last, they disappeared, and I found I was only gazing upon the domes of Samarcand, illuminated by the faint light of the rising moon!

{222}

CHAPTER XII.

SAMARCAND TO KARSHI THROUGH DESERT

NOMADS

KARSHI, THE ANCIENT NAKHSEB

TRADE AND MANUFACTURE

KERKI

OXUS

AUTHOR CHARGED WITH BEING RUNAWAY SLAVE

ERSARI TURKOMANS

MEZARI SHERIF

BELKH

AUTHOR JOINS KARAVAN FROM BOKHARA

SLAVERY

ZEÏD

ANDKHUY

YEKETUT

80

KHAIRABAD

MAYMENE

AKKALE.

Non succurrit tibi quamdiu circum Bactra haereas? --Q. Curtii Rufi lib. vii. 8.

[Samarcand to Karshi through Desert]

My new travelling companions were from Oosh Mergolan, and Namengan (Khanat of Khokand). It is unnecessary to describe them particularly. They were far from being to me like those friends from whom I had just parted; nor did we remain long together. I attached myself, in preference, to a young Mollah from Kungrat, who had travelled with us to Samarcand, and hoped to proceed, in my company, as far as Mecca. He was a young man, good-humoured, and as poor as myself, who looked up to me as one superior to himself in learning, and was disposed to serve me.

From Samarcand to Karshi there are three ways, first by Shehri Sebz, which may be styled almost a circuitous way, and is the longest; secondly, by Djam, only fifteen miles, but through a stony and mountainous country, and consequently difficult, if not impracticable, for carts; thirdly, through the desert. {223} barely eighteen miles in length. On setting out, we had, anyhow, to take the Bokhara road as far as the hill, whence Samarcand first becomes visible to the traveller approaching it from the former city. Here we turned off to the left. The way then passes through two villages, in the midst of land well cultivated. After proceeding three miles, we halted at the karavanserai, Robati Hauz, where the road divides into two others, that on the left passing by Djam, that on the right traversing a desert. We took the latter. In comparison with those deserts through which I had already made my way, this one, with respect to size, may be styled a moderate-sized field. It is everywhere visited by shepherds, from the convenience of its numerous wells of tolerably good water; in the neighbourhood of these the Ozbegs constantly pitch their tents. The wells are, for the most part, deep, and have each near them a somewhat elevated reservoir of stone or wood, always in the form of a square, into which is thrown the water drawn from the wells, for the use of cattle. As the buckets are small, and the shepherd would be soon tired by repeatedly using them, an ass, or more often a camel, is employed; the rope is attached to the saddle, and the animal draws up the bucket by walking a distance equal to the length of the cord. The appearance of these wells, of the drinking sheep, and the busy shepherd, has, in the stillness of those evening hours, something not unpoetic; and I was very much struck by the resemblance between this part of the desert and our Puszta (heaths) in Hungary.

{224}
In consequence of the strictness with which the police regulations were enforced everywhere by the Emir of Bokhara, the routes here are so safe, that not merely small karavans, but even single travellers, traverse the desert unmolested. On the second day we met at one of the wells a karavan coming from Karshi. There was amongst the travellers a young woman who had been treacherously sold by her own husband to an aged Tadjik for thirty Tilla. It was not until she reached the desert that she became fully aware of the cruel trick to which she was victim: the wretched creature, shrieking and weeping and tearing her hair, ran up to me like one distracted, and exclaimed, 'Hadjim (my Hadji), thou that hast read books, tell me where it is written that a Musselman can sell his wife who has borne him children!' I affirmed it to be a sin, but the Tadjik only laughed at me, for he had, probably, already an understanding with the Kazi Kelan (superior judge) of Karshi, and felt sure of his purchase.

As we advanced but slowly on account of the great heat, we took two days and three nights to reach Karshi. We first came in sight of it on reaching a plateau, where the road again divides into two, that on the right hand leading to Kette Kurgan, and that on the left conducting to the river that flows hither from Shehri Sebz, and disappears in the sand at a considerable distance beyond Karshi. From this point the whole way to the city, which is distant two miles, passes continually through cultivated land and numerous gardens, and as Karshi has no walls, one does not know before crossing the bridge that one is in the city.

Karshi, the ancient Nakhsheb, is, both from its size and its commercial importance, the second city in the Khanat of Bokhara; it consists of the city (proper) {225} and the citadel

(Kurgantche), which latter is on its north-western side, and weakly fortified. Karshi has, at present, ten karavanserais and a well-supplied bazaar, and, should no political disturbances occur to prevent, is considered likely to play an important part in the transit trade organised between Bokhara, Kaboul, and India. The inhabitants, estimated at 25,000 souls, are for the most part Özbegs, and form the nucleus of the troops of the Khan. The population consists, besides, of Tadjiks, Indians, Afghans, and Jews: the latter have the privilege of riding even in the interior of the city, which they are not allowed to do in any other part of the Khanat. With respect to its manufactures Karshi, less so, however, than Hissar (at a little distance from it), is distinguished by its fabrication of knives of different kinds. These are not only exported to all parts of Central Asia, but are conveyed by the Hadjis to Persia, Arabia, and Turkey, where they realise three times, and often four times, the cost price. One kind, with Damascus blades, and handles with gold and silver inlaid, is really worked with great taste, and might, both for durability and temper, put to shame the most famous produce of Sheffield and Birmingham.

[Nomads]
Amongst the letters of recommendation with which my friends had furnished me to different Khans and Mollahs on my way, one was addressed to a certain Ishan Hasan, who stood in high repute in Karshi. When I visited him he received me in a friendly manner, and advised me, as all cattle, and particularly asses, were cheap, to purchase one of these long-eared coursers, nor did he omit to tell me also to do like all other Hadjis, and employ what little money I had left in procuring knives, needles, thread, glass beads, {226} Bokhariot sacking, but, most of all, cornelians imported from Bedakhshan, and which are also cheap there; for he said that, as we were going amongst tribes of nomads, we should, by means of such merchandise, be able to gain something, and besides maintain ourselves better, for that for a single needle or a few glass beads (Mondjuck), one might often obtain bread and melons to support one a whole day. I saw at once that the good man was right, and proceeded the very same day, in company with the Mollah from Kungrat, to purchase some of the articles specified, so that, whilst one side of my Khurdjin knapsack was filled with my manuscripts, the other was occupied by a stock of cutlery. Thus I became simultaneously antiquary, haberdasher, Hadji, and Mollah, besides filling the accessorial functions of dispenser of blessings, Nefes, amulets, and other wonders.

Singular contrast! It is just a year ago that I exercised all those offices, and now I sit in the English metropolis confined within four walls, writing from eight to ten hours a day. There I had to do with nomads picking out from my glass beads those of lightest colour, and from my amulets those having the broadest red edgings; here I have to do with publishers, and stand with embarrassment before a critical and fastidious public, whose various and discordant requisitions are certainly more difficult to satisfy than the fashionable taste of a young Turkoman, or of a young brunette daughter of the Djemshidi!

[Karshi, the Ancient Nakhseb; Trade and Manufacture; Kerki]
It was quite a surprise for me to see in Karshi a public place of recreation not to be found upon the same scale either in Bokhara or Samarcand, or even in Persia itself. It is a large garden bearing the modest title Kalenterkhane (beggar's house), {227} extending along the bank of the river, and containing several walks and beds of flowers. Here the *beau monde* of Karshi are in motion from two o'clock in the afternoon until an hour after sunset. In different places the steaming Samovars (giant Russian teakettles) are in requisition, surrounded constantly by circles of customers, two or three deep; the sight of the gay crowd is, for the traveller in Central Asia, really something uncommon. The inhabitants of Karshi are in other respects distinguished by their cheerfulness and light-heartedness; they are, in fact, regarded as the Shirazi of the Khanat of Bokhara.

After a sojourn of three days, we started for Kerki, distant only fourteen miles: there is but one road. Our party now only consisted, in addition to myself, of Mollah Ishak (such was the name of the Mollah from Kungrat), and two other Hadjis. At the distance of two miles from Karshi we passed through a large and, as I understood, a rich village, named Feizabad, and spent half the night in the ruins of a cistern: there are many in these parts, all dating from the time of Abdullah Khan. Although security reigned everywhere, we were advised that we ought to be upon our guard when we were farther from Karshi, as there were already Turkomans about not to be depended upon. Posting our asses in a corner of the ruins, we laid ourselves down in the front part of it upon our knapsacks, and so slept alternately, until towards midnight. We then started again, in order to reach our intended station before noon. We arrived long before that period at the cistern Sengsulak. On seeing it at a distance surrounded by tents and feeding flocks, we rejoiced, for we felt now certain to find water, which we had before doubted, and therefore had loaded our {228} asses with that necessary article. The high dome-like arch of the cistern, although more than 200 years old, is quite uninjured, as also are some recesses in it that afford shade to travellers. The cistern, situated in the lower part of a valley, is completely filled, not only by the melting of the snows in the spring, but by rains. We found it then only three feet deep, and surrounded by 200 tents of the Özbegs, from the tribes of Kungrat and Nayman; their cattle, and their children in a complete state of nudity, were splashing about in it, and spoiling its flavour a little. As from here to Kerki is reckoned six miles, we wished, for the sake of our beasts, to make this tolerably long station a night journey, and to employ the day in sleeping. Our repose was soon disturbed, for the nomad girls had got scent of our glass beads. They hurried to us with huge wooden plates of camel's milk and mare's milk, to entice us to exchange.

An hour after sunset we started; it was a clear fine night. We had hardly got four leagues on our journey, when we all, simultaneously overpowered by sleep, sank down and slumbered with the reins of rope still in our hands. We were soon, however, awakened by horsemen, who reproached us with our imprudence, and incited us to continue our march. We sprang up, and, partly proceeding on foot and partly riding, reached at sunrise the Oxus. On the nearer bank stands the little citadel; on the further one, upon a steep hill, the frontier fortress round which lies spread the city Kerki.

[Oxus; Author charged with being runaway Slave.]

The Oxus, which flows between the two fortresses just mentioned, is nearly twice as broad as the Danube where it runs between Pesth and Ofen. The current is very strong, with banks of sand here and there. {229} Our passage over, as unluckily we were carried a little too far down the stream, lasted three hours. When things are most favourable for crossing--that is, during the summer months--the passage over where the river is deepest requires full half an hour, for it is unheard of, nay, impossible, for a ferry boat to cross without the boatman being obliged to step into the water and drag it by the rope over some shallow part. Happily, the heat was not as great as when I had before crossed, at Khanka; we did not, therefore, suffer much. The boatmen were humane and civil enough not to require from us any fare. Scarcely had we reached the opposite bank, when we were stopped by the Deryabeghi (intendant of the ferry) of the Governor of Kerki, who accused us of being runaway slaves making for Persia, our heretical fatherland. He forced us, bag and baggage, into the fortress, there to be heard by the Governor in person. Imagine my astonishment. My three colleagues, whose physiognomy, pronunciation, and language at once attested their origin, were not at all alarmed, and were, in fact, soon set free. With me they made a little difficulty, but, as I saw that they were about forcibly to take away my ass, I fell into a passion, and, employing alternately the dialects of Tartary and the Turkish dialect peculiar to Constantinople, I handed in my passport, demanding in a violent manner that they should show it to the Bi (governor), or that they should usher me to his presence.

On making this disturbance, I saw that the Toptchubashi (commandant of artillery) in the fortress, a Persian by birth, who had elevated himself from the condition of a slave to his present rank, whispered something in the ear of the Deryabeghi; he then {230} took me aside, and told me that he had been several times in Stamboul from Tebriz, his native city; that he could distinguish people from Roum very well; I might be easy, nothing would happen here either to me or my property; that all strangers were obliged to submit to the examination, because every emancipated slave on his way home was obliged to pay here, on the frontier, a tax of two ducats, and that often, to smuggle themselves through, they assumed different disguises. Soon afterwards, the servant returned who had shown my pass to the Governor; he gave it me back, with five Tenghe presented to me by the Bi, without any request on my part.

[Ersari Turkomans]

As Kerki is a frontier fortress, and is, so to say, the key of Bokhara on the side of Herat, let us describe it more in detail. As I before said, the fortifications are divided into two parts. The citadel on the right bank of the river is very small, and is defended by only four cannon, and guarded in time of peace by a few soldiers. The fortress itself, on the left bank, consists first of the castle built upon the hill, encircled by three walls, and having, as I heard, twelve cannon of iron and six of brass: the walls are of earth and tolerably strong, five feet broad and twelve feet high. The town, which is spread round the fortress, consists of 150 houses, three mosques, a small bazaar, and karavanserai: it is also defended by a good wall and deep ditch. The inhabitants are Özbegs and Turkomans, employed a little in trade, but more in agriculture. Near the walls of the city is the tomb of the famous Imam Kerkhi, the author of many commentaries. The province of Kerki extends from the vicinity of Chardjuy to the ford Hadji Salih (falsely called Hojasalu), on the bank of the Oxus, so far as the canals of {231} the said river run. This country is inhabited by the Ersari Turkomans, who pay tribute to the Emir only to secure themselves from hostilities on the part of the other tribes. In earlier and different times the sovereign of Bokhara had other possessions on the further side of the Oxus, but he was deprived of them by the victorious Dost Mohammed Khan, and now has nothing remaining there except Chardjuy and Kerki.

I heard, to my great regret, that Mollah Zeman, the chief of the karavan, proceeding from Bokhara to Herat, would not arrive for eight or ten days. I therefore considered it advisable to pass the interval rather in journeys amongst the Turkomans than in Kerki. I went with Mollah Ishak to the tribes Kizil Ayak and Hasan-Menekli, amongst whom there were Mollahs who had seen me at Bokhara with some of my friends. The Ersari Turkomans, who only migrated hither from Manghishlak 200 years ago, and have not recognised the supremacy of Bokhara except during the last forty years, have retained very little of the national characteristics of the Turkomans. They may be styled only semi-nomads, the greater part cultivating the land, and the remainder, still exclusively pastoral, having lost with their savage character all the primitive virtues of their kindred tribe. The exertions of Bokhara, in favour of civilisation, have stripped them at once of their sword and their integrity, giving them in exchange the Koran and hypocrisy. Never shall I forget the scenes that I witnessed as a guest in the house of one of the most considerable Ishans of these Turkomans. Khalfa Niyaz had inherited from his father sanctity, knowledge, and rank. He had a Tekkie (monastery), {232} where a limited number of students were instructed *à la* Bokhara. He had besides obtained an Izn (permission) from Mecca, to recite the sacred poems (Kaside Sherif): in doing so he used to place before him a cup with water into which he spat at the end of each poem; and this composition, into which the sanctity of the text had penetrated, was sold to the best bidder as a wonder-working medicine!

There is only one quality of the Turkomans that they have retained uncorrupted-- hospitality, which is displayed to all strangers whether they abide a day or a year; for throughout all Turkestan, if we except the Tadjiks, the proverb is unknown:--

Hôte et poisson,
En trois jours poison.

[Mezari Sherif]

I made an excursion also with my host to the Mezari Sherif ('the noble grave'). It is two days' journey from his Ova, and four or five from Kerki, and not very far from Belkh. As Mezari Sherif is said to be the tomb of Ali, it is throughout the whole of Turkestan an important place of pilgrimage. History tells that the miraculous grave at Shahi Merdan Ali ('king of the heroes,' as Mezar is also otherwise called) was discovered in the time of the Sultan Sandjar. Belkh being covered every where with ruins, it was supposed to have guarded its treasures ever since the time of the Divs (devils): the last-named Sultan, therefore, caused excavations to be made, and on one of these occasions a stone table of the purest white was found with the inscription, 'This is the tomb of Ali, the son of Abutahb, the mighty hero and companion of the Prophet.'

{233}

[Belkh]

This circumstance is only so far interesting that it enabled us to establish that the ruins of ancient Belkh, styled by the Orientals 'the mother of cities,' covered formerly a distance of five leagues. Now only a few heaps of earth are pointed to as the site of the ancient Bactra, and of the modern ruins there is nothing remarkable but a half-demolished mosque, built by the Sultan Sandjar of the race of the Seldjoukides; for in the middle ages Belkh was the capital of Islamite civilisation, and was styled Kubbet-ül Islam ('the dome of Islam'). It is singular that the bricks here are of the same size and quality as those in the ruins amongst the Yomuts; but I have been able to find amongst them no cuneiform inscriptions. Excavations would incontestably produce interesting results; but they would be impossible without recommendatory letters, backed by two or three thousand European bayonets.

Modern Belkh, regarded as the capital of the Afghan province of Turkestan, and occupied by the Serdar with his garrison, is only a winter residence, for in spring even the poorest inhabitant leaves it for Mezar, whose situation is more elevated, its temperature less oppressive, and its air less impure, than those of the ruins of the ancient Bactra; for whilst the latter is famous for poisonous scorpions, the former has a high reputation as producing the wonder-working red roses (Gül-i-Surkh). These flowers grow upon the pretended tomb of Ali, [Footnote 73] and have positively the sweetest smell and the finest colour of any I ever saw. Superstition fondly credits the story that they will not succeed in any other soil than that of Mezar. Every attempt, at least, to transplant it in Mezar itself has failed.

[Footnote 73: The real monument of Ali is in Nedjef.]
{234}

[Author joins Karavan from Bokhara; Slavery]

After a wearisome delay, we at last received intelligence of the arrival of the Herat karavan. I hurried to Kerki, and thought that I might proceed on my journey, when our departure was again postponed owing to a dispute about the tax imposed upon emancipated slaves. Mollah Zeman had in his karavan about forty of these, partly from Herat, partly from Persia, who journeyed homeward under his protection, which the poor men were obliged to purchase at a high rate, for otherwise they incurred the risk of being caught up and sold a second time. Although Zeman was well known to all the officers on the frontiers, he nevertheless had quarrels with them every time he passed, not so much on account of the tax itself, which is here fixed, but of the number of the slaves liable to it, which he always endeavoured to diminish and the authorities to increase. Every traveller not well known is presumed to be a slave, and is seized as such; and as every one seeks to enforce his own view of liability or exemption, there is no end to the shouting, quarrelling, and tumult. Finally, however, everything is left to the decision of the Kervanbashi, who, from his karavan of from 50 to 100 travellers, names such as emancipated slaves whose type, language, and other indications are unmistakable. Generally speaking, suspicion principally attaches to vagabonds and other travellers who journey with no apparent object in view; and as these for the most part assume the title of Hadjis, it is the policy of the Zeman to get together in Bokhara as many genuine Hadjis as possible, in whose ranks he then places his ex-slaves the false Hadjis.

{235}

They took a whole day to get through the bales of goods, the men, horses, camels, and asses. At last, they started, escorted by a custom-house officer, who kept strict watch to prevent any other travellers joining the karavan by circuitous routes. When we had got beyond the inhabited district--which is, in fact, the frontier of Bokhara--he turned back, and we proceeded on our way into the desert. We were in two days to reach the Khanat of Andkhuy.

[Zeid]

Whilst my heavily-laden ass was trotting on in the still night, the joyful thought for the first time occurred to me that I had turned my back upon the Khanat of Bokhara, and that I was actually on my way to that West which I loved so well. My travelling experience, thought I, may not be great, but I carry back with me what is worth more than anything--my life. I could not contain myself for joy when I thought that perhaps I might be so fortunate as to reach Persia, that Mecca of my warmest wishes. Our karavan, consisting of 400 camels, a few horses, and 190 asses, formed a long chain; and after sturdily marching the whole night, we reached, early in the morning, the station Zeid, which consists of a few wells of bad water at six miles' distance from Kerki. There were in the karavan, as I remarked at the first station, many others besides myself who were longing to reach the southernmost frontiers of Central Asia. These were the emancipated slaves, with whom Hadjis were intermixed, and I had an opportunity of witnessing the most heart-rending incidents. Near me was an old man--a father--bowed down by years. He had ransomed, at Bokhara, his son, a man in his thirtieth year, in order to restore a protector to his family left behind--that is to say, to his daughter-in-law a husband, to his children a father. The price was fifty ducats, and its payment had reduced the {236} poor old man to beggary. 'But,' said he to me, 'rather the beggar's staff than my son in chains.' His home was Khaf in Persia.

From the same city, not far from us, was another man, still of active strength, but his hair had turned grey with sorrow, for he had been despoiled by the Turkomans, some eight years ago, of life, sister, and six children. The unfortunate man had to wander from place to place a whole year in Khiva and Bokhara, to discover the spot in which those near members of his family were languishing in captivity. After long search, he found that his wife, sister, and two youngest children had succumbed under the severity of their servitude, and that, of the four children that survived, he could only ransom half. The remaining two having besides grown up, the sum demanded for them was beyond his means. Farther on sat a young man from Herat, who had ransomed his mother. Only two years ago, this woman, now in her fiftieth year, was, with her husband and eldest son, surprised by an Alaman. After seeing those near relatives both fall, in self-defence, under the lances and swords of the Turkomans, she experienced herself unceasing sufferings until sold for sixteen ducats in Bokhara. The owner, discovering a son in him who sought to ransom her, exacted a double amount, thus turning filial piety to cruelly usurious account. Nor must I omit to mention another unhappy case--that of an inhabitant of Tebber. He was captured eight years ago, and after the lapse of two years he was ransomed by his father. They were both returning home, and were three leagues from their native city, when they were suddenly attacked by the Turkomans, taken prisoners, led back to Bokhara, and again sold as slaves. Now, they were a second time freed, and were being conveyed to their homes.

{237}

But why any longer distress the reader with these cruelties? Unfortunately, the above are only a few sketches of that lamentable plague by which, for centuries, those districts, but more especially the north-eastern part of Persia, have been depopulated.

Amongst the Tekke Turkomans are reckoned at the present hour more than 15,000 mounted robbers, who are intent upon kidnapping expeditions night and day; and one can easily form an idea of how many houses and villages are devastated, how much family happiness destroyed, by these greedy free-booters.

We started from Zeid about noon. The whole country is one dry, barren plain, only occasionally producing a sort of thistle, the favourite fodder of the camels. It surprises us to see how these animals tear with their tongue and swallow a plant, to the sting of which the hardest hand is sensible.

[Andkhuy]

We continued to proceed in a south-westerly direction. They pointed out to us from a distance some Turkomans of the tribe Kara, watching for prey, and who would have been disposed even to attack our karavan had not its size rendered it unassailable. Towards evening we encamped. The adventurers galloped by us at two different points. We sent a few shots after them, and they made no second demonstration. An hour after sunset we set off again, and after advancing with the greatest caution the whole night, we arrived next morning at the ruins of Andkhuy.

{238}

The karavan took up its quarters at the end of the ancient city, near the Charbag of the Khan; and in its immediate proximity all those travellers also stationed themselves who, aware what notorious robbers the inhabitants were, did not dare to withdraw from the protection of the Kervanbashi. We found that they had determined that we should stay here a few days; because the regulations respecting the customs never cease to occasion delay, as the Khan or his Vizir always superintends in person. The Khan begins by demanding ordinarily exorbitant sums as the tax for men (i.e. emancipated slaves), for cattle, and bales of goods; and as he allows the matter to be discussed with himself, the question how far the tax is to be levied depends only upon the adroitness of the Kervanbashi and the leisure time at his disposal. To avoid staying through this tiresome operation, I went with the other Hadjis into the city, to seek shelter under the cool shade of an old Medresse, and also to open a shop at the bazaar, to realise by the sale of my cutlery the necessary food for the day, and a little money. Long did I wander about the ruins before I was able to find a place. I at last took up my position near the residence of the Khan, in the court of a mosque. The bazaar consisted only of a few warehouses where bread was sold, and of two or three shops for the sale of a little linen and cheap ready-made clothes. Our presence had given some animation to the market; our stall was surrounded by women and children from morning till evening; but still we could not get rid of our stock, for these people offered us in exchange only fruit and bread, instead of money; of course, we could not consent to such a barter for raw materials in a country where a single Tenghe (three-quarter franc) will purchase fifty melons. These melons are far from being so good as those I had seen on the banks of the Oxus; {239} but it is astonishing what a quantity of fruit, corn, and rice is raised in this desert-like neighbourhood, only scantily watered by a little salt stream flowing hither from Maymene. In summer a stranger finds this water--to the execrable taste of which the inhabitants are accustomed--quite undrinkable; and although it generates no worms (Rishte), like that in Bokhara, it is said to produce many other evil consequences. The climate, too, is in bad repute; and a Persian verse says with reason,

Andkhuy has bitter salt water, scorching sand, venomous flies, and even scorpions. Vaunt if not, for it is the picture of a real hell.

And yet, in spite of all these disadvantages, Andkhuy was, only thirty years ago, very flourishing. It is said to have had a population of 50,000 souls. They carried on an important traffic with Persia in the fine black sheep-skins called by us Astrakhan, and even seriously rivalled Bokhara, where this article is produced of first-rate quality. The camels of Andkhuy are the most in request throughout Turkestan, particularly a kind called Ner, distinguished by abundant hair streaming down from the neck and breast, a slim slender figure, and extraordinary strength. These animals have become scarce; the inhabitants themselves having for the most part either emigrated or perished.

Mollah Ishak had a countryman here, who was one of the most distinguished Imams, and as he had invited us, I found an opportunity to become acquainted with the chief residents of the spiritual order. I was much struck by the great disorder reigning in the regulations, both as to justice and religion. The Kazi Kelan (superior judge), who in Bokhara and {240} Khiva is a great man, plays here the part of a buffoon. Every one does as he thinks fit, and even the most atrocious crime can be compounded for by a present. The consequence is, that the inhabitants speak of Bokhara as the model of justice, of piety, and earthly grandeur, and would think themselves quite happy if the Emir would only condescend to take them under his sceptre. An old Özbeg remarked to me that 'even the Frenghi (English) (God pardon him his sins!) would be better than the present Musselman Government.' He added that he still remembered a Hekim Bashi (Moorcroft) who died in his uncle's house in the time of the Emir Haydar; that he was a clever magician and good physician; that he might have become as rich as he pleased; but with all these advantages he remained unassuming and condescending towards every one, even towards women. I made many enquiries respecting the death of this traveller, and all agreed in their accounts, that he had died of fever; which is indeed far more probable than the story of his having been poisoned.

Andkhuy contains at present about 2,000 houses, which form the city, and about 3,000 tents, which are either in its environs, or scattered over the oases in the desert. The number of inhabitants is estimated at 15,000. They are principally Turkomans, of the tribe Alieli, intermixed with Özbegs and a few Tadjiks. Formerly Andkhuy, like Khulum, Kunduz, and Belkh, formed a separate Khanat; but lying on the high road to Herat, it is more exposed to the attacks of the Emirs of Bokhara and Afghanistan, than those other places which I have mentioned. Down to the year 1840, it is said to have been tolerably flourishing. It was then subject to Bokhara, and was compelled to {241} oppose the victorious march upon the Oxus of Yar Mohammed Khan, who besieged it during four months, and at last only took it by storm. The city was plundered, and left a heap of ruins. The greater part of those inhabitants who could not fly fell under the swords of the merciless Afghans. The present sovereign, Gazanfer Khan, to preserve himself from utter destruction, threw himself into the arms of the Afghans, and thereby made bitter enemies of Bokhara on one side, and of the neighbouring Maymene on the other. Even during our stay in Andkhuy, he was obliged to join in person the Serdar of Belkh, and give battle to Maymene, which, however, inflicted upon the allies a signal defeat.

In the meantime all things were in confusion in our karavan. The Vizir, who wanted during the absence of the Khan to enrich himself by an enormous increase of the imposts, was already quarrelling with the Kervanbashi. From words, indeed, they soon came to blows; and as the inhabitants sided with the karavan, the members of the latter stoutly stood to their arms, and made up their minds for the worst. Happily the Khan, a well-disposed man, arrived at that very moment from the seat of war; he made up the differences by diminishing the immoderate tax imposed by his Vizir, and dismissed us upon our way with the recommendation to be careful, as the Turkomans, turning to account the confusion that reigned everywhere, were scouring the country and besetting all the ways. But this did not inspire in us much alarm, for in Andkhuy our karavan had swelled to double its former size, so that we had no cause to apprehend a surprise by robbers.

{242}

[Yeketut; Khaïrabad; Maymene]

We set out that very same afternoon, encamping at Yeketut, distant but a league from Andkhuy. It was the place appointed for our rendezvous. We proceeded hence during the night. The next station was on the bank of a stream coming from Maymene. Its bed, unusually deep in many places, is thickly planted with trees. From Andkhuy to Maymene they reckon twenty-two miles--a three days' journey for camels. Of this distance we had thus far performed eight miles; the remainder (fourteen miles) it would have been easy to accomplish, had we not been obliged to pass secretly by Khaïrabad, which should have been our second station, and reach next morning the district of Maymene. Khaïrabad belonged then to the Afghans, and the Kervanbashi was quite right in not venturing to approach it, as he knew that even in peace the Afghans committed virtual robbery under pretence of levying their customs; and it might be readily imagined how the military authorities would have treated the karavan had it fallen into their hands.

Some inhabitants of Khaïrabad who were in the karavan, on coming near their native city, wanted to separate from us; but they were forced to continue their journey, because treachery was apprehended, and, in case of discovery, the Afghans would have confiscated everything. Although the camels were heavily laden, the journey was continued, without interruption, from noon until eight o'clock next morning. The poor tired brutes were left behind; and great was our joy when we arrived the next morning, without accident, in the Khanat of Maymene. The last station was a harassing one, not merely from these apprehensions, but from the physical difficulties that it presented; for about nine miles from Andkhuy, {243} the country becomes more and more hilly, until, in the neighbourhood of Maymene, it is quite mountainous. Besides this, we had to cross a small portion of the dangerous Batkak (which consists of marshes), where, notwithstanding the heat of the season, there was mud in many places. This caused the camels and asses much suffering. I rode a sturdy little brute; but as his small feet sank so often, he got tired of pulling them out again, and gave me much trouble in shouting, entreating, and tugging before I could get him to advance from the spongy ground.

[Akkale]

We encamped at the foot of a small citadel named Akkale, which is distant from Maymene four leagues. The Kervanbashi made a present to the Hadjis of two sheep, as a grateful acknowledgment to God for having happily escaped from the peril to which the karavan had been exposed. As the senior, I was charged with the division of the donation. We ate that whole day, instead of bread, roast meat, and sang together in the evening some Telkins (hymns) to the accompaniment, under my direction, of a Zikr--that is, we shouted out to the full extent of our voices two thousand times, Ya hoo! ya hakk!

From this spot, our arrival was reported in Maymene. Towards evening an officer of the customs--a civil honest Özbeg--came to us, and wrote down his report. At night, we again started, and were in Maymene next morning.

{244}

CHAPTER XIII.

MAYMENE

ITS POLITICAL POSITION AND IMPORTANCE

REIGNING PRINCE

RIVALRY OF BOKHARA AND KABUL

DOST MOHAMMED KHAN

ISHAN EYUB AND MOLLAH KHALMURAD

KHANAT AND FORTRESS OF MAYMENE

ESCAPED RUSSIAN OFFENDERS

MURGAB RIVER AND BALA MURGAB

DJEMSHIDI AND AFGHAN

RUINOUS TAXES ON MERCHANDISE

KALÈ NO

HEZARE

AFGHAN EXACTIONS AND MALADMINISTRATION.

Wild warriors of the Turquoise hills, and those Who dwell beyond the everlasting snows   Of Hindoo Kosh, in stormy freedom bred,   Their fort the rock, their camp the torrent's bed.   Moore, *Veiled Prophet.*

[Maymene; Its Political Position and Importance; Reigning Prince; Rivalry of Bokhara and Kabul; Dost Mohammed Khan]

Before entering Maymene, let me describe the political state of that country, for as that city plays a part of great importance, some preliminary observations are here quite indispensable.

The whole tract of land on this side of the Oxus, as far as Hindukush and Herat, has, from ancient times, been the field of continual quarrels and warfare; and these have involved not only the small predatory states in its vicinity, Kunduz, Khulum, Belkh, Aktche, Serepul, Shiborgan, Andkhuy, Bedakshan, and Maymene, but the Emirs themselves, both of Bokhara and Kabul. These princes, to carry out their plans of conquest, have been ever ready to kindle the flames of dissension; sometimes, too, they have taken an active part in these differences. They {245} have striven to gain over to their respective causes some one of the above-named cities, or even actually to incorporate it, and to make use of it for the particular ends they had in view. The Emirs were, in fact, the principal rivals in the field. Until the commencement of this century, the influence of Bokhara had almost always predominated; but it has been in more recent tunes supplanted by the Afghan tribes of the Durani, Sadduzi, and Barekzi; and at last Dost Mohammed Khan succeeded, partly by force and partly by cunning, in bringing under his sceptre all the states I have mentioned, with the exception of Bedakhshan and Maymene. He formed the province Turkestan, naming for its capital Belkh. This city is made the seat of a Serdar, who has under his command ten thousand men, partly Paltan (regular troops), partly native militia, and three batteries of field-pieces. The possession of the mountainous Bedakhshan was not much coveted by the energetic Dost Mohammed Khan. Its native prince became a vassal, and the Afghan was for the time satisfied. The case stands differently with Maymene. It lies half-way on the route to Bokhara, and has been several times besieged, without success, both by Dost Mohammed Khan and by Yar Mohammed Khan. In 1862, when the grey Barekzi prince drew the sword to punish faithless Herat, the whole of Central Asia trembled; but Maymene again resisted, and was again victorious. The bravery of the Ozbegs there became proverbial, and an idea may be formed of the proud spirit of this city, when she could affirm, with truth, at the death of Dost Mohammed Khan, that she alone, of all the neighbouring states, had refused to do homage to the flag of the Afghans.

{246}

The death of Dost Mohammed Khan--an event of the highest importance to the destiny of Central Asia--was thought to threaten it with great change and political revolutions. The Emir of Bokhara was the first who sought to profit by the occasion, and, in spite of his notorious penuriousness, sent a subsidy of ten thousand Tilla to the little warlike Maymene; and an agreement was made that the Emir should cross the Oxus, and, uniting his forces with those of his ally, should make a simultaneous attack upon their common enemy, the Afghans. The reigning prince of Maymene, however, being a youth of fiery spirit, [Footnote 74] was too impatient to await his ally's approach, began the struggle with the forces at his own disposal, and succeeded in capturing some small places from the Afghans, a success which enabled him to ornament the gate of his fortress with three hundred long-haired Afghan skulls. During our stay in his city, they were making preparations to renew the contest on a larger scale.

[Footnote 74: He is in his 22nd year.]

[Ishan Eyub and Mollah Khalmurad]

When the karavan had encamped here, outside the town, I visited the Tekkie of a certain Ishan Eyub, to whom I had letters of recommendation from Hadji Salih. I spared no pains to gain his favourable opinion, for I thought it would be of service to me in the event of a ***rencontre*** which I expected to make in Maymene, and which I dreaded, as it might have the disagreeable effect of betraying my identity, and, my disguise once discovered, I might again be exposed to great danger. The person whom I so dreaded to meet was a certain Mollah Khalmurad, who had been known to me in Constantinople, and had given me lessons in the Turkish Djagatay {247} during a period of four months. The Mollah--a very cunning fellow--had already perceived on the Bosphorus that I was not the genuine Reshid Efendi for whom I was taken. Having been told of my intention of travelling to Bokhara, he had, indeed, formally tendered his services as cicerone, assuring me at the same time that he had served the English Mollah Yusuf (Dr. Wolff) in the same capacity. As I left him in doubt respecting my intentions, he proceeded to Mecca. I knew that his design had been to return home by Bombay and Karatchi, and was apprehensive of encountering him, for I was firmly convinced that in spite of the kindness with which I had loaded him, he was quite capable of denouncing me, if he had the slightest interest in doing so.

All communication being interrupted between Maymene and Bokhara by the Afghan campaign, I had the good fortune to escape his taking me by surprise in the latter city; but in Maymene I hardly expected to be so lucky, and, to foil any possible attack from this quarter, I felt it necessary to secure for myself some firm *locus standi*, which I might do by striving to win the good opinion and favour of Ishan Eyub, who was generally respected. After having been three days in the city, I took the initiative and made inquiries as to my man. 'What! Khalmurad?' said the Ishan in astonishment, 'thou hast been acquainted with him (peace to him, and long life to us!). He had the happiness of dying in Mecca, and, as he was my bosom friend, I have received his children into my house, and the little one there (pointing, as he said that, to a boy) is one of his sons.' I gave the child a whole string of glass beads, said three Fatihas for the {248} salvation of the soul of the departed, [Footnote 75] and my well-grounded apprehensions therefore at once ceased.

[Footnote 75: On my return to Teheran, I was told by my friend Ismael Efendi, then *Chargé d'affaires* of the Porte at the Persian Court, that a month before my arrival a Mollah from Maymene, whose description tallied exactly with that of my Mollah, whom we thought in the other world, had passed through and had spoken at the Embassy of me as of his former pupil in Djagatay. Khalmurad is consequently not dead, and some singular chance alone prevented our coming in contact.]

I began now to move about more at my ease. I soon opened a stall at the corner of a street, but, to my very great disappointment, my stock now was rapidly dwindling away. 'Hadji Reshid,' said one of my fellow-travellers, 'thou hast already eaten up half of thy knives, needles, and glass beads; thou wilt before long have devoured the other half, and thy ass to boot. What wilt thou then do?' He was right, thought I, for, in fact, what was I to do? My sombre prospects, and particularly the approaching winter, made me a little fearful, for I was still far from the Persian frontiers, and every attempt I made to replenish my case I saw fail.' A Dervish or a beggar,' I said, 'never passes hungry from the door of an Özbeg. Everywhere he has a well-founded hope of something, bread or fruits; here and there, too, an old article of attire, and this sends him, in his own opinion, richly provided on his way.'

That I must have suffered, and suffered much, the reader will well understand; but habit, and the hope of returning to Europe, enabled me to bear my burden. I slept sweetly enough in the open air, on the bare earth, esteeming myself especially happy in having no longer to dread constant discovery or a death by torture, for my Hadji character excited suspicion nowhere.

{249}

[Khanat and Fortress of Maymene]

The Khanat Maymene, so far as its peopled district extends, is eighteen miles broad and twenty miles long. Besides its capital, it contains ten villages and cantons, of which the most considerable are Kaisar, Khafir-kalè, Alvar, and Khodjakendu. The population, divided into settlers and nomads, is estimated at 100,000 souls; in point of nationality, they are for the most part Özbegs of the tribes of Min, Atchmayli, and Daz; they can bring into the field from five to six thousand cavalry, well mounted and well armed. They are distinguished, as I before mentioned, for their bravery. The present ruler of Maymene is Husein Khan, son of Hukumet Khan. The latter was, by order of his own brother, who is still living, and is uncle of the reigning prince, hurled down from the walls of the citadel, 'in order,' as he expressed himself, 'that his abler son might be placed at the head of affairs.' Now, as the latter was then still incapable of reigning, the motive of the atrocious crime is easy to be divined. Mirza Yakoub--that is the name of this amiable uncle--plays, indeed, the part of Vizir, but everybody knows that Husein Khan is only his instrument. In Maymene, at all events, the young prince was more liked than his uncle. The latter would be regarded, even amongst Europeans, as a man of agreeable exterior; in the eyes of the Özbegs he is, therefore, an Adonis. He is praised for his goodness of heart by men who forget how he enforces the tyrannical law by which the Khan, instead of inflicting corporal punishment or imposing fines, sends off his subjects to the slave-market of Bokhara. The Khans transmit every month a fixed number of these {250} unfortunates to that city. It is not considered strange, as it is an ancient custom. The city of Maymene stands in the midst of hills, and is only visible when approached within a distance of a quarter of a league. It is extremely filthy and ill built, and consists of 1,500 mud huts, and a bazaar built of brick, that seems about to fall; it has besides three mosques and two Medresse, the former constructed of mud, the latter of bricks. The inhabitants are Özbegs, with some Tadjiks, Heratis, about fifty families of Jews, a few Hindoos, and Afghans. These enjoy equal rights, and are not disturbed for reasons of religion or nationality. With respect to Maymene considered as a fortress, I was far from being able to discover in the simple city walls and fosses in the citadel, situated on its west side, the imposing stronghold said to be capable of resisting the Afghan artillery, mounted in English fashion, and of bidding defiance to all the power of Dost Mohammed Khan. The walls, made of earth, are twelve feet high, and about five broad; the fosse is neither broad nor particularly deep; the citadel is elevated and situated upon a conspicuous hill of steep ascent, but in the neighbourhood there are still higher hills, whence a battery could in a few hours reduce it to ashes. It is therefore probable that the renowned strength of Maymene consists rather in the bravery of its defenders than in its walls or ditches. One distinguishes at the first glance in the inhabitant the bold and fearless rider, and it is only the Özbeg of Shehri Sebz who can contest with him the palm. The resolute warlike character of the inhabitants of this little Khanat, and the possession, besides, of the mountainous pass at Murgab (river), will ever find enough to do for the Afghans, or any {251} other conquerors pressing forward from the south towards the Oxus; the fortifications of Kerki can offer but a weak resistance, and he who would wish to take Bokhara must destroy Maymene, or be sure of its friendly feeling.

In Maymene, the Kervanbashi and the principal merchants of our karavan were no longer detained by difficulties about the customs, but by arrangements affecting their private interests. They wanted to attend at least two or three horse-markets, for in these parts fine horses are to be purchased cheap, which the Özbegs and the Turkomans of the places around bring to the market. These are exported, for the most part, to Herat, Kandahar, and Kabul, and very frequently to India. Horses that I saw sold in Persia for thirty or forty ducats, fetch here from a hundred to a hundred and sixty Tenghe (from fourteen to fifteen ducats), and never did I behold in Bokhara, Khiva, or Karshi, horses so fine sold at prices so low; but it is not only with respect to these animals that the market of Maymene affords a rich choice; the natural produce of the country and home manufactures, such as carpets and other stuffs, made partly of wool and partly of camel's hair, are abundantly supplied by the Turkoman and Djemshidi women. It deserves notice that a considerable export trade is carried on to Persia and Bagdad in raisins (Kishmish), aniseed, and pistachio nuts: a hundred-weight of the aniseed costs here from thirty to forty Tenghe.

[Escaped Russian Offenders]

After a stay of eight days I returned to the karavan, that remained outside of the city, in order to inform myself as to the day when it would resume its journey. I heard here, to my astonishment, that they had been {252} searching for me the whole day to give my evidence to get four Roumi liberated, who had been arrested by order of the uncle of the Khan. According to the decree of the judge, nothing could free them from the suspicion of being run-away slaves, but the production of some credible witness to the genuineness of their Turkish origin. Before going to the Khan let me introduce my countrymen to the reader, as I had very nearly forgotten these highly interesting members of our karavan.

These people were nothing more or less than Russian criminals. They had been banished to Siberia, where they had for eight years been kept at hard labour in the Government of Tobolsk, and had escaped across the immense steppes of the Kirghis to Bokhara, and thence were striving to return to their own country by Herat, Meshed, Teheran, &c., to Gümrü (Elizabethpol). The history of their flight and other adventures is very long. I will only give a slight sketch of it.

In the last campaign between Russia and Turkey, they were engaged with a *razzia* (Tchapao), in the Caucasus, by command of Government, or as is more probable, on their own account. During this time they had fallen into the hands of a Russian patrol, and, as they well merited, were transported to Siberia. Here they were daily employed in the woods of Tobolsk with felling trees; but were kept at night in a prison, and not ill-treated, for they were fed with bread and soup, and often also with meat. Years elapsed before they learnt to speak Russian; but they did at last learn it from the soldiers that guarded them. Conversation being now rendered possible, confidence was inspired; bottles of brandy (Vodki) were tendered {253} reciprocally, and as, during last spring, one day, more than usual of the warming liquor had been handed to the two soldiers on guard, the captives seized the opportunity, and, instead of oaks, felled the robust Russians; exchanged their axes for the arms of those whom they had slaughtered, and after wandering up and down for a long time, and under perilous circumstances--in which they were obliged to feed even upon grass and upon roots--they finally reached some Kirghis tents, to them a haven of security; for the nomads regard it as a benevolent act to aid fugitives of that description. From the steppes of the Kirghis they passed by Tashkend to Bokhara, where the Emir gave them some money for journey expenses. Although on their way it had often been suspected that they were run-away slaves, it was not until they reached Maymene that they really incurred any serious danger.

At the urgent request of my fellow-travellers, and of the Kervanbashi, I went, accompanied by the Ishan Eyub, the very same day, to the citadel. Instead of seeing the Khan, we were received by his uncle; he admitted my testimony as competent, and the four fugitives were liberated. They thanked me with tears in their eyes; the whole karavan was rejoiced, and two days afterwards we resumed our journey to Herat.

The route passed continuously through a mountainous country. The first station, which was in a south-westerly direction, was reached in six hours. It is called Almar. This is the designation common to those villages, which lie there scattered at a little distance from each other. Hardly had the karavan taken up its quarters here, when the officers of the {254} customs at Maymene appeared, escorted by a few horsemen, and claimed to make a second examination. This led to shouting, quarrelling, and negotiations which lasted a few hours; but at last we were obliged to submit, and after the poor Kervanbashi and merchants had been once more fleeced for dues in respect of wares, cattle, and slaves, the march was resumed towards evening. After having passed the important place called Kaisar, we reached a little after midnight the station Narin. We had travelled five miles through valleys, small, fruitful, but abandoned; indeed, the whole of this fine district has been rendered unsafe by the thieving Turkomans, Djemshidi, and Firuzkuhi.

In Narin only a few hours' rest was taken, as we had before us a stage of seven hours. After having marched without cessation the whole day, we reached in the evening the village and station of Tchitchektoo, in the neighbourhood of which is a second village called Fehmguzar. As the Kervanbashi and some of the other travellers had business at the village Khodjakendu, which lies to the south east, at a distance of three leagues, amongst the hills, we halted here the whole day. The place itself is regarded as the frontier of Maymene, and at the same time of all Turkestan. A Yüzbashi named Devletmurad, who acts here as watcher of the frontiers, levied in this Khanat of Maymene a third custom-tax, by right of the Kamtchin pulu (whip-money) [Footnote 76]). {255} On my expressing my astonishment to a Herat merchant about this unjust proceeding, he replied, 'We thank God that they only tax us. Some time ago we could not pass Maymene and Andkhuy without risk, for the karavans were plundered by order of the Khan himself, and we lost everything.' Here in Tchitchektoo I saw the last of Özbeg nomads, and I will not deny that I parted from this open-hearted, honest people with great regret, for the nomads of their race whom I met in the Khanats of Khiva and Bokhara have left in my mind the most pleasing recollections of any natives of Central Asia.

[Footnote 76: It is the practice in Central Asia to give to the escort that accompanies you a sum of money; in Germany it is called drink-money, but in the East whip-money. This Yüzbashi had the right to exact payment from every passer-by, even although he had rendered no service as escort or guard.]

[Murgab River and Bala Murgab; Djemshidi and Afghan]

The karavan was here taken under the protection of an escort of Djemshidi, sent to meet us by their Khan from Bala Murgab, because the route henceforth lay through a tolerably broad valley, having the habitations of the Sarik Turkomans on the right side, and of the mountaineer robbers, the Firuzkuhi, on the left. The land is exceedingly fertile, but it lies there, unhappily, fallow and without an owner. As I heard, the karavan during its whole journey from Bokhara had not incurred such peril as it did here. Our guard consisted of thirty Djemshidi, well armed and well mounted, with the addition of about double the number of able-bodied men from the karavan; nevertheless, at every step in advance, vedettes were thrown out to our right hand and to our left upon the hills, and all were in the greatest anxiety. It can readily be imagined in what a state of mind were the poor emancipated slaves, who at great trouble and expense had escaped thus far, and who now saw themselves menaced with a new captivity.

The size of the karavan and the precautions taken happily saved us from surprise. We passed the whole day through magnificent meadows, which in {256} spite of the advanced season of the year, were covered with flowers and grass that came up to our knees: and after having reposed during the night we arrived the following morning at the ruins of the fortress Kalè Veli: it was peopled only two years ago, but had been surprised and plundered by a great Alaman of the Sarik-Turkomans. The inhabitants had been partly sold as slaves and partly massacred, the few empty houses still existing and the walls of the fortification will soon be a complete ruin. The Djemshidi horsemen, who thus far had only been our escort a single day, now demanded their whip-money; every one who travelled mounted or on foot was to pay it once, but the slaves twofold. The escort affirmed that their present claim was well founded, as they would not receive any portion of the toll-money paid to the Khan in Bala Murgab.

Towards evening, on the second day after we had left Tchitchektoo, we reached the end of that beautiful valley, and the way, leading to the river Murgab, traversed a rough mountainous pass, in many places very steep, and at the same time so narrow that loaded camels advancing singly could with difficulty wind their way through; it is said to be the only practicable passage leading over the mountain to the bank of the river. A body of troops that wished to cross the Murgab would have either to pass through the desert (and for this they must be on good terms with the Salor and the Sarik), or make their way through this pass, for which enterprise the friendship of the Djemshidi is essential, as their hostility might in the defiles be prejudicial even to the strongest army.

{257}

It was midnight when we arrived on the banks of the river; worn out by their painful mountainous journey, men and beasts all fell into a profound sleep.

On awaking next morning I found that we were in a long valley surrounded by lofty mountains, the central point, through which the clear green waters of the Murgab [Footnote 77] cut their way, affording a most charming picture to the eye.

[Footnote 77: The Murgab rises in the lofty mountains to the East which bear the name of Ghur; it flows in a north-westerly direction by Martchah and Pendjdeh until it loses itself in the sandy plain of Merv. It is pretended that at an earlier period it joined the Oxus, but this is an utter impossibility.]

We proceeded along the bank of the river for half an hour to find a ford, for the current is very strong, and, although not very deep, it cannot be crossed at all places, owing to the blocks of stone lying in its bed.

The crossing commenced with the horses, and then followed the camels, and our asses were to close the procession. Now, these animals, it is well known, have a great dread of mud and water. I thought it but a necessary measure of prudence to deposit my knapsack, containing my MSS.--the most precious result, the ***spolia opima***, of my journey--upon the back of a camel. Then seating myself upon the empty saddle I forced my ass into the river. When he made his first step upon the stony bottom of the rapid stream, I felt certain that something awful was going to happen: I strove to get down, but that was unnecessary, for a few steps further on my charger fell, amidst the loud laughter of our comrades standing upon the bank, and then afterwards, in great consternation, he made for the opposite bank, as I wished him to do. This cold morning bath in the clear waters of the transparent crystal Murgab was only so far {258} disagreeable to me that I had no change of clothes, so I was obliged to hide myself a few hours amongst some carpets and sacks until my clothes, which were entirely wet through, should dry in the sun. The karavan encamped near the citadel; in the interior, instead of houses there are only tents, and there the Khans or Chiefs of the Djemshidi reside.

This part of the valley of the Murgab bears the name of Bala Murgab [Footnote 78] (Upper Murgab); it extends from the frontiers of the lofty mountainous chain of the Hezares as far as Marchah (snake well), where dwell the Salor Turkomans; it is said of old to have been a possession of the Djemshidi, and that they were for a time dispossessed, but afterwards returned. To the south-west of the fortress the valley becomes so narrow, that it merits rather the name of a defile. Through the midst the Murgab rolls foaming away with the noise of thunder,--it is not until it has passed Pendjdeh, where the river becomes deeper and more sedate, that the valley spreads itself out and acquires a breadth of one or two miles. When Merv existed, there must have been here, too, a tolerable amount of civilisation; but at the present day Turkomans house themselves there, and upon their steps follow everywhere ruin and desolation.

[Footnote 78: Some said that this name designates merely the fortress. It may have been formerly a place of importance, for numerous ruins in the interior and in the environs indicate a bygone civilisation.]

The Djemshidi insist that they spring from Djemshid, the fabulous king of the Pishdadian family--a pretension naturally subject to doubt! They are, however, certainly of Persian descent. This is indicated not so much by their dialect as by their pure Irani type {259} of physiognomy; for it is retained amongst these nomads more faithfully than anywhere else, except in the southern provinces of Persia. Cast for centuries upon the extreme limit of Persian nationality, their numbers have melted away in consequence of constant warfare. They count now no more than about eight or nine thousand tents. The inhabitants live in a state of great destitution, scattered over the above-named valley and neighbouring mountains. As will be seen in the history of Khiva, a great part of them were forced by Allahkuli Khan to quit their country, and form a colony in that Khanat, where a new place of settlement was marked out for them in a fertile district (Köktcheg), abundantly watered by the Oxus. The change was for the better; but their irresistible attachment to their old mountainous homes led them to return thither. And there they still are located as new settlers, under no very brilliant circumstances.

In dress, manner of life, and character, the Djemshidi resemble the Turkomans. Their forays are just as much dreaded as those of the latter; but they cannot be so frequent, on account of the inferiority of their number. At present their Khans (they have two, Mehdi Khan and Allahkuli Khan) are notoriously vassals of the Afghans, and well recompensed as such by the Serdar of Herat. The Afghans, even in the time of Dost Mohammed Khan, took every possible step to win to their side the Djemshidi, in order, in the first place, to have in them a constant barrier-guard on the northern boundary of the Murgab against the incursions of the Maymenes; and, secondly, to paralyse the power of the Turkomans, of whose friendliness the greatest sacrifices never {260} could assure Dost Mohammed Khan. Mehdi Khan, the chief of the Djemshidi, of whom we before spoke, is said, at the siege of Herat, to have rendered essential service, and to have consequently gained not only the entire favour of the late Emir, but of his successor, the present king, Shir Ali Khan. Indeed, the latter left him guardian of his infant son, whom he had placed at the head of affairs in Herat. The extension, then, of the Afghan territory to the Murgab may be styled very precarious, for the Djemshidi may, at any moment, break out in open revolt, as they do not admit that the Serdar of Herat has the shadow of a right to their allegiance, and, least of all, should there be any hesitation or delay in the liquidation of their pay.

[Ruinous Taxes on Merchandise]

Here, as everywhere, our difficulties began and ended with questions respecting the customs. It had been said, all along, that with the left bank of the Murgab Afghanistan began, and that there the slave tax would cease to be exacted. It was a grievous mistake. The Khan of the Djemshidi, who treated in person with the Kervanbashi concerning the taxes, exacted more for goods, cattle, and slaves than the former claimants, and when the tariff was made known, the consternation, and with many the lamentation, knew no bounds. He even forced the Hadjis to pay two francs per ass--an extraordinary charge for all, but for me a very grievous one. But the greatest hardship was that which befell an Indian, who had purchased some loads of aniseed in Maymene for thirty Tenghe. The carriage to Herat cost him twenty Tenghes per load. He had also, up to this point, paid eleven Tenghes for customs, and now he was to pay thirty more, making for expenses about sixty-one Tenghes. The enormous duties imposed upon the {261} merchant, and with the authority of a sort of law, are a positive hindrance to all commercial transactions; and from the dreadfully tyrannical use made of their power by the princes, the inhabitants are prevented from profiting by the riches of nature that often ripen without any culture in the neighbourhood, and whose produce might bring a very good return, and satisfy the exigencies of domestic life. The mountainous fatherland of the Djemshidi has three special kinds of produce to which a genial Nature spontaneously gives birth, and which, belonging to no one, may be gathered by the hand of the first comer. These are:--(1) Pistachio nuts: (2) Buzgundj, a sort of nut used for dyeing: it is a produce of the pistachio tree. Of the former, a batman costs half a franc, and of the latter, from six to eight francs. (3) Terendjebin, a sort of sugary substance collected from a shrub like manna, having no bad flavour, and used in the making of sugar in Herat and Persia. The mountain Badkhiz (the word means 'where the wind rises') is rich in those three articles. The inhabitants are in the habit of collecting them, but the merchants, on account of the enormous subsequent charges, can only pay a small sum for them, and they thus afford but a sorry resource for the poor inhabitants. The Djemshidi women make several kinds of stuff of wool and goat's hair, and particularly a sort of cloth called Shal, which fetches good prices in Persia.

We lingered four days on the bank of the Murgab, in the vicinity of the ruins. Many hours did I spend in wandering by the side of this beautiful light green river, in order to visit the tents that lay scattered about in groups, with old torn pieces of felt for coverings, and presenting altogether a miserable dilapidated {262} appearance. In vain did I offer my glass beads, in vain my blessing and Nefes. What they stood in need of was not such articles of luxury, but bread. Religion itself is here but upon a feeble footing; and as I could not much build upon my character as Hadji and Dervish, I was obliged to relinquish the intention of a more extensive excursion to Marchah, where, according to report, there exist ruins of stone, with Munar (towers and pillars) perhaps dating from the time of the Parsees. The story did not seem to me very credible; otherwise the English, who had adequate knowledge of Herat and its environs, would have made researches. In the uncertainty, I did not care to expose myself to danger.

It is reckoned a four days' journey for horses from Bala Murgab to Herat. Camels require double the time, for the country is mountainous. Our camels could not certainly perform it in less, for they carried loads greater than usual.

Two high mountainous peaks, visible to the south of Murgab, were pointed out to us, and we were told that it would take us two days to reach them. They both bear the name Derbend (pass), and are far loftier, narrower, and easier of defence than the pass on the right bank of the Murgab, leading to Maymene. In proportion as one advances nature assumes a wilder and more romantic appearance. The elevated masses of rock, which form the first Derbend, are crowned with the ruins of an ancient fort, the subject of the most varying fables. Farther on, at the second Derbend, on the bank of the Murgab, there are the remains of an old castle. It was the summer residence of the renowned Sultan Husein Mirza, by whose order a stone bridge (Pul-Taban) was constructed, {263} of which traces are still distinguishable. In the time of this, the most civilised sovereign of Central Asia, the whole of the neighbourhood was in a flourishing state, and many pleasure-houses are said to have existed along the course of the Murgab.

Beyond the second pass we quitted the Murgab. The route turned to the right, in a westerly direction, towards a plateau closely adjoining a part of the desert peopled by the Salor. Here begins the lofty mountain Telkhguzar, which it takes three hours to pass over.

[Kalè No; Hezare]

Towards midnight we halted at a place called Mogor, whence next morning we reached the ruins of the former town and fortress, Kalè No, now surrounded by a few tents of the Hezare. They presented the appearance of still greater poverty than those of the Djemshidi. Kalè No, as I heard, had been, only fifty years ago, a flourishing town. It had served for a depôt to the karavans betaking themselves from Persia to Bokhara. The Hezare, the then possessors, became overbearing and presumptuous, claimed to give laws to Herat, and finally, by engaging in a struggle with this city, became the authors of their own downfall. They even made enemies of the Persians by their rivalry with the Turkomans in their predatory expeditions in Khorasan.

The Hezare here met with have, owing to their intermixture with the Irani, no longer been able to maintain their Mongoli type as pure as their brethren in Kabul. They are, too, for the most part Sunnites, whereas the latter profess everywhere the principles of the rival sect of the Shiites. If I am rightly informed, the northern Hezare first separated themselves from the southern in the time of Nadir {264} Shah; and the surrounding people forced them to embrace the doctrine of the rival sect (Sunnites), at least in part. It is said that the Hezare [Footnote 79] were brought by Djenghis Khan from Mongolia, their ancient seat, to the southern parts of Central Asia, and Shah Abbas was the cause of their conversion to Shiism. It is remarkable that they have exchanged their mother-tongue for the Persian, which is not generally spoken in the neighbourhood where they dwell. The Mongol dialect, or rather a jargon of it, is only preserved by a small portion of them who have remained isolated in the mountains near Herat, where they have for centuries been occupied as burners of charcoal. They style themselves, as well as the place they inhabit, Gobi.

[Footnote 79: The Hezare were styled Berber in Persia, a word used to designate the city Shehri-Berber, said to have existed on the mountains between Kabul and Herat, and of whose ancient grandeur, splendour, and magnificence wonders are recounted. Burnes says, in his work upon Kabul (p. 232), that 'the remains of this imperial city of the same name (Berber) are still to be seen.']

Baba Khan, the chief of the Hezare of Kalè No, ought at least from his poverty and weakness to acknowledge the supremacy of Herat, which is only at a distance of two days' journey. This was not the case; he also assumed the air of an independent Prince. Hardly had our karavan settled down near the ruins, when his Majesty appeared in person and demanded his customs: this gave rise to fresh quarrels and disputes. The Kervanbashi insisted upon sending an express to the Serdar of Herat to complain; the threat produced its effect, and instead of duties a famous sum was exacted for whip-money; and in levying it, the godless Khan not even allowing the Hadjis to escape, I was obliged to pay again for my ass the sum of two francs.

{265}

The merchants made here a large purchase of pistachio nuts and Berek, a light cloth for the fabrication of which the Hezare women are renowned, and is employed throughout the whole of the north of Persia and Afghanistan as an overgarment, called Chekmen.

From Kalè No the way again passes over lofty mountains to Herat; the distance is only twenty miles, but the journey is very fatiguing, and requires four days for its accomplishment. The first day's halt was at a village called Alvar, near the ruins of the robber-castle where Shir Ali Hezareh housed himself. The second day we passed by the summit Serabend, covered with everlasting snows, and where we suffered severely from frost, in spite of the immense masses of wood which we lighted to warm us. The third day, we descended continually: there are some very dangerous places, the path passing close to the edge of the precipice being only a foot broad; a false step may plunge man and camel down into the ravine below. We reached, however, without accident, the valley at Sertcheshme, whence, it is believed, springs a strong stream, that after bathing Herat on the north side falls into the Heri-Rud. On the fourth day we arrived at Kerrukh, which belongs to Herat, and is distant from it four miles.

[Afghan Exactions and Maladministration.]

Herat was still besieged by Dost Mohammed Khan when the karavan had set out for Bokhara in the spring. Six months had now elapsed, the report of their native city having been taken and plundered had reached them, and the reader may imagine the anxiety felt by every Herati to seek his house, property, family {266} and friends! Notwithstanding this, all were forced to wait here another day, until the officer of the customs, whose appearance on the scene, with his arrogant Afghan air, took us early in the morning by surprise, had got ready an exact list of all that had come and everything they had brought with them. I had pictured to myself Afghanistan as a land already half organised, where, through long contact with Western influence, at least something of order and civilisation had been introduced. I flattered myself that I was upon the eve of getting rid at once of my disguise and sufferings. I was cruelly deceived. The Afghan functionary, the first whom I had yet seen of that nation, threw into the shade all the inhumanity and barbarity of similar officers in Central Asia; all the dreadful things I had heard about the searches as to customs amongst the Afghans was only a painting 'couleur de rose' compared with what I here witnessed. The bales of goods that owners would not open were sent under guard to the town; the baggage of the travellers was examined and written down article by article; in spite of the coldness of the weather, every one was obliged to strip, and with the exception of shirt, drawers, and upper garment, every object of dress was declared liable to duty. The brute taxed the Hadjis most severely, he did not even spare their little stock of haberdashery; and, what is unheard of, he exacted five krans per head for the asses, animals for which so much had been already paid for duty, and which were themselves worth from twenty to twenty-five krans. As many were really so poor as to be unable to pay, he caused their asses to be sold; this revolting proceeding wrung me very hard; it left me, in fact, almost without resources.

{267}

Towards evening, when we thought that the plundering was over, the Governor of Kerrukh, who has the rank of a Mejir, [Footnote 80] made his appearance also to receive his whip-money. He was somewhat exacting, too, but his genuine soldier-like bearing, and his uniform buttoned tight over his chest (the first object that had greeted my eyes for so long a time that recalled European associations), produced upon me an indescribably cheering impression. Even now I laugh at the pettiness of my feelings, but I could not regard with indifference the end of the entire jest of which I had been the author. Bator Khan (that was his name) had remarked my look of surprise. This made him regard me more attentively; he was struck by my foreign features, and questioned the Kervanbashi; directed me to seat myself near him, and treated me with affability and consideration. In the course of the conversation, which he continually turned upon Bokhara, he laughed in my face, and yet so that he was not observed by others, as if to congratulate me upon the accomplishment of my object, for he thought that I had been sent upon a mission; and although I persisted in supporting the character I had so long assumed, he extended to me his hand at his departure, and wished to shake mine *à l'Anglaise*, but, seeing his design, I anticipated him, raised my arms, and was about to give him a Fatiha, when he withdrew laughing.

[Footnote 80: Mejir corresponds with the English 'Major,' from which it is borrowed. I devoted much attention to the words 'Djornel' and 'Kornel' used by the Afghans in their army, until it at last occurred to me that the former sprung from General, and the latter from Colonel.]

{268}

Next morning our karavan was to enter Herat, having spent more than six weeks on the way hither from Bokhara, a journey that may be easily accomplished in from twenty to twenty-five days.

From the details already furnished, it is apparent that trade on this route is not in a very splendid condition. We will now sum up, in Tenghe, the amount paid altogether for slaves, goods, and cattle at the different places:--

Paid in Tenghe at 75 centimes each.

Name of the Place	Paid for Bales of Goods	For Camels	Horses	Asses	Slaves
Kerki	20	5	?		2
Andkhuy	26	5	?		0
Maymene	28	5	?		5
Almar	--	3	?		
Fehmguzar	1	3	?		
Kalè Veli	--	5	?		

Murgab	30	5	?	5
Kalè-No	--	5	?	
Kerrukh	--	15	1 0	
Total	105	51 2	? 5	8

When we say, besides, that the interest of money at Herat is twenty per cent., we may form an idea of what the selling price must be to remunerate the merchant for his trouble!

{269}

CHAPTER XIV.

HERAT.

HERAT

ITS RUINOUS STATE

BAZAAR

AUTHOR'S DESTITUTE CONDITION

THE SERDAR MEHEMMED YAKOUB KHAN

PARADE OF AFGHAN TROOPS

INTERVIEW WITH SERDAR

CONDUCT OF AFGHANS ON STORMING HERAT

NAZIR NAIM THE VIZIR

EMBARRASSED STATE OF REVENUE

MAJOR TODD

MOSALLA, AND TOMB OF SULTAN HUSEIN MIRZA

TOMB OF KHODJA ABDULLAH ANSAEI, AND OF DOST MOHAMMED KHAN.

---Isidori Characeni, ***Mansiones Parthicae,*** 17, *apud Müller. Geograph. Gr. minores.*

[Herat; Its Ruinous State]

The traveller approaching from the north will certainly be surprised when, on turning round the mountain Khodja Abdullah Ansari, he sees lying before him the beautiful immense plain called Djölghei Herat, with its numerous canals and scattered groups of villages. Although trees, the principal ornament of every landscape, are here entirely wanting, he cannot but be convinced that he has reached the bounds of Turkestan, and with it of Central Asia, properly so called; for of this Herat is rightly named the gate, or key. Without going so far as the Orientals, in styling it 'Djennetsifat' (like Paradise), we cannot, nevertheless, deny to the surrounding country the character of loveliness and of fertility. Its natural advantages, {270} united with its political importance, have unhappily made it an apple of discord to adjoining nations, and when we consider the wars that have here been carried on, and the frequent sieges that the city has had to support, it is astonishing to us how rapidly the wounds inflicted seem to have scarred over. Only two months before we arrived, hordes of wild Afghans had here housed themselves, scattering desolation and devastation in every direction, and yet, even now, fields and vineyards looked flourishing, and the meadows were covered with high grass mixed with flowers.

Like all cities in the East, it has both ancient and modern ruins; and here, as everywhere else, we must pronounce the former the more beautiful and the nobler. The remains of the monuments on the Mosalla (place of prayer), remind us of the ruins of the ancient city of Timour; the round towers lying scattered singly about look like the immediate environs of Ispahan; but the city, and the fortress itself, in the state in which I saw it, form a ruin such as we rarely meet with, even in the East.

[Bazaar]

We entered by the gate Dervaze Arak. The houses which we passed, the advanced works, the very gate, looked like a heap of rubbish. Near the latter, in the inside of the city, is the Ark (citadel) having, from its elevation, served as a mark for the Afghan artillery; it lies there blasted and half demolished. The doors and windows have been stripped of their woodwork, for during the siege the inhabitants suffered most from the scarcity of fuel. In the bare openings of the walls are perched here and there a few wretched-looking Afghans or Hindoos--worthy guards of such a ruin. Each step we advance, we see greater indications of devastation. Entire quarters of the {271} town remain solitary and abandoned. The bazaar--that is to say, the arched part of it, where the quadrangle of the bazaar is united by its dome, and which has witnessed and resisted so many sieges--alone remains, and affords, in spite of its new population, dating only from three months ago, a really interesting sample of Oriental life--a blending of the characteristics of India, Persia, and Central Asia, better defined than even in the bazaar of Bokhara. It is only from the Karavanserai Hadji Resul to that of No that a throng, rightly so called, exists; and although the distance is small, the eye is bewildered by the diversity of races--Afghans, Indians, Tartars, Turkomans, Persians, and Jews. The Afghan parades about, either in his national costume, consisting of a long shirt, drawers, and dirty linen clothes, or in his military undress; and here his favourite garment is the red English coat, from which, even in sleep, he will not part. He throws it on over his shirt, whilst he sets on his head the picturesque Indo-Afghan turban. Others again, and these are the *beau monde*, are wont to assume a half Persian costume. Weapons are borne by all. Rarely does any one, whether civil or military, enter the bazaar without his sword and shield. To be quite *à la mode*, one must carry about one quite an arsenal, consisting of two pistols, a sword, poniard, hand-jar, gun, and shield. With the wild martial-looking Afghan we can only compare the Turkomanlike Djemshidi. The wretchedly-dressed Herati, the naked Hezare, the Teymuri of the vicinity, are overlooked when the Afghan is present. He encounters around him nothing but abject humility; but never was ruler or conqueror so detested as is the Afghan by the Herati.

{272}

The bazaar itself, dating from Herat's epoch of splendour, the reign of the Sultan Husein Mirza, and consequently about four hundred years old, deserved still, even in its ruins, the epithet beautiful. It is said, in earlier times, to have formed an entire street, from the Dervaze Arak to the Dervaze Kandahar. [Footnote 81] Of course, at present, the shops in the bazaar begin to open again, but only by degrees. The last siege and plundering of the city could not fail to prove a great discourager. Indeed, under the rapacious system of duties introduced by the Afghans, trade and manufacture have little prosperity opened to them; for it is extraordinary, indeed incredible, what taxes are extorted from both seller and purchaser, upon every article that is sold. They seem, besides, to be regulated by no fixed scale, but to be quite arbitrary. One has to pay a duty, for instance, for a pair of boots that has cost originally five francs, one and a half francs; for a cap, worth two francs, one franc; for a fur that has been purchased for eight francs, three francs; and so on. Every article imported or exported is stamped by tax-collectors, having offices in the bazaar and in different parts of the city.

[Footnote 81: Unlike the other gates this one suffered little during the siege. The Herati pretend that it can never be demolished, because built by the English, who lay brick over brick only as justice directs, unlike the Afghans, who mix the mortar with the tears of oppression.]

The original inhabitants of the city were Persians, and belonging to the race that spread itself from Sistan towards the north-east, and formed the ancient province of Khorasan, of which, until recent days, that remained the capital. In later times, the immigrations, of which Djenghis and Timour were the cause, {273} led to the infusion of Turco-Tartaric blood into the veins of the ancient population. The collective name Char-Aimak is the result, as well as the subdivision of the people into the Djemshidi, Firuzkuhi, Teïmeni or Timouri. These are races of different origin, and can only from a political point of view be regarded as one single nation. Thus far of the inhabitants of the Djölghei Herat.

The fortress itself is inhabited, for the most part, by Persians, who settled here in the last century, to maintain and spread the influence of their own country. They are now principally handicraftsmen or merchants. As for Afghans, one cannot find in the city more than one in five. They have become quite Persians, and are, particularly since the last siege, very hostile to their own countrymen. A Kabuli, or a Kaker from Kandahar, is as much regarded by him in the light of an oppressor, and therefore is as much detested, as by the aboriginal natives of Herat.

The diversified throngs I encountered in Herat produced a pleasing effect upon me. The Afghan soldiery in the English uniform, with shako--a covering for the head contrary to the prescriptions of the Koran, and the introduction of which into the Turkish army is regarded as impracticable [Footnote 82]--seemed {274} to lead to the conclusion that I had fallen upon a land where Islamite fanaticism had lost its formidable character, and where I might gradually discontinue my disguise. And when I saw many soldiers moving about with moustaches shaved off, and wearing whiskers--an appendage regarded as a deadly sin in Islam, and even in Constantinople as a renunciation of their religion--the hope seized me that perhaps I might meet here English officers; and how happy I should have considered myself to have found some son of Britain, whose influence, without doubt, from political circumstances, would have been here very great. I had, for the moment, forgotten that the Oriental is never what he seems, and my disappointment was, indeed, bitter.

[Footnote 82: The Osmanli insist that according to the Sunnet (tradition), Siper (a head-covering with a peak), and Zunnar (the cord round the loins of monks), are most rigorously forbidden as signs of Christianity. Sultan Mahmoud II., on introducing into Turkey for the first time a militia formed on the model of the European, was very desirous of substituting the shako for the highly inappropriate Fez, but the destroyer of the Janissaries did not venture to carry his wish into execution, for he would have been declared an ***apostate*** even by his best friends.]

[Author's Destitute Condition]

As I before remarked, my finances had melted away positively to nothing. I was obliged, on entering Herat, to sell at once even the ass upon which I rode. The poor brute, being quite worn out with his journey, brought me only twenty-six krans, out of which I was obliged to pay the tax upon the sale, and other little debts. The state in which I found myself was very critical. The want of bread admitted of remedy; but the nights had become quite cold, and in spite of my being inured to a life of hardship, my sufferings were great, when I slept in an open ruin, with scanty clothing, and on the bare earth. The thought that Persia might be reached in ten days cheered me up. Still, it was not so easy an enterprise to arrive thither. To go alone was impossible, and the karavan, preparing to go to Meshed, wished to wait still for an increase of travellers, and a more favourable opportunity; for the Tekke Turkomans not only rendered the journey exceedingly {275} unsafe, but plundered villages and karavans, and carried off captives before the very gates of Herat. During the first days of my arrival, I heard that a Persian envoy, named Mehemmed Bakir Khan, sent by the governor Prince of Khorasan to congratulate the young Serdar of Herat, proposed soon to return to Teheran. I immediately waited upon him, and begged him to take me with him. The Persian was very polite; but although I repeated to him over and over again the state of destitution in which I was, he paid no attention to that statement, and asked me (the dreadfully disfigured Hadji), if I had brought back with me any fine horses from Bokhara! Every word of his seemed to indicate a wish on his part to penetrate my secret. Seeing that I had nothing to expect, I left him. He quitted Herat soon after, accompanied by many of the Hadjis who had travelled with me from Samarcand and Kerki. All abandoned me--all but Mollah Ishak, my faithful companion from Kungrat, who had believed, when I said that in Teheran better fortunes awaited me, and who stood by me. The honest young man obtained our daily food and fuel by begging, and got ready besides our evening supper, which he even refused respectfully to share with me out of the same plate. Mollah Ishak forms, in another point of view, one of the most interesting of my episodes. He lives now, at this day, in Pesth, instead of being at Mecca, and in the sequel of my narrative we shall have occasion to speak of him.

[The Serdar Mehemmed Yakoub Khan; Parade of Afghan Troops]

Not to neglect any expedient to forward my journey on to Meshed, I went to the reigning Prince, Serdar Mehemmed Yakoub Khan, son of the present king of Afghanistan, a lad in his sixteenth year, who had been placed at the head of affairs in the conquered {276} province, his father, immediately after his accession to the throne, having been obliged to hasten away to Kabul, in order to prevent any steps being taken by his brothers to contest the throne with him. The young Prince resided in the Charbag, in the palace which had also served for the dwelling of Major Todd. It had, it is true, suffered much during the siege, but was naturally preferred, as a residence, to the citadel, which was a mere ruin. One part of that quadrangular court, a garden as they were in the habit of calling it, although I saw in it only a few trees, served as night quarters for him and his numerous retinue, whilst in the portions situate on the opposite side an Arz (public audience) of four or five hours' duration was held in a large long hall. The Prince was generally seated at the window in an armchair, dressed in military uniform, with high collars; and as the numerous petitioners, whom he was obliged officially to receive, very much wearied him, he made the Risale Company (the *élite* of the Afghan troops) exercise before his window, and seemed highly delighted with the wheeling of the columns, and the thundering word of command of the officer passing them in review, who, besides, pronounced the 'Right shoulder forward! Left shoulder forward!' with a genuine English accent.

[Interview with Serdar]

When I stepped into the court I have mentioned, accompanied by Mollah Ishak, the drill was at its most interesting point. The men had a very military bearing, far better than the Ottoman army, that was so drilled forty years ago. These might have been mistaken for European troops, if most of them had not had on their bare feet the pointed Kabuli shoe, and had not had their short trousers so tightly {277} stretched by their straps that they threatened every moment to burst and fly up above the knee. After having watched the exercises a short time, I went to the door of the reception-hall, which was filled by a number of servants, soldiers, and petitioners. If all made way for me, and allowed me undisturbed to enter the saloon, I had to thank the large turban I had assumed (my companion had assumed a similar one), as well as the 'anchorite' appearance which my wearisome journey had imparted. I saw the Prince as I have described; on his right hand sat his Vizir, and next to him there were ranged along against the wall other officers, Mollahs and Heratis; amongst these there was also a Persian, Imamverdi Khan, who on account of some roguery had fled hither from (Djam) Meshed. Before the Prince stood his keeper of the seal (Möhürdar), and four or five other servants. True to my Dervish character, on appearing I made the usual salutation, and occasioned no surprise to the company when I stepped, even as I made it, right up to the Prince, and seated myself between him and the Vizir, after having required the latter, a corpulent Afghan, to make room for me by a push with the foot. This action of mine occasioned some laughing, but it did not put me out of countenance. I raised my hands to repeat the usual prayer required by the law. [Footnote 83] Whilst I was repeating it, the Prince looked me full in the face. I saw his look of amazement, and when I was repeating the Amen, and all present were keeping time with me in stroking their beards, the Prince half rose from his chair, and, pointing {278} with his finger to me, he called out, half laughing and half bewildered, 'Vallahi, Billahi Schuma, Inghiliz hestid' ('By G--, I swear you are an Englishman!').

[Footnote 83: This is in Arabic, and to the following effect: 'God our Lord, let us take a blessed place, for of a verity Thou art the best quartermaster.']

A ringing peal of laughter followed the sudden fancy of the young king's son, but he did not suffer it to divert him from his idea; he sprang down from his seat, placed himself right before me, and, clapping both his hands like a child who has made some lucky discovery, he called out, 'Hadji, Kurbunet' ('I would be thy victim'), 'tell me, you are an Englishman in Tebdil (disguise), are you not?' His action was so naïve, that I was really sorry that I could not leave the boy in his illusion. I had cause to dread the wild fanaticism of the Afghans, and, assuming a manner as if the jest had gone too far, I said, 'Sahib mekun' ('have done'); 'you know the saying, "He who takes, even in sport, the believer for an unbeliever, is himself an unbeliever." [Footnote 84] Give me rather something for my Fatiha, that I may proceed further on my journey.' My serious look, and the Hadis which I recited, quite disconcerted the young man; he sat down half ashamed, and, excusing himself on the ground of the resemblance of my features, said that he had never seen a Hadji from Bokhara with such a physiognomy. I replied that I was not a Bokhariot, but a Stambuli; and when I showed him my Turkish passport, and spoke to him of his cousin, the son of Akbar Khan, Djelal-ed-din Khan, who was in Mecca and Constantinople in 1860, and had met with a distinguished reception from the Sultan, his manner quite changed; my passport went the round of the company, and met with approbation. The Prince gave me some krans, {279} and dismissed me with the order that I should often visit him during my stay, which I accordingly did.

[Footnote 84: Traditional sentence of the Prophet.]

'I SWEAR YOU ARE AN ENGLISHMAN!

However fortunate the issue of this amusing proceeding, it had still some consequences not very agreeable, as far as my continued stay in Herat was concerned. Following the Prince's example, every one wanted to detect in me the Englishman. Persians, Afghans, and Herati came to me with the express purpose of convincing themselves and verifying their suspicions. The most boring fellow was a certain Hadji Sheikh Mehemmed, an old man rejoicing in the reputation of being a great astrologer and astronomer, and really, as far as opportunity enabled me to judge, one well read in Arabic and Persian. He informed me that he had travelled with Mons. de Khanikoff, and had been of much service to him in Herat, and that the latter had given him a letter to the Russian ambassador in Teheran, of which he wished me to take charge. In vain did I try to persuade the good old man, that I had nothing to do with the Russians; he left me with his convictions unshaken. But what was most droll was the conduct of the Afghans and Persians; they thought they saw in me a man *à la* Eldred Pottinger, who made his first entry into Herat disguised as a horsedealer, and became later its master. They insisted that I had a credit here for hundreds, even thousands, of ducats, and yet no one would give me a few krans to purchase bread!

Ah, how long the time seemed that I had to pass in Herat waiting for the karavan! The city had a most gloomy troubled aspect; the dread of their savage conqueror was painted on the features of its inhabitants. The incidents of the last siege, its capture and plundering, formed the constant subjects of conversation.

{280}

[Conduct of Afghans on storming Herat]

According to the assertions of the Herati (which are, however, not founded in fact), Dost Mohammed Khan took the fortress, not by the bravery of the Kabuli, but by the treason of the garrison; they insist, too, that the beloved prince Sultan Ahmed was poisoned, and that his son Shanauvaz, who is almost deified by the Herati, did not obtain information of the treachery before a great part of the Paltan (soldiers) had already forced their way into the fortress. The struggle carried on by the besieged prince with his angry father-in-law was of the bitterest description, the sufferings borne and inflicted were dreadful, but worst of all were the sacking and plundering that took place unexpectedly some days after the actual capture, when many fugitive Herati returned with their property into the city. Four thousand Afghan soldiers, chosen expressly for the purpose from different tribes and regiments, rushed at a given signal, and from different sides of the city, upon the defenceless habitations, and are said not only to have carried off clothing, arms, furniture, whatever in fact met their eye, but forced every one to strip himself almost to a state of nudity, and to have left the half naked tenants behind them in their thoroughly denuded and emptied houses. They tore away even from the sick their bedding and clothing, and robbed infants of cradles, nay, of the very swathing clothes, valueless but to them! A Mollah, who had been robbed of all his books, told me that he had lost sixty of the finest MSS.; but the loss he most deplored was that of a Koran bequeathed to him by his grandfather. He entreated the plunderer to leave him this one book, from which he promised that he would pray for his despoiler. 'Do not trouble thyself,' said the Kabuli; {281} 'I have a little son at home who shall pray for thee from it. Come, give it me.'

[Nazir Naïm the Vizir]

Whoever is acquainted with the covetousness of the filthy grasping Afghan, may picture to himself how he would behave in plundering a city. The besiegers levied contributions upon the city during a day, upon the country around during months. These are indeed natural consequences of war, occurring even in civilised countries, and which we will not make the subject of excessive reproach against the Afghans. But it is a pity that, instead of seeking to heal the wounds which they have inflicted, their miserable policy seems now to aim at reducing the whole province still further to beggary; so that in a country, where undoubtedly they are called upon to play an important part, they have rendered themselves objects of detestation: for the inhabitants would at once again plunge into a hopeless contest rather than ever acknowledge the supremacy of the Afghans. Herat, that is said now again to show signs of fresh life, has been left in the hands of a good-humoured inexperienced child. His guardian, the Khan of the Djemshidi, has an understanding with the Turkomans, against whose incursions he ought to protect the country. The Alamans extend their depredations to within a few leagues of Herat; scarcely does any week elapse without villages being surprised and plundered, and the inhabitants being led away to captivity. The Vizir of the Prince, named Nazir Naïm, is a man whose coarse features are, as it were, the sign-post of stupidity; he has in the course of only two months so enriched himself that he has purchased for himself in Kabul two houses with vineyards. As the internal affairs of the city and province are left in his hands, he {282} is accustomed, during the whole time of his hours of business, to surround himself with litigants and place-hunters. He soon tires, and when questions or petitions are addressed to him respecting the government recently established, to get rid of the wearisome application he has ever ready the stereotyped answer: 'Her tchi pish bud' (Everything as before). In his absence of mind he returns the same answer when accusations are laid before him of murder or theft; the plaintiff surprised repeats his story, but obtains the eternal answer, 'Her tchi pish bud,' and so he must retire.

[Embarrassed State of Revenue; Major Todd]

A striking proof of the confusion that pervades everything is the circumstance, that in spite of unheard-of duties, in spite of endless imposts, the young Serdar cannot raise out of the revenues of the province of Herat a sum sufficient to defray the expenses of the civil functionaries and the garrison of fourteen hundred men. Mr. Eastwick [Footnote 85] reports, according to a statement made by the Prince Governor of the province of Khorasan, that the income of Herat amounts yearly to 80,000 Toman (38,000*l*.), but from this sum are to be maintained, besides the corps of civilians, five regiments of infantry, and about 4,000 cavalry, for which purpose the amount given is clearly insufficient. With a larger income, Herat of the present day has far fewer expenses; the terrified city is easily governed; and it can only be ascribed to maladministration that a subvention is required from Kabul to defray the expenses of the troops. {283} Had Dost Mohammed only lived a year longer to consolidate the government of the newly-conquered province, the incorporation of Herat with Afghanistan might have been possible. As it is, fear alone keeps things together. It needs only some attack, no matter by whom, to be made upon Herat, for the Herati to be the first to take up arms against the Afghans. Nor does this observation apply to the Shiite inhabitants alone, whose sympathies are, of course, in favour of Persia, but even to those of the Sunnite persuasion, who would certainly prefer the Kizilbash to their present oppressors; but I find no exaggeration in the opinion that they long most for the intervention of the English, whose feelings of humanity and justice have led the inhabitants to forget the great differences in religion and nationality. The Herati saw, during the government of Major Todd, more earnestness and self-sacrifice with respect to the ransoming of the slaves [Footnote 86] than they had ever even heard of before on the part of a ruler. Their native governments had habituated them to be plundered and murdered, not spared or rewarded.

[Footnote 85: 'Journal of a Diplomate's Three Years' Residence in Persia,' vol. ii. p. 244.]

[Footnote 86: The report is general in Herat that Stoddart was sent on a mission to Bokhara to ransom the Herati there pining in captivity.]

[Mosalla, and Tomb of Sultan Husein Mirza; Tomb of Khodja Abdullah Ansari, and of Dost Mohammed Khan.]

Two days before my departure, I suffered an Afghan to persuade me to make an excursion to a village in the vicinity named Gazerghiah, to pay a visit there to the tombs of Khodja Abdullah Ansari, and of Dost Mohammed Khan, in order, as it is said, to kill two flies with one blow. On the way I paid my parting visit to the fine ruins of Mosalla. The remains of the mosque and of the sepulchre, which the great Sultan Husein Mirza, caused to be built for {284} himself ten years before his death (901), are, as I before mentioned, an imitation of the monuments of Samarcand. [Footnote 87] Time would have long spared these works of art, but they suffered shamefully during the last two sieges, when the place became the quarters of Shiite fanaticism. It is to be regretted that European officers, like General Borowsky and General Bühler--the former a Pole, the latter an Alsatian, and both present in those campaigns, could not interfere to prevent such acts of Vandalism. Gazerghiah itself, at a league's distance from Herat, and visible, by its position on a hill from that city, has many monuments of interest in sculpture and architecture. They date from the epoch of Shahrookh Mirza, a son of Timour, and have been described at large by Ferrier, but with some slight mistakes, which one readily excuses in an officer who travels. The name of the saint at Gazerghiah, for instance, is Khodja Abdullah Ansari--the latter word signifying that he was an Arab, and of the tribe that shared the Hidjra (flight) with the Prophet. More than six hundred years ago, he passed from Bagdad to Merv, thence to Herat, where he died, and was declared a saint. He now stands in high repute as patron of both city and province. Dost Mohammed Khan directed himself to be buried at the feet of Khodja Abdullah Ansari, at once flattering the prejudices of his countrymen {285} and offending those of his enemies. The grave, which lies between the walls of the adjoining edifice and the sepulchre of the Khodja, had when I saw it no decoration, and not even a stone; for his son and successor preferred first to lay the foundation of his inheritance before completing the tomb of him who had bequeathed it to him. This does not, however, prevent the Afghans from performing their reverential pilgrimages. The saint will, before long, be thrown into the shade by his mighty rival; and yet he has but his deserts, for he is probably one of the numerous Arabian vagabonds, but Dost Mahommed Khan was the founder of the Afghan nation.

[Footnote 87: The sepulchre particularly has much resemblance to that of Timour. The decorations and inscriptions upon the tomb are of the most masterly sculpture it is possible to conceive. Many stones have three inscriptions carved out, one above the other, in the finest Sulus writing, the upper line, the middle one, and lower one, forming different verses.]

{286}

CHAPTER XV.

FROM HERAT TO LONDON.

AUTHOR JOINS KARAVAN FOR MESHED

KUHSUN, LAST AFGHAN TOWN

FALSE ALARM FROM WILD ASSES

DEBATABLE GROUND BETWEEN AFGHAN AND PERSIAN TERRITORY

BIFURCATION OF ROUTE

YUSUF KHAN HEZAREH

FERIMON

COLONEL DOLMAGE

PRINCE SULTAN MURAD MIRZA

AUTHOR AVOWS WHO HE IS TO THE SERDAR OF HERAT

SHAHRUD

TEHERAN, AND WELCOME THERE BY THE TURKISH CHARGE D'AFFAIRES, ISMAEL EFENDI

KIND RECEPTION BY MR. ALISON AND THE ENGLISH EMBASSY

INTERVIEW WITH THE SHAH

THE KAVVAN UD DOWLET AND THE DEFEAT AT MERV

RETURN BY TREBISOND AND CONSTANTINOPLE TO PESTH

AUTHOR LEAVES THE KHIVA MOLLAH BEHIND HIM AT

PESTH AND PROCEEDS TO LONDON

HIS WELCOME IN THE LAST-NAMED CITY.

'Tis sweet to hear the watch-dog's honest bark
Bay deep-mouth'd welcome as we draw nigh home.--Byron.

[Author joins Karavan for Meshed; Kuhsun, last Afghan Town]
 On the 15th November 1863, I quitted Herat, the gate of Central Asia or of India, as it is usually called, in order to complete my journey with the great karavan bound for Meshed. It consisted of 2,000 persons; half of whom were Hezare from Kabul, who in the greatest poverty and the most abject state of misery were undertaking with wives and children a pilgrimage to the tombs of Shiite saints. Although all formed one body, it had nevertheless many subdivisions. I was attached to a division consisting {287} of a troop of Afghans from Kandahar, who were trading with Persia in indigo or skins from Kabul, owing to my having made my agreement with the same Djilodar. I had been able to persuade him to allow me to take my seat on a lightly-loaded mule, under the engagement that I would pay him in Meshed as if I had had the sole use of it. By the pretension, now avowed by me, that in Meshed I should no longer be in a state of destitution, I began for the first time myself to throw a doubt upon the genuineness of the character I had hitherto assumed of a Hadji, but I did not dare completely to lay aside the mask, because the Afghans, more fanatical than the Bokhariots, would have probably avenged their insulted tenets upon the spot. The dubious light in which I stood afforded, however, a fund of interesting surmises to those by whom I was surrounded, for whilst some of them took me for a genuine Turk, others were disposed to think me an Englishman; the different parties even quarrelled on the subject, and it was very droll to observe how the latter began to triumph over the former, when it was observed that, in proportion as we drew nearer to Meshed, the bent posture of humility of the Dervish began more and more to give way to the upright and independent deportment of the European. Some Afghans, agents of wholesale indigo-houses in Moultan and Shikarpur, seemed quite to accommodate themselves to my metamorphosis; for although, whilst still in the district of Herat, they vaunted their characters of Gazi (men who have taken part in the war against the English), and boasted in the most extravagant manner of the victory in Kabul, they confided to me as we drew near {288} to Meshed that they were English subjects, and urged me to introduce them to the Vekil Dowlet (English consular agent), as his influence and protection would be of great service to them in their commercial affairs; and this they did without the slightest blush of shame. The Oriental is born and dies in a mask; candour will never exist in the East. Our way passed by Nukre, Kale Sefer Khan, Ruzenek, Shebesh and Kuhsun. At Shebesh the woody country begins, which extends along the bank of the Heri, and often serves the Turkomans for a retreat. In Kuhsun, where the territory of Herat ends, we were obliged to stay two days, to pay the last Afghan duties.
[False Alarm from Wild Asses]
 On the second day we saw from the tower of the karavanserai an immense cloud of dust approaching the village. 'The Turkomans!' 'the Turkomans!' was the cry on all sides. The consternation in karavan and village beggars all description: at last, the cloud coming closer, we saw an immense squadron of wild asses, at some hundred paces' distance; they wheeled round and vanished from our eyes in the direction of the desert.
[Debatable Ground between Afghan and Persian Territory; Bifurcation of Route; Yusuf Khan Hezareh]
 From this point to the Persian frontier, which commences at Kahriz and Taybad, lies a district without claimant or owner, over which from north to south as far as Khaf, Kaïn, and even Bihrdjan, the Tekke, Salor, and Sarik send forth their Alamans: these, consisting of hundreds of riders, fall unawares upon villages and hurry off with them into captivity, inhabitants and herds of cattle. In spite of its size, our karavan was further strengthened by an escort of all the men in Kuhsun capable of bearing arms. At Kafirkale we met another karavan coming from Meshed. I learnt {289} that Colonel Dolmage, an English officer in the Persian service, whom I had known before, was in the latter city. The tidings were a source of great satisfaction to me. After Kafirkale we came to the karavanserai Dagaru, where the route divides into two, the one going by Kahriz and Türbeti Sheikh Djam through a plain, the other, by Taybad, Riza, Shehrinow; the latter is very mountainous, and consequently the less dangerous of the two. The

principal part of the karavan proceeded along the former, whereas we were obliged to take the latter, as it was the pleasure of the Afghans that we should do so. Our way passed from Taybad through a waste deserted country named Bakhirz (perhaps Bakhiz), inhabited by the Sunnite Hezare, who migrated hither from Kalè No. There are five stations before reaching the plain of Kalenderabad. In Shehrinow I met the Sertib (general), Yusuf Khan, a Hezare chief, in the pay of Persia, and nevertheless its bitterest enemy. The policy of sending him to the frontier was in one respect good, as the Hezare are the only 'tribe capable of measuring themselves' with the Turkomans, and at the same time objects of dread to them: but in another point of view it may be doubted how far it is judicious, in the danger that menaces Persia on the side of the Afghans, to make use of enemies to guard the frontiers.

[Ferimon]

From Shehrinow we proceeded over Himmetabad and Kelle Munar, [Footnote 88]which is a station situate on the top of a mountain, consisting merely of a single tower, built as a precaution against surprises. The severe cold occasioned us much suffering, but the next day {290} we reached Ferimon, the first place we had come to whose inhabitants were Persians. Here a warm stable made me forget for some time the sufferings of many days past. At last, on the twelfth day after our departure from Herat, the gilded dome of the mosque and tomb of Imam Riza glittering from afar announced to me that I was approaching Meshed, the city for which I had so longed. That first view threw me into a violent emotion, but I must admit not so great as I expected to have experienced on the occasion. Without seeking to exaggerate the dangers that had attended my undertaking, I may speak of this point as the date of my regeneration; and is it not singular, that the reality of a liberation from a state of danger and restraint soon left me perfectly indifferent, and when we were near the gates of the city I forgot Turkomans, desert, Tebbad, everything!

[Footnote 88: The word signifies 'hill of skulls.']

[Colonel Dolmage]

Half an hour after my arrival, I paid a visit to Colonel Dolmage, who filled many important offices here for the Prince-Governor, and stood in high estimation everywhere. He was still engaged in his official place of business, when his servants summoned him to me; they announced me as a singular Dervish from Bokhara. He hastened home, regarded me fixedly for a long time, and only when I began to speak did he recognise me, and then his warm embrace and tearful eye told me that I had found not only a European, but a friend. The gallant Englishman offered me his house, which I did not reject, and I have to thank his hospitality that I so far recovered from the hardships of my journey as to be able, in spite of the winter, in a month's time to continue my journey to Teheran.

{291}

[Prince Sultan Murad Mirza]

Colonel Dolmage introduced me also, during my stay in Meshed, to the Prince Governor, Sultan Murad Mirza, the uncle of the reigning Shah. This prince, the son of that Abba Mirza, whose English predilections are so well known, is surnamed 'the kingdom's naked sword;' [Footnote 89] and he deserves the title, for it is to be ascribed only to his constant watchfulness and energy that Khorasan, under his administration, has not suffered more from the incursions of the Turkomans, and that the roads begin everywhere to assume an appearance of bustle and animation. I paid him several visits, and was always received with particular kindness and affability. We conversed for hours together respecting Central Asia, upon which subject he is tolerably well informed. His delight was great when I related to him how the bigoted and suspicious Emir of Bokhara, who styles himself, to the disgust of all the Shiites, 'Prince of the true believers,' [Footnote 90] had suffered himself to be blessed by me.

[Footnote 89: 'Husam es Saltanat.']

[Footnote 90: Emir-ul-Muminim, a title ascribed by the Shiites to Ali alone.]

To the praises rightly bestowed upon Sultan Murad Mirza by M. de Khanikoff and Mr. Eastwick, I will only add that in point of energy, sound judgment, and patriotism, there are few who resemble him in Persia, or scarcely even in Turkey; but, alas! it is not a single swallow that makes a summer, and his abilities will never find a worthy field of exertion in Persia.

[Author avows who he is to the Serdar of Herat]

On account of the scantiness of my European wardrobe, I was obliged to continue my turban as well as my Oriental dress, both in Meshed and during the remainder of my journey to Teheran; but, as the {292} reader will very well understand, I had said adieu to all disguise as a

Dervish. My acquaintance with the European officer above mentioned had already told my fellow-travellers sufficiently who and what I was. My character and mission afforded a field to the Afghans for the most varying and extravagant conclusions, and, as it was easy for me to perceive that they would soon inform the young Prince of Herat of the fact, I thought it better at once myself to anticipate them, and make, in the customary form, my own communication. In a letter to the young prince, I congratulated him on his perspicacity, and told him that, although not an Englishman, I was next door to one, for that I was a European; that he was an amiable young man, but that I would advise him another time, when any person was obliged by local circumstances to travel incognito through his country, not to seek publicly and rudely to tear off his mask.

[Shahrud]

After having passed Christmas with the hospitable English officer whom I have mentioned, I began, on the day following (December 26), my journey to Teheran without either joining any karavan, or having any companion except my friend the Mollah. We were both mounted on good horses, my own property, as were also other articles that we took with us, consisting of culinary vessels and bedding, and, in fact, every possible travelling convenience; and in spite of my having, in the middle of winter, to perform twenty-four stations, I shall never forget the pleasure that I experienced in the journey that brought me, each step that I advanced, nearer to the West, that I loved so well. I even performed without escort the four stations from Mezinan to Shahrud, where {293} Persians, from fear of the Turkomans, proceed accompanied by pieces of artillery. In the last city I met, in the karavanserai, an Englishman from Birmingham, who was stopping there to purchase wool and cotton. What was the astonishment of the Briton when he heard a man in the dress of a Dervish, with an immense turban on his head, greet him in this distant land with a 'How do you do?' In his amazement his countenance assumed all hues; thrice he exclaimed, 'Well, I--,' without being able to say more. But a little explanation rid him of his embarrassment; I became his guest, and spent a famous day with him and another European, a well-informed Russian, who acted there as agent for the mercantile house of Kawkaz.

From Shahrud I took ten days to reach the Persian capital. Towards evening on the 19th of January, 1864, I was at a distance of two leagues, and, singular to say, I lost my way at the village Shah Abdul Azim, owing to the obscurity; and when, after searching about a long time in all directions, I at last reached the gate of the city, I found it shut, and I was obliged to pass the night in a karavanserai at the distance of only a few paces. The next morning I hastened, to avoid being noticed by any one in my droll costume, through the streets of Teheran to the Turkish Embassy.

[Teheran, and Welcome there by the Turkish Charge d' Affaires, Ismael Efendi; Kind Reception by Mr. Alison and the English Embassy]

The reader will easily understand in what tone of mind I again entered that edifice which, ten months before, I had left with my head full of such vague and adventurous plans. The intelligence that my benefactor Haydar Efendi had left Teheran affected me very much, although his successor, Ismael Efendi, accredited as *Chargé d'affaires* at the Persian Court, {294} gave me an equally kind and hearty reception. This young Turkish diplomatist, well known for his particularly fine breeding and excellent character, rendered me by his amiability eternally his debtor. He immediately vacated for me an entire suite of rooms at the Embassy, so that the comforts I enjoyed during two months in Teheran made me forget all the hardships and sufferings of my most fatiguing journey; indeed, I soon found myself so strong again that I felt capable of commencing a similar tour. No less kindness and favour awaited me at the English Embassy. The distinguished representative of the Queen, Mr. Alison, [Footnote 91] as well as the two secretaries, Messrs. Thompson and Watson, really rejoiced at the happy and successful termination of my journey; and I have to thank their kind recommendations alone, that on my arrival in England, to publish the narrative of my travels, I met with so much unhoped-for, and I may add, too, so much unmerited support. Nor can I omit here also to offer my acknowledgments for the courtesy shown to me by the Imperial *chargé d'affaires*, the Count Rochechouart.

[Footnote 91: This gentleman had, by an act of great generosity, the same winter that I returned to Teheran, caused much sensation in the Persian capital. Such a lesson is the best that can be given to Orientals, and far more meritorious and pregnant of consequence than all the hypocritical morality of which others make a vaunt.]

[Interview with the Shah; The Kavvan ud Dowlet and the Defeat at Merv]

The King having expressed a desire to see me, I was officially presented by Ismael Efendi. The youthful Nasr-ed-din Shah received me in the middle of his garden. On being introduced by the minister for foreign affairs and the chief adjutant, I was much astonished to find the ruler of all the countries of Iran {295} watching our approach with an eye-glass, attired in a simple dress, half Oriental and half European. [Footnote 92] After the customary salutations, the conversation was directed to the subject of my journey. The King enquired in turn about all his royal brethren in distant places, and when I hinted at their insignificance as political powers, the young Shah could not refrain from a little gasconade, and made an observation aside to his Vizir. 'With fifteen thousand men we could have done with them all.' Of course, he had quite forgotten the exclamation after the catastrophe at Merv: 'Kavvam! Kavvam! redde mihi meas legiones.' [Footnote 93] The subject of Herat was also touched upon. Nasr-ed-din Shah questioned me as to the state in which the city was then. I replied that Herat was a heap of ashes, and that the Herati were praying for the welfare of His Majesty of Persia. The King caught at once the meaning of my words, and, in the hasty manner of speaking usual with {296} him, which reminded me of the fox in the fable, he added, 'I have no taste for such ruined cities.' At the close of my audience, which lasted half an hour, the King expressed his astonishment at the journey I had made, and left me, as a mark of especial favour, the ribbon of the fourth class of the Order of the Lion and the Sun, after which I was obliged to write for him a short summary of my travels.

[Footnote 92: The under garments retain for the most part the native cut, the over ones alone follow European fashions--a real picture of our civilisation in the East.]

[Footnote 93: The unfortunate campaign against Merv, really (as I observed) directed against Bokhara, was commanded by an incapable Court favourite, bearing the title Kavvam eddowlet ('stability of the kingdom'). The disastrous defeat there suffered by the Persians at the hands of the Tekke is only to be ascribed to this officer's incompetency. He looked upon the Turkomans at Merv with the same contempt with which Varus had contemplated the Cherusci in the woods of the Teutones, but the Persian was too cowardly to face the death of the Roman General. Neither was his sovereign an Augustus. He exclaimed, it is true, 'Redde mihi meas legiones,' but he nevertheless allowed himself to be appeased by a payment of 24,000 ducats; and the base coward, even at the present day, fills a high post in Persia.]

[Return by Trebisond and Constantinople to Pesth]

On the 28th March, the very same day on which, in the previous year, I had commenced my journey through Central Asia, I quitted Teheran on my route to Trebisond by Tabris. As far as the latter city we had the finest spring weather, and it is unnecessary for me to say what my feelings were when I called to mind the corresponding date in the past year. Then each step in advance took me further towards the haunts of savage barbarism, and of unimaginable dangers; now, each step carried me back nearer to civilised lands, and my own beloved country. I was very much touched by the sympathy which, on my way, I received from Europeans, as in Tabris, from my distinguished Swiss friends, Messrs. Hanhart & Company, and Mr. Abbot, the English Vice-consul; in Trebisond, from the Italian Consul Mr. Bosio, and also from my learned friend, Dr. O. Blau, and particularly from Herr Dragorich, the former the Prussian, the latter the Austrian Consul. All these gentlemen, by their obligingness and friendly reception, bound me to them eternally. They knew the hardships that attend travelling in the East, and their acknowledgment of them is the sweetest reward that can fall to the lot of the traveller.
{297}
As, after having been in Kurdistan, I was no longer able to distinguish in the countenance of the Osmanli anything Oriental, so now I could see in Stamboul nothing but, as it were, a gorgeous drop curtain to an unreal Eastern existence. I could only indulge myself with a stay of three hours on the shore of the Bosphorus. I was glad, however, still to find time to wait upon the indefatigable savant and diplomat Baron von Prokesh-Osten, whose kind counsels with reference to the compilation of my narrative I have kept constantly before my eyes. Hence I proceeded to Pesth by Küstendje, where I left behind me my brother Dervish [Footnote 94] from Kungrat, who had accompanied me all the way from Samarcand; for the joy of tarrying long in my fatherland was not allowed me, as I was desirous, before the close of the season, of delivering an account of my journey to the Royal Geographical Society of England--an object furthered and obtained for me by the kind recommendations of my friends. I arrived in London on the 9th of June, 1864, where it cost me incredible trouble to accustom myself to so sudden and extreme a change as that from Bokhara to London.

[Footnote 94: It is needless for me to picture to the reader how this poor Khivite, transplanted by me to the capital of Hungary instead of being permitted to proceed to Mecca, was amazed, and how he talked! What most astonished him was the good nature of the Frenghis, that they had not yet put him to death, a fate which, drawing his conclusions from the corresponding experience amongst his countrymen, he had apprehended.]

Wonderful, indeed, is the effect of habit upon men! Although I had advanced to the maximum of these extremely different forms of existing civilisation, as it were, by steps and by degrees, still everything appeared to me here surprisingly new, as if what I had {298} previously known of Europe had only been a dream, and as if, in fact, I were myself an Asiatic. My wanderings have left powerful impressions upon my mind. Is it surprising, if I stand sometimes bewildered, like a child, in Regent Street or in the saloons of British nobles, thinking of the deserts of Central Asia, and of the tents of the Kirghis and the Turkomans?

{299}

PART II.

TURKOMANS

KHIVA

BOKHARA

KHOKAND

CHINESE TARTARY

ROUTES

AGRICULTURE AND TRADE

POLITICAL RELATIONS

RUSSIANS AND ENGLISH

{300}

{301}

CHAPTER XVI.

BOUNDARIES AND DIVISION OF TRIBES

NEITHER RULERS NOR SUBJECTS

DEB

ISLAM

CHANGE INTRODUCED BY THE LATTER ONLY EXTERNAL

INFLUENCE OF MOLLAHS

CONSTRUCTION OF NOMAD TENTS

ALAMAN, HOW CONDUCTED

PERSIAN COWARDICE

TURKOMAN POETS

TROUBADOURS

SIMPLE MARRIAGE CEREMONIES

HORSES

MOUNDS, HOW AND WHEN FORMED

MOURNING FOR DEAD

TURKOMAN DESCENT

GENERAL POINTS CONNECTED WITH THE HISTORY OF THE TURKOMANS

THEIR PRESENT POLITICAL AND GEOGRAPHICAL IMPORTANCE.

Non se urbibus tenent et ne statis quidem sedibus. Ut invitavere pabula, ut cedens et sequens hostis exigit, its res opesque secum trahens, semper castra habitant; bellatrix, libera, indomita. --Pomp. Mela, de Situ Orbis, 1. ii. c. 4.

THE TURKOMANS IN THEIR POLITICAL AND SOCIAL RELATIONS.

Boundaries and Divisions.

The Turkomans or Türkmen, [Footnote 95] as they style themselves, inhabit for the most part that tract of desert land which extends on this side of the river Oxus, from the shore of the Caspian Sea to Belkh, and from the {302} same river to the south as far as Herat and Astrabad. Besides the partially productive soil which they possess along the Oxus, Murgab Tedjend, Görghen, and Etrek, where they actually busy themselves a little with agriculture, the country of the Turkomans comprises that immense awful desert where the traveller may wander about for weeks and weeks without finding a drop of sweet water or the shade of a single tree. In winter the extreme cold and the thick snow, in summer the scorching heat and the deep sand, present equal dangers; and storms only so far differ from each other in these different seasons, as the graves that they prepare for the karavans are dry or moist.

[Footnote 95: This word is compounded of the proper name Türk, and the suffix *men* (corresponding with the English suffix *ship, dom*); it is applied to the whole race, conveying the sense that the nomads style themselves pre-eminently ***Türks***. The word in use with us, Turkoman, is a corruption of the Turkish original.]

To describe with more exactitude the divisions of the Turkomans, we will make use of their own expressions. According to our European ideas, we name their main divisions, stocks or tribes, because we start from the assumption of *one* entire nationality. But the Turkomans, who, as far as history records, never appear united in any single body, mark their principal races by the name Khalk (in Arabic *people*), and designate them as follows:--

I. Tchaudor.
II. Ersari.

III. Alieli.
IV. Kara.
V. Salor.
VI. Sarik.
VII. Tekke.
VIII. Göklen.
IX. Yomut.

Employing, then, the expression adopted by these nomads themselves, and annexing the corresponding words and significations, we have--

Turkoman words.	Primitive sense.	Secondary sense.
Khalk.	People.	Stock or tribe.
Taife.	People.	Branch.
Tire.	Fragment.	Lines or clans.

{303}

The Khalks are divided into Taife, and these again into Tire. We proceed to touch briefly upon all these main stocks, devoting, however, our particular attention to the Tekke, Göklen, and Yomuts, who are settled to the south, as occasion permitted me to visit and to become more acquainted with these from personal contact.

I. TCHAUDOR.

These inhabit the southern part of the district between the Caspian Sea and the Aral Sea, counting about 12,000 tents; their principal Tire, or branches, extending from the former sea as far as Köhne Urgendj, Buldumsaz, Porszu, and Köktcheg in Khiva, are--

Abdal.
Bozadji.
Igdyr.
Burundjuk.
Essenlu.
Sheikh.
Karatchaudor.

II. ERSARI.

These dwell on the left bank of the Oxus, from Tschihardschuj as far as Belkh. They are divided into twenty Taife, and still more numerous Tire. The number of their tents is said to amount to from fifty to sixty thousand. As they inhabit for the most part the bank of the Oxus, and are tributary to the Emir of Bokhara, they are often alluded to as the Lebab-Türkmen, or Bank-Turkomans.

III. ALIELI.

These, who have their principal seat at Andkhoy, form only three little Tire, not counting more than three thousand tents.

{304}

IV. KARA.

A small but exceedingly savage tribe of Turkomans, who, for the most part, are found loitering about in the vicinity of certain wells in the great sandy desert between Andkhoy and Merv. They are pitiless robbers, and are warred against as such by all the surrounding tribes.

V. SALOR.

This is the oldest Turkoman tribe recorded in history. It was already renowned for its bravery at the time of the Arabian occupation. Its numbers were then probably greater, for they have suffered very much from incessant wars. They number only eight thousand tents, although it is not ten years since they were in possession of the important point of Merve. They are now-a-days supplanted by the Tekke in Martschah and its vicinity. They consist of the following Taife and Tire:--

Taife.	Tire.
Yalavadj	Yasz, Tiszi, Sakar, Ordukhodja.
Karaman	Alam, Gördjikli, Beybölegi.
Ana bölegi	Yadschi, Bokkara, Bakaschtlöre, Timur.

VI. SARIK.

These do not stand in less repute for bravery than the tribe of Salor. Their numbers, too, are less than they were formerly. At present the Sariks [Footnote 96] inhabit {305} the regions about Pendschdeh, on the bank of the Murgab. With the exception of their neighbours the Djemshidi, they are in hostile relations with all the Turkomans. They are separated into the following Taife and Tire:--

Taife.	*Tire.*
Khorasanli	Bedeng, Khodjali, Kizil, Huszeïnali.
Biradj	Kanlibash, Kultcha, Szudjan.
Sokhti	Tapyr, Mumatag, Kurd, Kadyr.
Alascha	Kodjeck, Bogadja, Huszein Kara, Szaad, Okensziz.
Herzegi	Yerki, Djanibeg, Kurama, Jatan, Japagy.

The number of their tents, I was told, amounts to ten thousand.

[Footnote 96: The women of this tribe, Sarik, have a peculiar renown as manufacturers of a tissue called Agary. It is formed of the hair of the young camel (three or four days old), which, after being boiled in milk, during four or five days acquires an elasticity and consistence as of a silk pulp; this substance they afterwards draw out and weave into the material so called. It is of particular beauty and strength, and is in high esteem and of great value as a material for forming the overdress of men. It is to be met with in Persia, and always fetches high prices.]

VII. TEKKE.

These form at this day the greatest and most powerful tribe of the Turkomans. They are separated into two principal encampments--the first at Akhal (to the east of Tedjend), and the second at Merv. According to the best accounts, they have sixty thousand tents. Possessing less land that is capable of being cultivated than the other Turkoman tribes, they are, so to say, almost forced by nature itself to commit acts of robbery, and are a real scourge in the hand of God to the north-easterly portions of Persia, to Herat and its neighbourhood. I have only been able to ascertain the following subdivisions; there are probably many others:--

{306}

Taife.	Ta	Tire.
Ötemiscli		Kelletscho, Sultansiz, Szitschmaz Kara Ahmed.
Bakhshi		Perreng, Topaz, Körszagry, Aladjagöz, Tashajak Aksefi Goh, Marsi, Zakir, Kazilar.
Toktamish		Bokburun Amanshah, Göktche Beg, Kara, Khar, Kongor, Yussuf, Jazi, Arik Karadja.

VIII. GÖKLEN.

Judging by the position and the relations in which I found these, I am justified in characterising them as belonging to the most peaceable and most civilised Turkomans. Willingly occupying themselves with the pursuits of agriculture, they are subject, most of them, to the King of Persia. They dwell in the lovely region so famed in history, that of the ancient Gurgan (now the ruins of Shehri Djordjan). Their branches and clans are as follows:--

Taife.	Taif	Tire.
kir	Tshadlli	Gökdish, Alamet, Toramen, Khorta, Karavul, Kösze, Kulkara, Baynal.
dlli	Beg	Pank, Amankhodja, Boran, Karishmaz.
	Kayi	Djankurbanli, Erkekli, Kizil Akindjik, Tckendji Bok Khodja Kodana Lemek Kaniasz, Dari.
balkan	Kara	Tshotur, Kapan, Szigirsiki, Pashej, Adjibég
k	Kyry	Giyinlik Szufian, Dehene Karakuzu, Tcheke, Gökese Kabaszakal, Ongüt, Kongor.
ndir	Baji	Kalaydji, Körük, Yapagi Yadji Keszir Yasagalik Töreng.
kesz	Ger	Mollalar, Kösze Ataniyaz Mehrem Börre.
ak	Jang	Korsüt Madjiman, Kötü, Dizegri, Szaridsche, Ekiz.
grik	Szen	Karashur, Akshur, Kutchi, Khar, Sheikhbégi.

		Aj	
0.	Dervisch		Otschu, Kodjamaz, Dehli, Tchikszari, Arab, Adschem, Kandjik.

{307}
These ten branches are said to contain ten thousand tents, a number, perhaps, not exaggerated.

IX. YOMUT.

The Yomuts inhabit the East shore of the Caspian Sea and some of its islands. Their original appellation is Görghen Yomudu (Yomuts of the Görghen). Besides these there are the Khiva-Yomudu (Yomuts of Khiva), who have chosen for their abode the other end of the desert, close upon the Oxus.

The particular places in the desert where the Yomuts first above mentioned are wont to encamp, beginning to reckon them from the Persian frontier upward, are as follows:--

1. ***Khodja Nefes***., at the lower mouth of the Görghen, an encampment of from forty to sixty tents, furnishes a strong contingent to the audacious pirates that render the Persian coast so insecure.

2. ***Gömüshtepe***, more particularly a winter quarter, not habitable in summer on account of the prevalence of virulent fevers. It extends, as already mentioned, in the upper mouth of the Görghen, which is here tolerably deep, and which, from the wonderful number of fish that it yields, is of great service to this tribe.

3. ***Hasankuli***, on the shore of the gulf of this sea, having the same name. This place is densely peopled in summer, and produces tolerably good melons.

{308}

4. ***Etrek*** lies to the left of Hasankuli, on the banks of the river of like appellation, which, at a distance of six miles from this place, precipitates itself into the sea.

5. ***Tchekishlar***, also a Yaylak (summer abode), near to the hill on the sea-shore, named Ak Tepe.

6. ***Tcheleken***, [Footnote 97] an island only distant a few miles from the continent. The inhabitants are peaceful traders.

[Footnote 97: Better written Tchereken from the Persian Tchar-ken, the four mines, so called on account of the four principal productions of the island.]

The Yomuts are divided into the following branches and clans:--

Taife.	*Tire.*
Atabay	Schene, Düngirtchi, Tana Kisarka, Kesze, Temek
Djafer bay, having again two divisions,	
a. Yarali	Iri Tomatch, Kızıl Sakallı, Arigkoseli, Tchokkan borkan, Onuk Tomatch.
b. Nurali	Kelte, Karindjik, Gazili Kör, Hasankululu kör Pankötek.
Sheref Djuni, of whom one part dwells in Görghen, and the other in Khiva,	
a. Görghen	Karabölke, Teredji, Telguj Djafun
b. Khiva	Oküz, Salak, Ushak, Kodjuk, Meshrlk, Imreli.

113

The Ogurdjali, hardly ever busying themselves with marauding and robbery, refuse to recognise the Yomuts as of their tribe, and dealing themselves peaceably with Persia, with which they have great activity of commerce, they have become subjects of {309} the Shah, to whom they pay a yearly tribute of 1000 ducats. The Persians, however, do not interfere in their internal government.

The Yomuts themselves are accustomed to count the number of their tents in the aggregate at from forty to fifty thousand. Their calculations are as little to be guaranteed as the statements of the other tribes, for the greatness of their numbers always constitutes, with these nomads, a question of national pride.

Let us now add together the different tribes:--

Tribes.	No. of Tents.
Tchaudor	12,000
Ersari	50,000
Alieli	3,000
Kara	1,500
Salor	8,000
Sarik	10,000
Tekke	60,000
Göklen	12,000
Yomut	40,000
Total	196,500

Reckoning to each tent five persons, we have a sum-total of 982,500 souls; and as I have myself diminished the Turkoman statements by at least a third, we may regard this as the lowest possible estimate of the whole population.

POLITICAL CONDITION OF THE TURKOMANS.

What surprised me most during my sojourn amongst this people, was my inability to discover any single man among them desirous of commanding, or any individual inclined to obey. The Turkoman himself {310} is wont to say, 'Biz bibash khalk bolamiz (We are a people without a head), and we will not have one. We are all equal, with us everyone is king.' In the political institutions of all the other nomads, we occasionally discover some sign, more or less defined --some shadow of a government, such as the Aksakal amongst the Turks, the Rish Sefid amongst the Persians, or the Sheikh amongst the Arabs. Amongst the Turkomans we find no trace of any such character. The tribes have, it is true, their Aksakals; but these are, in effect, merely ministers to each particular circle, standing, to a certain degree, in a position of honourable distraction. They are liked and tolerated so long only as they do not make their supremacy felt by unusual commands or extravagant pretensions.

'How, then,' the reader will enquire, 'can these notorious robbers'--and the savageness of their nature is really unbounded--'live together without devouring each other?' The position in which they stand is really surprising; but what shall we say to the fact that, in spite of all this seeming anarchy, in spite of all their barbarism, so long as enmity is not openly declared, *less robbery and murder, fewer breaches of justice and of morality*, take place amongst them than amongst the other nations of Asia whose social relations rest on the basis of Islam civilisation? The inhabitants of the desert are ruled, often tyrannised over, by a mighty sovereign, invisible indeed to themselves, but whose presence is plainly discerned in the word 'Deb'--*custom, usage*. [Footnote 98:]

[Footnote 98: 'Deb' is a word of Arabian origin, derived from 'Edeb' (morality).]

{311}

Among the Turkomans the 'Deb' is obeyed; everything is practised or abominated according to its injunctions. Next to the 'Deb' we may refer also, in exceptional cases, to the influence of religion. The latter, however, which came to them from Bokhara, where so much fanaticism prevails, is far from being so influential as has been said. It is generally supposed that the Turkoman plunders the Persian because the latter belongs to the detested sect of the Shiites. It is a gross error: I am firmly convinced that the Turkoman would still cling to his plundering habits, which the 'Deb' sanctions, even if he had for his neighbours the Sunnite Turks instead of the Persians. What I advance derives the strongest confirmation from other considerations--from the frequency of the attacks made by the Turkomans upon the countries belonging to Sunnites, upon Afghanistan, Maymene, Khiva, and even Bokhara. Later experience, too, convinced me that the greater number of the slaves in Central Asia belong to the religious sect of the Sunnites. I once put the question to a robber, renowned for his piety, how he could make up his mind to sell his Sunnite brothers as slaves, when the Prophet's words were, 'Kulli Iszlam hurre (Every Musselman is free)'? 'Behey!' said the Turkoman, with, supreme indifference; 'the Koran, God's book, is certainly more precious than man, and yet it is bought or sold for a few krans. What more can you say? Yes, Joseph, the son of Jacob, was a prophet, and was himself sold. Was he, in any respect, the worse for that?'

{312}

It is very remarkable how little the 'Deb' has suffered in its struggle of eight centuries with Mahommedanism. Many usages, which are prohibited to the Islamite, and which the Mollahs make the object of violent attack, exist in all their ancient originality; and the changes effected by Islam, not only amongst the Turkomans, but amongst all the nomads of Middle Asia, were rather confined to the external forms of the religion previously existing. What they before found in the Sun, fire, and other phenomena of nature, they saw now in Allah-Mohammed: the nomad is ever the same, now as two thousand years ago; nor is it possible for any change to take place in him till he exchanges his light tent for a substantial house; in other words, till he has ceased to be nomad.

To return to the subject of the influence of the Aksakals, I may be permitted to remark that these, as my experience amongst the Yomuts enables me to say, are, in points of external relations, [Footnote 99] really fair representatives of the general wishes of the particular tribe, but they are no envoys entrusted with full powers, and how powerless they really are, Russia and Persia have had many opportunities of learning. These two countries have, at great expense, sought to attach the Aksakals to their interest, in order, through them, to put a stop to the habit of plundering and robbery; a policy that up to the present day has had but little success.

[Footnote 99: For instance, where Persia, Russia, or other Turkoman tribes not directly allied, are concerned.]

The Mollahs enjoy greater respect, not so much from being Islamites, as from the more general reputation for religion and mystery which attaches to their character, and which is the object of the dread of the {313} superstitious nomads. The Mollahs, educated in Khiva and in Bokhara, are cunning people, who from the beginning assume the appearance of holiness, and make off as soon as they have once filled their sacks. But the chief support of the social union is the firm cohesion, not merely of the particular divisions, but of the whole tribe. Every Turkoman nay, even the child of four years--knows the taife and tire to which he belongs, and

115

points with a certain pride to the power or to the number of his particular branch, for that really is the shield that defends him from the capricious acts of others; and, indeed, in the event of one member suffering from the hand of violence, the whole tribe is bound to demand satisfaction.

With regard to the particular relations of the Yomuts with neighbouring tribes and countries, I have found that they live in an inveterate and irreconcilable enmity with the Göklen. At the time I was in Etrek, negotiations were on foot for a treaty of peace with the Tekke, which was a lucky circumstance as far as our journey was concerned. I learned, however, later, that the peace never was concluded: in fact, it may be considered, and particularly by Persia, a fortunate circumstance that the union of tribes, in so high a degree warlike, should be impossible; for the provinces of Persia, and particularly Mazendran, Khorasan, and Sigistan, are constantly exposed to depredations of particular tribes--Tekke and Yomut need only to combine to produce unceasing injury. The Turkoman is intoxicated with the successes that have always attended his arms in Iran, and he only deigns to laugh at the menaces of that country, even when it seeks to carry them into effect {314} by the actual march of an army. The position of Russia is very different, whose might the Yomuts have hitherto learned both to know and to fear merely from the petty garrison at Ashourada. I heard that about four years ago the Russians, in violation of all their treaties with Persia, had attacked the encampment of Gömüshtepe with an armed force barely 120 strong, and that the Turkomans, although they far outnumbered them, betook themselves to flight, allowing their assailants to plunder and burn their tents. A report as to the 'infernal' arms made use of by the Russians spread itself amongst the Tekke; but what the nomads find it so difficult to withstand, is no doubt the excellent discipline of their opponents.

SOCIAL RELATIONS.

But now to accompany the Turkoman into his home and his domestic circle. We must first commence by speaking of the nomad himself, of his dress, and his tent.

The Turkoman is of Tartaric origin; but has only retained the type of his race in cases where circumstances have conspired to prevent any intermixture with the Iranis. This is remarkably the case with the Tekke, the Göklen, and the Yomuts; for amongst them the pure Tartar physiognomy is only met with in those branches and families which have sent fewer Alaman to Persia, and have consequently introduced amongst themselves fewer black-haired slaves. Still the Turkoman, whether he has departed more or less from the original type, is always remarkable for his bold penetrating glance, which distinguishes him from {315} all the nomads and inhabitants of towns in Central Asia, and for his proud military bearing; for although I have seen many young men of martial demeanour amongst the Kirghis, Karakalpak, and Özbegs, it was only in the Turkoman that I always found an absolute independence, an absence of all constraint. His dress is the same as that worn at Khiva, with some slight modification for man and woman, by the addition of little articles of luxury from Persia. The part of the attire of most importance is the red silk shirt that the ordinances of the Koran forbid, but which is still worn by both sexes; with the Turkoman women it constitutes in reality the whole home attire. My eye had great difficulty in habituating itself to the sight of old matrons and mothers of families, marriageable maidens and young girls, moving about in shifts reaching to the ankle. The covering of the head for the man is a fur cap, lighter and more tasty than the awkward cap of the Özbeg, or the large towering hat of the Persian. They employ also the Tchapan, an over-dress resembling our dressing-gown, which comes from Khiva, but of which they curtail the proportions when they take part in a Tchapao (predatory expedition). The women, when dressing themselves for holidays, are accustomed also to bind a shawl round the waist over their long shift, which hangs down in two slips; high-heeled boots, red or yellow, are also indispensable; but the objects that are most coveted, and that give them most pleasure, are the trinkets, rings for neck, ear, or nose, and étuis for amulets, and resembling cartouch-boxes, which are often seen hanging down on their left side and on their right: as with us the ribbons which are used in the different orders of knighthood. These accompany every movement of the body with a clear sound, as it were, of bells.

{316}

The Turkoman is very fond of such clatter, and attaches articles that produce it either to his wife or his horse; or when the opportunity there fails him, he steals a Persian, and suspends chains upon him. To render the lady's attire complete, a Hungarian dolmany (Hussar jacket) is hung from the shoulders, which is only permitted to be so long as to leave visible the ends of her hair plaited with a ribbon.

The tent of the Turkoman, which is met with in the same form throughout all Central Asia and as far as the remote parts of China, is very neat and in perfect accordance with the life led by the nomad. We annex a representation [See plate] in three forms:--1st, the framework cut in wood; 2nd, the same when covered with pieces of felt; 3rd, its interior. With the exception of the woodwork, all its component parts are the product of the industry of the Turkoman woman, who busies herself also with its construction and the putting together the various parts. She even packs it up upon the camel, and accompanies it in the wanderings of her people, close on foot. The tents of the rich and poor are distinguished by their being got up with a greater or less pomp in the internal arrangements. There are only two sorts:--1. Karaoy (black tent, that is, the tent which has grown brown or black from age);--2. Akoy (white tent, that is, one covered in the interior with felt of snowy whiteness; it is erected for newly-married couples, or for guests to whom they wish to pay particular honour).

TENT IN CENTRAL ASIA.
(A-- Framework. B--Covered with Felt. C--Interior.)

{317}
Altogether the tent as I met with it in Central Asia has left upon my mind a very pleasing impression. Cool in summer and genially warm in winter, what a blessing is its shelter when the wild hurricane rages in all directions around the almost boundless steppes! A stranger is often fearful lest the dread elements should rend into a thousand pieces so frail an abode, but the Turkoman has no such apprehension; he attaches the cords fast and sleeps sweetly, for the howling of the storm sounds in his ear like the song that lulls the infant in its cradle! The customs, usages, and occupations of the Turkomans might furnish matter for an entire volume, so great and so remarkable is the distinction between their manner of life and our own. I must, however, here limit myself to a few traits in their characters, and only touch upon what is indispensable to my narrative. The leading features in the life of a Turkoman are the Alaman (predatory expedition) or the Tchapao (the surprise). The invitation to any enterprise likely to be attended with profit, finds him ever ready to arm himself, and to spring to his saddle. The design itself is always kept a profound secret even from the nearest relative; and as soon as the Serdar (chief elect) has had lavished upon him by some Mollah or other the Fatiha (benediction), every man betakes himself at the commencement of the evening by different ways to a certain place, before indicated as the rendezvous.

The attack is always made either at midnight, when an inhabited settlement, or at sunrise, when a karavan or any hostile troop is its object. This attack of the Turkomans, like that of the Huns and Tartars, is rather to be styled a surprise. They separate themselves {318} into several divisions, and make two, hardly ever three, assaults upon their unsuspecting prey; for, according to a Turkoman proverb, 'Try twice, turn back the third time.' ['Iki deng ütschde döng.'] The party assailed must possess great resolution and firmness to be able to withstand a surprise of this nature; the Persians seldom do so. Very often a Turkoman will not hesitate to attack five or even more Persians, and will succeed in his enterprise. I have been told by the Turkomans, that not unfrequently one of their number will make four or five Persians prisoners. 'Often,' said one of these nomads to me, 'the Persians, struck with a panic, throw away their arms, demand the cords, and bind each other mutually; we have no occasion to dismount, except for the purpose of fastening the last of them.' Not to allude to the defeat of 22,000 Persians by 5,000 Turkomans on a very recent occasion, I can state as an undoubted fact the immense superiority of the sons of the desert over the Iranis. I am inclined to think that it is the terrible historical prestige of the Tartars of the north that robs the boldest Persian of his courage; and yet how dear has a man to pay for his cowardice! He who resists is cut down; the coward who surrenders has his hands bound, and the horseman either takes him up on his saddle (in which case his feet are bound under the horse's belly), or drives him before him: whenever from any cause this is not possible, the wretched man is attached to the tail of the animal, and has for hours and hours--yes, for days and days--to follow the robber to his desert home. Those who are unable to keep up with the horseman generally {319} perish. [Footnote 100] What awaits him in that home the reader already knows. Let me add an anecdote of an occurrence which I myself witnessed. It occurred in Gömüshtepe. An Alaman returned richly laden with captives, horses, asses, oxen, and other movable property. They proceeded to the division of the booty, separating it into as many portions as there had been parties to the act of violence. But besides they left in the centre one separate portion; this was done to make all good, as I afterwards remarked. The robbers went up each in his turn to examine his share. One was satisfied; a second also; the third examined the teeth of the Persian woman who had been allotted to him, and observed that his share was too small, whereupon the chief went to the centre heap and placed a young ass by the side of the poor Persian slave; an estimate was made of the aggregate value of the two creatures, and the robber was contented: this course was often repeated; and although my feelings revolted at the inhumanity of the proceeding, I could not refrain from laughing at the droll composition of these different shares of spoil.

[Footnote 100: I once heard a young girl say that her mother had been killed and left in the desert, because unable to follow the Turkomans in their rapid flight.]

The main instrument, the one to which the Turkoman gives the preference over all others in his forays, is, beyond all question, his horse, which is really a wonderful creature, prized by the son of the desert more than his wife, more than his children, more than his own life. It is interesting to mark with what carefulness he brings him up, how he clothes him to resist cold and heat, what magnificence he displays in the {320} accoutrements of his saddle, in which he, perhaps in a wretched dress of rags, makes a strange contrast with the carefully-decorated steed. These fine animals are well worth all the pains bestowed upon them, and the stories recounted of their speed and powers of endurance are far from being exaggerated. By origin the Turkoman horse is Arabian, for even at the present day those of the purest blood are known by the name Bedevi (Bedoueen). The horses of the Tekke stand very high and are very fast, but are far from possessing the bottom or powers of endurance of the smaller horses of the Yomuts.

The profit arising to the nomads by their abominable practice of kidnapping by no means compensates for the perils which it entails, for it is not often that it diminishes the poverty to which the son of the desert is born. And what if he is able to save a few small coins? His mode of living, simple in the extreme, would rarely call for such; and I have known many Turkomans who, in spite of a condition of increased prosperity, have continued to eat dried fish, and have allowed themselves bread but once in the week, just like the very poorest to whom the price of wheat renders bread almost inaccessible.

In his domestic circle, the nomad presents us a picture of the most absolute indolence. In his eyes it is the greatest shame for a man to apply his hand to any domestic occupation. He has nothing to do but to tend his horse; that duty once over, he hurries to his neighbour, or joins one of the group that squat on the ground before the tents, discussing topics connected with politics, recent raids, or horseflesh. In the meantime the inevitable Tchilim, a sort of Persian pipe, in which the tobacco is not moistened, passes from hand to hand.

{321}

It is only during evening hours, particularly in the winter time, that they love to listen to fairy tales and stories; it is regarded as an enjoyment of a still higher and more elevated nature, when a Bakhshi (troubadour) comes forward, and to the accompaniment of his Dütara (a two-stringed instrument) sings a few songs of Köroglu, Aman Mollah, or the national poet, Makhdumkuli, whom they half deify. The latter, regarded as a sort of saint, was a Turkoman of the Göklen tribe; he died about eighty years ago. Makhdumkuli died, as I heard from Kizil Akhond, during the civil wars between the Yomuts and the Göklens--his generous spirit could not endure to contemplate the spectacle of brother struggling in murderous combat with brother, whose wives and children were reciprocally captured and sold to slavery.

In his biography, clouded with fable, I found him represented as a wondrous man, who, without going to Bokhara or Khiva, was divinely inspired in all books and all sciences. Once being on horseback, he was surprised by an overpowering sleep; he saw himself, in fancy, transported to Mecca into a circle where the Prophet and the first Khalifs were assembled. With a thrill of reverence and awe he looked round and perceived that Omar, the patron of the Turkomans, was beckoning to him. He approached the latter, who blessed him and struck him a slight blow on the forehead, whereupon he awoke. From that instant the sweetest poesy began to flow from his lips, and his books will long occupy with the Turkomans the first place after the Koran. In other respects the collection {322} of poems by Makhdumkuli is of particular interest: first, as furnishing us with a pure specimen of the Turkoman dialect; secondly, because the method, particularly of that part which relates to precepts as to horse-breeding, arms, and the Alaman, is such as we rarely find in the literature of the Oriental nations.

How charming to me, too, those scenes, which can never pass from my memory, when on festal occasions, or during the evening entertainments, some Bakhshi used to recite the verses of Makhdumkuli! When I was in Etrek, one of these troubadours had his tent close to our own; and as he paid us a visit of an evening, bringing his instrument with him, there flocked around him the young men of the vicinity, whom he was constrained to treat with some of his heroic lays. His singing consisted of certain forced guttural sounds, which we might rather take for a rattle than a song, and which he accompanied at first with gentle touches of the strings, but afterwards, as he became more excited, with wilder strokes upon the instrument. The hotter the battle, the fiercer grew the ardour of the singer and the enthusiasm of his youthful listeners; and really the scene assumed the appearance of a romance, when the young nomads, uttering deep groans, hurled their caps to the ground, and dashed their hands in a passion through the curls of their hair, just as if they were furious to combat with themselves.

And yet this ought not to surprise us. The education of the young Turkoman is in every respect calculated to bring him to this tone of mind. Only one in a thousand can read and write: horses, arms, battles, and robberies, are the subjects that exercise, in youth, the imaginations of all. I once heard even the honest {323} Khandjan, who intended to read a lesson to his son, recount that a certain young Turkoman had already kidnapped two Persians, and 'of him' (pointing to his son) 'he feared he should never be able to make a man.'

TARTAR HORSE RACE--PURSUIT OF A BRIDE.

Some customs and usages of the Turkomans are very remarkable, as we have but faint traces of them amongst the other nomads of Central Asia. But there is also the marriage ceremonial where the young maiden, attired in bridal costume, mounts a high-bred courser, taking on her lap the carcase of a lamb or goat, and setting off at full gallop, is followed by the bridegroom and other young men of the party, also on horseback; but she is always to strive, by adroit turns, &c., to avoid her pursuers, that no one of them approach near enough to snatch from her the burden on her lap. This game, called Kökbüri (green wolf), is in use amongst all the nomads of Central Asia.

To mention another singular usage, sometimes two, sometimes four days after the nuptials, the newly-married couple are separated, and the permanent union does not begin until after the expiration of an entire year.

Another singular custom has reference to the mourning for the decease of a beloved member of the family. It is the practice, in the tent of the departed one, each day for a whole year, without exception, at the same hour that he drew his last breath, for female mourners to chant the customary dirges, in which the members of the family present are expected to join. In doing so, the latter proceed with their ordinary daily employments and occupations; {324} and it is quite ridiculous to see how the Turkoman polishes his arms and smokes his pipe, or devours his meal, to the accompaniment of these frightful yells of sorrow. A similar thing occurs with the women, who, seated in the smaller circumference of the tent itself, are wont to join in the chant, to cry and weep in the most plaintive manner, whilst they are at the same time cleaning wool, spinning, or performing some other duty of household industry. The friends and acquaintances of the deceased are also expected to pay a visit of lamentation, and that even when the first intelligence of the misfortune does not reach them until after months have elapsed. The visitor seats himself before the tent, often at night, and, by a thrilling yell of fifteen minutes' duration, gives notice that he has thus performed his last duty towards the defunct. When a chief of distinction, one who has really well earned the title of Bator (valiant), perishes, it is the practice to throw up over his grave a Joszka [Footnote 101] (large mound); to this every good Turkoman is bound to contribute at least seven shovelfuls of earth, so that these elevations often have a circumference of sixty feet, and a height of from twenty to thirty feet. In the great plains these mounds are very conspicuous objects; the Turkoman knows them all, and calls them by their names,--that is to say, by the names of those that rest below.

[Footnote 101: This custom existed amongst the ancient Huns, and is in use in Hungary even at the present day. In Kashau (Upper Hungary) a mound was raised a few years ago, at the suggestion of Count Edward Karolyi, in memory of the highly-respected Count St. Széchenyi.]

{325}

Let me conclude this short account of the Turkomans with a still briefer review of their history, in which I shall confine myself to what, in these particulars, I have heard regarded as traditions still commanding credit amongst them. 'We all spring,' said to me my learned friend Kizil Akhond, 'from Manghischlak. Our ancestors were Szön Khan and Eszen Ili. Yomut and Tekke were the sons of the first, Tchaudor and Göklen of the second. Manghischlak was in the most ancient times called Ming Kiszblak (a thousand winter quarters), and is the original home, not only of those of our race who have separated and migrated to Persia, but of the Ersari, Salor, and the rest of the tribes. Our saints of the olden times, as Ireg Ata [Footnote 102] and Sari-er, repose within the confines of Manghischlak; and especially fortunate is he who has been able to visit their tombs.' Khandjan told me that, so late as one hundred and fifty years ago, the Turkomans had very rarely any other dresses than those which they prepared of sheepskins, or the hides of horse or wild ass; that nowadays this was all changed, and the only thing that remains to remind us of the old national costume is the fur cap.

[Footnote 102: Ireg Ata means 'the great father' in Hungarian; Oreg Atya, 'old father.']

The animosities prevailing amongst the different tribes often lead to the reciprocal insulting reproach of 'descendants of slaves.' The time when they left their common country cannot be fixed with exactitude. Ersari, Sarik, and Salor were already, at the time of the Arabian occupation, in the eastern part of the desert, on this side of the Oxus. Tekke, Göklen, and Yomut took possession of their present country at a {326} later period, perhaps in the time of Djinghis Khan and Timour. The change of abode of these last-mentioned tribes took place only by partial emigrations, and, indeed, cannot even at the present day be said to be more than half complete, for many Yomuts and Göklens still loiter about their ancient seat with singular predilection. During the middle ages, the Turkoman horsemen were for the most part to be met with in the service of the Khans of Khiva and Bokhara; often, also, under the banners of Persia. The renown of their bravery, and particularly of their furious charges, spread far and wide; and certain of their leaders, like Kara Yuszuf, who took part with the tribe Salor in the campaigns of Timour, acquired historical celebrity. The Turkomans contributed much to the **Turkecising** of North Persia, at the epoch when the family of the Atabegs ruled in Iran; and beyond all dispute it is they who contributed the largest contingent to the Turkish population on the other side of the Caucasus, to Azerbaydjan, Mazendran, and Shiraz. [Footnote 103]

[Footnote 103: There are even now four or five of the smaller Turkish tribes living a nomadic life in the district around Shiraz. Their Ilkhani (chieftain), with whom I became acquainted in Shiraz in 1862, told me that he can raise from them 30,000 horsemen, and some, as the Kashkai and the Allahverdi, had been transplanted hither by Djinghis Khan. In Europe this fact has not been appreciated; and even Burnes, in other respects well informed, thinks he has found, in a place of like name in the vicinity of Samarcand, the **Turki shirazi** mentioned by Hafiz in his songs.]

{327}

It is remarkable that in spite of the bitter hostility reigning between the Turkomans and their Shiite brethren in Persia, the former still always especially name Azerbaydjan as the seat of a higher civilisation; and whenever the Bakhshi is asked to sing something more than usually beautiful and original, Azerbaydjanian songs are always called for: nay, even the captive Irani, if of Turkish origin, may always expect more merciful treatment, for the Turkoman says, 'He is our brother, this unbeliever.' [Footnote 104]

[Footnote 104: 'Kardashi miz dir ol Kafir.']

The last risings of the Turkomans in mass occurred under Nadir Shah and Aga Mehemed Khan. Nadir, helped by these tribes and by the Afghans, at the commencement of the last century, shook Asia out of her slumber; and the second conqueror above mentioned availed himself of the sword of the Turkomans to found his dynasty. Nomads are well aware of the fact, and make the ingratitude of the Kadjar a subject of frequent complaint, who, since the time of Feth Ali Shah, have, they say, entirely forgotten them, and even withdrawn the lawful pensions of several of their chiefs.

To form an idea of the political importance of the nomads, we need only cast a glance at the map of Central Asia. We there see at once that they have become, from their position, the guardians of the southern frontiers of the entire Asiatic Highlands of Turkestan, as they name it themselves. The Turkoman is, without any possibility of contradiction, next to the Kiptchak, the most warlike and savage race of Central Asia: in his rear, in the cities of Khiva, Bokhara, and Khokand, we find the seat of cowardice and effeminacy; and had he not constituted himself as it were into a barrier of iron, things would never have remained, in the three countries just mentioned, in the condition in which they were after the time of Kuteibe and Ebu Muszlim, [Footnote 105] and in which they still continue.

[Footnote 105: The former conquered Turkestan in the time of Khalif Omar; the latter, having first been Governor of Merv, fought for a long time the battle of independence, in conjunction with the Turkomans and Kharesmians against his master, the sovereign of Bagdad.]

{328}

Civilisation, some may think, has a predilection for the way that leads from the south to the north; but how can any spark penetrate to Central Asia, as long as the Turkomans menace every traveller and every karavan with a thousand perils?

{329}

CHAPTER XVII.

KHIVA, THE CAPITAL

PRINCIPAL DIVISIONS, GATES, AND QUARTERS OF THE CITY

BAZAARS

MOSQUES

MEDRESSE OR COLLEGES; HOW FOUNDED, ORGANISED, AND ENDOWED

POLICE

KHAN AND HIS GOVERNMENT

TAXES

TRIBUNALS

KHANAT

CANALS

POLITICAL DIVISIONS

PRODUCE

MANUFACTURES AND TRADE

PARTICULAR ROUTES

KHANAT, HOW PEOPLED

ÖZBEGS

TURKOMANS

KARAKALPAK

KASAK (KIRGHIS)

SART

PERSIANS

HISTORY OF KHIVA IN FIFTEENTH CENTURY

KHANS AND THEIR GENEALOGY.

Les principaux Tartares firent asseoir le Khan sur une pièce de feutre et lui dirent: 'Honare les grands, sois juste et bienfesant envers tous; sinon tu seras si misérable que tu n'auras pas même le feutre sur lequel tu es assis.'
Voltaire, Essai sur les Moeurs, c. lx.

A. KHIVA, THE CAPITAL.

As we are speaking of an Oriental city, what need to say that the interior of Khiva is very different from what its exterior would lead us to expect! First, reader, you must have seen a Persian city of the lowest rank, and then you will understand my meaning when I say that Khiva is inferior to it; or picture to yourself three or four thousand mud houses standing in different directions in the most irregular manner with uneven and unwashed walls, and fancy these surrounded by a wall ten feet high, also made of mud, and again you have a conception of Khiva.
{330}

Its Divisions.

The city is divided into two parts: (**a**) Khiva proper; and (**b**) Itch Kale, the citadel with its encircling wall, which can be shut off from the outer city by four gates; and consists of the following Mahalle (quarters): Pehlivan, Uluyogudj, Akmesdjid, Yipektchi, Koshbeghimahallesi.

The city, properly so called, has nine gates, and ten Mahalle (quarters). [Footnote 106]
[Footnote 106: That is to say, towards the north, Urgendj dervazesi,(Dervaze, a Persian word, meaning gate.) Gendumghia dervazesi, Imaret dervazesi; towards the east, Ismahmudata dervazesi, Hazaresp dervazesi; to the south, Shikhlair dervazesi, Pishkenik dervazesi, Rafenek dervazesi; and to the west, Bedrkhan dervazesi. There are ten Mahalle (quarters), that is to say,
1. Or.
2. Kefterkhane.
3. Mivesztan, where the fruit is sold.
4. Mehterabad.
5. Yenikale.
6. Bala Havuz, where there is a large reservoir of water surrounded by plane trees, serving as a place of recreation.
7. Nanyemezorama. (This word means 'village that eats no bread.')
8. Nurullahbay.
9. Bagtche.
10. Rafenek.

Bazaars.

Bazaars or shops for sale equal to those which we meet with in Persia, and in other Oriental cities, do not exist in Khiva. The following only deserve any mention. Tim, a small well-built bazaar, with tolerably high vaulted ceilings, containing about 120 shops and a karavanserai. Here are exposed all the cloth, {331} hardware, fancy articles, linen, and cotton that the Russian commerce supplies, as well as the inconsiderable produce proceeding from Bokhara and Persia. Around the Tim are also to be seen Nanbazari (bread market), Bakalbazari (grocers), Shembazari (the soap and candle market), and the Sertrashbazari (from ten to twelve barbers' rooms, where the heads are shaved: I say the heads, for the man would be regarded as out of his senses or would be punished with death who should have his beard shaved).

I must also class amongst the bazaars the Kitchik Kervanserai, where the slaves brought by the Tekke and the Yomuts are exposed for sale. But for this article of business Khiva itself could not exist, as the culture of the land is entirely in the hands of the slaves. When we come to speak of Bokhara, we will treat this subject more at large.

Mosques.

There are few mosques in Khiva of much antiquity or artistic construction. Those that follow alone deserve notice. (1) Hazreti Pehlivan, an edifice four centuries old, consisting of one large and two small domes; it contains the tomb of Pehlivan Ahmed Zemtchi, a revered saint, patron of the city of Khiva. Its exterior promises little, although the Kashi (ornamental tiles) of the interior are tasteful, but unfortunately the place itself is dark, and the insufficiency of the lighting of the interior leaves much that the eye cannot distinguish. Both inside the dome and in the courts leading to it there are always swarms of blind practitioners of the *memoria technica*, who know the Koran by heart from frequent {332} repetition, and are ever reciting passages from it. (2) Another mosque is the Djüma-a-Mesdjidi, which the Khan attends on Fridays, and where the official Khutbe (prayer for the ruling sovereign) is read. (3) Khanmesdjidi, in the interior of the citadel. (4) Shaleker, which owes its construction to a farmer. (5) Atamurad Kushbeghi. (6) Karayüzmesdjidi.

Medresse (Colleges).

The number of colleges and their magnificent endowments are, in Central Asia, always a criterion of the degree of prosperity and religious instruction of the population; and when we consider the limited means at their disposal, we cannot but laud the zeal and the readiness to make sacrifices, evinced both by King and subject, when a college is about to be founded and endowed. Bokhara, the oldest seat of Islamite civilisation in Central Asia, is a pattern in this respect; but some colleges exist in Khiva also, and of these we shall particularly mention the following:

(1) Medemin [Footnote 107]Khan Medressesi, built in 1842, by a Persian architect, after the model of a Persian karavanserai of the first rank. On the right is a massive tower, somewhat loftier than the two-storied Medresse, but which, owing to the death of the builder, remains imperfect. This college has 130 cells, affording accommodation for 260 students; it enjoys a revenue of 12,000 Khivan Batman of wheat, and 5,000 Tilla (2,500*l.* sterling) in money. To give the reader an idea of this institution, I will state the manner in which this revenue is apportioned, in order to show the parties composing the *personnel*.

[Footnote 107: Abbreviation of Mehemmed Emin.]
{333}

	Batman.	Tilla.
Akhond (professors) receive yearly	3,000	50
Iman	2,000	0
Muezzin (caller to prayers)	200	(
Servants	200	(
Barber	200	(

Muttewali, or inspectors, receive a tithe of the whole revenue; the residue is divided amongst the students, who form three classes:

1st class	0	6
2nd class	0	3
3rd class	5	1

(2) Allahkuli Khan Medressesi has 120 cells, and the yearly revenue of the pupils is fifty Batman and two Tilla (1*l.* sterling).

(3) Kutlug Murad Inag Medressesi. Each cell produces fifty Batman and three Tilla.

(4) Arab Khan Medressesi has only a few cells, but is richly endowed.

(5) Shirgazi Khan Medressesi.

These Medresse are the only edifices in the midst of the mud huts that deserve the name of houses. Their courts are for the most part kept clean, are planted with trees, or used as gardens. Of the subjects in which instruction is given we will speak hereafter, remarking only by the way, that the lectures themselves are delivered in the cells of the professors, to groups of scholars ranged together according to the degree of their intellectual capacity.

{334}

Police.

In each quarter of the town there is a Mirab, [Footnote 108] responsible by day for the public order of his district, in case of any rioting, theft, or other crime. The charge of the city after sunset is entrusted to the four Pasheb (chief watchmen), who are bound to patrol the whole night before the gate of the citadel. Each of them has eight under-watchmen subject to his orders, who are at the same time public executioners. These, in all thirty-two in number, go about the city, and arrest everyone who shows himself in the streets half an hour after midnight. Their particular attention is directed to burglars, or to the heroes of the intrigues proscribed by the law: woe to those caught *in flagrante delicto!*

[Footnote 108: A Mirab is the same as the Turkish Subashi, a functionary, that has played his part from the Chinese frontier to the Adriatic, and still continues to do so.]

B. THE KHAN AND HIS GOVERNMENT.

That the Khan of Khiva can dispose despotically, according to his good pleasure, of the property and lives of his subjects, scarcely requires to be mentioned. In his character of Lord of the Land, he is what every father is at the head of his family: just as the latter, when he pleases, gives ear to a slave, so the Khan pays attention occasionally to the words of a minister; nor is there any barrier to the capricious use of his authority, except that inspired by the Ulemas, when these have at their head such men as, by their learning and irreproachable lives, have conciliated the affection of the people, and rendered themselves objects of dread to the Khan. Matters stand so with almost all the Governments of Asia, but this is not altogether to be ascribed to the defects or entire absence of forms of government. No; in all times, and in all epochs of history, forms intended for controlling the tyrannical and capricious exercise of {335} power have existed in theory, and have only remained inoperative from that weakness of character and that deficiency of the nobler sentiments in the masses at large which have, throughout the East, ever favoured, as they still continue to do, every crime of the sovereign.

According to the Khivan Constitution, which is of Mongol origin, he is

(1) Khan or Padisha, who is chosen for the purpose from the midst of a victorious race. At his side stand the

(2) Inag, [Footnote 109] four in number, of whom two are the nearest relatives of the King, and the two others merely of the same race. One of the former is always the regular Governor of the province of Hezaresp.

[Footnote 109: The literal meaning of the word is younger brother.]

(3) Nakib, the spiritual chief, must always be a Seid (of the family of the Prophet). He has the same rank as the Sheikh-ül-Islam in Constantinople. [Footnote 110]

[Footnote 110: In Constantinople the Nakib-ül-Eshref, the chief of the Seïds, is in rank below the Sheikh-ül-Islam.]

(4) Bi, not to be confounded with Bey, with which it has only a similar verbal meaning. The Bi is, in the battle, always at the right hand of the Khan.

(5) Atalik, a sort of councillor of state, who can only be Özbegs, and whose number the Khan can fix.

(6) Kushbeghi. [Footnote 111]

[Footnote 111: Vizir, or first Court Minister of the Khan: with him begins the 'corps' of ministers properly so called, holding their place at the will of the ruler.]

(7) Mehter, a sort of officer who has the charge of the internal affairs of the court and country. The Mehter must always be from the Sart (ancient Persian population of Khiva).

{336}

(8) Yasaulbashi, two in number, principal guards, whose functions are those of introduction at the Arz (public audience). The Divan, a sort of secretary, at the same time accountant, is of the same rank.

(9) Mehrem, also two in number, having merely the office of chamberlains and confidants, yet possessing great influence with the Khan and his Government.

(10) Minbashi, commander of 1,000 horsemen. [Footnote 112]

[Footnote 112: The collective military forces of the Khan of Khiva were computed, I was told, at 20,000 men, but this number can be doubled in the time of peril.]

(11) Yüzbashi, commander of 100 horsemen.

(12) Onbashi, commander of 10 horsemen.

These twelve divisions form the class of officials, properly so called, and are styled Sipahi. They are also divided as follows: some whom the Khan cannot remove from office, some who have a fixed stipend, and the rest who are only in active service in time of war.

The high officials are rewarded with lands, and the regular troops receive from the Khan horses and arms, and are exempt from all taxes and imposts.

Thus far of the secular officers.

The Ulema or priests, of whom the Nakib is the chief, are subdivided as follows:--

(1) Kazi Kelan, superior judge and chief of jurisdiction throughout the Khanat.

(2) Kazi Ordu, who attends the Khan as superior judge in his campaigns.

(3) Alem, the chief of the five Muftis.

(4) Reis, who is inspector of the schools, and exercises a surveillance over the administration of the laws respecting religion.

{337}

(5) Mufti, of whom there is one in every considerable city.

(6) Akhond, professor or elementary teacher.

The first three belong to the higher rank of officials, and on entering upon their functions, are richly provided for by the Khan. The three others draw their stipends from the Vakf (pious foundations) paid to them in money and produce; but it is, besides, the usage for the Khan to make them certain presents every year, at the festivals of the Kurban and the Noruz. The Ulemas of Khiva do not stand in as high repute for learning as those of Bokhara, but they are far from being so presumptuous and arrogant as the latter; and many are animated by a sincere zeal to improve their countrymen as far as they can, and to soften the rude habits contracted by constant wars.

Taxes.

In Khiva these are of two kinds:--

(*a*) Salgit, corresponding with our land-tax. For every piece of ground capable of cultivation, measuring ten Tanab (a Tanab contains sixty square ells), the Khan receives a tax of eighteen Tenghe (about ten shillings.) From this the following are exempt: the warriors (Nöker or Atli), the Ulemas, and Khodja (descendants from the Prophet).

(*b*) Zekiat (customs), in accordance with which imported wares pay 2-1/2 per cent, on their value, whereas for oxen, camels, and horses [Footnote 113] a Tenghe per head, and for sheep half a Tenghe per head, were payable yearly.

[Footnote 113: Only those, however, are obliged to pay who have more than ten, which constitute a herd.]

{338}

The collection of the Salgit is left to the Kushbeghi and Mehter, who make circuits for the purpose every year through the principal districts, and hold the Yasholu [Footnote 114] responsible for the collection in the particular departments.

[Footnote 114: 'The great of age,' as the grey beards are denominated in Khiva.]

The collection of the Zekiat is controlled by a favourite Mehrem of the Khan, who visits, attended by a secretary, the tribes of nomads; and, as it is impossible to count the cattle, he every year taxes each tribe at a rate fixed after negotiation with his Yasholu. Of course, in this operation, the principal profit finds its way into the sack of the Mehter; and the Khan last year was made to believe that the Karakalpak had only 6,000 oxen, and the Yomuts and Tchaudors only 3,000 sheep taxed last year, which was, as I heard, only a third of the truth.

Justice.

This is administered in the mosques, and the private dwellings of the Kazis and Muftis, on whom the jurisdiction devolves. But every individual may prefer his complaint before the governor of the city or the province, who then makes his decision after Urf (i. e., as it seems to him right). Each governor, and even the Khan himself, must every day hold a public audience of at least four hours' duration, a duty the neglect of which illness can alone excuse; and, as no one can be excluded, the ruler is often forced to listen to and settle even the pettiest family differences amongst his subjects. I have been told that the Khan finds it fine sport to witness the quarrels of married couples, {339} maddened with anger which he himself takes care to foment. The father of the country is obliged to hold his sides for laughter to see, sometimes, man and wife thrashing each other around the hall, and finally falling wrestling in the dust.

C. KHIVA, THE KHANAT.

The Khanat of Khiva, known in history under the name of Kharezm, [Footnote 115] and called also in adjoining countries Ürgendj, is surrounded on all sides by deserts; its extreme frontiers to the south-east are formed by the city of Fitnek, to the north-west by Kungrat and Köhne Ürgendj, to the south by Medemin and Köktcheg. Without attempting to give the superficial measurement of the land occupied by fixed settlers, or ascertain precisely the number of the inhabitants, let me rather content myself by furnishing as complete a description as circumstances admit of the topography of the Khanat, and leave the geographer, if so disposed, to apply himself to the arithmetical calculation.

[Footnote 115: Kharezm is a Persian word signifying warlike, rejoicing in war.]

But we may with less hesitation enlarge upon the extraordinary fruitfulness of the soil, to be ascribed, not so much to appropriate modes of cultivation, as to the excellent irrigation, and the fertilising waters of the Oxus.

Canals.

These in Khiva are of two sorts--(*a*) Arna, those formed by the river itself, which have from time to time been merely widened and deepened by the {340} inhabitants; (*b*) Yap, canals dug to a width of one or two fathoms, for the most part fed from the Arna. With these the whole of the land that is under cultivation is covered, as with a net. Amongst the Arna deserve particular mention--

1. Hazreti Pehlivan Arnasi, which, breaks in between Fitnek and Hezaresp, passes before Khiva, and is lost in the sand after having flowed through Zey and the district of the Yomuts.

2. Gazavat Arnasi forms a break between Khanka and Yenghi Ürgendj, passes also to the west before Gazavat, and loses itself in the territory of the Yomuts.

3. Shahbad Arnasi has its beginning above Yenghi Ürgendj, passes by Shabad Tash-haus and Yillali, and disappears at Köktcheg.

4. Yarmish Arnasi breaks in opposite Shahbaz Veli, and flows through the districts between Kiat Kungrat and Yenghi Ürgendj.

5. Kilitchbay Arnasi separates Khitai and Görlen, goes by Yillali, and disappears in the sand behind Köktcheg.

6. Khodjaili Arnasi. On the further bank are--

7. Shurakhan Arnasi, which commences from the place of the same name, and disappears to the northeast, after having watered Yapkenary and Akkamish.

8. Iltazar Khan Arnasi, which traverses the land of the Karakalpak.

Divisions.

The political divisions of Khiva correspond with the number of those cities having particular Bay, or governors, this entitling them to the name of separate districts. At this present moment the following {341} {342} divisions subsist, of which the most interesting are Khiva, the capital, Yenghi Ürghendj, the most manufacturing, Köhne Ürgendj, famous for having long been the capital of the Khanat, but now only a miserable village. There only remain of its former splendour (*a*) two ruins of towers, one more considerable, the other smaller, designed in the same massive style as the other towers in Central Asia. The legend recounts that these owe their demolition to the fury of the Calmucks, because at a distance they seemed to be near, yet fly before the approaching assailants; (*b*) the Dome of the Törebegkhan, inlaid with tastefully enamelled bricks; (*c*) Mazlum Khan Solugu.

Principal Towns or Divisions, with the Villages belonging to them, and their distance from the Oxus.

Name	Distance from Oxus	Villages
	Tash	

		or mile	
.	Khiva	6	**To the West:** Bedrkhan, Kinik, Akyap, Khasian, Tashayak, Töyesitchti. **To the South:** Sirtcheli, Shikhlar, Rafenek Engrik, Pesckenik, Pernakaz Akmesdjid. **To the East:** Sayat, Kiat, Shikhbaghi, Kettebag. **To the North:** Gendumghiah, Perishe, Khalil, Neyzekhasz, Gauk, Tcharakhshik, Zirsheytan Ordumizan.
.	Hezaresp	1	Djengeti, Shikharik, Khodjalar Himetbaba, Bitjaktchi, Ishanteshepe, Bagat, Nogman, Besharik.
.	Jenghi Ürgendj	1-1/4	Gaibulu Shabadboyu, Kutchilar, Oroslar, Sabundji, Akhonbaba, Karamaza Kiptchaklar.
.	Kungrat	Bank	Kiet, Nogai, Sarsar, Sakar.
.	Tash-haus	6	Kamishli Kuk, Kongrudlar, Karzalar Yarmish boyu, Bastirmali.
.	Görlen	1	Djelair, Yonushkali, Eshim, Vezir, Alchin, Bashkir, Tashkali, Kargali.
.	Khodja Ili	2	Ketmendji Ata, Djarnike Naymanlar (in the woods), Kamishtchali Dervish Khodja.
.	Tchimbay	On the further bank	
.	Shahbad	4	Khodjalar, Kefter Khane, Kökkamish.
0.	Shurakhan	On the opposite side	
1.	Kilidj bay	4-1/2	Klalimbeg Bagalan Alieliboyu, Bozjapboyu.
2.	Mangit	1/2	Permanatcha, Kiatlar, Kenegöz.
3.	Kiptchak	On bank	Basuyapboyu, Nogai ishan Kandjirgali, Kanlilar.

4.	Khitai	1-1/2	Akkum, Yomurlutam, Kulaulu.
5.	Ak derbendand Djamli	7	
6.	Kiet	2	
7.	Khanka	1	Meder, Godje, Khodjalar, Shagallar.
8.	Fitnek	2	
9.	Shabaz Veli	2	
0.	Djagatai	4-1/2	
1.	Ambar	5	Bastirmali Veyenganka Peszi.
2.	Yenghi ya	Opposite bank	Altchin, Vezir.
3.	Nôks		
4.	Köktcheg	9	
5.	Köhne Urgendj	6	
6.	Kiat Kungrat [between Görlen and Yenghi Urgendj]	2	
7.	Nokhasz [between Khanka and Hezaresp]	2	
8.	Rahmetbirdi beg [near Oveisz Karaayne mountain]	Opposite bank	
9.	Kangli	1	
0.	Yilali [between Medemin and Tashhaus]	8	

1.   Koshköpür

2.   Gazavat   6

{343}
D. PRODUCTS, MANUFACTURES, AND TRADE OF KHIVA.

The fertility of the Khivan soil has already been several times mentioned; we must, however, allude to the following produce as especially excellent:--corn; rice, particularly that from Görlen; silk, the finest of which is from Shahbad and Yenghi Ürgendj; cotton; Ruyan, a kind of root, prized for the red colour extracted from it; and fruits, the superior merit of which not Persia and Turkey alone, but even Europe itself, would find it difficult to contest. I particularly refer to the apples of Hezaresp, the peach and pomegranate of Khiva, but, above all, to the incomparable and delicious melons, renowned as far even as remote Pekin, so that the sovereign of the Celestial Empire never forgets, when presents flow to him from Chinese Tartary, to beg for some Ürkindji melons. Even in Russia they fetch a high price, for a load of winter melons exported thither brings in return a load of sugar.

{344}
With respect to Khivan manufactures, in high repute is the Ürgendj Tchapani, or coat from Ürgendj; the material is a striped stuff of two colours (of wool or silk, often made of the two threads mingled), this is cut to the fashion of our dressing gowns. Khiva is also renowned for its articles in brass, Hezaresp for its gowns, and Tash-hauz for its linens.

The principal trade is with Russia. Karavans, consisting of from one to two thousand camels, go to Orenburg in spring, and to Astrakhan in autumn, conveying cotton, silk, skins, coats for the Nogai Tartars, Shagreen leather, and fruits to the markets of Nishnei (which they call also Mäkariä); they bring back in return kettles or other vessels of cast-iron (here called Djöghen), chintz (the kinds used by us to cover furniture, but here employed for the fronts of women's shifts), fine muslin, calicoes, clothing, sugar, iron, guns of inferior quality, and fancy goods in small quantities. There is a great export trade in fish, but the Russians have their own fisheries, which are protected by three steamers, stationed on the sea of Aral, and which navigate as far as Kungrat, in accordance with a treaty concluded six years ago by the last Russian embassy sent to Khiva. With Persia and Herat [Footnote 116] the trade is inconsiderable; the reason is that the routes leading thither are occupied by the Turkomans. Between Khiva and Astrabad the intercourse is entirely in the hands of the Yomuts, who bring {345} with them every year 100 or 150 camels, loaded with box-wood (to make combs) and naphtha. With Bokhara, on the contrary, more important transactions take place. They export thither gowns and linen, and receive in exchange tea, spices, paper, and light fancy goods, there manufactured. For the home trade they hold every week, in each city, one or two markets; even in parts confined exclusively to nomads, and where houses as such do not exist, a market-place (Bazarli-djay), consisting of one or more mud huts, is constructed. A market in this country assumes the appearance of a fair or festival. The Central Asiatic visits it often from a distance of ten or twenty miles, purchasing perhaps a few needles or other trifles; but his real object is the love of display, for on such occasions he mounts his finest horse and carries his best weapons.

[Footnote 116: In Herat, it is true, and in its environs, the Khiva-Tchapani (coat from Khiva) is much appreciated and bought at a high price, but the article itself reaches them through Bokhara.]

MARKET ON HORSEBACK--AMONGST THE ÖZBEGS.

E. HOW THE KHANAT IS PEOPLED.

Khiva is peopled by 1. Özbegs; 2. Turkomans; 3. Karakalpak; 4. Kasak (called by us Kirghis); 5. Sart; 6. Persians.

1. Özbegs.

This is the designation of a people for the most part inhabiting settled abodes, and occupying themselves with the cultivation of the earth. They extend from the southern point of the sea of Aral as far as Komul (distant a journey of forty days from Kashgar), and are looked upon as the prominent race in the three Khanats. According to their divisions they fall into thirty-two principal Taife (tribes). [Footnote 117]

129

[Footnote 117: As--1. Kungrat; 2. Kiptchak; 3. Khitai; 4, Manghit; 5. Nöks; 6. Nayman; 7. Kulan; 8. Kiet; 9. Az; 10. Taz; 11. Sayat; 12. Djagatay; 13. Uygur; 14. Akbet 15. Dörmen 16. Öshün; 17. Kandjigaly; 18. Nogai; 19. Balgali; 20. Miten; 21. Djelair; 22. Kenegöz; 23. Kanli; 24. Ichkili; 25. Bagurlü; 26. Altchin; 27. Atchmayli; 28. Karakursak; 29. Birkulak; 36. Tyrkysh; 31. Kettekeser; 32. Ming.]

{346}
This division is old, but it is very remarkable that even these particular tribes are scattered almost indiscriminately over the ground above mentioned, and it seems astonishing and, indeed, almost incredible, that Özbegs of Khiva, Khokand, and Yerkend, differing in language, customs, and physiognomy, represent themselves nevertheless as members, not only of one and the same nation, but of the very same tribe or clan.

I will here only remark that in Khiva most of the tribes have representatives, and the Khivite has a legitimate pride in the purity of his ancient Özbeg nationality, as contrasted with that of Bokhara and Kashgar. At the very first sight, however, the Khivan Özbeg betrays the mixture of his blood with the Iran elements, for he has a beard, always to be regarded in the Turanis as a foreign peculiarity, but his complexion and form of countenance indicate very often genuine Tartar origin. Even in the traits of his character, the Khivan Özbeg is preferable to his relatives in the other races. He is honest and open-hearted, has the savage nature of the nomads that surround him without the refined cunning of Oriental civilisation. He ranks next to the pure Osmanli of Turkey, and it may be said of both that something may still be made out of them.

{347}
Khiva is less instructed in the doctrine of Islamism than Bokhara, a circumstance that has had much influence in producing the following result: the retention by the Khivan Özbeg not only of many of the national usages of heathenism, but also of the religious observances of the Parsees. A predilection in favour of music and the national poetry of the Turks, more passionately cultivated by the nomads of Central Asia than by any civilised nation, has been here more strictly maintained than in Khokand, Bokhara, and Kashgar. The Khivan players on the Dutar (a guitar with two strings), and Koboz (lute) are in high renown throughout all Turkestan; and not only is Nevai, the greatest of the Özbeg poets, familiar to every one, but no ten years elapse without the appearance of lyrists of the second or third rank. I became acquainted in Khiva with two brothers; one, Munis, wrote excellent poems, of which it is my purpose later to publish several, and the other, Mirab, had the extraordinary patience to translate into the Özbeg-Turkish dialect the great historical work of Mirkhond to render it more accessible to his son, who was nevertheless acquainted with Persian. The work employed him twenty years, but he was ashamed to communicate the fact to any one, for a man who busies himself with any other branch of learning than religion is there regarded as a very superficial person.

Many centuries have elapsed since their first settlement, and yet the Khivan customs still retain the impress of the early heroic age. Mimic battles, wrestling, and particularly horse races, occur frequently. In the latter very brilliant prizes await the winners. Every wedding of distinction is honoured by a race of 9, 19, 29, which means that the winner receives from the giver of the festival, of all or part of his property, 9, 19, 29, for instance 9 sheep, 19 goats. {348} and so on; these often yield him a considerable sum. Smaller races of less importance consist of what is styled Kökbüri (green wolf), of which we have already spoken when treating of the Turkomans. There are festivals and sports in Khiva which have been handed down from the primitive inhabitants, who were fire-worshippers; they once existed in other parts of Central Asia before the introduction of Islam, but they are at the present day quite forgotten.

2. *Turkomans.*

Of these we have already spoken at large. There are in Khiva (*a*) Yomuts who inhabit the borders of the desert, from Köhne to Gazavat, the district of Karayilghin, Köktcheg, Özbegyap, Bedrkend, and Medemin. (*b*) Tchaudor, who wander about also in the land around Köhne, namely, near Kizil Takir, and Porsu, but more to the west, in the country between the Aral and Caspian Seas. Of Göklen there are very few.

3. *Karakalpak.*

These inhabit the further bank of the Oxus, opposite Görlens, far away up close to Kungrat, in the vicinity of extensive forests, where they occupy themselves with the breeding of cattle; they have few horses and hardly any sheep. The Karakalpak pique themselves upon possessing the most beautiful women in Turkestan; but on the other side they are themselves described as being the greatest idiots, and I have heard many anecdotes confirming this assertion. [Footnote 118]

[Footnote 118: Of this nation I have found ten principal tribes--
1. Baymakli.
2. Khandekli.
3. Terstamgali.
4. Atchamayli.
5. Kaytchili Khitai.
6. Ingakli.
7. Kenegöz.
8. Tomboyun.
9. Shakoo.
10. Ontönturûk.]

{349}
Their number is computed at 10,000 tents. From time out of mind they have been subject to Khiva. Forty years ago they rebelled under their leader, Aydost, who invaded Kungrat, but were, at a later date, defeated by Mehemmed Rehim Khan. Eight years have hardly elapsed since they rose again under their chief, Zarlig, who is said to have had under him 20,000 horsemen, and to have committed great devastations until they were utterly routed and dispersed by Kutlug Murad. Their last insurrection took place three years ago, under Er Nazar, who built himself a stronghold, but was nevertheless overcome.

4. *Kasak (Kirghis)* .

Of these, very few remain subject to Khiva, they having, in recent times, for the most part fallen under the dominion of Russia, We shall speak more fully of this great nomadic nation of Central Asia when we come to treat of Bokhara.

5. *Sart.*

These are called Tadjik in Bokhara and Khokand, and are the ancient Persian population of Kharezm. Their number here is small. They have, by degrees, exchanged their Persian language for the Turkish. The Sart is distinguishable, not less than the Tadjik, by his crafty, subtle manners. He is no great favourite with the Özbeg, and in spite of the Sart and Özbeg having lived five centuries together, very few mixed marriages have taken place between them.

{350}

6. *Persians.*

These are either slaves, of whom there are about 40,000, or freed men, besides a small colony in Akderbend and Djamli. In other respects, as far as material existence is concerned, the slave in Khiva is not badly off. Craftier than the plain straightforward Özbeg, he soon enriches himself, and many prefer, after having purchased their freedom, to settle in the country rather than return to Persia. The slave is styled in Khiva, Dogma, and his offspring, Khanezad (house-born). The blemish of the captivity to which he has been subjected is only effaced in the third generation.

F. MATERIALS FOR A HISTORY OF KHIVA IN THE 19TH CENTURY.

1. *Mehemmed Emin Inag.*

On the sudden retreat of Nadir Shah, [Footnote 119] who had, without a blow, rendered himself master of the Khanat, the Kirghis of the small horde (or Üstyurt Kazaghi, or Kasaks of the upper Yurt, as they style themselves) took the lead of affairs in Khiva. They ruled until the end of the last century, at which time an Özbeg chieftain of the tribe of Konrad rose and laid claim to the throne. His name was Mehemmed Emin Inag (1792-1800), by which title he meant to express his descent from the last Özbeg family that had reigned. He succeeded in getting together a small army, and marched against the Kasak Prince. But the latter, who was still in considerable force, defeated his adversary several times, till he finally fled to Bokhara, where he lived some years in retirement. His partisans,{351} however, continued the struggle until they gained several advantages; they then despatched a deputation of forty horsemen to inform

Mehemmed Emin; whereupon that prince returned and again placed himself at the head of affairs, and this time with better result, for he drove away the Kasaks. Mounting the throne he became the founder of the present reigning family, who were his successors, in an unbroken order of succession, as shown in the accompanying genealogical account.--*See next page*.

[Footnote 119: After he had, in 1740, conquered Yolbarz (Lion) Shah, and a few months later had retired to Kelat.]

2. *Iltazar Khan* (1800-1804).

This prince made war with Bokhara, because the latter supported the sinking power of the Kasaks. Whilst he was occupied in the neighbourhood of Chardjuy, the Yomuts, at the instigation of the Bokhariots, dashed upon Khiva and got possession of the city, and plundered it under the guidance of their chief, Tapishdeli. Iltazar, endeavouring to return with rapidity, was, in his retreat, routed by the Bokhariots, and died in flight in the waters of the Oxus. He was succeeded on the throne by his son,

3. *Mehemmed Rehim* (1804-1826);

Called also Medrehim. He lost no time in turning his arms against the Yomuts, drove them out of the capital, and made them richly atone for the booty they had taken. Equal success attended him in his dealings with the Karakalpaks. These, led by Ajdost, resisted him at first, but he compelled them to submit. He was not so fortunate in his attack upon Kungrat, where one of his relatives contested the throne with him.

{352}

Family Tree

{353}

The struggle lasted 17 years. It is remarkable that he continued, during the whole of this time, the siege of the above-named city; and the obstinate defender, laughing at all the efforts of the enemy, called out to him, it is said, one day from the top of the tower: 'Utch ay savun (three months sour milk), Utch a kavun (three months melons), Utch ay kabak (three months pumpkins), Utch a tchabak' (three months fish); meaning thereby that he had food for the four seasons of the year, which he could procure within the precincts of the city; that he had no occasion for bread, and that he could last a long time without being reduced by famine.

To revenge the death of his father, Medrehim marched against Bokhara, where, at that time, Emir Seid, a weak-minded prince who assumed the Dervish character, held the reins of government. The Khivites devastated many cities up to the very gates of Bokhara, making numerous prisoners. The Emir was informed, and he exclaimed, 'Akhir Righistan amandur!' which means that he had still a place of security, Righistan, [Footnote 120] and that he had no occasion to fear. After having committed great ravages, Medrehim returned laden with spoil. Towards the close of his reign, he reduced to subjection, at Astrabad, the Tekke and the Yomuts.

[Footnote 120: A place of public resort in the city of Bokhara.]

{354}

4. *Allah Kuli Khan* (1826-1841).

This prince inherited from his father a well-filled Hazne (treasury), as well as powerful influence amongst the neighbouring nations. His anxiety to preserve it involved him in several wars. In Bokhara the feeble Seid had been succeeded by the energetic Nasr Ullah, who, seeking to avenge the disgraceful defeat of his father, began a war in which the Khivan Crown Prince was routed.

At the time the news arrived that the Russians were marching from Orenburg upon Khiva, and that the hostility of the Emir of Bokhara was only owing to the instigations of the unbelievers, the consternation was great, for it was reported that the Muscovite force amounted to more than eighty thousand men, with a hundred cannon; and as they had waited long in the vain hope of receiving help from the 'Inghiliz' in Herat, the Khan despatched, about ten thousand horsemen, led by Khodja Niyazbay, against the Russians, who had already forced their way from the Ughe plain as far as the lake of Atyolu, six miles distant from Kungrat. The Khivites recount that they surprised the enemy, and that such a slaughter ensued as is seldom heard of. Many were made prisoners; and in Kungrat two Russians were pointed out to me who had remained behind from that campaign as prisoners, had afterwards become public converts to

Islamism, and had in consequence been set free by the Khan, who had loaded them with presents: they had even contracted marriages there. [Footnote 121]

[Footnote 121: The above is the version of the affair according to the Khivites themselves. It is, however, well known that the expedition that marched against Khiva, under the command of General Perowszky, consisted of only from ten to twelve thousand men. The principal cause of the Russian disaster was unquestionably the severe cold; still a battle did actually take place, and the Özbegs, to whom Captain Abbot ascribes so much cowardice, did inflict considerable injury upon the corps of occupation after it had fallen into disorder.]

{355}
After the victory, the Khan had raised entrenchments in the neighbourhood of Dövkara, on both sides. The garrisons of these were placed under the control of Khodja Niyazbay. These, however, have been abandoned, and have remained in ruins for the last ten years. To return thanks to God for the happy termination of the war with the Russians, Allahkuli founded a Medresse (college), which he richly endowed.

On the other side the war with Bokhara continued; the Göklens were also subdued, and a great number of them sent to colonise Khiva. It is an old but singular custom in this country that a whole tribe is taken altogether and forced to submit to a transportation which transfers them to Khiva itself; there they receive every possible succour, and as their own feelings of animosity continue to exist, there is no difficulty in maintaining over them a close surveillance.

5. *Rehim Kuli Khan* (1841-1843).

This prince succeeded to his father, and immediately found that he had enough to do with the Djemshidi, a Persian tribe inhabiting the eastern bank of the Murgab, of whom the Khivites had taken 10,000 tents with their chiefs, and had settled there as a colony on the bank of the Oxus, near Kilidjbay. On the other side the Sarik, at that time masters of Merv, began hostilities with the Özbegs. The younger brother of the Khan, Medemin Inag, was sent against them with 15,000 horsemen; but on the dreadful journey between Khiva and Merv, many {356} soldiers fell sick. As the Emir of Bokhara was at the same time besieging the city of Hezaresp, the Inag turned his arms quickly against the latter, defeated him, and then concluded a peace. About this time died Rehim Kuli Khan, and

6. *Mehemmed Emin Khan* (1843-1855)

seized the reins of government, to which not perhaps the law of inheritance (for the deceased Khan left sons), but his former services, gave him a good claim. Mehemmed Emin Khan is regarded as the most glorious monarch that Khiva can boast in modern times; for he restored to the kingdom of Kharezm, wherever possible, its ancient limits which it had lost 400 years before; and at the same time, by the subjection of all the nomads in the surrounding country, he raised the reputation of the Khanat, and considerably increased its revenues.

Two days had not elapsed after his having been raised to the White Felt [Footnote 122]--a proceeding tantamount in Khiva and Khokand to accession to the throne--when he marched in person against the Sarik, the bravest of all the Turkoman tribes; for he longed to bring under his sceptre the fruitful plain of Merv. After six campaigns he succeeded in capturing the citadel of Merv as well as another fortress called Yolöten, in the same vicinity. Scarcely had he got back to Khiva, when the Sarik again rose in rebellion, and put to the sword the officer left in command at Merv with the whole garrison. A new campaign was commenced with great rapidity, in which the Djemshidi, old {357} enemies of the Sarik, also took part, and, led on by their chief Mir Mehemmed, were conquerors, and, to the chagrin and vexation of all the Özbeg heroes, made their triumphal entry into Khiva.

[Footnote 122: The enacting of this ceremonial, I was told, has been ever since the time of Genghis Khan, and still is, the exclusive privilege of the grey-beards of the tribe of Djagatay.]

The Sarik was consequently reduced to subjection: nevertheless the Tekke, who at that time dwelt in Karayap and Kabukli, between Merv and Akhal, evincing feelings of hostility by refusing the payment of their yearly tribute, Medemin saw himself forced again to use a sword, still reeking with Turkoman blood, against another of these tribes. After three campaigns, during which many men and animals perished in the sandy desert, the Khan succeeded in overpowering a part of the insurgents, and left a garrison composed of Yomuts and Özbegs, under their two leaders, to keep them in check. By mishap differences broke out between the chieftains; the leader of the Yomuts returned to Khiva, and was there hurled down by order of the offended Khan from the top of a lofty tower.

133

This act made all the Yomuts enemies of Mehemmed Emin; allying themselves secretly with the Tekke, they were, a little later, the cause of his death. At this time Medemin had collected a force of 40,000 horsemen, consisting of Özbegs and other tributary nomads; of these he despatched a part against the Russians, who were then approaching Khiva, and marching from the eastern shore of the Sea of Aral upon the entrenchments of Khodja Niyazbay. He proceeded with the rest of his forces to Merv, with the intention of putting an end by a decisive blow to the never-ceasing disorders amongst the Turkomans. He speedily took Karayap, and was preparing to assail Sarakhs {358} (the ancient Syrinx), when one day, whilst resting in his tent, pitched on a hill in the vicinity of Merv, [Footnote 123] in the very centre of his camp, he was surprised by some daring hostile horsemen, and in spite of his cry, 'Men Hazret em' (I am the Khan), his head was struck off, without any of his retinue having had time to hasten to his rescue. At the sight of the severed head, which the Turkomans sent as a present to the Shah of Persia, [Footnote 124] a panic seized his troops, who retired nevertheless in good order, and whilst on their way called to the throne Abdullah Khan.

[Footnote 123: With respect to this hill we are told that it was here also that Ebu Muslim, the mighty vassal and afterwards enemy of the Kahlifs of Bagdad, met with his death.]

[Footnote 124: The Shah, who had reason to dread Medemin--for after the fall of Sarakhs, he would certainly have assailed Meshed--respected the gory head of his enemy, and had a small chapel built for it before the gate (D. Dowlet). But he afterwards had it demolished because it was said that pious Shiites might mistake it for the tomb of an Imamzade, a holy Shiite, and it might so give occasion to a sinful act.]

7. *Abdullah Khan* (1855-6).

Scarcely had this prince reached the alarmed capital when differences arose respecting the right to the throne, and Seid Mahmoud Töre, a claimant who had some preferable right from seniority, drew his sword in the presence of all the Mollahs and great personages, and avowed his intention to make good his claim by immediately striking the Khan dead. He was first pacified and afterwards placed in confinement. The Yomuts on their side had gained over two princes with the intent to place them on the throne; but their intrigue was discovered whilst it was yet time; the {359} unfortunate princes were strangled; and as for the Yomuts, their criminality being plain to all, it was determined to punish them. The Khan advanced against them at the head of a few thousand horsemen but the Yomuts protesting their innocence, and their grey-beards, with naked swords suspended from their necks (symbolising their submission), coming bare-footed to meet him, they were this time forgiven. Two months later, the tribe again beginning to show hostile sentiments, the Khan became incensed, assembled in great haste 2,000 horsemen, and attacked the Yomuts who were in open rebellion. The affair terminated unfortunately. The Özbegs were put to flight; and when a search was made for the Khan, it was found that he was amongst the first that had fallen, and that his body had been thrown with the others, without distinction of person, into a common grave. They named, as his successor, his younger brother,

8. *Kutlug Murad Khan* (reigned three months only).

He had fought at the side of the late Khan, and was returning covered with wounds. He soon armed afresh to continue the struggle that had cost his brother his life, when the chiefs of the Yomuts made overtures of peace, with the promise that they would appear in Khiva to do homage, and bring with them the cousin of the Khan, who had fallen into their hands in the last engagement, and whom they had proclaimed Khan.

{360}
Kutlug Murad and his ministers put faith in these professions. The day was fixed for their appearance, when they appeared accordingly, but with a force of 12,000 men, and bringing with them their best horses and arms of parade. On the morning of the presentation, the Khan received his cousin, and the latter, whilst in the act of embracing him, treacherously stabbed the sovereign with his poniard. The Khan fell to the ground, and the Turkomans rushed upon the royal servants who were present. During the consternation that prevailed, the Mehter ascended the wall of the citadel, and, announcing from the battlements the atrocious crime, called upon the Khivites to put to death all the Yomuts within the walls of the city. The incensed populace attacked the Turkomans, who, paralysed by fear, offered no resistance. They fell, not only by the weapons of Khivites, but even by the knives of the women. The streets of Khiva ran literally with blood, and it took six days' labour to dispose of the dead bodies.

For a period of eight days after this butchery Khiva remained without a sovereign. The crown was tendered to the formerly capable Seid Mahmoud Töre; but his passionate fondness for the indulgence of the intoxicating opium was an obstacle, and he abdicated his rights in favour of his younger brother,

9. *Seid Mehemmed Khan* (1856--still reigning).

The incapacity of this prince is well known, and the reader has seen many instances of it. During this reign Khiva has been much devastated by the civil war with the Yomuts, and colonies founded by the previous Khans have been ruined and unpeopled. Whilst Yomuts and Özbegs were thus destroying one {361} another, and hurrying off mutually their women and children to slavery, the Djemshidi making their way in, according to the proverb, 'Inter duos litigantes tertius est gaudens,' and assailing the unarmed population, plundered the whole of Khiva, from Kitsdj baj to Fitnek, and richly laden with spoil, and accompanied by 2,000 Persian slaves, who had freed themselves in the confusion, returned to the banks of the Murgab.

Poverty, cholera, pestilence, and depopulation led necessarily to a peace; then a pretender to the throne, supported by Russian influence, named Mehemmed Penah, unfurled the banner of revolution, and despatched an embassy by Manghishlak to Astrakhan to implore the protection of the Russian Padishah. The intrigue took wind, and the envoys were put to death on their way. Later, however, when the Russian Imperials (gold pieces) had been expended, Mehemmed Penah was murdered by his own partisans, and the ringleaders were formed into parcels (that is to say, they had their hands bound to their body with wetted leather), and were so forwarded to Khiva, where a cruel end awaited them.

{362}

CHAPTER XVIII.

THE CITY OF BOKHARA.

CITY OF BOKHARA, ITS GATES, QUARTERS, MOSQUES, COLLEGES

ONE FOUNDED BY CZARINA CATHERINE

FOUNDED AS SEMINARIES NOT OF LEARNING BUT FANATICISM

BAZAARS

POLICE SYSTEM SEVERER THAN ELSEWHERE IN ASIA

THE KHANAT OF BOKHARA

INHABITANTS: ÖZBEGS, TADJIKS, KIRGHIS, ARABS, MERVI, PERSIANS, HINDOOS, JEWS

GOVERNMENT

DIFFERENT OFFICIALS

POLITICAL DIVISIONS

ARMY

SUMMARY OF THE HISTORY OF BOKHARA.

. . . regnata Cyro   Bactra . . . Tanaisque discors.   Horace, *Ode* iii. 29, 27-8.

The circumference of Bokhara, represented to me as a day's journey, I found actually not more than four miles. The environs, though tolerably well cultivated, are in this respect far inferior to the country around Khiva.

Bokhara has eleven gates, [Footnote 125] and is divided into two principal parts, Deruni Shehr (inner city), and Beruni Shehr (outer city); and into several quarters, the chief of which are Mahallei Djuybar, Khiaban, Mĭrekan, Malkushan, Sabungiran. Although we have given {363} the reader, in a preceding chapter, some idea of the great buildings and public places, we will here condense in a short account our particular observations.

[Footnote 125: Dervaze Imam, D. Mezar, D. Samarcand, D. Oglau, D. Talpatch, D. Shirgiran, D. Karaköl, D. Sheikh Djelal, D. Namazgiah, D. Salakhane, D. Karshi.]

Mosques.

The Bokhariot pretends that his native city possesses 365 mosques, counting the small as well as the large ones, so that the pious Musselman may find a different one to attend each day in the year. I have not been able to discover more than the half of that number. The following are the only ones that deserve mention:--

1. Mesdjidi Kelan, built by Timour, but restored by Abdullah Khan, which is thronged on Fridays, as the Emir then says his prayers there.

2. Mesdjidi Divanbeghi, built, with the reservoir and Medresse bearing the same name, by a certain Nezr, 1029 (1629), who was Divanbeghi (state secretary) of the Emir Imankuli Khan.

3. Mirekan.

4. Mesdjidi Mogak. This is a subterranean building, in which, according to one tradition, the primitive Musselmans, according to another, the last Fire-worshippers, held their meetings. The former version seems more probable; for, first, the Guebres could have found more suitable spots outside of the city, in the open air; and secondly, many Kufish inscriptions there point to an Islamite origin.

{364}

Medresse (Colleges).

The Bokhariot prides himself upon the number of these colleges, and fixes them at his favourite figure, 365. There are, however, not more than 80. The most celebrated are the following:--

1. The Medresse Kökeltash, built in 1426; it has 150 cells, each of which costs from 100 to 120 Tilla. [Footnote 126] The students in the first class receive an annual sum of five Tillas.

[Footnote 126: On the first foundation of a Medresse, the cells are given as presents, but the subsequent proprietors can only obtain them upon the payment of a fixed price.]

2. M. Mirarab was erected in 1529, and has 100 cells, each of which costs from 80 to 90 Tilla, and pays interest 7 per cent.

3. Koshmedresse (pair of colleges) of Abdullah Khan, built in 1372. It has about 100 cells, but not so valuable as the preceding ones.

4. M. Djuybar was erected in 1582, by a grandson of the great scholar and ascetic of the same name. It is most richly endowed; each cell pays 25 Tilla, but it is not very full, being at the extreme end of the city.

5. M. Tursindjan, where each cell yields five Tilla yearly.

6. M. Emazar, founded by the Czarina Catherine, through her ambassador. It has 60 cells, each paying three Tilla.

We may remark, generally, that the colleges of Bokhara and Samarcand are the cause why so high an idea not only prevailed throughout Islam, but existed for a long time even amongst Europeans, as to the learning of the superior schools in Central Asia. The readiness to make the sacrifice which the foundation of such establishments supposes, may by a superficial observer be easily mistaken and ascribed to a higher motive. {365} Unhappily, merely blind fanaticism lies at the root; and the same thing occurs here as took place during the middle ages, for, with the exception of what is given in a few books upon Mantik (logic) and Hikmet (philosophy), there is no instruction at all but in the Koran, and religious casuistry. Now and then, perhaps, one may be found who would like to busy himself with poetry and history, but his studies must be in secret, as it is regarded as a disgrace to devote oneself to any such frivolous subjects. The aggregate number of students has been represented to me as about 5,000; they flock thither, not merely out of all parts of Central Asia, but also from India, Kashmir, Afghanistan, Russia, and China. The poorer receive an annual pension from the Emir, for it is by means of these Medresse, and its severe observance of Islamism, that Bokhara is able to exercise a spiritual influence upon neighbouring countries.

Bazaars.

There are none here like those in the chief cities of Persia. Very few are vaulted or built of stone; the larger ones are covered over either with wood or reed mattings laid across long perches. [Footnote 127]

[Footnote 127: They are separated into different parts, as Tirm Abdullah Khan, the above-mentioned prince, had them built according to Persian models on his return from Persia in 1582. Restei Suzenghiran, haberdashers; R. Saraffan, where the money-changers and booksellers station themselves; R. Zergheran, workers in gold; R. Tchilingheran, locksmiths; R. Attari, dealers in spices; R. Kannadi, confectioners; R. Tchayfurnshi, tea-dealers; R. Tchitfuroshi, dealers in chintz; Bazari Latta, linendrapers; Timche darayfurushi, grocers; and so on.]

{366}

Each bazaar has its particular Aksakal, responsible to the Emir for order, as well as for taxes. In addition to the bazaars there are, perhaps, altogether about thirty small karavanserais, used partly as warehouses, and partly for the reception of strangers.

Police.

The system of police in Bokhara is more severe than in any other city of known parts of Asia. By day the Reis himself perambulates the bazaars and public places, and he sends out his numerous dependents and spies; and about two hours after sunset no one dares to show himself in the streets, neighbour cannot visit neighbour, and the sick man runs the risk of perishing for want of medical aid, for the Emir has declared that the Mirshebs (night-watchers) may even arrest himself should they meet him abroad during the forbidden hours.

THE KHANAT OF BOKHARA.

Inhabitants.

The actual frontiers of the Khanat are: on the east, the Khanat of Khokand, and the mountains of Bedakhshan; on the south, the Oxus, with the districts on the further side, Kerki and Chardjuy; on the west and north, the Great Desert. The positive line of demarcation cannot be defined, and it is equally impossible to fix the number of inhabitants. Without going too far, they may, perhaps, be set down at two millions and a half, consisting generally {367} of those having fixed habitations and those leading a nomad life, or, if we take the principle of nationality, of Özbegs, Tadjiks, Kirghis, Arabs, Mervi, Persians, Hindoos, and Jews.

Özbegs.

The Ozbegs, part of the thirty-two tribes, are already particularised in our account of Khiva, but they are sensibly distinguishable from the kindred race in Kharezm, both by the conformation of the face and by the character. The Özbeg Bokhariots have dwelt in closer connection with the Tadjiks than the Khivites have done with the Sarts, and have consequently paid the penalty by losing much of their national type, and of their Özbeg straightforwardness and honesty. As the dominant population in the Khanat (for the Emir himself is also an Özbeg of the tribe Manghit), the Özbegs form the nerve of the army, but the superior officers are rarely taken out of their ranks.

Tadjiks.

The Tadjiks, the aboriginal inhabitants of all the cities of Central Asia, are represented still in the greatest number here; hence Bokhara is the only place where the Tadjik can point to his origin with pride, assigning as he does, for frontiers to his primitive fatherland, Khorasan, [Footnote 128] Khoten (in China) to the east, the Caspian to the west, Khodjend to the north, and India to the south. It is a pity that this people, in spite of the high antiquity of their origin, and their {368} grandeur in time gone by, should have attained the very highest stage of vice and profligacy: if they are to be taken as a specimen of antique Asia, the cradle of our race, it must, indeed, have presented in those early ages a sorry appearance.

[Footnote 128: Khor means 'sun,' and son 'district;' hence the whole word signifies 'district of the sun.']

Kirghis.

Kirghis [Footnote 129] or Kasaks, as they style themselves, are not numerous in the Khanat of Bokhara, but we will, nevertheless, record here a few notes which we have made respecting this people, numerically the greatest, and by the peculiarity of its nomad life the most original, in Central Asia.

[Footnote 129: Kir means field, gis or gez is the root of the word gizmelt (wander). The word Kirghiz signifies, in Turkish, a man that wanders about the fields, a nomad, and is used to denote all nations leading the pastoral life. It is also employed to designate a tribe; but they are only a subdivision of the Kazaks, to be met with in Khokand in the vicinity of Hazneti in Turkestan.]

I have often, in my wanderings, fallen upon particular encampments of Kirghis, and whenever I wished to acquire information as to their number, they laughed at me, and said, 'Count first the sand in the desert, and then you may number the Kirghis.' There is the same impossibility in defining their frontiers. We know only that they inhabit the Great Desert that lies between Siberia, China, Turkestan, and the Caspian Sea; and such localities to move in, as well as their social condition, suffice to show how likely we are to err when we at one time ascribe Kirghis to the Russian dominions, and at another transfer them to the Chinese. Russia, China, Khokand, {369} Bokhara, and Khiva, exercise dominion over the Kirghis only so long as the taxing officers, whom they send, sojourn amongst those nomads. The Kirghis regard the whole procedure as a *razzia* on a gigantic scale, and they are grateful to find that those who commit it are content to receive merely a percentage or some tax that is tantamount. The revolutions that have taken place in the world for hundreds, nay, perhaps thousands of years, have wrought very little influence upon the Kirghis; it is, therefore, in this nation, which we can never behold as one mass, but in small sections, that we especially see the most faithful picture of those customs and usages which characterise the Turani races of ancient times, and which constitute so extraordinary a mingling of savage qualities and of virtues.

We are surprised to perceive in them so great a disposition to music and poetry; but their aristocratical pride is particularly remarkable. When two Kirghis meet, the first question is, 'Who are thy seven fathers--ancestors?' [Footnote 130] The person addressed, even if a child in his eighth year, has always his answer ready, for otherwise he would be considered as very ill-bred.

[Footnote 130: 'Yeti atang kimdir.']

In bravery the Kirghis is inferior to the Özbeg, and still more so to the Turkoman. Islamism, with the former, is on a far weaker footing than with the others I have mentioned. Nor are any of them, except the wealthy Bays, accustomed to search the cities for Mollahs to exercise the functions of teachers, chaplains, and secretaries at a fixed salary, payable in sheep, horses, and camels.

{370}

The Kirghis, even after frequent contact, must still, in the eyes of us Europeans, appear wonderful beings. We behold in them men who, whether the heat is scorching or the snow a fathom deep, move about for hours daily in search of a new spot for their purpose: men who have never heard bread even named, and who support themselves only upon milk and meat. The Kirghis look upon those who have settled down in town or country as sick or insane persons, and they compassionate all whose faces have not the pure Mongol conformation. According to their aesthetic views, that race stands at the very zenith for beauty; for God made it with bones prominent like those of the horse--an animal, in their eyes, the crowning work of creation.

3. Arabs.

These Arabs are the descendants of those warriors who, under Kuteïbe, in the time of the third Khalif, took part in the conquest of Turkestan, where they subsequently settled. They retain, however, with the exception of their physiognomy, very little resemblance to their brethren in Hedjaz or Arak. I found very few of them who even spoke Arabic. Their number is said to be 60,000, and they are mostly settled in the environs of Vardanzi and Vafkend.

{371}

4. *Mervi.*

The Mervi are the descendants of the 40,000 Persians transplanted from Merv to Bokhara by the Emir Said Khan, when about the year 1810 he took that city by aid of the Sarik. The race sprang originally from the Turks of Azerbaydjan and Karabag, whom Nadir Shah transferred from their ancient homes to Merv. Next to the Tadjiks, the Mervi is the most cunning amongst the inhabitants of Bokhara, but he is far from being so cowardly as the former.

5. *Persians.*

The Persians in Bokhara are partly slaves, partly such as have paid their own ransom and then settled in the Khanat. Here, in spite of all religious oppression--for as Shiites they can only practise their religion in secret--they readily apply themselves to trade and handicraft, because living is here cheaper and the gain easier than in their own country. The Persian, so far superior in capacity to the inhabitants of Central Asia, is wont to elevate himself from the position of slave to the highest offices in the state. There are hardly any governors in the province who do not employ in some office or other Persians, who were previously his slaves, and who have remained faithful to him. They swarm even in the immediate proximity of the present Emir, and the first dignitaries in the Khanat belong to the same nation. In Bokhara, the Persians are looked upon as men more disposed to intercourse with the Frenghis; men who have knowledge of diabolical arts: but the Emir would bitterly rue it if Persia threatened him with invasion, which it had already thought of; for with his army in its present state, he could do but little; the chief commanders, Shahrukh Khan, Mehemmed Hasan Khan, also are Persians; and their Toptchibashi, chiefs of artillery, Zeinel Bey, Mehdi Bey, and Lesker Bey, belong to the same nation.

{372}

6. *Hindoos.*

Of Hindoos there are but 500. They form no families, and, scattered throughout the capital and provinces, they have in some wonderful manner got all the management of money into their hands, there being no market, not even a village, where the Hindoo is not ready to act as usurer. Bowing with the deepest submissiveness, like the Armenian in Turkey, he nevertheless all the time fleeces the Özbeg in fearful fashion; and as the pious Kadi for the most part carries on business in common with the worshipper of Vishnoo, it is rarely that the victim escapes.

7. *Jews.*

The Jews in the Khanat are about 10,000 in number, dwelling for the most part in Bokhara, Samarcand, and Karshi, and occupying themselves rather with handicrafts than with commerce. In their origin they are Jews from Persia, and have wandered hither from Kazvin and Merv, about 150 years ago. They live here under the greatest oppression, and exposed to the greatest contempt. They only dare to show themselves on the threshold when they pay a visit to a 'believer;' and again, when they receive visitors, they are bound in all haste to quit their own houses, and station themselves before their doors. In the city of Bokhara they yield yearly 2,000 Tilla Djizie (tribute), which the chief of their whole community pays in, receiving, as he does so, two slight blows on the cheek, prescribed by the Koran as a sign of submission. The rumour of the privileges accorded to {373} the Jews in Turkey has attracted some to Damascus, and other places in Syria; but this emigration can only occur secretly, otherwise they would have to atone for the very wish by confiscation or death. It is surprising what a letter correspondence is maintained by them through the Hadjis proceeding every year from Turkestan to Mecca. My companions also had charge of many letters, which they everywhere delivered at the addresses indicated.

Government.

The form of government in Bokhara has retained very few of the primitive Persian or Arabian characteristics, the Turco-Mongolian element predominating, and giving its tone to the whole. Although powerfully influenced by its hierarchy, the constitution is a military despotism. At its head stands the Emir, as generalissimo, prince, and chief of religion.

The military and civil dignitaries are divided into (*a*) Kette Sipahi (higher functionaries), (*b*) Orta Sipahi (middle functionaries), and (*c*) Ashaghi Sipahi. To the first two classes it is the rule to admit only Urukdar (personages of good family), for they are nominated on account of Yerlik (handwriting), or Billig (insignia). [Footnote 131] A practice, however, of appointing emancipated Persian slaves is of old date.

[Footnote 131: Yerlik and Billig are old Turkish words, the former signifying 'writing'--the root is yer, Hungarian ir, Turkish yaz; the latter meaning 'mark,' in Hungarian bélyeg.]

{374}

The following list or sketch furnishes a view of the different functionaries, from the Emir downwards:--

Kette Sipahi

1. Atalik.

2. Divanbeghi (Secretary of State).

3. Pervanedji, the 'butterfly man,' as he is termed at Court, because he is sent about by the Emir in different directions, on important errands.

Orta Sipahi

4. Tokhsabay, properly Tughsahibi (one who has as a banner a Tugh or horse's tail).

5. Inag.

6. Miakhor (Constable).

Ashaghi Sipahi

7. Choragasi, properly Chehre agasi (the 'face-man'), so called because at the audience he stands facing the Emir.

8. Mirzabasbi (Principal Writer).

9. Yasaulbeghi and Kargaulbeghi.

10. Yüzbashi.

11. Pendjabashi.

12. Onbashi.

Besides these, we have still to mention the officers about the Emir's person and court. At their head stands the Kushbeghi, or Vizir, the Mehter, Desturkhandji (steward), and Zekiatchi (receiver of the customs). The latter, in his quality of finance minister, is also chief master of the Emir's household. Next come the Mehrem (chamberlains), whose number varies with circumstances. These are sent, upon extraordinary occasions, as commissioners into the provinces. Every subject, if not content with the decision of the Governor as to his right, can appeal to the Emir, whereupon a Mehrem is assigned to him, as attorney, who travels back with him to his province, examines the affair, and lays it before the Emir for his final decision. There are, besides, Odadji (door-keepers), Bakaul (provision-masters), and Selamagasi, {375} who on public processions return, instead of the Emir, the salutation 'Ve Aleïkum es selam.' These functions and offices exist only nominally under the present Emir, whose aversion to all display or pomp has made him leave many vacant.

The Political Division of the Khanat.

The political division of the Khanat, like that of Khiva, is based upon the number of its large cities, and Bokhara consists at present of the following districts, which we here prefer to classify according to their size and population:--1. Karaköl; 2. Bokhara; 3. Karshi; 4. Samarcand; 5. Kerki; 6. Hissar; 7. Miyankal, or Kermineh; 8. Kette Kurgan; 9. Chardjuy; 10. Djizzak; 11. Oratepe; 12. Shehri Sebz. The latter equals Samarcand in size, but, owing to its continual struggles with the Emir, cannot be considered as wholly subject to the Khanat.

Governors of the rank of Divanbeghi, or Pervanedjis, have allowed to them a fixed share in the revenue of the province under their administration, but in extraordinary emergencies they are obliged to forego the claim. Under the direct orders of each Governor there is a Tokhsaboy, a Mirzabashi, a Yasaulbeghi, and several Mirakhor and Chohragasi.

{376}

Army.

The standing army of the Khanat is stated to consist of 40,000 horsemen, but can be raised to 60,000. Of these troops Bokhara and Karshi are said to supply the greater proportion; the former are especially renowned for their bravery. Such is the account of their numbers current in Bokhara, but I have found it exaggerated; because the Emir, in his campaign against Khokand, where his army never exceeded 30,000 men, was forced to maintain an auxiliary force at a heavy expense--an expense which the stingy Mozaffar-ed-din never would have incurred, if the foregoing computation had been correct. The pay, only made in time of war, consists of 20 Tenghe (about 11*s.* 2*d.*) monthly, with which the horseman has to keep himself and horse. In addition to this, half the booty made belongs to the soldiery.

It is really singular that, with the great population subject to him, the prince sets no greater native force on foot; singular, also, that he takes no auxiliaries from the 50,000 Ersari who are tributary to him, but prefers applying to the Tekke, or even taking Sariks into his service, at a yearly expense of 4,000 Tilla.

Short Outline of the History of Bokhara.

Efrasiab, the great Turani warrior, and one of the greatest heroes of ancient Iran, is regarded as the founder of Bokhara. Extravagant fables form the basis of its earlier history. Of the accounts which they embody, we only accept the following fact, that the incursions of the Turkish hordes were from the oldest times the terror of those districts whose Persian population had separated themselves from their brethren in Iran so early as the epoch of the Pishdadian. The first thread of real history, properly so called, only begins at the epoch of the occupation by {377} the Arabs; and we can only regret that these daring adventurers have not transmitted to us more notices than those which we find scattered in the pages of Tarikhi Taberi and some other Arabian authorities. Islam did not so easily as in other countries strike its roots in Mavera-ül Nehr (the land between the Oxus and the Jaxartes), and the Arabs found, on their return to the different cities after an absence of any duration, that the work of proselytism had ever to be begun afresh. Up to the time of its conquest by Djenghis Khan (1225), Bokhara and Samarcand, as well as the city, at that time considerable, of Merv (Mervi Shah Djihan or Merv, 'king of the world'), Karshi (Nakhsheb), and Belkh (Um-ül Bilad, 'mother of cities'), were regarded as belonging to Persia, although the government of Khorasan, as it was then called, was the subject of an extraordinary firman of investiture from Bagdad. On the invasion of the Mongols, the Persian element was entirely supplanted, the Özbegs everywhere seized the reins of government, and Timour, the lame conqueror from Shehri Sebz (green city), was satisfied with nothing less than making Samarcand the capital of all Asia. The design perished with him, and the special history, properly so called, of Bokhara begins with the house of the Sheïbani, whose founder, Ebulkheir Khan, broke the power of the descendants of Timour in their hereditary dominions. A grandson of the last Sheïbani Mehemmed Khan enlarged the limits of Bokhara from Khodjend to Herat; and when he ventured to attack Meshed also, he was defeated by Shah Ismael, and perished in 916 (1510), in the battle. One of the ablest amongst his successors was Abdullah Khan (born 1544). {378} He conquered Bedakhshan, Herat, and Meshed afresh, and, from his efforts in favour of civilisation and commerce, deserves to be placed at the side of the great sovereign of Persia, Shah Abbas II. In his time the routes of Bokhara were provided with karavanserais and fine bridges, the ways through the deserts with cisterns for water; and the ruins of all his constructions of this description still bear his name. His son, Abdul Mumin Khan, 1004 (1595), was unable to retain long his seat on the throne; he was murdered; and after the invasion of the Kirghis chief Tököl, who laid all the country waste, fell even the last offspring of the house of Sheïbani.

In the long disturbance and civil war that ensued, the candidates who disputed the throne were especially Veli Mehemmed Khan (a remote collateral representative of the Sheïbani), and Baki Mehemmed Khan; and as the latter, 1025 (1616), fell in battle at Samarcand, the former founded his dynasty, which is said to have survived at the time of Ebul Feïz Khan, who, in 1740, was compelled to implore Nadir Shah for peace. In the period that succeeds, the sovereigns who have most distinguished themselves have been Imamkuli Khan, and Nazir Mehemmed Khan. By their liberal support of the Ishan class, they have contributed much to the religious fanaticism that exists in Bokhara, and which has reached there, as well as throughout Turkestan, such a point as was never before attained by Islam in any age or country. Ebul Feïz was treacherously murdered by his own Vizir Rehim Khan, as was also his son after him. Subsequently to the death of the murderer, who had governed under the title of Vizir, but with independent authority, Danial Beg, of the race of the Mangit, seized the reins of government. He was succeeded by the Emirs Shah Murad, Said Khan, and Nasrullah Khan.

{379}

As the history of the three last-mentioned sovereigns has been already handled by Malcolm, Burnes, and Khanikoff, and as we can adduce no fresh materials, we leave that period untouched. But we propose in a subsequent chapter to treat of the war waged by Bokhara with Khokand during the last three years.

{380}

CHAPTER XIX.

KHANAT OF KHOKAND.

INHABITANTS

DIVISION

KHOKAND
TASHKEND

KHODJEND

MERGOLAN

ENDIDJAN

HAZNETI
TURKESTANA

OOSH

POLITICAL
POSITION

RECENT WARS.

Khokand, or Fergana as the ancients style it, is bounded on the east by Chinese Tartary, on the west by Bokhara and the Jaxartes, on the north by the great horde of Nomads, and on the south by Karateghin and Bedakhshan. Its superficial extent we cannot positively affirm; but it is certainly larger than the territory of either Bokhara or Khiva. It is also better peopled than the latter Khanat.

Judging by the number of cities and other circumstances, Khokand, at the present day, may be said to contain more than three millions of inhabitants, consisting of the following races:-

(1) Özbegs form that part of the population having fixed habitations; and, as I remarked when I spoke of Khiva, they have a type quite distinct from the Özbegs either of that Khanat or of Bokhara. As the Özbegs have been for hundreds of years the dominant race in Turkestan, and adopted the institutions of Islam earlier than any other nomad people of these parts, the name itself has become invested with a certain prestige of {381} breeding and **bon ton**, so that the Kirghis, Kiptchak, and Kalmuk, from the moment that they settle in cities, generally abandon their several nationalities, and assume the denomination of Özbegs. In Khokand this has been also long the case, and it may be affirmed, without exaggeration, that half of those who so style themselves are to be regarded merely as a mixture of the nomad races just referred to.

Judging from his outside appearance, as he presents himself in his clumsy loose clothes, the Özbeg of Khokand seems a very helpless person. We had many opportunities of witnessing his unexampled cowardice, and had it not been for the protection of the nomads, his cities would have long fallen under the dominion of China, Russia, or Bokhara.

(2) Next to the Özbegs come the Tadjiks, who, although they may not constitute a more numerous, still form a more compact population here than in the Khanat of Bokhara, and, as is nowhere else the case, people entire villages and towns. Accordingly, the city of Khodjend, the villages Velekendaz and Kisakuz (near Khodjend) are exclusively inhabited by this primitive Persian race, and the important cities of Namengan, [Footnote 132] Endigan, and Mergolan, are said to have belonged to them more than four hundred years ago.

[Footnote 132: These three words respectively signify (1)Nemengan (originally Nemek kohn), salt mine; (2) Endekgan, from Endek, small; and (3) Murghinan, hen and bread. These etymologies I learnt from my friends; perhaps they are not to be received as absolutely correct, but their Persian origin is unquestionable.]

{382}

As far as their national character is concerned, the Tadjiks of Khokand are not much better than those of the same race in Bokhara. The sole circumstance I find noticeable is that their language, both in its grammatical forms and its vocabulary, is purer than that of the other Tadjiks. This is particularly the case in Khodjend, the inhabitants of which make use of a dialect that has retained many of the forms of expression observable in the writings of the oldest Persian poet Rudeki, by birth a Bokhariot. In the other cities of Khokand, particularly in those on the Chinese frontiers, Tadjiks are rarely met with.

(3) Kasaks form the majority in the Khanat. They lead a nomad life in the mountainous districts between the lake of Tchaganak and Tashkend, and pay to their prince the same amount of tribute as they do in Khiva to the Khan. Amongst the Kirghis of Khokand some are in affluent circumstances, possessing in Hazreti Turkestan, or in other places, houses, which, however, they do not themselves inhabit. In other respects, in spite of their superiority in number, the Kirghis have, owing to their want of bravery, little influence in the Khanat.

(4) Kirghis--or the Kirghis properly so called, a tribe of the great Kasak horde live in the southern part of the Khanat between Khokand and Sarik Köl, and from their warlike qualities are always made use of by the different factions to carry out their revolutionary projects. Their tents are said to be fifty thousand in number, consequently they are about as numerous as the Tekke Turkomans.

(5) The Kiptchak are, in my opinion, the primitive original Turkish race. Amongst all the branches of this great family, spread from Komul to as far as the Adriatic Sea, the Kiptchaks have remained most faithful in {383} physiognomy and character, language and customs, to their ancestral type. The name, the etymology of which has been clouded with fables by Rashideddin Tahibi, has little interest for the reader. There is said to have been formerly a mighty nation bearing the same designation, and the Kiptchaks of the present day, although counting only from five to six thousand tents, pretend that Deshti Kiptchak, [Footnote 133] as Turkestan is named in the documents of Oriental history, was conquered, and peopled by their ancestors.

Notwithstanding their small numbers, the Kiptchaks continue to exercise, even at the present day, the greatest influence upon political affairs in Khokand. They nominate the Khans, and sometimes even dethrone them; and often five hundred of their horsemen have taken possession of a city, without the Khan daring to resist them. I have not been able to detect, in the Turkish that they speak, a single Persian or Arabic word, and their dialect may be regarded as the best point of transition from the Mongolian language to that of the Djagatai. The same remark may be made respecting the type of their physiognomy as of their language; for these stand in a similar relation to those of the other races of Central Asia. In their slanting eyes, beardless chins, and prominent cheekbones, they resemble the Mongols, and are for the most part of small stature, but extraordinary agility. In bravery they stand, as was remarked before, superior to all nations of Central Asia, and form, incontestably, the truest specimen remaining to us of the immense hordes that revolutionised all Asia.

[Footnote 133: Deshti Kiptchak as far as the frontiers of Bolgar (in Russia?) is the denomination most in use.]

{384}
With respect to its divisions, the Khanat of Khokand falls into different districts, designated here, too, only by the names of the most remarkable cities. Its capital is Khokand, [Footnote 134] or Kokhandi Latif ('enchanting Khokand'), as it is termed by the natives. It lies in a beautiful valley, and is in circumference six times as large as Khiva, three times as Bokhara, and four times as Teheran. The southern portion of the city, in which the Khan has his palace, was not, until recently, surrounded by a wall. The northern part is open. The number of inhabitants and houses is proportionably small. The latter are surrounded by large orchards, so that one often requires a quarter of an hour to pass by ten or fifteen houses. As for the architecture, the Khokandi is in the habit of admitting the superiority of that of Bokhara; and from this circumstance one may easily form an idea of the architectural beauty of the city. Only four mosques are of stone, as is also a small portion of the extensive bazaar. In this they expose for sale, at low prices, exclusively Russian merchandise, and the native silk and woollen manufactures; besides which tasty articles in leather, saddles, whips, and equipments for riding, made in the capital, enjoy a high repute.

[Footnote 134: The word Khokand is said to be derived from Khob-kend, 'beautiful place' or 'village.']

After Khokand, Tashkend deserves to be mentioned. It is the first commercial town in the Khanat, and, as I heard on all sides, is at present the residence of many affluent merchants, having extensive trading relations with Orenburg and Kizildjar (Petropavlosk). Tashkend, which has the transit trade between Bokhara, Khokand, and Chinese Tartary, is one of the most {385} important cities of Central Asia; and at the same time the object towards which Russia is quietly striving, and from which her most advanced frontier (Kalè Rehim) is within a few days' journey. Once in possession of Tashkend, a place important also in a military point of view, Russia would find little difficulty in possessing herself of the Khanats of Bokhara and Khokand, for what might prove difficult for the Russian bayonet would be facilitated by intestine discord, the flames of which the Court of St. Petersburg never ceases to foment between the two Khanats.

After Tashkend the following are the most remarkable places: Khodjend, that has about 3,000 houses, many manufactories for Aladja (a sort of cotton stuff), eighteen Medresse, and twice that number of mosques; Mergolan, a large city, the principal city of Khokandi learning and the present residence of the Khodja Buzurk, chief of the order of the Makhdum Aazam. This dignitary refused his blessing to the present Emir of Bokhara on his triumphant entry into the city, and the latter did not venture, nor was he in fact able in any way to punish him. Endidjan, where the best Atresz (heavy substantial silks) in the Khanat are manufactured; Namengan, about which the Kiptchaks are located. The following also deserve mentioning:--Hazreti Turkestana with the grave there, in high repute, of Khodj Ahmed Jaszavi, the author of a book (Meshreb) [Footnote 135] upon morals and religion, which is even at the present day a favourite work both amongst the nomads and the settlers in Khokand; {386} Shehri Menzil and Djust, where the famous knives are manufactured which, after those of Hissar, fetch the highest price in Turkestan; Shehrikhan, a place where the best silk is produced; and Oosh, on the eastern frontier of the Khanat, called Takhti Suleiman, Suleiman's throne, which is visited yearly by a great number of pilgrims; the place of pilgrimage itself consists of a hill in the city of Oosh where, amidst the ruins of an old edifice built of large square stones and ornamented by columns, the visitor is first shown, not only a throne hewn out of marble, but the place where Adam, the first prophet (according to the teachings of Islam), tilled the ground. The latter fable was introduced very *apropos*, as the inventor wished to accustom the nomads to agriculture through the medium of their religion.

[Footnote 135: I was able to bring back with me to Europe a copy of this very original book written in Turkish, which I hope to publish with a translation.]

Anyhow, Oosh is not without interest to our antiquarians. The ruins themselves, and particularly the columns, as they were described to me, lead to the suspicion of a Grecian origin; and if we were searching for the most eastern colony founded by Alexander, we might readily suppose Oosh to be the very spot where the daring Macedonian marked by some monument the most easterly frontier of his gigantic empire. [Footnote 136]

[Footnote 136: Appian mentions (De Rebus Syriacis, lvii.) many cities founded by the Greeks and by Seleucus, amongst others one [Greek text], of which Pliny (vi. 16) seems to speak when he says: 'Ultra Sogdiana, oppidum Tarada, et in ultimis eorum finibus Alexandria ab Alexandro magno conditum.' That point or its vicinity seems to have marked the extreme limit of progress on that side of all the great conquerors of classical antiquity; for there, says Pliny, were altars placed by Hercules, Bacchus, Cyrus, Semiramis, and Alexander: 'Finis omnium eorum ductus ab illâ parte terrarum, includente flumine Jaxarte, quod Scythae Silin vocant.' And indeed with respect to the city 'Alexandreschata' Arrian (***Exped. Alexand***. 1. iv. c. i. 3, and c. iv. 10), agrees with Pliny, telling us that this great hero intended it as a barrier against the people on the further bank of the river, and colonised it with Macedonian veterans, Greek mercenaries, and such of the adjacent barbarians as were so disposed. This city was built on the banks of the Jaxartes, and most consider it to be the modern Khodjend. What if Oosh should have been the spot where stood the columns of Alexander (***Curtius***, vii. 6)? And yet the supposition that Alexander firmly possessed himself of any land beyond the Jaxartes is hardly consistent with the account of Arrian. Curtius (1. vii. 9) describes the remains of the altars of Bacchus as 'monuments consisting of stones arranged at numerous intervals, and eight lofty trees with their stems covered with ivy.']

{387}

With respect to the political position of the Khanat of Khokand, its independence dates as far back as that of Bokhara and Khiva. The present reigning family pretends to descend in a direct line from Djenghis Khan, which is very improbable, as his family was dethroned by Timour; and after Baber, the last descendant of Timour in Khokand, the Sheïbani, as well as other chieftains from the races Kiptchak and Kirghis, seized alternately the reins of government. The family at present on the throne, or perhaps, I should rather say, now disputing its claim to it with Bokhara, is of Kiptchak origin, and has only been 80 years at the head of affairs. The institutions in Khokand bear very slight traces of Arabian or Persian elements, and the Yaszao Djenghis (code of Djenghis) is the legal authority which they follow. Here also a singular ceremonial deserves notice. The Khan at his coronation is raised in the air upon a white felt, and shoots arrows to the north, south, east, and west. [Footnote 137]

[Footnote 137: It is singular that this custom exists even in the present day at the coronation of kings in Hungary. The king on the Hill of Coronation, on horseback, and invested with all the insignia of royalty, is required to brandish his sword respectively to the four points of the compass.]

{388}

A.

THE WAR BETWEEN BOKHARA AND KHOKAND IN THE TIME OF THE EMIR NASRULLAH.

The animosity between Khokand and Bokhara is of ancient date. After the Sheïbani family began to take the head of affairs in Turkestan, Khokand, with the exception of some cities still held by the Kiptchaks, was incorporated into the Khanat of Bokhara. It tore itself away again afterwards, and during its independence attached itself to its neighbours, Kashgar, Yarkend, and Khoten, then also still independent; but after these latter States had been themselves incorporated by the Emperor of China into his dominions, Khokand, as its enemies to the east seemed too powerful, thought itself bound to recommence its differences with Bokhara, and the war that was going on during our stay in Central Asia was only a continuation of the struggle that Mehemmed Ali, Khan of Khokand, and his rival the Emir Nasrullah, had begun.

Mehemmed Ali Khan is termed by the Khokandi their greatest monarch in recent times. Whilst this prince, by extending the frontiers and by advancing internal prosperity, had on the one hand contributed much to lend a certain splendour to his Khanat, yet on the other he had in the same degree stimulated the envious cupidity of the wicked Emir Nasrullah. {389} But what most displeased the latter was that the Khan should have formed a friendly alliance with Khiva, the principal enemy of Bokhara, and should have given a friendly reception to the Emir's own uncle and rival, who had fled to Khokand for safety. Others also assign as an additional cause the hospitality they had shown to Captain Conolly; but in any case abundant ground of dissension existed, and a rupture was regarded as inevitable.

In 1839, Mehemmed Ali, having defeated the Russians at Shehidan, [Footnote 138] considered a contest with the Emir as near at hand; and, himself preferring to be the assailant, marched towards the frontiers of Bokhara in the vicinity of Oratepe, and was already threatening Djizzak and Samarcand, when the Emir, after vainly trying intrigues, marched against him with a superior force of Özbeg horsemen and 300 of the newly-formed militia (Serbaz), under the conduct of their chief and organiser Abdul-Samed Khan. Upon this Mehemmed Ali held it prudent to retreat. Nasrullah laid siege to Oratepe, which, after three months, he took; but his treatment of the inhabitants made them his bitterest enemies: and scarcely had he returned to Bokhara, when, having a secret understanding with Mehemmed Ali, they fell upon the Bokhariot garrison and massacred all, soldiers as well as officers.

[Footnote 138: According to the account of this affair given by the Khokandi, a strong detachment of Cossacks, after having gone round Hazreti Turkestan from the right bank of the Jaxartes, had advanced towards Tashkend, and on their march were surprised and dispersed by the Khokandi with great loss.]

{390}

As soon as the intelligence of this event was conveyed to Nasrullah, he in the greatest haste, and in still greater anger, called together all his forces and marched against Oratepe. Mehemmed Ali again retreated, and was accompanied by a great part of the inhabitants who feared the incensed Emir; but this time escape was impossible: his enemy followed him step by step until he could retreat no further. In the battle which then took place at Khodjend, he was defeated, and the city became the prize of the conqueror. The Khan again retreated, but, finding himself still pursued and even his capital menaced, he sent a flag of truce to his victorious enemy. A peace was concluded at Kohne Badem, by which Mehemmed Ali bound himself to cede Khodjend with many other places. That such conditions were little calculated to lead to a sincere reconciliation is easily intelligible. The malicious Emir, intending still further to offend his vanquished enemy, named as governor of the conquered province the brother and rival of Mehemmed Ali, who had previously fled to Bokhara. But nevertheless he was here wrong in his calculation. The mother of the two Khokandi princes reconciled them, and before the Emir had got wind of what had occurred, Khodjend and the other cities united themselves again with Khokand, and he had now to measure himself with two enemies instead of one.

The fury of the Bokhariot tyrant knew no bounds, nor is it difficult to understand that his thirst for revenge would prompt him to make extraordinary armaments. In addition to his ordinary army, consisting of 30,000 horsemen and 1,000 Serbaz, he took into his pay 10,000 Turkomans of the Tekke and Salor tribes, and hurrying with forced marches towards {391} Khokand, he took Mehemmed Ali so by surprise that he was even obliged to fly from his own capital, but, overtaken and made prisoner near Mergolan, he was, with his brother and two sons, executed ten days afterwards in his own capital. [Footnote 139]After him most of his immediate partisans fell by the hands of the executioners, and their property was confiscated. The Emir returned to Bokhara laden with booty, having first left Ibrahim Bi, a Mervi by birth, with a garrison of 2,000 soldiers in the conquered city.

[Footnote 139: To excuse this act of shame, Nasrullah spread the report that Mehemmed Ali had married his own mother, and had consequently been punished by death.]

Three months had scarcely elapsed when the Kiptchaks, who had until now observed a neutrality, weary of the Bokhariots, took the city, made its garrison prisoners, and set on the throne Shir Ali Khan, son of Mehemmed Ali. [Footnote 140] In order to prevent being a second time surprised as before, the Khokandi now conceived the idea of surrounding a portion of the city, where the residence of the Khan was, with a wall; the plan {392} was soon carried out by the forced labour of the prisoners of war, who had formed part of the Emir's garrison. It was to be anticipated that the Emir would seek his revenge; no one, therefore, was surprised to see soon after this occurrence 15,000 Bokhariots, under the conduct of a Khokandi pretender to the throne, an old *protegé* of Nasrullah, make their appearance before Khokand. But even on the march Musselman Kul (so he was named) appeared to have reconciled himself with his countrymen; the gates of the city were soon opened to him; and although Nasrullah had sent him hither with the promise of making him Khan, his first step was to turn his arms against that prince, and, joining with his countrymen, to put to flight the Bokhariots who had escorted him thither.

[Footnote 140: The genealogy of the reigning house in Khokand, beginning with Mehemmed Ali, is as follows:--]

Mehemmed Ali (1841).	Shir Ali	---------------------------------	
(a) By first Wife. (b) By second Wife.			Mollah Khan.
--------------------------------- Sofi Beg.			
Sarimsak. Sultan Murad. Khudayar.			
Shah Murad. Several young children.			

The Emir, although now four times overreached, still would not give way, but again sent an army under the command of Shahrukh Khan, who already held the rank of commander-in-chief. [Footnote 141] But the latter did not advance beyond Oratepe, for the news that the Emir had fallen sick at Samarcand, and had subsequently returned to Bokhara, put an end to the whole campaign. A few days after the illness had attacked the prince, the world was freed by his death of one of the greatest of tyrants.

[Footnote 141: The infamous Abdul Samed Khan, the murderer of Conolly, Stoddart, and Naselli, had in the meantime been overtaken by a righteous punishment. The Emir, who had sent him to Shehri-Sebz, was at last convinced of his treason, and, not being able to reach him by forcible means, sought to employ artifice to get possession of his person. Abdul Samed evaded his fate a long time, but finally fell into the snare laid for him, and, aware of the presence of the executioner in the ante-room, he rent up his belly with his own poniard, to irritate by his death a master so like himself in character.]

{393}

I heard from good authority that the death of the Emir Nasrullah was solely owing to a paroxysm of rage at the constant ill success that attended his campaigns against Khokand, and the unprecedented obstinacy with which the city of Sheri-Sebz [Footnote 142] resisted, for although he had taken the field thirty times against it, and had been then besieging it six months, it was all without effect. Upon this occasion his adversary was a certain Veliname, whose sister he had married to obtain by the connection a faithful vassal in the brother of his wife. Now it happened that the news of the capture reached the Emir when on his deathbed; although half senseless, the tyrant ordered his rebel brother-in-law to be put to death with all his children. But as circumstances prevented him from feasting his eyes with that spectacle of blood, in the evening, a few hours before his death, he summoned to his presence his wife, the sister of Veliname; the unhappy woman, who had borne him two children, trembled, but the dying Emir was not softened--she was executed close to his couch, and the abominable tyrant breathed his last breath with his glazing eye fixed upon the gushing blood of the sister of his detested enemy.

[Footnote 142: Sheri-Sebz, previously named Kesh, is the native city of Timour, and renowned for the warlike character of its inhabitants.]

{394}

B.

THE WAR BETWEEN BOKHARA AND KHOKAND WAGED BY THE EMIR MOZAFFAR-ED-DIN.

In the meantime affairs in Khokand had taken a different turn. Musselman Kul had been put to death, and in his place Khudayar Khan had been raised to the 'white felt.' At his first accession, the latter showed great ardour and activity. He was engaged victoriously in several combats with the Russians, who were pressing on from the Jaxartes. Whilst he was thus occupied on the frontiers, Mollah Khan was nominated Khan in his capital; but as he had only inconsiderable forces to oppose to those of his rival, he thought it better to fly to Bokhara, and seek the aid of the Emir Mozaffar-ed-din for the recovery of his throne. This prince, immediately after the death of his father, besieged the city Sheri-Sebz, which, in spite of the vengeance of which it had already been the object, and the blood that had flowed there, was again in open revolt. He was before the walls of Tchiragtchi, a stronghold belonging to Sheri-Sebz, when the intelligence reached him that the governor of Oratepe, a native of Sheri Sebz, had allied himself with the Khokandi, and that Mollah Khan was already marching at their head against Djizzak.

The Emir Mozaffar-ed-din, urged on by his guest and *protegé*, Khudayar Khan, could not restrain himself. He abandoned his position before Sheri-Sebz, although he was pressing it hard, and rushed at the head of 15,000 men against Khokand, whose Khan (Mollah Khan) threatened, from his acknowledged ability, to prove a formidable antagonist. Adopting the unscrupulous policy of his father, Mozaffar-ed-din caused him to be assassinated in a conspiracy which the Emir had himself set on foot. In the great confusion that ensued, he next made himself master of the capital, and then set Khudayar at the head of the government, after the legitimate heir, Shahmurad, had fled to the Kiptchaks.

{395}

Khudayar Khan had scarcely exercised four months the royal functions so new to him, when the Kiptchak, with Shahmurad at their head, assailed, and forced him a second time to fly to Bokhara. The Emir, seeing himself so slighted and mocked at in his character as protector, hastily assembled all his forces to wreak his vengeance upon Khokand in some exemplary manner; and after having sent on before him Shahrukh Khan with 40,000 men, and Mehemmed Hasan Bey with thirty pieces of artillery, he hastened after them himself, escorted by a few hundred Tekke, with the fixed design not to return until he had reduced under his sceptre all as far as the frontiers of China.

In Khokand the firm intention of the young Emir was well known, so also was his cupidity; and he met, accordingly, with the most resolute resistance. The Ulemas pronounced the Emir, who was invading their country, to be Kafir (an unbeliever), and preached against him the Djihad (war of religion). All flew to arms, but in vain. The Emir attached to his own dominions not only Khokand, but all the territory as far as the Chinese frontiers. The greatest resistance which he met with was from the Kiptchaks, under their chieftain Alem Kul. These were attacked by the Turkomans; and the combat that ensued must have proved highly interesting, for two of the most savage of the primitive races of Tartary stood there face to face. After the death of the Alem Kul in the battle, his wife set herself at the head of the horde. The war was continued; but at last a peace was made with the {396} Emir. The Khanat, from which the conqueror had sent all the cannon, and immense stores of arms and treasures, to Bokhara, was divided into two parts. Khokand fell to the share of Sahmurad, the darling of the Kiptchaks, Khodjend to Khudayar Khan. Mozaffar-ed-din returned to his capital. I met him on his way thither on August 15, 1863.

Since this time, yet so recent, Khokand has probably experienced several other changes. Similar dissensions formerly occurred between Kashgar, Khoten, and Yarkend; and as those continued until all their territory was incorporated by China, so is it here probable that Russian occupation will soon put an end to these miserable civil wars.

{397}

CHAPTER XX.

CHINESE TARTARY.

APPROACH FROM WEST

ADMINISTRATION

INHABITANTS

CITIES.

The traveller who journeys on during twelve days in an easterly direction from Oosh, will reach the Chinese territory at the point where stands the city of Kashgar. The way thither leads him over a mountainous country, where the Kiptchaks are wandering about with their herds. No villages, it is said, ever existed in this district, except in the time of Djenghis Khan, and then only here and there. At the present day it is not possible to trace even their ruins. Places blackened by fire and heaps of stones indicate the spots used by travellers and karavans for their stations. Although the Kiptchaks are wild and warlike, they do not attack solitary travellers. Large karavans coming from China are bound to pay a moderate tribute, in other respects no one is disturbed. At the distance of a single day's journey from Kashgar one arrives at a blockhouse, the first post of the Chinese, occupied by 10 soldiers and an accountant. No one is permitted to proceed unless furnished with a pass drawn up by the Aksakal in Namengan, who acts as a sort of paid agent for the Chinese. After {398} the traveller has exhibited his pass, he is interrogated in detail respecting everything that he has seen and heard in foreign parts. The accountant makes two copies of the report, one is given to the nearest post to be compared with the answer to a similar interrogation there; this document is forwarded to the governor whom it concerns. According to the statements of Hadji Bilal and my other friends, in Chinese Tartary it is most advisable on such occasions to employ the formula 'Belmey-men' (I know not). [Footnote 143] It is not the practice to force a man to reply in detail, and indeed no one has power to compel him to do so, and the accountant himself prefers the shorter answer, which lightens the functions he has to perform.

[Footnote 143: The Chinese have besides a proverb quite in accordance with this rule, for they say:
'Bedjidu yikha le
Djidu shi kha-le.'

'I know not, is one word; I know, is ten words,' that is to say, 'Saying "I know not," you have said everything; but saying "I know," your interrogator will put more questions, and you will have necessarily more to say.']

Under the name of Chinese Tartary we generally understand that angular point of the Chinese Empire that stretches away to its west towards the central plateau of Asia, and which is bounded on the north by the great hordes of Kirghis, and in the south by Bedakhshan, Cashemir, and Thibet. The country from Hi to Köhne Turfan is said to have been subject to the sovereignty of China for several centuries; but it is only 150 years since Kashgar, Yarkend, Aksu, and Khoten have been {399} incorporated. These cities had been continually at war with one another, until several of the leading personages with the Yarkend chief, Ibrahim Bey, at their head, desirous to put an end to the dissensions, called in the Chinese, who, after long hesitating, assumed the sovereignty, and have governed these cities upon a different system from that in force in the other provinces of the Celestial Empire.

(a.) Administration.

As I heard from an authentic source (for as I have stated, my friend and informant, Hadji Bilal, was the chief priest of the governor), each of these provinces had two authorities, one Chinese and military, the other Tartar-Musselman and civil. Their chiefs are equal in rank, but the Tartar is so far subordinate to the Chinese that it is only through the latter that one can communicate with the supreme authority at Pekin. The Chinese officials inhabit the fortified part of the city, and consist of

1. Anban, who is distinguished by a ruby button on his cap, and by a peacock feather. His yearly salary is 36 Yambu, [Footnote 144] about £800. Under him are the

[Footnote 144: A Yambu is a massive piece of silver with two ears or handles, in form like our weights. In Bokhara it is taken for forty Tilla.]

2. Da-lui, secretaries, four in number, of whom the first has the superintendence of the correspondence, the second the administration of the expenditure, the third the penal code, and the fourth the police.

3. Dji-zo-tang, keeper of the archives.

{400}

The court of the supreme Chinese officer is denominated Ya-mun, and is accessible at all times to every one who wishes to prefer his complaint against any subordinate officer for maladministration, or in any other case of supposed failure of justice. And here we meet with a characteristic trait of Chinese government. Immediately before the gate of the court stands a colossal drum; this every plaintiff strikes once if his desire is to summon a secretary, whereas he must beat twice if his intention is to see the Anban himself. Whether it be day or night, summer or winter, the sound of distress must be attended to, or at least very rarely is it neglected. Even in Europe such a mode of summoning, I think, might be desirable in the case of many a drowsy functionary of justice.

The Tartar-Musselman corps of officials intrusted with the administration of justice in civil cases, with the collection of the taxes and customs, or other such functions touching their domestic concerns, and which do not devolve upon the Chinese authorities, are as follows:--

1. Vang, or Hakim, upon the same footing as the Anban, both as to rank and pay.

2. Ishnadji, or Cosnadji as he is designated by the Tartars, who has the control and inspection of the revenue.

3. Ishkaga (the word signifies doorkeeper), a sort of master of ceremonies, chamberlain, and chief intendant.

4. Shang Beghi, a kind of secretary, interpreter, and functionary, serving as medium between the Chinese and Musselman authorities.

{401}

5. Kazi Beg, the kadi or judge.

6. Örtengbeghi, postmaster, responsible for all the post-houses existing in his district. The system of posts in the country has much resemblance with the Persian Tchapar; the Government farms out certain roads, and it is the duty of the postmaster to take care that the farmers of them everywhere provide good horses for the public service. The distance from Kashgar to Komul is reckoned 40 stations, which the Örteng performs generally in 16, but on extraordinary emergencies, in 12 or even 10 days. From Komul to Pekin is counted 60 stations, which may also be performed in 15 days, consequently the whole distance from Kashgar to Pekin, which is a journey of 100 stations, is usually performed by the courier in about a month. [Footnote 145]

7. Badjghir, collector of customs.

[Footnote 145: It is remarkable that the postilions, almost always Kalmuks, are able to accomplish these sharp rides, consisting each of thirty days and thirty nights, several times each year. With us such a performance on horseback would be regarded as something extraordinary. The ride of Charles XII. from Demotika to Stralsund, and that of the Turkish courier, from Szigetvar (in Hungary, where Solyman the Magnificent died) to Kutahia in eight days, are famous in history. For the first see Voltaire's 'Life of Charles XII.,' and for the second 'Saadeddin Tadj et Tevarikh.']

(b.) Inhabitants.

The greater part of the population of Chinese Tartary, that is to say, of the four provinces, occupy fixed habitations, and busy themselves with agriculture. With respect to nationality, they style themselves Özbegs, but the first glance detects their Kalmuk {402} origin. Özbegs, in the sense understood in Bokhara and Khiva, have never existed in Chinese Tartary. When the word is used here, it signifies a mixed race that has sprung from the union of Kalmuks, who invaded the country from the north, and of Kirghis, with the original inhabitants of Persian race; and it deserves particular mention, that in places where the ancient Persian population was thicker (now it has entirely vanished), the Irani type is more dominant than in the contrary case. Next to these pseudo-Özbegs come the Kalmuks and the Chinese. The former are either military or lead the life of nomads; the latter, who occupy themselves with commerce and handicrafts, are merely to be found in the principal cities, and there only in insignificant numbers. Lastly, we must also name the Tungani or Tongheni, who are spread over the country from Ili to far beyond Komul. In nationality they are Chinese; in religion, however, Musselmans, and belonging all to the Shafeï sect. [Footnote 146] Tungani or Tongheni means, in the dialect of Chinese Tartary, converts (in Osmanli Turkish, dönme), and, as is confidently asserted, these Chinese, who count a million of souls, were converted in the time of Timour by an Arabian adventurer, who came with the above-named conqueror from Damascus to Central Asia, and roamed about in Chinese Tartary as a wonder-working saint. These Tungani distinguish themselves not only by their gross fanaticism, but by their hate for those of their countrymen who are not Musselmans; and in spite of their constituting the most advanced post of Islam on the side of the East, they nevertheless send every year a strong contingent of Hadjis to Mecca.

[Footnote 146: The Sunnites number four Mezheb (sects) amongst themselves, i.e. Hanifeï, Shafeï, Maleki, and Hambali. All four stand in equal estimation, and to give the preference to any one is regarded as a sin.]

{403}

As for the general character of the population, I found the Chinese Tartar honest, timid, and, to speak plainly, bordering upon stupidity; his relation to the inhabitants of the other cities in Central Asia is about the same as that of the Bokhariot to the Parisian or the Londoner. Extremely modest in their aspirations, my fellow-travellers have yet often delighted me by the enthusiastic terms which they used when they spoke of their poor homes. The splendour and lavish expenditure discernible in Roum and Persia, and even Bokhara, displease them; and although they are governed by a people differing from themselves in language and religion, still they prefer their own to the Musselman government in the three Khanats. But it would really seem as if they had no cause to be dissatisfied with the Chinese. Every one from the age of fifteen years upwards, with the exception of Khodjas (descendants of the Prophet) and Mollahs, pay to Government a yearly capitation tax of five Tenghe (three shillings). The soldiers [Footnote 147] are enlisted, but not by compulsion; and the Musselman regiments have besides the advantage of remaining unmixed and forming a single body, and, except in some little external points, [Footnote 148] are not in the slightest degree interfered with. {404} But the higher officials do not escape so easily; they are obliged to wear the dress prescribed to their rank, long moustaches, and pigtail; and, most dreadful of all, they must on holidays appear in the Pagodas, and perform a sort of homage before the unveiled portrait of the emperor, by touching the ground three times with the forehead. The Musselmans assert that their countrymen filling high offices hold on such occasions, concealed between their fingers, a small scrap of paper, with 'Mecca' written upon it, and that by this sleight of hand their genuflection becomes an act of veneration, not to the sovereign of the Celestial Empire, but to the holy city of the Arabian Prophet.

[Footnote 147: I am told, that there are at present in the four districts of Chinese Tartary about 120,000 soldiers, forming the garrisons of the four principal towns. One part of them, armed with spear and sword, is called ***Tchan-ping***, the others, who bear muskets, are known by the designation of ***Shüva***.]

[Footnote 148: Such, for instance, as (1) the robes being made to reach the kaees, and of blue linen, a costume regarded by the Musselmans with abhorrence as distinctive marks of the Chinese; (2) the permitting the moustache to grow, whereas Islam rigidly enjoins that the hair covering the upper lip shall be cut close.]

In social matters it is easy to conceive how two such discordant elements as the Chinese and Musselmans live together. Warm friendly relations seem, under the circumstances, impossible; but I fancy that I can discern, nevertheless, that no peculiar animosity exists between the two classes. The Chinese, who are the minority, never allow the Tartars to feel that they are rulers, and the authorities distinguish themselves by the greatest impartiality. As conversion to the dominant religion is singularly displeasing to the Chinese, it is not surprising that their efforts carefully tend not only to make the Musselmans exact in the performance of their religious duties, but to punish severely those who, in this respect, offend. Does a Musselman omit to pray, the Chinese are wont to say {405} to him, 'Behold how ungrateful thou art; we have some hundreds of gods, and, nevertheless, we satisfy them all. Thou pretendest to have but one God, and yet that one thou canst not content!' Even the Mollahs, as I often had occasion to observe, extol the conscientiousness of the Chinese officials, although they deal with their religion in the most unsparing terms. So, also, the Tartars are never tired of praising the art and cleverness of their rulers, and there is no end to their laudatory strains when they once begin to speak upon the subject of the power of the Djong Kafir (great unbelievers), i.e., the genuine Chinese. [Footnote 149]

[Footnote 149: The taking of Pekin by the Anglo-French army has not remained hidden from them. When I asked Hadji Bilal, how that was reconcilable with the boasted omnipotence of the Chinese, he observed that the Frenghis had employed cunning, and had begun by stupefying all the inhabitants of Pekin with opium, and then had naturally and easily made their way into the slumbering city.]

And is it not again most astonishing that all the followers of Islamism, including those who are farthest to the west, as well as those to be found on its most distant eastern boundaries, whether Turks, Arabs, Persians, Tartars, or Özbegs, ridicule and mock at their own faults just in the same degree as they praise and extol the virtues and merits of the nations not Mohammedan? This is the account I heard everywhere. They admit that taste for the arts, humanity, and unexampled love of justice are attributes of the Kafir (unbelievers), and yet you hear them, with their eyes glancing fire, using an expression like that attributed to a Frenchman, after the battle of Rosbach, 'God be praised that I am a Musselman! [Footnote 150]

[Footnote 150: 'El hamdü lilla ena Müszlim.']

{406}

(c.) Cities.

Amongst the cities, of which we give a list in the account of routes in Chinese Tartary, the most flourishing are Khoten and Yarkend. The largest are Turfan Ili and Komul; and the objects of most pious veneration, Aksu and Kashgar. In the last, which boasts 105 mosques (probably, however, only mud huts destined for prayer), and twelve Medresse, there is the venerated tomb of Hazreti Afak, the national saint of Chinese Tartary. Hazreti Afak means 'his highness the Horizon,' a phrase by which is meant to be expressed the infinity of the talents of the saint. His actual name was Khodja Sadik. He contributed much to form the religious character of the Tartars. It is said that Kashgar originally was more considerable, and that its population was more numerous than is the case at present. This decay is owing alone to the invasion of the Khokandi Khodja, who every year surprise the city, drive the Chinese into their fortifications, and remain there plundering and despoiling, until the besieged garrison have despatched their formal interrogatory to Pekin, and have obtained official permission to assume the offensive. The Khokandi Khodja, a troop of greedy adventurers, have thus for years been in the habit of plundering the city, and yet the Chinese never cease to be Chinese.

CHAPTER XXI.

COMMUNICATION OF CENTRAL ASIA WITH RUSSIA, PERSIA, AND INDIA

ROUTES IN THE THREE KHANATS AND CHINESE TARTARY.

Of all the foreign countries with which Central Asia is in relation, Russia is that with which it has the most active correspondence.

(*a*) From Khiva the karavans proceed to Astrakhan and Orenburg, whence many wealthy merchants reach Nishnei Novogorod, and even St. Petersburg.

(*b*) From Bokhara an uninterrupted correspondence--particularly active in summer--is kept up with Orenburg. This is the most usual journey, and is performed in from fifty to sixty days. Extraordinary circumstances may, indeed, render it longer or shorter; but except in times of unusual disturbances amongst the Kirghis, even the smallest karavans undertake it.

(*c*) From Tashkend karavans go to Orenburg and Kizil Djar (Petropavlosk). They reach the first in from fifty to sixty days, and the latter in from fifty to seventy. These are always the most numerous karavans, the district they traverse being the most dangerous.

(*d*) The route from Namengan and Aksu to Pulat (Semipalatinsk) is frequented for the most part by Khokandi karavans, which proceed under strong escort, and arrive at their destination in forty days. Solitary travellers may pass among the Kirghis unmolested. Of course, I mean when they travel like Dervishes. Many of my fellow-travellers had performed the journey to Mecca by Semipalatinsk, Orenburg, Kasan, and Constantinople.

Thus far I have spoken of the communications of Central Asia towards the north. Towards the south they are far less important. Khiva is accustomed to send one or two small karavans to Persia by the way of Astrabad and Deregöz. Bokhara shows somewhat more activity; but no karavans have passed by Merv to Meshed during the last two years, the Tekke having interrupted all communication. The most frequented route is by Herat, at which city the karavans separate, accordingly as they proceed to Persia or Afghanistan and India. The way by Karshi and Belkh to Kabul is only of secondary importance, because the difficulties of surmounting the Hindukush offer constant and serious obstacles, and during the last two years this route has not been much frequented.

Besides the above-named communication on a great scale, we must mention the slender thread of correspondence maintained by single pilgrims or beggars from the most hidden parts of Turkestan with the remotest parts of Asia. Nothing is more interesting than these vagabonds, who leave their native nests without a farthing in their pockets to journey for thousands of miles in countries of which they previously hardly know the names; and amongst nations entirely different from their own in physiognomy, {409} language, and customs. Without further consideration, a poor inhabitant of Central Asia, [Footnote 151] following the suggestions of one sole dream, betakes himself to Arabia, and even to the most westerly parts of the Turkish Empire. He has nothing to lose. He seeks to see the world, and so follows blindly his instinct. The world I say, but I mean his world, beginning with China, and ending with the limits of the Turkish Empire. As for Europe, he admits, indeed, that it may be beautiful, but he regards it as so filled with magic and diabolical arts that he would never venture thither, even though he held in his hand the surest thread to guide him on his way through so perilous a labyrinth.

[Footnote 151: I say poor, for the rich rarely submit to the toil and inconvenience of a pilgrimage; but they have an expedient, for they find deputies. Their representatives supplied with the necessary funds are sent on to Mecca, where in their prayers they substitute the name of the sender for their own, but the latter only so far profits that he has the honour after his decease of having engraved upon his tomb the affix to his name, 'Hadji.']

Experience convinced me that the farther we advance in Turkestan, the greater is the disposition to perform these annual pilgrimages and toilsome journeys. The number of the Hadjis proceeding yearly from Khiva is, on an average, from ten to fifteen; from Bokhara, thirty to forty; but from Khokand and Chinese Tartary, between seventy and eighty. If we add thereto the rage of the Persians for pilgrimages to the holy places in Meshed, Kerbela, Kom, and Mecca, it is impossible not to be surprised at the great zeal in favour of such ramblings still prevalent in Asia. The seed from which sprang the migration of its ancient races, continues still to {410} exist, and but for the civilisation of the West and its mighty influence, that press closely upon Asia on all sides, who knows what revolutions might not already have taken place!

THE ROUTES IN THE THREE KHANATS.

A.

Routes in the Khanat or Khiva and the adjacent Country.
1. *From Khiva to Gömüshtepe.*

(a) Ortayolu, the middle of the three routes indicated by me in the commencement of my work, and which I myself took, has the following stations, and can be traversed easily on horseback in fourteen or fifteen days.

1. Akyap.
2. Medemin.
3. Shor Göl (lake).
4. Kaplankir.
5. Dehli Ata.
6. Kahriman Ata.
7. Koymat Ata.
8. Yeti Siri.
9. Djenak.
10. Ulu Balkan.
11. Kitchig Balkan.
12. Kören Taghi (a mountain chain).
13. Kyzyl Takir.
14. Bogdayla.
15. Etrek.
16. Gömüshtepe.

(b) The route termed Tekke Yolu can be traversed on horseback in ten days, and is said to consist of the following stations:--

1. Medemin.
2. Döden.
3. Shahsenem.
4. Ortakuju.
5. Alty Kuyruk.
6. Chirlalar.
7. Chin Mohammed.
8. Sazlik.
9. Etrek.
10. Gömüshtepe.

{411}

This route seems infested by the Turkoman Alamans; the reason appears clear, because by the ordinary way they can go so rapidly over large tracts of land.

2. *From Khiva to Meshed.*

The routes are two: the one by Hezaresp and Deregöz southwards through the desert (the traveller can perform this journey on horseback in twelve days); the other way passes by Merv, and has the following principal stations or wells:--

1. Dari. [Footnote 152]
2. Sagri.
3. Nemekabad.
4. Shakshak.
5. Shur ken.
6. Akyap.
7. Merv.

[Footnote 152: Dari is reached on the first day from Khiva.]

3. From Khiva to Bokhara (a high road).

From	To	Farsz. Parasangs [2-4 miles]
Khiva	Khanka	6
Khanka	Shurakhan	5
Shurakhan	Ak Kamish	6
Ak Kamish	Töyeboyun	8
Töyeboyun	Tünüklü	6
Tünüklü	Utch udjak	10
Utch udjak	Karaköl	10
Karaköl	Bokhara	9
		60

{412}

4. From Khiva to Khokand.

There is a route through the desert without touching Bokhara. At Shurakhan, one leaves the Khanat of Khiva, and reaches Khodjend ordinarily in from ten to twelve days inclusive. The journey may, however, be shortened by turning off to Djizzak. This was the route taken by Conolly in company of a Khokandi prince, whom he had met in Khiva.

5. From Khiva to Kungrat and the Shore of the Aral Sea.

From	To	Tash or Farsz
Khiva	Yenghi Urgendj	4
Yenghi Urgendj	Görlen	6
Görlen	Yenghi Yap	3

From	To	Tash
Yenghi Yap	Khitai	3
Khitai	Manghit	4
Manghit	Kiptchak	1
Kiptchak	Kamli	2
Kamli	Khodja Ili	22 (desert)
Khodja Ili	Kungrat	4
Kungrat	Hekim Ata	4
Hekim Ata	Tchortan göl	5
Tchortan göl	Bozatav	10
Bozatav	Shore of the Sea	5

Making together 73 Tash, a distance which, when the way is not in bad condition, may be travelled in twelve stations.

6. *From Khiva to Kungrat, by Köhne.*

From	To	Tash or Farsz.
Khiva	Gazavat	3
Gazavats	Tashhau	7
Tashhaus	Köktcheg	2
Köktcheg	Kizil Takir	7
Kizil Takir	Porsu	6
Porsu	Köhne Urgendj	9

155

| Köhne Urgendj | Khodja Ili | 6 |

{413}
And thence to Kungrat, as already mentioned, there are four Tash, making together 44 Tash, a nearer way, consequently, than the one by Görlen, but less eligible and less frequented. First, it is not safe; and secondly, it is wearisome, on account of the desert and the route itself.

7. *From Khiva to Fitnek.*

From	To	Tash or Farsz.
Khiva	Sheikh Mukhtar	3
Sheikh Mukhtar	Bagat	3
Bagat	Ishantchepe	2
Ishantchepe	Hezaresp	2
Hezaresp	Fitnek	6
		16

Adding to this number the 73 already given in the sum of the distances in route marked (5), we see that the greatest distance traversed by the Oxus in the Khanat is not more than 89 Tash or Farszakhs.

{414}

B.

ROUTES IN THE KHANAT OF BOKHARA AND THE ADJACENT COUNTRY.

1. *From Bokhara to Herat.*

From	To	Tash or Farsz.
Bokhara	Khoshrobat	3
Khoshrobat	Tekender	5
Teke	Tche	5

nder		rtchi	
rtchi	Tche	Kara hindi	5
Kara hindi	Kara	Kerki	7
	Kerki	Zeid (Well)	8
	Zeid	Andk huy	10
huy	Andk	Batka k	5
k	Batka	May mene	8
mene	May	Kaisa r	4
r	Kaisa	Nari n	6
n	Nari	Chik ektu	6
ektu	Chik	Kalé Veli	6
Veli	Kalé	Murg ab	4
ab	Murg	Derb end	3
end	Derb	Kalè No 8	
No	Kalè	Sertc heshme	9
heshme	Sertc	Herat	
	Total		108

This distance can be travelled on horseback in from 20 to 25 days.

2. *From Bokhara to Merv.*

The traveller must here first go to Tchardjuy, from which city there are three different routes.

(*a*) By Rafatak. There is one well, and its distance is 45 Farszakhs.

{415}

(*b*) By Ütchhadji. Two wells, and distance 40 Farszakhs.
(*c*) By Yolkuyu. This is the route most to the east; the distance is 50 Farszakhs.

3. *From Bokhara to Samarcand (usual road).*

From	To	Farsz. Parasangs
Bokhara	Mezar	5
Mezar	Kermine R.	6
Kermine R.	Mir	6
Mir	Kette Kurgan	5
Kette Kurgan	Daul	6
Daul	Samarcand	4
		32

This journey is performed by two-wheeled loaded carts in six days. Mounted on a good horse, one may accomplish it in three: the couriers take but two days, but they travel night and day.

4. *From Samarcand to Kerki.*

From	To	Farsz.
Samarcand	Robati Haus	
Robati Haus	Nayman	
Nayman	Shur kuduk	
Shur kuduk	Karshi	
Karshi	Feizabad	
Feizabad	Seng	

bad sulak

sulak Seng i Kerk

2

{416}

5. *From Samarcand to Khokand by Khodjend.*

From	To	arsz.
Samarcand	Yenghi Kurgan	
Yenghi Kurgan	Djizzag	
Djizzag	Zamin	
Zamin	Djam	
Djam	Savat	
Savat	Oratepe	
Oratepe	Nau	
Nau	Khodjend	
Khodjend	Karaktchikum	
Karaktchikum	Mehrem	
Mehrem	Besharik	
Besharik	Khokand	

6

This journey takes eight days in a cart (two-wheeled), and may be much shortened by going straight from Oratepe to Mehrem, which requires only eight hours, so that there is a gain of six Tash

6. *From Samarcand to Tashkend and the Russian Frontiers.*

From	To	ash
Samarcand	Yenghi Kurgan	
Yenghi Kurgan	Djizzag	
Djizzag	Djinas	6
Djinas	Zenghi Ata	
Zenghi Ata	Tashkend	
		3

Five days' journey farther on from here is, as I learnt from the accounts of many different persons, the first Russian fort and post of the Cossacks.
{417}

ROUTES IN THE KHANAT OF KHOKAND.

1. *From Khokand to Oosh (a straight road).*

From	To	ash
Khokand	Karaultepe	
Karaultepe	Mergolan	
Mergolan	Sherikhan	
Sherikhan	Endigan	
Endigan	Oosh	
		9

160

The journey can be performed in two-wheeled carts in four days.

2. From Khokand to Oosh (by Namengan).

From	To
Khokand	Bibi Uveida
Bibi Uveida	Sehri Menzil
Sehri Menzil	Kirghis kurgan
Kirghis kurgan	Namengan
Namengan	Üsch kurgan
Üsch kurgan	Gömüshtepe
Gömüshtepe	Oosh

5

Besides these two principal roads, there is a mountainous route from Tashkend to Namengan; offering, however, many perilous places, which entail the necessity of much laborious exertion. Although the distance is only 45 miles, one requires ten days to {418} traverse it. It passes by the following places: Toy Tepe, Karakhitai Tilav, Koshrobat, Mollamir, Babatarkhan, Shehidan (where the Russians were defeated by Mehemmed Ali Khan), Kamishkurgan, Pnngan, Haremseray, Uygur, Pop, Seng, Djust, Törekurgan, Namengan.

D.

ROUTES IN CHINESE TARTARY.

The distance from **Kashgar** to **Yarkend** is reckoned 36 miles (Tash), journeyed over by karavans and carts in seven days. On the third day from Kashgar, the traveller reaches a place called Yenghi Hissar, which is occupied by a strong garrison of soldiers.

From **Kashgar** to **Aksu**, the distance is 70 miles; a karavan takes to perform it twelve days.

From **Aksu** to **Ushturban**, lying to the south, the traveller requires two days. Proceeding still farther to the east, we reach Komul in twenty-eight days, as follows:—

From	To	Days' Journey

Aksu	Bay	3
Bay	Saram	1
Saram	Kutcha	2
Kutcha	Shiar	2
Shiar	Bögür	4
Bögür	Kurli	3
Kurli	Kohne Turfan	8
Kohne Turfan	Komul	3
		26

Adding twelve days for the journey from Kashgar to Aksu, this makes, for the whole distance from the latter city, forty days.
{419}

CHAPTER XXII.

GENERAL VIEW OF AGRICULTURE, MANUFACTURES, AND TRADE.

AGRICULTURE

DIFFERENT KINDS OF HORSES

SHEEP

CAMELS

ASSES

MANUFACTURES

PRINCIPAL SEATS OF TRADE

COMMERCIAL ASCENDANCY OF RUSSIA IN CENTRAL ASIA.

(a.) Agriculture.

Taken altogether, it is incredible how fertile all the cultivable land is in these three Khanats, which rise like oases out of the monstrous deserts of Central Asia. In spite of the primitive system of culture adopted, fruit and corn are luxuriantly abundant, one might even say, in many places, superabundant. The excellence of the fruit in Khiva has been already mentioned; and although Bokhara and Khokand cannot be placed, in this respect, in the same rank with Khiva, the following produce of those Khanats deserve, nevertheless, mention, e.g., the grapes, of extraordinary excellence (of which there are ten kinds), the 'magnificent pomegranates,' and particularly the apricots, which are exported in immense quantities to Persia, Russia, and Afghanistan. Corn is met with everywhere in the three Khanats, and is of five kinds: wheat, barley, Djugheri (Holcus saccharatus), millet, (Tarik), and rice. The best wheat and Djugheri are {420} said to be found in Bokhara and Khiva, a genial soil; whereas Khokand is in high repute for millet. Barley is nowhere of very good quality, and is made use of, either alone or mixed with Djugheri, as fodder for horses.

In cattle-breeding the inhabitants of Turkestan concentrate their attention on three animals alone, namely, the horse, the sheep, and the camel.

The horse is regarded by the Central Asiatic as his *alter ego*. Different races are met with here, possessing too different qualities and excellences. Volumes might be written to show how it is reared, and what are its varieties; but this not being my province, I will confine myself to a few observations. As countless as the stocks and branches of the nomads themselves, so countless are the races and families of their horses. The following classification deserves to be noted:--

(1) The Turkoman horse: and here a main distinction exists between the Tekke and the Yomut breeds. The former, of which the favourite races are the Körogli and the Akhal, are distinguished by extraordinary height (sixteen to seventeen hands). They are slightly built, have handsome heads, majestic carriage, wonderful speed, but no bottom. The latter, those of the Yomuts, are smaller, finely formed, and unite speed with unparalleled endurance and strength. [Footnote 153] In general, the Turkoman horse is distinguished by a slender barrel, thin tail, handsome head and neck (it is a pity that the mane is cut off), {421} and a particularly fine and glossy coat; the latter quality is owing to its being kept covered, summer and winter, with several housings of felt. With respect to the value, a good Turkoman horse may be had at a price varying from one hundred to three hundred ducats, but never under thirty ducats.

[Footnote 153: I have seen many horses of this description which had carried each his Turkoman rider with a slave behind him in the saddle at a constant rapid gallop for thirty hours.]

(2) The Özbeg horse resembles the Yomut, but its form is more compact, and denotes more power; its neck short and thick, rather suited, like our hacks, for journeys than serviceable in war or Alamans.

(3) The Kasak horse, in a half wild state, small, with long hair, thick head, and heavy feet. He is seldom fed by hand, but is accustomed to seek himself his subsistence, summer and winter, in the pastures.

(4) The Khokandi sumpter or cart-horse is a cross between the Özbeg and the Kasak breeds, and is remarkable for its great strength. Of these four races, the genuine Turkoman horses have only been exported to Persia, and the Özbeg horses to Afghanistan and India.

The sheep is everywhere of the race with fat tails; the finest are met with in Bokhara. Its flesh is the best I have tasted in the East.

There are three kinds of camels, the one-humped and the two-humped, the latter called by us the Bactrian, and only met with amongst the Kirghis, and the Ner, of which we have already spoken when treating of Andkhuy.

Finally, I must not omit to mention the asses. The finest are those of Bokhara and Khiva. Of these the Hadjis export yearly many to Persia, Bagdad, Damascus, and Egypt.

{422}

(b.) Manufactures.

Two hundred years ago, when Turkey was less accessible to our European commerce than is the case at the present day, the native manufactures of Engürü (Angora), Broussa, Damascus, and Aleppo were certainly more active. Central Asia is even now far more remote from us than was Turkey in the times alluded to; our trade there is still very weakly represented--the consequence is that the greater part of the articles requisite for clothing or household purposes are the produce of native industry, of which we will give in this place a short account.

The principal seats of Central Asiatic manufactures are Bokhara, Karshi, Yenghi Ürgendj, Khokand, and Namengan. Out of these cities come the different stuffs, whether of cotton, silk, or linen, as well as the articles manufactured from leather, which supply the native demand. The principal and most widely-diffused material is the so-called Aladja, a stuff employed for the dresses of man and woman. In Khiva it is woven of cotton and raw silk, in Bokhara and Khokand of cotton alone. As there are no distinct tailors' shops, the manufacturer busies himself also with the scissors and the needle, so that a great part of the produce consists in ready-made clothes. When we were in Bokhara, the high prices of clothing were a general complaint. The following were those then current:--

{423}

[Prices in Tenghe]

Dresses	1st Class	2nd Class	3rd Class
Khivan	30	20	8
Bokhariot	20	12	8
Khokandi	12	8	5

Besides the Aladja, they fabricate stuffs of silk, woollen shawls for turbans, linen, for the most part very coarse and bad, and from the latter a sort of calico, with dark red figures, used as coverlets for bedding throughout Turkestan and Afghanistan.

In the manufacture of leather they are famous; they excel us in the preparation of shagreen ('Sagri' in the Tartar language), which, as is well known, is green, with little elevations like bladders. With the exception of Russia leather--which they import from that country, and employ in fashioning their water-skins--their coverings for the feet, and their harness and accoutrements for horses, are manufactured of native leather. Bokhara and Khokand produce these articles of the best quality. Khiva has only one kind of thick yellow leather, employed both for soles and upper leather. Of fine leather they prepare the Meskh (under-shoes like stockings); and of the coarser kinds, the Koush, or upper galoshes.

Paper manufactured in Bokhara and Samarcand enjoys a high repute throughout Turkestan and the adjoining countries. It is made of raw silk, is very smooth and thin, and well adapted for the Arabic{424} writing. Articles of iron and steel, as the raw material is wanting, are only weakly represented. The rifled guns from Hezaresp, the swords and knives from Hissar, Karshi, and Djust, are in great renown.

An important manufacture of Central Asia, which reaches us in Europe by way of Persia and Constantinople, is that of carpets, which is, however, the exclusive product of the industry and skill of the Turkoman women. Besides the beautifully pure colouring and solidity of the texture, what most surprises us is how these simple nomad women preserve so well the symmetry of the outline of figures, and even betray often a better taste than many manufacturers in Europe. One carpet gives work always for a number of girls and young women. An old woman places herself at their head as directress. She first traces, with points, the pattern of the figures in the sand. Glancing at this, she gives out the number of the different threads required to produce the desired figures. In the next place, the workers in felt demand notice, but the Kirghis women here distinguish themselves most.

(c.) *Trade.*

As it was before mentioned, in the chapter respecting the mode of communication, that Russia maintains the most extensive and regular relations with Central Asia, so also must it be stated that it is Russian trade which deserves to be styled the most ancient and the most considerable. It is a trade ever on the increase, and, at least in this field, remains without a rival. The extraordinary progress which it has made in these regions is best seen from the following most {425} authentic data. M. de Khanikoff [Footnote 154] states, in his work published in 1843, that every year a number of from five to six thousand camels is employed in the transport trade; that goods are imported into Russia from Central Asia to the value of from three to four millions of roubles; and that the export trade, which in 1828 amounted to £23,620, had risen, in 1840, to £65,675 16*s*. This estimate applies to the years from 1828 to 1845. Her Majesty's Secretary of Embassy at St. Petersburg, Mr. T. Saville Lumley, in his Report upon the Russian trade with Central Asia, drawn up with great industry and ability, informs us that, in the period from 1840 to 1850, the export trades rose to £1,014,237, and the import trade to £1,345,741. [Footnote 155]

[Footnote 154: See the English translation of his work by the Baron Bode, 1850. Madden.]

[Footnote 155: The Report above alluded to furnishes itself all the necessary details: we have appended them as given by Mr. Lumley himself.]

Table of the Trade between Russia and the Countries of Central Asia for the Decennial Period from 1840 to 1850.

EXPORTED. [Amounts in Pounds Sterling]

	Bokhara	Khiva	Kokan	Total
Specie, gold and silver	213,969	15,210	375	229,554
Copper	45,776	1,856	2,043	49,675
Iron, hardware, various metals	82,127	9,331	10,979	102,437
Cotton, manufactures in	156,707	58,915	7,559	223,181
Wool, ditto	50,467	25,869	1,976	78,312
Silk, ditto	10,550	4,799	71	15,420
Leather	81,543	37,921	4,069	123,533
Wooden ware	8,595	460	826	9,881
Dye stuffs and colours	48,635	17,904	693	67,232
Miscellaneous goods	85,416	27,567	2,031	115,012
Total	783,785	199,830	30,622	1,014,237

{426}
Even without these data, a glance alone at the bazaars of Bokhara, Khiva, and Karshi would suffice to convince us of the importance of this branch of Russian trade; and it is by no means any exaggeration to assert that there is no house, and even no tent, in all Central Asia where there is not some article of Russian manufacture. The most important trade is carried on in cast iron, for the most part consisting of kettles and water cans, and imported from South Siberia; but particularly from the manufactories in the Ural Mountains. In the trade with Bokhara, Tashkend, and Khiva alone, more than three thousand camels are employed in the transport of this one article. After cast iron come raw iron and brass, Russian cotton goods, cambric, muslins, tea-kettles, army and miscellaneous cutlery.

IMPORTED. [Amounts in Pounds Sterling]

	Bokhara	Khiva	Kokan	Kotal	Total
Cotton, raw and twist in	333,177	76,255	2,718	2,150	414
Cotton, manufactures in	498,622	88,960	14,180	11,802	60
Silk, raw, and manufactures in	17,443	3,088	160	1,691	20
Wool, manufactures in	428	1,322	52	802	1,
Madder	7,351	26,201	7	,559	33
Furs, lamb-skins	151,773	6,297	6,995	10,065	16
Precious stones and pearl	17,856	703	..	,559	18
Fruit, dried	27,784	2,147	16,883	1,814	44
Shawls, Cashmere	24,242	..	..	,242	24
Miscellaneous goods	19,664	4,452	3,941	,057	28
Total	1,096,380	209,425	39,936	345,741	1,

For further details see 'Reports by Her Majesty's Secretaries of Embassy and Legation on the Manufactures, Commerce, &.c.,' 1862, No. V. p. 313.

{427}

Cloth, from its high price, meets with few purchasers, and is seldom found. The before-named articles are transported from Bokhara and Karshi, not only to the remaining parts of Turkestan, but to Maymene and Herat, and even as far as Kandahar and Kabul. The latter two cities are, indeed, nearer to Peshawur and Karatchi; but give, nevertheless, the preference to the Russian merchandise, although far inferior to that of England.

The circumstance may seem surprising to the reader, and yet the reasons are simple. Orenburg is just as distant from Bokhara as Karatchi, which, being in the Indian territory of Great Britain, might form the outpost of English commerce. The route thence by Herat to Central Asia would be far more practicable and more convenient than that leading through the desert to Russia. That the English trade is here supplanted by the Russian is, in my humble opinion, to be ascribed to the following causes:--(1) The commercial relations of Russia with Tartary are now several centuries old, and in comparison with it that of England deserves to be denominated new, and it is notorious how tenaciously Orientals cling to old usages and customs. (2) The Russians occupying adjoining frontiers, in matters affecting the taste and requisitions of the Central Asiatics, are more experienced than the English manufacturers of Birmingham, Manchester, and Glasgow, &c., an evil only to be remedied by European travellers being able to move about more freely in these regions than is the case at the present day, when journeys, not only in Bokhara, {428} but even in Afghanistan, are attended by so much risk and peril. (3) The

Herat route, in spite of its possessing every element of convenience, has very much to deter foreign merchants, in consequence of the organised system of what may be styled bandit governments, as may be seen from what was before said upon the subject. [Footnote 156]

[Footnote 156: See Chapter XIV.]

Besides these commercial relations with Russia, Turkestan maintains also others, almost uninterruptedly, by the way of Herat with Persia, whither it sends lambs' wool, dried fruit, materials for red colouring, and certain native stuffs, receiving in exchange a great quantity of opium [Footnote 157] from Meshed, some English wares through the house of Ralli & Company, sugar and cutlery. There is a route from Meshed to Bokhara which can be performed in ten days, but the karavans are forced to take the circuitous way by Herat, which requires thrice as much time. From Kabul is exported to Bokhara a sort of cotton shawl, with blue and white stripes, called by the Tartars Pota, and by the Afghans Lunghi. It is used universally for summer turbans, and looks like an English manufacture, which may perhaps be imported by way of Peshawar; it is the only article having a good sale, because in accordance with the national taste. The Kabuli besides bring indigo and different kinds of spices, receiving in return Russian calicoes, tea, and paper. {429}

[Footnote 157: Opium, called here Teryak, is prepared in the south-eastern part of Persia as follows:--The head of the poppy has incisions made in it lengthways on three of its sides at a fixed time in the evening, and when only half ripe. The next morning after it has been so cut a dew-like substance shows itself at the place; this must be removed before sunrise, and, after having been boiled, the resulting product is the Teryak. It is singular that from the three places where the poppy has been cut issue substances of different quality, and of these that in the middle is most esteemed.]

With China there is only an insignificant trade in tea and porcelain; but these articles are quite different from those seen in Europe. The Chinese seldom set foot over the frontier, the communication here being almost entirely kept up by Kalmucks and Musselmans.

Lastly, let me not omit to allude to the trade carried on in Persia, India, Arabia, and Turkey, by the Hadjis. The reader may think that I am jesting; but still my experience justifies me in saying that this also merits the name of commercial transaction. The fifty or sixty Hadjis who came with me from Central Asia to Herat transported with them about forty dozens of silk handkerchiefs from Bokhara, about two thousand knives, thirty pieces of silk stuff from Namengan, a large quantity of Khokandi Dappi (caps upon which the turban is wound), &c. These were the Hadjis upon one route only. As for the imports, account must also be held of the Hadjis; for it is very easy to understand that the largest part of the European cutlery that finds its way to Central Asia has been introduced by them.

{430}

CHAPTER XXIII.

INTERNAL AND EXTERNAL POLITICAL RELATIONS OF CENTRAL ASIA.

INTERNAL RELATIONS BETWEEN BOKHARA, KHIVA, AND KHOKAND

EXTERNAL RELATIONS WITH TURKEY, PERSIA, CHINA, AND RUSSIA.

(a.) *Internal Relations.*

From what I have said in the previous pages upon the subject of the recent history of Khiva and Khokand, one may form a tolerably good idea of the terms upon which the different Khanats live with each other. I will, nevertheless, here collect a few facts to render it easier to appreciate the whole situation.

Let us begin with Bokhara. This Khanat, which, even previously to the introduction of Islamism, played a capital part, has, notwithstanding all the revolutions that have since occurred, always preserved its superiority, and it is regarded at the present day as the cradle of the civilisation of Central Asia. Khokand and Khiva, as well as the other small Khanats to the south, and even Afghanistan itself, have never ceased to recognise its spiritual supremacy. They praise and extol the Mollahs as well as the Islamite learning; of the 'noble Bokhara;' but their love of it extends only thus far, for all attempts made by the Emirs of {431} Bokhara to make use of their spiritual influence to increase their political power have failed of success, not only in the Khanats but even in the respective cities. Near-sighted politicians might infer, from the wars carried on by the Emir Nasrullah with Khiva and Khokand, that Bokhara, from apprehension of a Russian invasion, is disposed to organise an alliance by means gentle or foul. But this is not the case. Bokhara had never any such plans. The campaigns of the Emir are but predatory expeditions; and I am firmly convinced that should Russia proceed actively to carry out her designs on Central Asia, the three Khanats, so far from giving each other any mutual support in the moment of peril, would by their dissensions furnish the common enemy with the very best arms against themselves. Khiva and Khokand are then to be regarded as the constant enemies of Bokhara: still Bokhara does not look for any serious danger in those quarters, and the only rival that she really fears in Central Asia is one that is day by day becoming more formidable to her--Afghanistan.

That this fear reached its highest point during the victorious march of Dost Mohammed Khan towards the Oxus, need scarcely be mentioned. Emir Nasrullah was well aware that he should never be forgiven by the aged Afghan for his infamous jest played upon him, or rather his son, when the latter sought his hospitality in Bokhara; [Footnote 158] and as it was affirmed that Dost Mohammed had been reconciled with the English, and had become even an English mercenary, the apprehension of the Emir was still further increased by the {432} suspicion that he was but a tool in the hands of the English to avenge the bloody deaths of Conolly and Stoddart. Dark, indeed, must the pictures have been of the future destiny of his Khanat, that the Tartar tyrant carried with him into his grave. Not less was the apprehension entertained by his son and successor, the reigning Emir, on his accession. Mozaffar-ed-din was in Khokand when the intelligence reached him of the death of Dost Mohammed. The messenger received a present of 1000 Tenghe; the very same day a festival was improvised, and in the evening the Emir, to complete the number of his legal wives, took to his bed his fourth spouse, the youngest daughter of Khudayar Khan. The great dread has, indeed, passed away, but a feeling of 'respect' continues still to exist; for in Bokhara it is very well known that the Afghans, as fruit of the alliance with England, can now dispose of some thousands of well-drilled regular troops.

[Footnote 158: See Ferrier's 'History of the Afghans,' p. 336.]

Conscious of the superiority of the Afghans, and its own inability to cope with them, it is the policy of Bokhara to do them as much harm as possible by their intrigues. As the Afghans have allied themselves with England it is not difficult to decry them throughout Turkestan as apostates from Islam, and consequently during the last few years the commercial intercourse with Kabul has much diminished. As before mentioned, the Tekke and Salor stand constantly in the pay of Bokhara. At the siege of Herat it was a matter of great surprise to the aged Dost that, in spite of all the presents which he made to them, the Turkomans continued to molest him, and to carry off prisoners even from his own army. He had quite forgotten his real enemies--the gold pieces of Bokhara; for the sympathies of the Turkomans are ever with those that pay best. Thus far of the internal policy of Bokhara.

{433}

Khiva has been much enfeebled by the continual wars it has had to maintain with its own tributaries--who are ever ready to renew the contest--the Yomuts, Tchaudors, and Kasaks. The superiority of numbers is on the side of Bokhara; and if the Emir has hitherto been unable to conquer Khiva, the sole cause is the bravery of the Özbeg population. Allahkuli was, as I heard, the first who sent an ambassador to Bokhara and Khokand (probably it was at the suggestion of Conolly), in order to organise a system of mutual aid and defensive alliance against that power of Russia which was ever on the increase. Not only did Bokhara decline to enter into such alliance, but it even evinced a disposition to enter into relations with Russia. Khokand, on the other hand, as well as Shehri Sebz, and Hissar (cities which were then at war with the Emir), declared their readiness to adhere to the proposition of Khiva. But this union never assumed any other form but that of a wish, never was carried into effect; and how difficult its realisation would be is best shown by an ancient Arab proverb, adopted by the Central Asiatics as descriptive of their own national character, and which is to the following effect: 'In Roum are blessings, in Damascus beneficence, in Bagdad science; but in Turkestan nought but rancour and animosity.' [Footnote 159]

[Footnote 159: 'El bereket fi Rum el muruvet fi Sham el ilm fi Bagdad, el togz ve adavet fi Mavera ül-nehr.']

{434}

Khokand, owing to the continual dissensions between the Kiptchaks, Kirghis, and Kasaks, is a prey to the same evil as Khiva. When we add to this the unexampled cowardice of its Özbeg inhabitants, it will no longer appear surprising if, in spite of its having the greatest population and the most extensive territory of the three Khanats, it has, nevertheless, been continually conquered by Bokhara.

(b.) External Relations.

In its political relations with foreign countries, Central Asia, comes only in contact with Turkey, Persia, China, and Russia.

The Sultan of Constantinople is regarded as Chief of Religion and Khalif, and as it was the practice in the middle ages for the three Khanats of Turkestan to receive, as badges of investiture from the Khalif of Bagdad, a sort of court office, this old system of etiquette has not been abandoned even at the present day; and the princes, on their accession to the throne, are wont still to solicit, through the medium of an extraordinary embassy to Stamboul, these honorary distinctions. The Khan of Khiva assumes his rank as Cupbearer, the Emir of Bokhara as Reis (guardian of religion), and the Khan of Khokand as Constable. These courtly functions have always been in high estimation, and I have been informed that the different functionaries fulfil formally once every year the corresponding duties. But the bond that unites them with Constantinople goes thus far, and no farther. The Sultans cannot exercise any political influence upon the three Khanats. The inhabitants of Central Asia, indeed, are in the habit of associating with the word Roum (as Turkey is here called) all the power and splendour of ancient Rome, {435} with which, in the popular opinion, it is identified; but the princes seem to have seen through this illusion, nor would they be disposed to recognise the paramount grandeur of the Sultan unless the Porte associated its 'Firman of Investiture,' or its 'Licences to Pray,' with the transmission of some hundreds or thousands of piastres. In Khiva and Khokand these Firmans from Constantinople continue to be read with some demonstration of reverence and respect. The former Khanat was represented in Constantinople during a period of ten years, by Shükrullah Bay; the latter, during the reign of Mollah Khan, had only four years ago an ambassador, Mirza Djan, at the court of the Sultan. These envoys were, in accordance with ancient usages, sometimes maintained for long periods of years at the cost of the State, a charge not altogether convenient as far as its budget for foreign affairs was concerned, but nevertheless altogether essential and necessary to the pretension to a spiritual superiority in Asia.

The Ottoman Empire could only have gained effectual political influence in these remote regions of the East when it was roused from its slumbering Oriental existence before the time of Peter the Great. In its character of Turkish dynasty, the house of Osman might, out of the different kindred elements with which it is connected by the bond of common language, religion, and history, have founded an empire extending from the shore of the Adriatic far into China, an empire mightier than that which the great Romanoff was obliged to employ not only force but cunning to put together, out of the most discordant and heterogeneous materials. {436} Anatolians, Azerbaydjanes, Turkomans, Özbegs, Kirghis, and Tartars are the respective members out of which a mighty Turkish Colossus might have arisen, certainly better capable of measuring itself with its greater northern competitor than Turkey such as we see it in the present days.

With *Persia*, its nearest neighbour, Khiva and Bokhara interchange ambassadors but rarely. The fact that Persia avows the principles of the Shiite sect, forms in itself just such a wall of separation between these two fanatical nations as Protestantism created between the two great classes of Christians in Europe three centuries ago. To this feeling of religious animosity let us add, also, the traditional enmity between the Iranian and Turanian races that has become matter of history, and we may then easily form an idea of the gulf that separates the sympathies of nations that nature has made inhabitants of adjoining countries. Persia, which, according to the natural course of events, should form the channel to convey to Turkestan the benefits of modern civilisation, is far from producing there even the slightest effect. Powerless to defend even her own frontiers from the Turkomans, the disgraceful defeat she sustained, as before mentioned, at Merv, in an expedition directed, in fact, against Bokhara, has utterly destroyed her prestige. Her power is the object of very little apprehension in the three Khanats, for the Tartars affirm that God gave the Persians head (understanding) and eyes, but no heart (courage).

{437}

With respect to *China*, its political relations with Central Asia are so rare and insignificant, that they scarcely merit any mention. Once, perhaps, in a century a correspondence takes place. The Emirs are in the habit of sending occasionally envoys to Kashgar, but the Chinese, on their side, never venture so far into Turkestan as Bokhara. With Khokand negotiations take place more frequently, but it sends only functionaries of inferior rank to the Musselman barbarians.

With *Russia* political relations are upon a very different footing. Having been for centuries in possession of the countries that border upon the deserts of Turkestan on the north, an extensive commercial intercourse has rendered Russia more observant of what is going on in the three Khanats than their other neighbours, and has caused a series of efforts of which the only possible termination seems to be their complete occupation. The very obstacles which nature has interposed have rendered, indeed, the progress of Russia slow, but perhaps her progress is only on that account the more certain. The three Khanats are the only members now wanting to that immense Tartar kingdom that Ivan Vasilyevitch (1462-1505) imagined, and which he began actually to incorporate with his Russian dominions, and which, since the time of Peter the Great, has been the earnest though silent object of his successors.

In the Khanats themselves this Russian policy has not passed entirely unnoticed. Princes and people are well aware of the danger that threatens them, and it is only Oriental indifference and religious enthusiasm that lull them in the fond sleep of security. {438} The majority of the Central Asiatics with whom I conversed upon this subject, contented themselves by observing that Turkestan has two strong defences: (1) the great number of saints who repose in its territory, under the constant protection of the 'noble Bokhara;' (2) the immense deserts by which it is surrounded. Few men, and these only merchants, who have resided long in Russia, would regard a change in their government with indifference, for although they have the same detestation for everything that is not Mohammedan, yet, at the same time, they never cease to extol the love of justice and the spirit of order that distinguish the 'Unbelievers.'

{439}

CHAPTER XXIV.

THE RIVALRY OF THE RUSSIANS AND ENGLISH IN CENTRAL ASIA.

ATTITUDE OF RUSSIA AND ENGLAND TOWARDS CENTRAL ASIA

PROGRESS OF RUSSIA ON THE JAXARTES.

Rivalry between England and Russia in Central Asia I heard in England, on my return, affirmed to be an absurdity. 'Let us,' it was said, 'hear no more of a question so long ago worn out and out of fashion. The tribes of Turkestan are wild, rude, and barbarous; and it is a matter upon which we congratulate ourselves, if Russia takes upon herself the onerous and meritorious task of civilisation in those regions. England has not the slightest cause to watch such a policy with envy or jealousy.'

Full of horror at the scenes of cruelty witnessed by me in Turkestan, of which I have endeavoured to give a faint sketch in the preceding pages, I long argued over the question with myself, whether these political views which men sought to instill into me were really in every respect well founded. It is clear, and, indeed, has long been so, to my mind, that Christian civilisation, incontestably the noblest and most glorious attribute that ever graced human society, would be a benefit to Central Asia. The part, however, of {440} the question that has a political bearing I could not so easily dispose of; for although I regard the subject in all its different points of view, and drive my conjectures ever so far, I can never entirely realise the idea that England can behold with indifference any approach of Russia to her Indian dominions.

The epoch of political Utopias is past. We are far from being so inspired with a Russophobia as to regard the time as at hand when the Russian Cossack and the English Sepoy shall knock their noses together while acting as sentinels upon their respective frontiers. The drama of a collision of the two great colossi in Central Asia, which political dreamers imagined years ago, continues still far from actual performance. The question moves, it is true, slowly, but still always in a forward direction. Let me, following the natural course of events, without undue warmth endeavour to acquaint the reader with the motives that influence me when I disapprove of the indifference of the English to the Russian policy in Central Asia.

In the first place, let us enquire whether Russia is really pressing on towards the south; and if so, what, up to the present moment, has been the extent of her actual advance. Until twenty-five years ago, very little attention had been devoted to Russian policy in Central Asia. The occupation of Afghanistan by the English, and the Russo-Persian alliance and expedition against Khiva, were the causes that first led to the subject of Turkestan being touched upon in the diplomatic correspondence between the cabinets of St. Petersburg and London. Since that time a tolerable calm has ensued. England, discouraged by {441} the failure of her plans, withdrew at once, but Russia still keeps silently advancing, and essential changes have taken place with respect to her frontiers on the side of Turkestan. On the western part of Central Asia--for instance, on the Sea of Aral and its shores--Russian influence has considerably increased. With the exception of the mouth of the Oxus, the entire west of the Aral Sea is recognised Russian territory. Upon that sea itself there are, at this day, three steamers to which the Khan of Khiva has given permission to advance as far as Kungrat. [Footnote 160] It is given out that they are there to protect their fisheries; but they may probably have another destination, and every one in Khiva knows that the recent revolutions in Kungrat, as well as other frequent skirmishes between Kasaks and Özbegs, have a certain connection with these fishing boats.

But these are only secondary plans. The real line of operations is rather to be sought along the left bank of the Jaxartes. Here we find the Russian outposts supported by an uninterrupted chain of forts and walls, pushed on as far as Kale Rehim, distant thirty-two miles from Tashkend, which city may, as I have remarked, be regarded as a key to all conquests in Central Asia. This route, which traverses fewer deserts than any other, is also in different respects {442} well chosen. An army would be here exposed, indeed, to more surprises; but these can be resisted more easily than the fury of the elements. On the eastern frontiers of Khokand also, beyond Namengan, the Russians continue to move nearer and nearer; and in the time of Khudayar Khan many collisions had already taken place there between the Khokandi and the Russians.

[Footnote 160: That the Russian vessels do not pass higher up the Oxus is alone attributable to the numerous sandbanks in that river, which rapidly shift their places. I am astonished that Barnes expresses himself so lightly respecting its navigability. Boatmen who have passed all their lives on the Oxus assured me that the sandbanks change position so often that the experience and observation of one day are useless for the day that follows.]

The continued progress of the Russian designs in Central Asia is then beyond all doubt. As I before said, the interests of civilisation make us wish the most entire success to the Russian arms; but still the remote consequences of an acquisition once made suggest a highly important and complicated enquiry. The question whether Russia will content herself even with Bokhara, or will allow the Oxus to become the final boundary of her influence and of her designs, is difficult to answer. Without plunging into any deep considerations of policy, I may remark that it seems very probable that the court of St. Petersburg, in return for her persevering policy of sacrifices pursued across deserts for years and years, at great expense and labour, will seek some richer compensation than is to be found in the oases of Turkestan. I should like, indeed, to see the politician who would venture to affirm that Russia, once in possession of Turkestan, would be able to withstand the temptation of advancing, either personally or by her representatives, into Afghanistan and Northern India, where political intrigues are said to find always a fruitful soil. At the time when the Russian columns, under the orders of Peroffsky, threw their ominous shadow from the west shore of the Aral Sea as far as Kabul--at the {443} time when the spectre of Vitkovitsh [Footnote 161] appeared in that city and in Kandahar, the possibility of such complications as those alluded to was foreseen. And cannot that which has once occurred, when the necessity arises, occur a second time? [Footnote 162]

[Footnote 161: This was the name of the Russian agent sent by the court of St. Petersburg to Afghanistan in 1838, with large sums of money to be employed in intrigues against England.]

[Footnote 162: Whilst I write the above, a St. Petersburg correspondent of the *Daily Telegraph* (10th October 1864) sends the intelligence that the Russians have already taken Tashkend. The authenticity of the statement may perhaps be doubted, but that the Russians are in movement in that quarter is certain.]

Without, therefore, lending to the question the foul colouring of envy or jealousy, I consider myself justified in disapproving of England's indifference to the plans of Russia in Central Asia. Such is my humble opinion; but whether the British Lion is to come in direct hostile collision with the Russian Bear in those regions, or in brotherly fashion they are to share and share alike, is a question which, in accordance with the precept, 'Ne sutor ultra crepidam,' I in my character of a Dervish, devoted to philological studies, will not venture nearer to approach.

LONDON

PRINTED BY SPOTTISWOODE AND CO

NEW-STREET SQUARE

Albemarle Street, London,
November, 1863.

MR. MURRAY'S

GENERAL LIST OF WORKS.

ALBERT (Prince).
THE PRINCIPAL SPEECHES AND ADDRESSES of H.R.H. THE PRINCE CONSORT; with an Introduction giving some Outlines of his Character. Portrait. 8vo. 10*s*. 6*d*.

ABBOTT'S (Rev. J.)
Philip Musgrave; or, Memoirs of a Church of England Missionary in the North American Colonies. Post 8vo. 2*s*.

ABERCROMBIE'S (John)
Enquiries concerning the Intellectual Powers and the Investigation of Truth. 16th *Edition*. Fcap. 8vo. 6*s*. 6*d*.

Philosophy of the Moral Feelings. 12*th Edition.* Fcap. 8vo. 4*s*.

ACLAND'S (Rev. Charles)
Popular Account of the Manners and Customs of India. Post 8vo. 2*s*.

AESOP'S FABLES.
A New Translation. With Historical Preface. By Rev. Thomas James. With 100 Woodcuts, by Tenniel and Wolf. 50*th Thousand*. Post 8vo. 2*s*. 6*d*.

AGRICULTURAL (The) Journal.
Of the Royal Agricultural Society of England. 8vo. *Published half-yearly.*

AIDS TO FAITH:
a Series of Essays on, By various Writers. Edited by William Thomson, D.D., Lord Archbishop of York. 8vo. 9*s*.

CONTENTS.

Rev. H. L. Mansel--*On Miracles*.

Bishop Fitzgerald--*Christian Evidences.*

Rev. Dr. McCaul--*On Prophecy.*

Rev. F. C. Cook.--*Ideology and Subscription.*

Rev. Dr. McCaul--*Mosaic Record of Creation.*

Rev. George Rawlinson--*The Pentateuch.*

Archbishop Thomson--*Doctrine of the Atonement.*

Rev. Harold Browne--*On Inspiration.*

Bishop Ellicott--*Scripture and its Interpretation.*

AMBER-WITCH (The).
The most interesting Trial for Witchcraft ever known. Translated from the German by Lady Duff Gordon. Post 8vo. 2*s*.

ARMY LIST (MONTHLY)
Published by Authority. Fcap. 8vo. 1*s*. 6*d*.

ARTHUR'S (LITTLE)
History of England. By Lady Callcott. 120*th Thousand*. With 20 Woodcuts. Fcap. 8vo. 2*s*. 6*d*.

ATKINSON'S (Mrs.)
Recollections of Tartar Steppes and their Inhabitants. With Illustrations. Post 8vo. 12*s*.

AUNT IDA'S Walks and Talks;
a Story Book for Children, By a Lady. Woodcuts. 16mo. 5*s.*
AUSTIN'S (John)
Lectures on Jurisprudence; or, the Philosophy of Positive Law. 3 Vols. 8vo. 39*s.*
AUSTIN'S (Sarah)
Fragments from German Prose Writers. With Biographical Notes. Post 8vo. 10*s.*
ADMIRALTY PUBLICATIONS; Issued by direction of the Lords Commissioners of the Admiralty:--
A MANUAL OF SCIENTIFIC ENQUIRY, for the Use of Travellers. Edited by Sir John F. Herschel, and Rev. Robert Main. **Third Edition**. Woodcuts. Post 8vo. 9*s.*

AIRY'S ASTRONOMICAL OBSERVATIONS Made At Greenwich. 1836 to 1847. Royal 4to. 50*s.* each.

AIRY'S ASTRONOMICAL RESULTS. 1848 to 1858. 4to. 8*s.* each.

AIRY'S APPENDICES TO THE ASTRONOMICAL OBSERVATIONS.

1836.--I. Bessel's Refraction Tables.
II. Tables for converting Errors of R.A. and N.P.D. into Errors of Longitude and Ecliptic P.D. 8*s.*
1837.--I. Logarithms of Sines and Cosines to every Ten Seconds of Time. 8*s.*
II. Table for converting Sidereal into Mean Solar Time. 8*s.*
1842.--Catalogue of 1439 Stars. 8*s.*

1845.--Longitude of Valentia. 8*s.*

1847.--Twelve Years' Catalogue of Stars. 14*s.*

1851.--Maskelyne's Ledger of Stars. 6*s.*
1852.--I. Description of the Transit Circle. 5*s.*
II. Regulations of the Royal Observatory. 2*s.*
1853.--Bessel's Refraction Tables. 3*s.*

1854.--I. Description of the Zenith Tube. 3*s.*
II. Six Years' Catalogue of Stars. 10*s.*
1856.--Description of the Galvanic Apparatus at Greenwich Observatory. 8*s.*
AIRY'S MAGNETICAL AND METEOROLOGICAL OBSERVATIONS. 1840 to 1847. Royal 4to. 50*s.* each.

AIRY'S ASTRONOMICAL, MAGNETICAL, AND METEOROLOGICAL OBSERVATIONS, 1848 to 1860. Royal 4to. 50*s.* each.

AIRY'S ASTRONOMICAL RESULTS. 1859. 4to.

AIRY'S MAGNETICAL AND METEOROLOGICAL RESULTS. 1848 to 1859. 4to. 8*s.* each.

AIRY'S REDUCTION OF THE OBSERVATIONS OF PLANETS. 1760 to 1830. Royal 4to. 60*s.*

AIRY'S REDUCTION OF THE LUNAR OBSERVATIONS. 1750 to 1830. 2 Vols. Royal 4to. 50*s.* each.

AIRY'S REDUCTION OF THE LUNAR OBSERVATIONS. 1831 to 1851. 4to. 20*s.*

BERNOULLI'S SEXCENTENARY TABLE. London, 1779. 4to.

BESSEL'S AUXILIARY TABLES FOR HIS METHOD OF CLEARING LUNAR DISTANCES. 8vo.

BESSEL'S FUNDAMENTA ASTRONOMIAE; *Regiomontii* 1818. Folio. 60*s.*

BIRD'S METHOD OF CONSTRUCTING MURAL QUADRANTS. **London**, 1768. 4to. 2s. 6d.

BIRD'S METHOD OF DIVIDING ASTRONOMICAL INSTRUMENTS. **London**, 1767. 4to. 2s. 6d.

COOK, KING, AND BAYLY'S ASTRONOMICAL OBSERVATIONS. **London**, 1782. 4to. 21s.

EIFFE'S ACCOUNT OF IMPROVEMENTS IN CHRONOMETERS. 4to. 2s.

ENCKE'S BERLINER JAHRBUCH, for 1830. Berlin, 1828. 8vo. 9s.

GROOMBRIDGE'S CATALOGUE OF CIRCUMPOLAR STARS. 4to. 10s.

HANSEN'S TABLES DE LA LUNE. 4to. 20s.

HARRISON'S PRINCIPLES OF HIS TIME-KEEPER. Plates. 1797. 4to. 5s.

HUTTON'S TABLES OF THE PRODUCTS AND POWERS OF NUMBERS. 1781. Folio. 7s. 6d.

LAX'S TABLES FOR FINDING THE LATITUDE AND LONGITUDE. 1821. 8vo. 10s.

LUNAR OBSERVATIONS at GREENWICH. 1783 to 1819. Compared with the Tables, 1821. 4to. 7s. 6d.

MASKELYNE'S ACCOUNT OF THE GOING OF HARRISON'S WATCH. 1767. 4to. 2s. 6d.

MAYER'S DISTANCES of the MOON'S CENTRE from the PLANETS. 1822, 3s.; 1823, 4s. 6d. 1824 to 1836, 8vo. 4s. each.

MAYER'S THEORIA LUNAE JUXTA SYSTEMA NEWTONIANUM. 4to. 2s. 6d.

MAYER'S TABULAE MOTUUM SOLIS ET LUNAE. 1770. 4to. 5s.

MAYER'S ASTRONOMICAL OBSERVATIONS MADE AT GOTTINGEN, from 1756 to 1761. 1826. Folio. 7s. 6d.

NAUTICAL ALMANACS, from 1767 to 1866. 8vo. 2s. 6d. each.

NAUTICAL ALMANACS, SELECTIONS FROM THE ADDITIONS up to 1812. 8vo. 5s. 1834-54. 8vo. 5s.

NAUTICAL ALMANACS, SUPPLEMENTS, 1828 to 1833, 1837 and 1838. 8vo. 2s. each.

NAUTICAL ALMANACS, TABLE requisite to be used with the N.A. 1781. 8vo. 6s.

POND'S ASTRONOMICAL OBSERVATIONS. 1811 to 1836. 4to. 21s. each.

RAMSDEN'S ENGINE for Dividing Mathematical Instruments. 4to. 5s.

RAMSDEN'S ENGINE for Dividing Straight Lines. 4to. 5s.

SABINE'S PENDULUM EXPERIMENTS TO DETERMINE THE FIGURE OF THE EARTH. 1825. 4to. 40s.

SHEPHERD'S TABLES for Correcting Lunar Distances. 1772. Royal 4to. 21s.

SHEPHERD'S TABLES, GENERAL, of the MOON'S DISTANCE from the SUN, and 10 STARS. 1787. Folio. 5s. 6d.

TAYLOR'S SEXAGESIMAL TABLE. 1780. 4to. 15s.

TAYLOR'S TABLES OF LOGARITHMS. 4to. 3*l.*

TIARK'S ASTRONOMICAL OBSERVATIONS for the Longitude of MADEIRA. 1822. 4to. 5s.

TIARK'S CHRONOMETRICAL OBSERVATIONS for Differences of LONGITUDE between Dover, Portsmouth, and Falmouth. 1823. 4to. 5s.

VENUS and JUPITER: Observations of, compared with the Tables. **London**, 1822. 4to. 2s.

WALES' AND BAYLY'S ASTRONOMICAL OBSERVATIONS. 1777, 4to. 21s.

WALES' REDUCTION OF ASTRONOMICAL OBSERVATIONS MADE IN THE SOUTHERN HEMISPHERE. 1764-1771. 1788. 4to. 10s. 6*d*.
 BABBAGE'S (Charles)
 Economy of Machinery and Manufactures. ***Fourth Edition***. Fcap. 8vo. 6s.

Ninth Bridgewater Treatise. 8vo. 9s. 6 *d*.

Reflections on the Decline of Science in England, and on some of its Causes. 4to. 7s. 6*d*.
 BAIKIE'S (W. B.)
 Narrative of an Exploring Voyage up the Rivers Quorra and Tshadda in 1854. Map. 8vo. 16s.
 BANKES' (George)
 Story of Corfe Castle, with documents relating to the Time of the Civil Wars, &. Woodcuts. Post 8vo. 10s. 6s.
 BARBAULD'S (Mrs.)
 Hymns in Prose for Children. With 112 Original Designs by Barnes, Wimperis Coleman, and Kennedy. Engraved by Cooper. Small 4to.
 BARROW'S (Sir John)
 Autobiographical Memoir, including Reflections, Observations, and Reminiscences at Home and Abroad. From Early Life to Advanced Age. Portrait. 8vo. 16***s.***

Voyages of Discovery and Research within the Arctic Regions, from 1818 to the present time. 8vo. 15***s***.

Life and Voyages of Sir Francis Drake. With numerous Original Letters. Post 8vo. 2s.
 BATES' (H. W.)
 Naturalist on the River Amazons during eleven years of Adventure and Travel. Second Edition, Illustrations. 2 Vols. Post 8vo.
 BEES AND FLOWERS.
 Two Essays. By Rev. Thomas James. Reprinted from the "Quarterly Review." Fcap. 8vo. 1*s.* each.
 BELL'S (Sir Charles)
 Mechanism and Vital Endowments of the Hand as evincing Design. ***Sixth Edition***. Woodcuts. Post 8vo. 6***s.***
 BENEDICT'S (Jules)
 Sketch of the Life and Works of Felix Mendelssohn-Bartholdy. ***Second Edition.*** 8vo. 2s. 6*d*.
 BERTHA'S
 Journal during a Visit to her Uncle in England. Containing a Variety of Interesting and Instructive Information.***Seventh Edition***. Woodcuts. 12mo.
 BIRCH'S (Samuel)
 History of Ancient Pottery and Porcelain: Egyptian, Assyrian, Greek, Roman and Etruscan. With 200 Illustrations. 2 Vols. Medium 8vo. 42s.
 BLUNT'S (Rev. J. J.)
 Principles for the proper understanding of the Mosaic Writings, stated and applied, together with an Incidental Argument for the truth of the Resurrection of our Lord. Being the HULSEAN LECTURES for 1832. Post 8vo. 6s. 6*d*.

Undesigned Coincidences in the Writings of the Old and New Testament, an Argument of their Veracity: containing the Books of Moses. Historical and Prophetical Scriptures, and the Gospels and Acts. 8*th Edition*. Post 8vo. 6*s*.

History of the Church in the First Three Centuries. *Third Edition*, Post 8vo. 7*s*. 6*d*.

Parish Priest; His Duties, Acquirements and Obligations. *Fourth Edition*. Post 8vo. 7*s*. 6*d*.

Lectures on the Right Use of the Early Fathers. *Second Edition*. 8vo. 15*s*.

Plain Sermons Preached to a Country Congregation. *Second Edition*. 3 Vols. Post 8vo. 7*s*. 6*d*. each.

Literary Essays, reprinted from the Quarterly Review. 8vo. 12*s*.
BLACKSTONE'S COMMENTARIES
on the Laws of England. Adapted to the present state of the law. By R. Malcolm Kerr, LL.D. *Third Edition*. 4 Vols. 8vo. 63*s*.
BLACKSTONE'S COMMENTARIES
For Students. Being those Portions which relate to the British Constitution and the Rights of Persons. Post 8vo. 9s.
BLAKISTON'S (Capt.)
Narrative of the Expedition sent to explore the Upper Waters of the Yang-Tsze. Illustrations. 8vo. 18*s*.
BLOMFIELD'S (Bishop)
Memoir, with Selections from his Correspondence. By his Son. 2*nd Edition.* Portrait, 2 Vols, post 8vo. 18*s*.
BOOK OF COMMON PRAYER.
Illustrated with Coloured Borders, Initial Letters, and Woodcuts. A new edition. 8vo.
BORROWS (George)
Bible in Spain; or the Journeys, Adventures, and Imprisonments of an Englishman in an Attempt to circulate the Scriptures in the Peninsula. 3 Vols. Post 8vo. 27*s*.; or *Popular Edition*, 16mo, 3*s*. 6*d*.

Zincali, or the Gipsies of Spain; their Manners, Customs, Religion, and Language. 2 Vols. Post 8vo. 18*s*; or *Popular Edition*, 16mo, 3*s*. 6*d*.

Lavengro; The Scholar--The Gipsy--and the Priest. Portrait. 3 Vols. Post 8vo. 30*s*.

Romany Rye; a Sequel to Lavengro. *Second Edition*. 2 Vols. Post 8vo. 21*s*.

Wild Wales: its People, Language, and Scenery. 3 Vols. Post 8vo. 30*s*.
BOSWELL'S (James)
Life of Samuel Johnson, LL.D. Including the Tour to the Hebrides. Edited by Mr. Crokee. Portraits. Royal 8vo. 10*s*.
BRACE'S (C. L.)
History of the Races of the Old World. Designed as a Manual of Ethnology. Post 8vo. 9*s*.
BRAY'S (Mrs.)
Life of Thomas Stothard, R.A. With Personal Reminiscences. Illustrated with Portrait and 60 Woodcuts of his chief works. 4to.
BREWSTER'S (Sir David)
Martyrs of Science, or the Lives of Galileo, Tycho Brahe, and Kepler. Fourth Edition. Fcap. 8vo. 4*s*. 6*d*.

More Worlds than One. The Creed of the Philosopher and the Hope of the Christian. *Eighth Edition*. Post 8vo. 6*s*.

Stereoscope: its History, Theory, Construction, and Application to the Arts and to Education. Woodcuts. 12mo. 5*s*. 6*d*.

Kaleidoscope: its History, Theory, and Construction, with its application to the fine and Useful Arts. *Second Edition*. Woodcuts. Post 8vo. 5 *s*. 6*d*.

BRINE'S (Capt.)
Narrative of the Rise and Progress of the Taeping Rebellion in China. Plans. Post 8vo. 10s. 6d.

BRITISH ASSOCIATION REPORTS. 8vo.
York and Oxford, 1831-32, 13s. 6d.

Cambridge, 1833, 12s.
Edinburgh, 1834, 15s.
Dublin, 1835, 13s. 6d.
Bristol, 1836, 12s.
Liverpool, 1837, 16s. 6d.
Newcastle, 1838, 15s.
Birmingham, 1839, 13s. 6d.
Glasgow, 1840, 15s.
Plymouth, 1841 13s. 6d.
Manchester, 1842, 10s. 6d.
Cork, 1843, 12s.
York, 1844, 20s.
Cambridge, 1845, 12s.
Southampton, 1846, 15s.
Oxford, 1847, 18s.
Swansea, 1818, 9s.
Birmingham, 1849, 10s.
Edinburgh, 1850, 15s.
Ipswich, 1851, 16s. 6d.
Belfast, 1852, 16s.
Hull, 1853, 10s. 6d.
Liverpool, 1854, 18s.
Glasgow, 1855, 15s.;
Cheltenham, 1856, 18s.;
Dublin, 1857, 15s. ;
Leeds. 1858, 20s.
Aberdeen, 1859, 15s.
Oxford, 1860.
Manchester, 1861. 15s.

BRITISH CLASSICS.
A New Series of Standard English Authors, printed from the most correct text, and edited with elucidatory notes. Published occasionally in demy 8vo. Volumes, varying in price.

Already Published.

GOLDSMITH'S WORKS. EDITED NY PETER CUNNINGHAM, F.S.A. Vignettes. 4 Vols. 30s.

GIBBON'S DECLINE AND FALL OF THE ROMAN EMPIRE. Edited by William Smith, LL.D. Portrait and Maps. 8 Vols. 60s.

JOHNSON'S LIVES OF THE ENGLISH POETS. Edited by Peter CUNNINGHAM, F.S.A. 3 Vols. 22s. 6d.

BYRON'S POETICAL WORKS. Edited, with Notes. 6 vols. 45s

In Preparation.

WORKS OF POPE. With Life, Introductions, and Notes, by Rev. Whitwell Elwin. Portrait.

HUME'S HISTORY OF ENGLAND. Edited, with Notes.

LIFE AND WORKS OF SWIFT. Edited by JOHN FORSTER.
BROUGHTON'S (Lord)
Journey through Albania and other Provinces of Turkey in Europe and Asia, to Constantinople, 1809--10, *Third Edition.* Illustrations. 2 Vols. 8vo. 30s.

Visits to Italy. ***3rd Edition***. 2 vols. Post 8vo. 18*s*.

BUBBLES FROM THE BRUNNEN OF NASSAU.
By an Old Man. ***Sixth Edition***. 16mo. 5*s*.

BUNYAN (John) and Oliver Cromwell.
Select Biographies. By Robert Southey. Post 8vo. 2*s*.

BUONAPARTE'S (Napoleon)
Confidential Correspondence with his Brother Joseph, sometime King of Spain. ***Second Edition***. 2 vols. 8vo. 26*s*.

BURGHERSH'S (Lord)
Memoir of the Operations of the Allied Armies under Prince Schwarzenberg and Marshal Blucher during the latter end of 1813--14. 8vo. 21*s*.

Early Campaigns of the Duke of Wellington in Portugal and Spain. 8vo. 8*s*. 6***d***.

BUEGON'S (Rev. J. W.)
Memoir of Patrick Fraser Tytler. ***Second Edition***. Post 8vo. 9*s*.

Letters from Rome, written to Friends at Home. Illustrations. Post 8vo. 12*s*,

BURN'S (Lieut.-Col.)
French and English Dictionary of Naval and Military Technical Terms. ***Fourth Edition***. Crown 8vo, 15*s*.

BURNS' (Robert)
Life. By John Gibson Lockhart. ***Fifth Edition***. Fcap. 8vo. 3*s*.

BURR'S (G. D.)
Instructions in Practical Surveying, Topographical Plan Drawing, and on sketching ground without Instruments. ***Third Edition***. Woodcuts. Post 8vo. 7*s*. 6*d*.

BUTTMAN'S LEXILOGUS;
a Critical Examination of the Meaning of numerous Greek Words, chiefly in Homer and Hesiod. Translated by Rev. J. E. Fishlake. ***Fifth Edition***. 8vo. 12*s*.

BUXTON'S (Sir Fowell)
Memoirs. With Selections from his Correspondence. By his Son. Portrait. ***Fifth Edition***. 8vo. 16*s*. ***Abridged Edition***, Portrait. Fcap. 8vo. 2*s*. 6*d*.

BYRON'S (Lord)
Life, Letters, and Journals. By Thomas Moore. Plates. 6 Vols. Fcap. 8vo. 18*s*.

Life, Letters, and Journals. By Thomas Moore. Portraits. Royal 8vo. 9*s*.

Poetical Works. Portrait. 6 Vols. 8vo. 45*s*.

Poetical Works. Plates. 10 Vols. Fcap. 8vo. 30*s*.

Poetical Works. 8 Vols. 24mo. 20*s*.

Poetical Works. Plates. Royal 8vo. 9*s*.

Poetical Works. Portrait. Crown 8vo. 6*s*.

Childe Harold. With 80 Engravings. Small 4to. 21*s*.

Childe Harold. With 30 Vignettes. 12mo. 6*s*.

Childe Harold. 16mo. 2*s*. 6*d*.

Childe Harold. Vignettes. 16mo. 1*s*.

Childe Harold. Portrait. 16mo. 6*d*.

Tales and Poems. 24mo. 2*s*. 6*d*.

Miscellaneous. 2 Vols. 24mo. 5*s*.

Dramas and Plays. 2 Vols. 24mo. 5*s*.

Don Juan and Beppo. 2 Vols. 24mo. 5*s*.

Beauties. Selected from his Poetry and Prose. Portrait, Fcap. 8vo. 3*s*. 6*d*.
    CARNARVON'S (Lord)
        Portugal, Gallicia, and the Basque Provinces. From Notes made during a Journey to those Countries. ***Third Edition***. Post 8vo. 3*s*. 6*d*.

Recollections of the Druses of Lebanon. With Notes on their Religion. ***Third Edition***. Post 8vo. 5*s*. 6*d*.
    CAMPBELL'S (Lord)
        Lives of the Lord Chancellors and Keepers of the Great Seal of England. From the Earliest Times to the Death of Lord Eldon in 1838. ***Fourth Edition***. 10 Vols. Crown 8vo. 6*s*. each.

Lives of the Chief Justices of England. From the Norman Conquest to the Death of Lord Tenterden. ***Second Edition***. 3 Vols. 8vo. 42*s*.

Shakspeare's Legal Acquirements Considered. 8vo. 5*s*. 6*d*.

Life of Lord Chancellor Bacon. Fcap. 8vo. 2*s*. 6*d*.
    CAMPBELL (George)
        Modern India. A Sketch of the System of Civil Government. With some Account of the Natives and Native Institutions. ***Second Edition***. 8vo. 16*s*.

India as it may be. An Outline of a proposed Government and Policy. 8vo. 16*s*.
    CAMPBELL (Thos.)
        Short Lives of the British Poets. With an Essay on English Poetry. Post 8vo. 3*s*. 6*d*.
    CALVIN'S (John)
        Life. With Extracts from his Correspondence By Thomas H. Dyer. Portrait. 8vo. 15*s*.
    CALLCOTT'S (Lady)
        Little Arthur's History of England 130*th* ***Thousand***. With 20 Woodcuts. Fcap. 8vo. 2*s*. 6*d*.
    CASTLEREAGH (The) DESPATCHES,
        from the commencement of the official career of the late Viscount Castlereagh to the close of his life. Edited by the Marquis of Londonderry. 12 Vols. 8vo. 14*s*.each.
    CATHCART'S (Sir George)
        Commentaries on the War in Russia and Germany, 1812-13. Plans. 8vo. 14*s*.

Military Operations in Kaffraria, which led to the Termination of the Kaffir War, ***Second Edition***. 8vo. 12*s*.
    CAVALCASELLE (G. B.).
        Notices of the Lives and Works of the Early Flemish Painters. Woodcuts. Post 8vo. 12*s*.
    CHAMBERS' (G. F.)
        Handbook of Descriptive and Practical Astronomy. Illustrations. Post 8vo. 12*s*.
    CHANTREY (Sir Francis).
        Winged Words on Chantrey's Woodcocks. Edited by Jas. P. Muirhead. Etchings. Square 8vo. 10*s*. 6*d*.
    CHARMED ROE (The);
        or, The Story of the Little Brother and Sister. By Otto Speckter. Plates 16mo. 5*s*.
    CHURTON'S (Archdeacon) Gongora.
        An Historical Essay on the Age of Philip III. and IV. of Spain. With Translations. Portrait. 2 Vols. Small 8vo. 15*s*.
    CLAUSEWITZ'S (Carl Von)
        Campaign of 1812, in Russia. Translated from the German by Lord Ellesmere. Map. 8vo. 10*s*. 6*d*.
    CLIVE'S (Lord)
        Life. By Rev. G. R. Gleig, M.A. Post 8vo. 3*s*. 6*d*.
    COBBOLD'S (Rev. R. H.)
        Pictures of the Chinese drawn by a Native Artist, described by a Foreign Resident. With 24 Plates. Crown 8vo. 9*s*.
    COLCHESTER (The) PAPERS.

The Diary and Correspondence of Charles Abbott, Lord Colchester, Speaker of the House of Commons, 1802-1817. Edited by His Son. Portrait. 3 Vols. 8vo. 42s.
COLEEIDGE'S (Samuel Taylor)
Table-Talk. **Fourth Edition.** Portrait. Fcap. 8vo. 6s.
COLEEIDGE (Henry Nelson)
Introductions to the Greek Classic Poets. **Third Edition**. Fcap. 8vo. 5s. 6d.
COLEEIDGE (Sir John)
on Public School Education, with especial reference to Eton. **Third Edition**. Fcap. 8vo. 2s.
COLONIAL LIBRARY.
[See Home and Colonial Library.]
COOK'S (Rev. F. C.)
Sermons Preached at Lincoln's Inn Chapel, and on Special Occasions. 8vo.
COOKERY (Modern Domestic).
Founded on Principles of Economy and Practical Knowledge, and adapted for Private Families. By a Lady. **New Edition**. Woodcuts. Fcap. 8vo. 5s.
CORNWALLIS (The) Papers and Correspondence
during the American War,--Administrations in India,--Union with Ireland, and Peace of Amiens. Edited by Charles Ross. **Second Edition**. 3 Vols. 8vo. 63s.
COWPER'S (Mart Countess)
Diary while Lady of the Bedchamber to Caroline Princess of Wales. Portrait. 8vo.
CRABBE'S (Rev. George)
Life, Letters, and Journals. By his Son. Portrait. Fcap. 8vo. 3s.

Poetical Works. With his Life.' Plates. 8 Vols. Fcap. 8vo. 24s.

Life and Poetical Works. Plates. Royal 8vo. 7s.
CROKER'S (J. W.)
Progressive Geography for Children. Fifth Edition. 18mo. 1s. 6d.

Stories for Children, Selected from the History of England. **Fifteenth Edition**. Woodcuts. 16mo. 2s. 6d.

Boswell's Life of Johnson. Including the Tour to the Hebrides. Portraits. Royal 8vo. 10s.

Lord Hervey's Memoirs of the Reign of George the Second, from his Accession to the death of Queen Caroline. Edited with Notes. Second Edition. Portrait. 2 Vols. 8vo. 21s.

Essays on the Early Period of the French Revolution. 8vo. 15s.

Historical Essay on the Guillotine. Fcap. 8vo. 1s.
CROMWELL (Oliver) and John Bunyan.
By Robert Southey. Post 8vo. 2s.
CROWE'S (J. A.)
Notices of the Early Flemish Painters; their Lives and Works. Woodcuts. Post 8vo. 12s.
CROWE'S AND CAVALCASELLE'S
History of Painting in Italy, from 2nd to 16th Century. Derived from Historical Researches as well as inspection of the Works of Art in that Country. Illustrations. 2 Vols. 8vo.
CUNNINGHAM'S (Allan)
Poems and Songs. Now first collected and arranged, with Biographical Notice. 24mo. 2s. 6d
CUNNINGHAM (Capt. J. D.)
History of the Sikhs. From the Origin of the Nation to the Battle of the Sutlej. **Second Edition.** Maps. 8vo. 15s.
CURETON (Rev. W.)
Remains of a very Ancient Recension of the Four Gospels in Syriac, hitherto unknown in Europe. Discovered, Edited, and Translated. 4to. 24s.
CURTIUS' (Professor)
Student's Greek Grammar, for the use of Colleges and the Upper Forms. Translated under the Author's revision. Edited by Dr. Wm. Smith. Post 8vo. 7s. 6d.

Smaller Greek Grammar for the use of the Middle and Lower Forms, abridged from the above. 12mo. 3*s.* 6*d.*

 CURZON'S (Hon. Robert)
 Visits to the Monasteries of the Levant. **Fourth Edition**. Woodcuts. Post 8vo. 15*s.*

Armenia and Erzeroum. A Year on the Frontiers of Russia, Turkey, and Persia. **Third Edition**. Woodcuts. Post 8vo. 7*s.* 6*d.*

 CUST'S (General)
 Annals of the Wars of the 18th & 19th Centuries. 9 Vols. Fcap. 8vo. 5*s.* each.
 DARWIN'S (Charles)
 Journal of Researches into the Natural History of the Countries visited during a Voyage round the World. Post 8vo. 9*s.*

Origin of Species by Means of Natural Selection; or, the Preservation of Favoured Races in the Struggle for Life. Post 8vo. 14*s.*

Fertilization of Orchids through Insect Agency, and as to the good of Intercrossing. Woodcuts. Post 8vo. 9*s.*

 DAVIS'S (Nathan)
 Visit to the Ruined Cities of Numidia and Carthaginia. Illustrations. 8vo. 16*s*
 DAVY'S (Sir Humphry)
 Consolations in Travel; or, Last Days of a Philosopher. **Fifth Edition**. Woodcuts. Fcap. 8vo. 6*s.*

Salmonia; or, Days of Fly Fishing. **Fourth Edition**. Woodcuts. Fcap. 8vo. 6*s.*

 DELEPIERRE'S (Octave)
 History of Flemish Literature and its celebrated Authors. From the Twelfth Century to the present Day. 8vo. 9*s.*
 DENNIS' (George)
 Cities and Cemeteries of Etruria. Plates. 2 Vols. 8vo. 42*s.*
 DIXON'S (Hepworth)
 Story of the Life of Lord Bacon. Portrait. Fcap, 8vo. 7*s.* 6*d.*
 DOG-BREAKING;
 the Most Expeditious, Certain, and Easy Method, whether great excellence or only mediocrity be required. By Lieut.-Col. Hutchinson. **Third Edition**. Woodcuts. Post 8vo. 9*s.*
 DOMESTIC MODERN COOKERY.
 Founded on Principles of Economy and Practical Knowledge, and adapted for Private Families. **New Edition**. Woodcuts. Fcap. 8vo. 6*s.*
 DOUGLAS'S (General Sir Howard)
 Life and Adventures; From Notes, Conversations, and Correspondence. By S. W. Fullom. Portrait. 8vo. 15*s.*

On the Theory and Practice of Gunnery. **5*th* Edition**. Plates. 8vo. 21*s.*

Military Bridges, and the Passages of Rivers in Military Operations. **Third Edition**. Plates. 8vo. 21*s.*

Naval Warfare with Steam. **Second Edition**. 8vo. 8*s.* 6*d.*

Modern Systems of Fortification, with special reference to the Naval, Littoral, and Internal Defence of England. Plans. 8vo. 12*s.*

 DRAKE'S (Sir Francis)
 Life, Voyages, and Exploits, by Sea and Land. By John Barrow. **Third Edition**, Post 8vo. 2*s.*
 DRINKWATER'S (John)
 History of the Siege of Gibraltar 1779-1783. With a Description and Account of that Garrison from the Earliest Periods. Post 8vo. 2*s.*
 DU CHAILLU'S (Paul B.)
 EQUATORIAL AFRICA, with Accounts of the Gorilla, the Nest-building Ape, Chimpanzee, Crocodile, &c. Illustrations. 8vo. 21*s.*
 DUDLEY'S (Earl of)
 Letters to the late Bishop of Llandaff. **Second Edition**. Portrait. 8vo. 10*s.* 6*d.*

DUFFERIN'S (Lord)
Letters from High Latitudes, being some Account of a Yacht Voyage to Iceland, &c., in 1856. **Fourth Edition**. Woodcuts. Post 8vo. 9*s*.

DYER'S (Thomas H.)
Life and Letters of John Calvin. Compiled from authentic Sources. Portrait. 8vo. 15*s*.

History of Modern Europe, from the taking of Constantinople by the Turks to the close of the War in the Crimea. Vols. 1 & 2. 8vo. 30*s*.

EASTLAKE'S (Sir Charles)
Italian Schools of Painting. From the German of Kugler. Edited, with Notes. **Third Edition**. Illustrated from the Old Masters. 2 Vols. Post 8vo. 30*s*.

EASTWICK'S (E. B.)
Handbook for Bombay and Madras, with Directions for Travellers, Officers, &c. Map. 2 Vols. Post 8vo. 24*s*.

EDWARDS' (W. H.)
Voyage up the River Amazon, including a Visit to Para. Post 8vo. 2*s*.

ELDON'S (Lord)
Public and Private Life, with Selections from his Correspondence and Diaries. By Horace Twiss. **Third Edition**. Portrait. 2 Vols. Post 8vo. 21*s*.

ELLIS (Rev. W.)
Visits to Madagascar, including a Journey to the Capital, with notices of Natural History, and Present Civilisation of the People, **Fifth Thousand**. Map and Woodcuts. 8vo. 16*s*.

ELLIS (Mrs.)
Education of Character, with Hints on Moral Training. Post 8vo. 7*s*. 6*d*.

ELLESMERE'S (Lord)
Two Sieges of Vienna by the Turks. Translated from the German. Post 8vo. 2*s*.

Second Campaign of Radetzky in Piedmont. The Defence of Temeswar and the Camp of the Ban. From the German. Post 8vo. 6*s*. 6*d*.

Campaign of 1812 in Russia, from the German of General Carl Von Clausewitz. Map. 8vo. 10*s*. 6*d*.

Poems. Crown 4to. 24*s*.

Essays on History, Biography, Geography, and Engineering. 8vo. 12*s*.

ELPHINSTONE'S (Hon. Mountstuart)
History of India--the Hindoo and Mahomedan Periods. **Fourth Edition**. Map. 8vo. 18*s*.

ENGEL'S (Carl)
Music of the Most Ancient Nations; particularly of the Assyrians, Egyptians, and Hebrews, with Special Reference to the Discoveries in Western Asia and in Egypt. Illustrated. 8vo.

ENGLAND (History of)
from the Peace of Utrecht to the Peace of Versailles, 1713--83. By Lord Mahon. **Library Edition**, 7 Vols. 8vo. 93*s*.; or **Popular Edition**, 7 Vols. Post 8vo. 36*s*.

From the First Invasion by the Romans, down to the 14th year of Queen Victoria's Reign. By Mrs. MARKHAM. 118*th* **Edition**. Woodcuts. 12mo. 6*s*.

ENGLISHWOMAN IN AMERICA.
Post 8vo. 10*s*. 6*d*.

ERSKINE'S (Admiral)
Journal of a Cruise among the Islands of the Western Pacific, including the Fejees, and others inhabited by the Polynesian Negro Races. Plates. 8vo. 16*s*.

ESKIMAUX and English Vocabulary,
for Travellers in the Arctic Regions. 16mo. 3*s*. 6*d*.

ESSAYS FROM "THE TIMES."
Being a Selection from the LITERARY Papers which have appeared in that Journal. **Seventh Thousand**. 2 vols. Fcap. 8vo. 8*s*.

EXETER'S (Bishop of)
Letters to the late Charles Butler, on the Theological parts of his Book of the Roman Catholic Church; with Remarks on certain Works of Dr. Milner and Dr. Lingard, and on some parts of the Evidence of Dr. Doyle. **Second Edition**. 8vo. 16*s*.

FALKNER'S (Fred.)
Muck Manual for the Use of Farmers. A Treatise on the Nature and Value of Manures. **Second Edition**. Fcap. 8vo. 5s.

FAMILY RECEIPT-BOOK.
A Collection of a Thousand Valuable and Useful Receipts. Fcap. 8vo. 5s. 6d.

FANCOURT'S (Col.)
History of Yucatan, from its Discovery to the Close of the 17th Century. With Map. 8vo. 10s. 6d.

FARRAR'S (Rev. A. S.)
Sermons on Science in Theology. 8vo. 9s.

Critical History of Free Thought in reference to the Christian Religion. Being the Bampton Lectures, 1862. 8vo. 16s.

FARRAR (F. W.)
Origin of Language, based on Modern Researches. Fcap. 8vo. 5s.

FEATHERSTONHAUGH'S (G. W.)
Tour through the Slave States of North America, from the River Potomac to Texas and the Frontiers of Mexico. Plates. 2 Vols. 8vo. 26s.

FELLOWS' (Sir Charles)
Travels and Researches in Asia Minor, more particularly in the Province of Lycia. **New Edition**. Plates. Post 8vo. 9s.

FERGUSSON'S (James)
Palaces of Nineveh and Persepolis Restored; an Essay on Ancient Assyrian and Persian Architecture. Woodcuts. 8vo. 16s.

Rock-Cut Temples of India, described with 75 Photographs taken on the Spot. By Major Gill. Medium 8vo.

Handbook of Architecture. Being a Concise and Popular Account of the Different Styles prevailing in all Ages and Countries in the World. With 850 Illustrations. 8vo. 26s.

History of the Modern Styles of Architecture, completing the above work. With 312 Illustrations. 8vo. 31s. 6d.

FERRIER'S (T. P.)
Caravan Journeys in Persia, Afghanistan, Herat, Turkistan, and Beloochistan, with Descriptions of Meshed, Balk, and Candahar, &c. **Second Edition**. Map. 8vo. 21s.

History of the Afghans. Map. 8vo. 21s.

FISHER'S (Rev. George)
Elements of Geometry, for the Use of Schools. **Fifth Edition**. 18mo. 1s. 6d.

First Principles of Algebra, for the Use of Schools. **Fifth Edition**. 18mo. 1s. 6d.

FLOWER GARDEN (The).
An Essay. By Rev. Thos. James. Reprinted from the "Quarterly Review." Fcap. 8vo. 1s.

FORBES' (C. S.)
Iceland; its Volcanoes, Geysers, and Glaciers. Illustrations. Post 8vo. 14s.

FORD'S (Richard)
Handbook for Spain, Andalusia, Ronda, Valencia, Catalonia, Granada, Gallicia, Arragon, Navarre, &c. **Third Edition**. 2 Vols. Post 8vo. 30s.

Gatherings from Spain. Post 8vo. 3s. 6d.

FORSTER'S (John)
Arrest of the Five Members by Charles the First. A Chapter of English History re-written. Post 8vo. 12s.

Debates on the Grand Remonstrance, 1641. With an Introductory Essay on English freedom under the Plantagenet and Tudor Sovereigns. **Second Edition**. Post 8vo. 12s.

Oliver Cromwell, Daniel De Foe, Sir Richard Steele, Charles Churchill, Samuel Foote. Biographical Essays. **Third Edition**. Post 8vo. 12s.

FORSYTH'S (William)
New Life of Cicero. Post. 8vo.

FORTUNE'S (Robert)
Narrative of Two Visits to the Tea Countries of China, between the years 1843-52, with full Descriptions of the Tea Plant. **Third Edition**. Woodcuts. 2 Vols. Post 8vo. 18*s*.

Chinese,--Inland,--on the Coast,--and at Sea, 1853-56. Woodcuts. 8vo. 16*s*.

Yedo and Peking. Being a Journey to the Capitals of Japan and China. With Notices of the Agriculture and Trade of those Countries, Illustrations. 8vo. 15*s*.

FRANCE (History of).
From the Conquest by the Gauls to the Death of Louis Philippe. By Mrs. Markham. 56*th Thousand*. Woodcuts. 12mo. 6*s*.

FRENCH (The) in Algiers;
The Soldier of the Foreign Legion-- and the Prisoners of Abd-el-Kadir. Translated by Lady Duff Gordon. Post 8vo. 2*s*.

GALTON'S (Francis)
Art of Travel; or, Hints on the Shifts and Contrivances available in Wild Countries. **Third Edition**. Woodcuts. Post 8vo. 7*s*. 6*d*.

GEOGRAPHICAL (The) Journal.
Published by the Royal Geographical Society of London. 8vo.

GERMANY (History of).
From the Invasion by Marius, to the present time. By Mrs. Markham. **Fifteenth Thousand**. Woodcuts. 12mo. 6*s*.

GIBBON'S (Edward)
History of the Decline and Fall of the Roman Empire. **A New Edition**. Preceded by his Autobiography. Edited, with Notes, by Dr. Wm. Smith. Maps. 8 Vols. 8vo. 60*s*.

(The Student's Gibbon); Being an Epitome of the above work, incorporating the Researches of Recent Commentators. By Dr. Wm. Smith. **Ninth Thousand**. Woodcuts, Post 8vo. 7*s*. 6*d*.

GIFFARD'S (Edward)
Deeds of Naval Daring; or, Anecdotes of the British Navy. New Edition. Fcap. 8vo. 3*s*. 6*d*.

GOLDSMITH'S (Oliver) Works.
A New Edition. Printed from the last editions revised by the Author. Edited by Peter Cunningham. Vignettes. 4 Vols. 8vo. 30*s*. (Murray's British Classics.)

GLADSTONE'S (Right Hon. W. E.)
Financial Statements of 1853, 60, and 63; also his Speeches on Tax-Bills, 1861, and on Charities, 1863. 8vo.

GLEIG'S (Rev. G. R.)
Campaigns of the British Army at Washington and New Orleans. Post 8vo. 2*s*.

Story of the Battle of Waterloo. Post 8vo. 3*s*. 6*d*.

Narrative of Sale's Brigade in Affghanistan. Post 8vo. 2*s*.

Life of Robert Lord Clive. Post 8vo. 3*s*. 6*d*.

Life and Letters of Sir Thomas Munro. Post 8vo 3*s*. 6*d*.

GORDON'S (Sir Alex. Duff)
Sketches of German Life, and Scenes from the War of Liberation. From the German. Post 8vo. 3*s*. 6*d*.

French in Algiers. 1. The Soldier of the Foreign Legion. 2. The Prisoners of Abd-el-Kadir. From the French. Post 8vo. 2*s*.

GORDON'S (Lady Duff)
Amber-Witch: A Trial for Witchcraft. From the German. Post 8vo. 2*s*.

GOUGER'S (Henry)
Personal Narrative of Two Years' Imprisonment in Burmah. **Second Edition**. Woodcuts. Post 8vo. 12*s*.

GRENVILLE (The) PAPERS.
Being the Public and Private Correspondence of George Grenville, including his Private Diary. Edited by W. J. Smith, 4 Vols. 8vo. 16*s*. each.

GREY'S (Sir George)

Polynesian Mythology, and Ancient Traditional History of the New Zealand Race. Woodcuts. Post 8vo. 10s. 6d.

GEOTE'S (George)
History of Greece. From the Earliest Times to the close of the generation contemporary with the death of Alexander the Great. **Fourth Edition**. Maps. 8 vols. 8vo. 112s.

GEOTE'S (Mrs.)
Memoir of Ary Scheffer. Post 8vo. 8s. 6d.

Collected Papers. 8vo. 10s. 6d.

HALLAM'S (Henry)
Constitutional History of England, from the Accession of Henry the Seventh to the Death of George the Second. **Seventh Edition**. 3 Vols. 8vo. 30s.

History of Europe during the Middle Ages. **Tenth Edition**. 3 Vols. 8vo. 30s.

Literary History of Europe, during the 15th, 16th and 17th Centuries. **Fourth Edition**. 3 Vols. 8vo. 36s.

Literary Essays and Characters. Selected from the last work. Fcap. 8vo. 2s.

Historical Works. History of England,--Middle Ages of Europe,--Literary History of Europe. 10 Vols. Post 8vo. 6s. each.

HALLAM'S (Arthur)
Remains; in Verse and Prose. With Preface, Memoir, and Portrait Fcap. 8vo. 7s. 6d.

HAMILTON'S (James)
Wanderings in North Africa. Post 8vo. 12s.

HART'S ARMY LIST.
(Quarterly and Annually.) 8vo. 10s. 6d. and 21s.

HANNAH'S (Rev. Dr.)
Bampton Lectures for 1863; the Divine and Human Elements in Holy Scripture. 8vo.

HAY'S (J. H. Drummond)
Western Barbary, its wild Tribes and savage Animals. Post 8vo. 2s.

HEAD'S (Sir Francis)
Horse and his Rider. Woodcuts. Post 8vo. 5s.

Rapid Journeys across the Pampas. Post 8vo. 2s.

Descriptive Essays. 2 Vols. Post 8vo. 18s.

Bubbles from the Brunnen of Nassau. 16mo. 5s.

Emigrant. Fcap. 8vo. 2s. 6d.

Stokers and Pokers; or, N.-Western Railway. Post 8vo. 2s.

Defenceless State of Great Britain. Post 8vo. 12s.

Faggot of French Sticks. 2 Vols. Post 8vo. 12s.
a Fortnight in Ireland. Map. 8vo. 12s.

HEAD'S (Sir Edmund)
Shall and Will; or, Future Auxiliary Verbs. Fcap. 8vo. 4s.

HAND-BOOK
TRAVEL-TALK. English, German, French, and Italian. 18mo. 3s. 6d.

NORTH GERMANY, Holland, Belgium, and the Rhine to Switzerland. Map. Post 8vo. 10s.

KNAPSACK GUIDE TO BELGIUM AND THE RHINE. Post 8vo. (*In the Press*.)

SOUTH GERMANY, Bavaria, Austria, Styria, Salzberg, the Austrian and Bavarian Alps, the Tyrol, Hungary, and the Danube, from Ulm to the Black Sea. Map. Post 8vo. 10s.

KNAPSACK GUIDE TO THE TYROL. Post 8vo. (*In the Press*.)

PAINTING. German, Flemish, and Dutch Schools. Edited by Dr. Waagen. Woodcuts. 2 Vols. Post 8vo. 24*s*.

LIVES OF THE EARLY FLEMISH PAINTERS, with Notices of their Works. By Crowe and Cavalcaselle. Illustrations. Post 8vo. 12*s*.

SWITZERLAND, Alps of Savoy, and Piedmont. Maps. Post 8vo. 9*s*.

KNAPSACK GUIDE TO SWITZERLAND. Post 8vo. (***In the Press***.)

FRANCE, Normandy, Brittany, the French Alps, the Rivers Loire, Seine, Rhone, and Garonne, Dauphiné, Provence, and the Pyrenees. Maps. Post 8vo. 10*s*.

KNAPSACK GUIDE TO FRANCE. Post 8vo. (***In the Press***.)

PARIS AND ITS Environs. Map. Post 8vo. (***Nearly Ready***.)

SPAIN, Andalusia, Ronda, Granada, Valencia, Catalonia, Gallicia, Arragon, and Navarre. Maps. 2 Vols. Post 8vo, 30*s*.

PORTUGAL, Lisbon, &c. Map. Post 8vo.

NORTH ITALY, Piedmont, Liguria, Venetia, Lombardy, Parma, Modena, and Romagna. Map. Post 8vo. 12*s*.

CENTRAL ITALY, Lucca, Tuscany, Florence, The Marches, Umbria, and the Patrimony of St. Peter's. Map. Post 8vo. 10*s*.

ROME AND ITS Environs. Map. Post 8vo. 9*s*.

SOUTH ITALY, Two Sicilies, Naples, Pompeii, Herculaneum, and Vesuvius. Map. Post 8vo. 10*s*.

KNAPSACK GUIDE TO ITALY AND ROME. 1 Vol. Post 8vo. (***In Preparation***.)

SICILY, Palermo, Messina, Catania, Syracuse, Etna, and the Ruins of the Greek Temples. Map. Post 8vo. (***In the Press***.)

PAINTING. The Italian Schools. From the German of Kugler. Edited by Sir Charles Eastlake, R.A. Woodcuts. 2 Vols. Post 8vo. 30*s*.

LIVES OF THE EARLY ITALIAN PAINTERS, and Progress of Painting In Italy, from CIMABUE to BASSANO. By Mrs. Jameson. Woodcuts. Post 8vo. 12*s*.

DICTIONARY OF ITALIAN PAINTERS. By A Lady. Edited by Ralph Wornum. With a Chart. Post 8vo. 6*s*. 6*d*.

GREECE, the Ionian Islands, Albania, Thessaly, and Macedonia. Maps. Post 8vo. 15*s*.

TURKEY, Malta, Asia Minor, Constantinople, Armenia, Mesopotamia, &c. Maps. Post 8vo. (***In the Press***.)

EGYPT, Thebes, the Nile, Alexandria, Cairo, the Pyramids, Mount Sinai, &c. Map. Post 8vo. 15*s*.

SYRIA & PALESTINE, Peninsula of Sinai, Edom, and Syrian Desert. Maps. 2 Vols. Post 8vo. 24*s*.

BOMBAY AND MADRAS. Map. 2 Vols. Post 8vo. 24*s*.

DENMARK, Norway and Sweden. Maps. Post 8vo. 15*s*.

RUSSIA, The Baltic and Finland. Maps. Post 8vo. 12*s*.

MODERN LONDON. A Complete Guide to all the Sights and Objects of Interest in the Metropolis. Map. 16mo. 3*s*. 6*d*.

WESTMINSTER ABBEY. Woodcuts. 16mo. 1*s*.

KENT AND SUSSEX, Canterbury, Dover, Ramsgate, Sheeroess, Rochester, Chatham, Woolwich, Brighton, Chichester, Worthing, Hastings, Lewes, Arundel, &c. Map. Post 8vo. 10*s*.

SURREY, HANTS, Kingston, Croydon, Reigate, Guildford, Winchester, Southampton, Portsmouth, and Isle of Wight. Maps. Post 8vo. 7*s*. 6*d*.

BERKS, BUCKS, AND OXON, Windsor, Eton, Reading, Aylasbury, Uxbridge, Wycombe, Henley, the City and University of Oxford, and the Descent of the Thames to Maidenhead and Windsor. Map. Post 8vo. 7*s*. 6*d*.

WILTS, DORSET, AND SOMERSET, Salisbury, Chippenham, Weymouth, Sherborne, Wells, Bath, Bristol, Taunton, &c. Map. Post 8vo. 7*s*. 6*d*.

DEVON AND CORNWALL, Exeter, Ilfracombe, Linton, Sidmouth, Dawlish, Teignmouth, Plymouth, Devonport, Torquay, Launceston, Truro, Penzance, Falmouth, &c. Maps. Post 8vo. 7*s*. 6*d*.

NORTH AND SOUTH WALES, Bangor, Carnarvon, Beaumaris, Snowdon, Cooway, Menai Straits, Carmarthen, Pembroke, Tenby, Swansea, The Wye, &c. Maps. 2 Vols. Post 8vo. 12*s*.

CATHEDRALS OF ENGLAND--Southern Division, Winchester, Salisbury, Exeter, Wells, Chichester, Rochester, Canterbury. With 110 Illustrations. Vols. Crown 8vo. 24*s*.

CATHEDRALS OF ENGLAND--Eastern Division, Oxford, Peterborough, Norwich, Ely, and Lincoln. With 90 Illustrations. Crown 8vo. 18*s*.

CATHEDRALS OF ENGLAND--Western Division, Bristol, Gloucester, Hereford, Worcester, and Lichfield. Illustrations. Crown 8vo.
a FAMILIAR QUOTATIONS. From English Authors. **Third Edition**. Fcap. 8vo. 5*s*.
    HEBER'S (Bishop)
    Journey through India. **Twelfth Edition**. 2 Vols. Post 8vo. 7*s*.

Poetical Works. **Sixth Edition**. Portrait. Fcap. 8vo. 6*s*.

Sermons Preached in England. **Second Edition**. 8vo.

Hymns for Church Service. 16mo. 2*s*.
    HEIRESS (The) in Her Minority,
    or, The Progress of Character. By the Author of "Bertha's Journal." 2 Vols. 12mo. 18*s*.
    HERODOTUS,
    A New English Version. Edited with Notes and Essays, historical, ethnographical, and geographical. By Rev. G. Rawlinson, assisted by Sir Henry Rawlinson and Sir J. G. Wilkinson. **Second Edition**. Maps and Woodcuts, 4 Vols. 8vo. 48*s*.
    HERVEY'S (Lord)
    Memoirs of the Reign of George the Second, from his Accession to the Death of Queen Caroline. Edited, with Notes, by Mr. Croker. **Second Edition**. Portrait. 2 Vols. 8vo. 21*s*.
    HESSEY (Rev. Dr.).
    Sunday--Its Origin, History, and Present Obligations. Being the Bampton Lectures for 1860. **Second Edition**. 8vo. 16*s*.
    HICKMAN'S (Wm.)
    Treatise on the Law and Practice of Naval Courts-Martial. 8vo. 10*s*. 6*d*.
    HILLARD'S (G. S.)
    Six Months in Italy. 2 Vols. Post 8vo. 16*s*.
    HOLLWAY'S (J. G.)

Month in Norway. Fcap. 8vo. *2s.*
HONEY BEE (The).
An Essay. By Rev. Thomas James. Reprinted from the "Quarterly Review." Fcap. 8vo. 1*s.*
HOOK'S (Dean)
Church Dictionary. ***Eighth Edition***. 8vo. 16*s.*
HOOK'S (Theodore)
Life. By J. G. Lockhart. Reprinted from the "Quarterly Review." Fcap. 8vo. 1*s.*
HOOKER'S (Dr. J. D.)
Himalayan Journals; or, Notes of an Oriental Naturalist in Bengal, the Sikkim and Nepal Himalayas, the Khasia Mountains, &c. ***Second Edition***. Woodcuts. 2 Vols. Post 8vo. 18*s.*
HOPE'S (A. J. Beresfohd)
English Cathedral of the Nineteenth Century. With Illustrations. 8vo. 12*s.*
HORACE
(Works of). Edited by Dean Milman. With 300 Woodcuts. Crown 8vo. 21*s.*

(Life of). By Dean Milman. Woodcuts, and coloured Borders. 8vo. 9*s.*
HUME'S (David)
History of England, from the Invasion of Julius Caesar to the Revolution of 1688. Abridged for Students. Correcting his errors, and continued to 1858. ***Twenty-fifth Thousand***. Woodcuts. Post 8vo. 7*s.* 6***d***.
HUTCHINSON (Col.)
on the most expeditious, certain, and easy Method of Dog-Breaking. ***Third Edition***. Woodcuts. Post 8vo. 9*s.*
HUTTON'S (H. E.)
Principia Graeca; an Introduction to the Study of Greek. Comprehending Grammar, Delectus, and Exercise-book, with Vocabularies. ***Third Edition***. 12mo. 3*s.* 6***d***.
HOME AND COLONIAL LIBRARY.
A Series of Works adapted for all circles and classes of Readers, having been selected for their acknowledged interest and ability of the Authors. Post 8vo. Published at 2*s.* and 3*s.* 6***d***. each, and arranged under two distinctive heads as follows:--
CLASS A.

HISTORY, BIOGRAPHY, AND HISTORIC TALES.
1. SIEGE OF GIBRALTAR. By John Drinkwater. 2*s.*

2. THE AMBER-WITCH. By Lady Duff Gordon. 2*s.*

3. CROMWELL AND BUNYAN. By Robert Southey. 2*s.*

4. LIFE OF SIR FRANCIS DRAKE. by John Barrow.

5. CAMPAIGNS AT WASHINGTON. By Rev. G. R. Gleig. 2*s.*

6. THE FRENCH IN ALGIERS. By Lady Duff Gordon. 2*s.*

7. THE FALL OF THE JESUITS. 2*s.*

8. LIVONIAN TALES. 2*s.*

9. LIFE OF CONDE. By Lord Mahon. 3*s.* 6***d***.

10. SALE'S BRIGADE. By Rev. G. R. Gleig. 2*s.*

11. THE SIEGES OF VIENNA. By Lord Ellesmere, 2*s.*

12. THE WAYSIDE CROSS. By Capt. Milman. 2*s.*

13. SKETCHES of GERMAN LIFE. By Sir A. Gordon. 3*s.* 6***d***.

14. THE BATTLE of WATERLOO. By Rev. G. R. Gleig. 3*s.* 6***d***.

15. AUTOBIOGRAPHY OF STEFFENS. 2*s.*

16. THE BRITISH POETS. By Thomas Campbell. 3*s.* 6*d.*

17. HISTORICAL ESSAYS. Lord Mahon. 3*s.* 6*d.*

18. LIFE OF LORD CLIVE. By Rev. G. R. Gleig. 3*s.* 6*d.*

19. NORTH-WESTERN RAILWAY. By Sir F. B. Head. 2*s.*
a 20. LIFE OF MUNRO. By Rev. G. R. Gleig. 3*s.* 6*d.*
    CLASS B

VOYAGES, TRAVELS, AND ADVENTURES.
    1. BIBLE IN SPAIN. By George Borrow. 3*s.* 6*d.*

2. GIPSIES OF SPAIN. By George Borrow. 3*s.* 6*d.*

3 & 4. JOURNALS IN INDIA. By Bishop Herer. 2 vols. 7*s.*

5. TRAVELS IN THE HOLY LAND. By Irby and Manoles. 2*s.*

6. MOROCCO AND THE MOORS. By J. Drummond Hay. 2*s.*

7. LETTERS FROM THE BALTIC. By a Lady. 2*s.*

8. NEW SOUTH WALES. By Mrs. Meredith. 2*s.*

9. THE WEST INDIES. By M. G. Lewis. 2*s.*

10. SKETCHES OF PERSIA. By Sir John Malcolm. 3*s.* 6*d.*

11. MEMOIRS OF FATHER RIPA. 2*s.*

12 & 13. TYPEE AND OMOO. By Hermann Melville. 2 Vols. 7*s.*

14. MISSIONARY LIFE IN CANADA. By Rev. J. Abbott. 2*s.*

15. LETTERS FROM MADRAS. By a Lady. 2*s.*

16. HIGHLAND SPORTS. by Charles St. John. 3*s.* 6*d,*

17. PAMPAS JOURNEYS. By Sir F. B. Head. 2*s.*

18. GATHERINGS FROM SPAIN. By Richard Ford. 3*s.* 6*d.*

19. THE RIVER AMAZON. W. H. Edwards. 2*s.*

20. MANNERS & CUSTOMS OF INDIA. By Rev. C. Acland. 2*s.*

21. ADVENTURES IN MEXICO. By G. F. Ruxton. 3*s.* 6*d.*

22. PORTUGAL AND GALLICIA. By Lord Carnarvon. 3*s.* 6*d.*

23. BUSH LIFE IN AUSTRALIA. By Rev. H. W. Haygarth. 2*s.*

24. THE LIBYAN DESERT. By Bayle St. John. 2*s.*

25. SIERRA LEONE. By a Lady. 3*s.* 6*d.*

[*** Each work may be had separately.]
    IRBY AND MANGLES'
      Travels in Egypt, Nubia, Syria, and the Holy Land. Post 8vo. 2*s.*
    JAMES' (Rev. Thomas)

Fables of AEsop. A New Translation, with Historical Preface. With 100 Woodcuts by Tenniel and Wolf. *Thirty-eighth Thousand*. Post 8vo. 2s. 6d.

JAMESON'S (Mrs.)

Lives of the Early Italian Painters, from Cimabue to Bassano, and the Progress of Painting in Italy. *New Edition*. With Woodcuts. Post 8vo. 12s.

JESSE'S (Edward)

Scenes and Occupations of Country Life. *Third Edition*. Woodcuts. Fcap. 8vo. 6s.

Gleanings in Natural History. *Eighth Edition*. Fcap. 8vo. 6s.

JOHNSON'S (Dr. Samuel)

Life. By James Boswell. Including the Tour to the Hebrides. Edited by the late Mr. Crokes. Portraits. Royal 8vo. 10s.

Lives of the most eminent English Poets. Edited by Peter Cunningham. 3 vols. 8vo. 22s. 6d. (Murray's British Classics.)

JOURNAL OF A NATURALIST.

Woodcuts. Post 8vo. 9s 6d.

JOWETT (Rev. B.)

on St. Paul's Epistles to the Thessalonians, Galatians, and Romans, *Second Edition*. 2 Vols. 8vo. 30s.

KEN'S (Bishop) Life.

By A Layman. *Second Edition*. Portrait. 2 Vols. 8vo. 18s.

Exposition of the Apostles' Creed. Extracted from his "Practice of Divine Love." Fcap. 1s. 6d.

Approach to the Holy Altar. Extracted from his "Manual of Prayer" and "Practice of Divine Love." Fcap. 8vo. 1s. 6d.

KING'S (Rev. S. W.)

Italian Valleys of the Alps; a Tour through all the Romantic and less-frequented "Vals" of Northern Piedmont. Illustrations. Crown 8vo. 18s.

KING'S (Rev. C. W.)

Antique Gems; their Origin, Use, and Value as Interpreters of Ancient History, and as illustrative of Ancient Art. Illustrations. 8vo. 42s.

KING EDWARD VIth's

Latin Grammar; or, an Introduction to the Latin Tongue, for the Use of Schools. *Sixteenth Edition*. 12mo. 3s. 6d.

First Latin Book; or, the Accidence, Syntax, and Prosody, with an English Translation for the Use of Junior Classes. *Fourth Edition*. 12mo. 2s. 6d.

KIRK'S (J. Foster)

History of Charles the Bold, Duke of Burgundy. Portrait. 2 Vols. 8vo.

KUGLER'S

Italian Schools of Painting. Edited, with Notes, by Sir Charles Eastlake. *Third Edition*. Woodcuts. 2 Vols. Post 8vo. 30s.

German, Dutch, and Flemish Schools of Painting. Edited, with Notes, by Dr. Waagen. *Second Edition*. Woodcuts. 2 Vols. Post 8vo. 24s.

LABARTE'S (M. Jules)

Handbook of the Arts of the Middle Ages and Renaissance. With 200 Woodcuts. 8vo. 18s.

LATIN GRAMMAR

(King Edward VIth's). For the Use of Schools. *Sixteenth Edition*. 12mo. 3s. 6d.

First Book (King Edward VIth's); or, the Accidence, Syntax, and Prosody, with English Translation for Junior Classes. *Fourth Edition*. 12mo. 2s. 6d.

LAYARD'S (A. H.)

Nineveh and its Remains. Being a Narrative of Researches and Discoveries amidst the Ruins of Assyria. With an Account of the Chaldean Christians of Kurdistan; the Yezedis, or Devil-worshippers; and an Enquiry into the Manners and Arts of the Ancient Assyrians. *Sixth Edition*. Plates and Woodcuts. 2 Vols. 8vo. 36s.

Nineveh and Babylon; being the Result of a Second Expedition to Assyria. *Fourteenth Thousand*. Plates. 8vo. 21s. Or *Fine Paper*, 2 Vols. 8vo. 30s.

Popular Account of Nineveh. 15*th* **Edition**. With Woodcuts. Post 8vo. 5*s*.
LEAKE'S (Col.)
Topography of Athens, with Remarks on its Antiquities. Second Edition. Plates. 2 Vols. 8vo. 30*s*.

Travels in Northern Greece. Maps. 4 Vols. 8vo. 60*s*.

Disputed Questions of Ancient Geography. Map. 8vo. 6*s*. 6*d*.

Numismata Hellenica, and Supplement. Completing a descriptive Catalogue of Twelve Thousand Greek Coins, with Notes Geographical and Historical. With Map and Appendix. 4to, 63*s*.

Peloponnesiaca. 8vo. 15*s*.

Degradation of Science in England. 8vo. 3*s*. 6*d*.
LESLIE'S (C. R.)
Handbook for Young Painters. With Illustrations. Post 8vo. 10*s*. 6*d*.

Autobiographical Recollections, with Selections from his Correspondence. Edited by Tom Taylor. Portrait. 2 Vols. Post 8vo. 18*s*.

Life of Sir Joshua Reynolds. With an Account of his Works, and a Sketch of his Cotemporaries. By Tom Taylor. 2 Vols. 8vo. (**In the Press**.)
LETTERS FROM THE BALTIC.
By a Lady. Post 8vo. 2*s*.
LETTERS FROM MADRAS.
By a Lady. Post 8vo. 2*s*.
LETTERS FROM SIERRA LEONE.
By a Lady. Post 8vo. 3*s*. 6*d*.
LEWIS' (Sir G. C.)
Essay on the Government of Dependencies. 8vo. 12*s*.

Glossary of Provincial Words used in Herefordshire and some of the adjoining Counties. 12mo. 4*s*. 6*d*.
LEWIS' (Lady Theresa)
Friends and Contemporaries of the Lord Chancellor Clarendon, illustrative of Portraits in his Gallery. With a Descriptive Account of the Pictures, and Origin of the Collection. Portraits. 3 Vols. 8vo. 42*s*.
LEWIS' (M. G.)
Journal of a Residence among the Negroes in the West Indies. Post 8vo. 2**LEWIS'** s.
LIDDELL'S (Dean)
History of Rome. From the Earliest Times to the Establishment of the Empire. With the History of Literature and Art. 2 Vols. 8vo. 28*s*.

Student's History of Rome. Abridged from the above Work. 25*th* **Thousand**, With Woodcuts. Post 8vo. 7*s*. 6*d*.
LINDSAY'S (Lord)
Lives of the Lindsays; or, a Memoir of the Houses of Crawford and Balcarres, With Extracts from Official Papers and Personal Narratives. **Second Edition**. 3 Vols. 8vo. 24*s*.

Report of the Claim of James, Earl of Crawford and Balcarres, to the Original Dukedom of Montrose, created in 1488. Folio. 15*s*.

Scepticism; a Retrogressive Movement in Theology and Philosophy. 8vo. 9*s*.
LISPINGS from LOW LATITUDES;
or, the Journal of the Hon. Impulsia Gushington. Edited by Lord Dufferin. With 24 Plates, 4to. 21*s*.
LITTLE ARTHUR'S HISTORY OF ENGLAND.
By Lady Callcott. 120*th* **Thousand**. With 20 Woodcuts. Fcap. 8vo. 2*s*. 6*d*
LIVINGSTONE'S (Rev. Dr.)
Popular Account of his Missionary Travels in South Africa, Illustrations. Post 8vo. 6*s*.

LIVONIAN TALES.
By the Author of "Letters from the Baltic." Post 8vo. 2s.
LOCKHART'S (J. G.)
Ancient Spanish Ballads. Historical and Romantic. Translated, with Notes. Illustrated Edition. 4to. 21s. Or, *Popular Edition*, Post 8vo. 2s. 6d.

Life of Robert Burns. *Fifth Edition*, Fcap. 8vo. 3s.
LONDON'S (Bishop of)
Dangers and Safeguards of Modern Theology. Containing Suggestions to the Theological Student under present difficulties. *Second Edition*, 8vo. 9s.
LOUDON'S (Mrs.)
Instructions in Gardening for Ladies. With Directions and Calendar of Operations for Every Month. *Eighth Edition.* Woodcuts. Fcap. 8vo. 5s.

Modern Botany; a Popular Introduction to the Natural System of Plants. *Second Edition*, Woodcuts. Fcap. 8vo. 6s.
LOWE'S (Sir Hudson)
Letters and Journals, during the Captivity of Napoleon at St. Helena. By William Foesyth. Portrait. 3 Vols. 8vo. 45s.
LUCAS' (Samuel)
Secularia; or, Surreys on the Main Stream of History. 8vo. 12s.
LUCKNOW:
A Lady's Diary of the Siege. *Fourth Thousand.* Fcap. 8vo. 4s. 6d.
LYELL'S (Sin Charles)
Principles of Geology; or, the Modern Changes of the Earth and its Inhabitants considered as illustrative of Geology. *Ninth Edition.* Woodcuts. 8vo. 18s.

Visits to the United States, 1841-46. *Second Edition.* Plates. 4 Vols. Post 8vo. 24s.

Geological Evidences of the Antiquity of Man. *Second Edition.* Illustrations. 8vo. 14s.
MAHON'S (Lord)
History of England, from the Peace of Utrecht to the Peace of Versailles, 1713--83. *Library Edition*, 7 Vols. 8vo. 93s. *Popular Edition*, 7 Vols. Post 8vo. 35s.

"Forty-Five;" a Narrative of the Rebellion in Scotland. Post 8vo. 3s.

History of British India from its Origin till the Peace of 1783. Post 8vo. 3s. 6d.

Spain under Charles the Second; 1690 to 1700. *Second Edition.* Post 8vo. 6s. 6d.

Life of William Pitt, with Extracts from his MS. Papers. *Second Edition.* Portraits. 4 Vols. Post 8vo. 42s.

Condé, surnamed the Great. Post 8vo, 3s. 6d.

Belisarius. *Second Edition.* Post 8vo. 10s. 6d.

Historical and Critical Essays. Post 8vo. 3s. 6d.

Miscellanies. *Second Edition.* Post 8vo. 5s. 6d.

Story of Joan of Arc. Fcap. 8vo. 1s.

Addresses. Fcap. 8vo. 1s.
McCLINTOCH'S (Capt. Sir F. L.)
Narrative of the Discovery of the Fate of Sir John Franklin and his Companions in the Arctic Seas. *Twelfth Thousand.* Illustrations. 8vo. 16s.
McCULLOCH'S (J. R.)
Collected Edition of Ricardo's Political I Works. With Notes and Memoir. *Second Edition.* 8vo. 16s.
MAINE (H. Sumner)

on Ancient Law: its Connection with the Early History of Society, and its Relation to Modern Ideas. **Second Edition**. 8vo. 12*s*.

MALCOLM'S (Sir John)

Sketches of Persia. **Third Edition**. Post 8vo. 3*s*. 6*d*.

MANSEL (Rev. H. L.)

Limits of Religious Thought Examined. Being the Bampton Lectures for 1858. **Fourth Edition**. Post 8vo. 7*s*. 6*d*.

MANTELL'S (Gideon A.)

Thoughts on Animalcules; or, the Invisible World, as revealed by the Microscope. **Second Edition**. Plates. 16mo. 6*s*.

MANUAL OF SCIENTIFIC ENQUIRY,

Prepared for the Use of Officers and Travellers. By various Writers. Edited by Sir J. F. Herschel and Rev. R. Main. **Third Edition**. Maps. Post 8vo. 9*s*. (**Published by order of the Lords of the Admiralty**.)

MARKHAM'S (Mrs.)

History of England, From the First Invasion by the Romans, down to the fourteenth year of Queen Victoria's Reign. 156*th Edition*. Woodcuts. 12mo. 6*s*.

History of France. From the Conquest by the Gauls, to the Death of Louis Philippe. **Sixtieth Edition**. Woodcuts. 12mo. 6*s*.

History of Germany. From the Invasion by Marius, to the present time. **Fifteenth Edition**. Woodcuts. 12mo. 6*s*.

History of Greece. From the Earliest Times to the Roman Conquest. By Dr. Wm. Smith. Woodcuts. 16mo. 3*s*. 6*d*.

History of Rome, from the Earliest Times to the Establishment of the Empire. By Dr. Wm. Smith. Woodcuts. 16mo. 3*s*. 6*d*.

MARKHAM'S (Clements, E.)

Travels in Peru and India, for the purpose of collecting Cinchona Plants, and introducing Bark into India. Maps and Illustrations. 8vo. 16*s*.

MARKLAND'S (J. H.)

Reverence due to Holy Places. **Third Edition**. Fcap. 8vo. 2*s*.

MARRYAT'S (Joseph)

History of Modern and Mediaeval Pottery and Porcelain. With a Description of the Manufacture. **Second Edition**. Plates and Woodcuts. 8vo. 31*s*. 6*d*.

MARRYAT'S (Horace)

Jutland, the Danish Isles, and Copenhagen. Illustrations. 2 Vols. Post 8vo. 24*s*.

Sweden and Isle of Gothland. Illustrations. 3 Vols. Post 8vo. 28*s*.

MATTHIAE'S (Augustus)

Greek Grammar for Schools. Abridged from the Larger Grammar. By Blomfield. **Ninth Edition**. Revised by Edwards. 12mo. 3*s*.

MAUREL'S (Jules)

Essay on the Character, Actions, and Writings of the Duke of Wellington. **Second Edition**. Fcap. 8vo. 1*s*. 6*d*.

MAXIMS AND HINTS

on Angling and Chess. By Richard Penn. Woodcuts. 12mo. 1*s*.

MAYNE'S (R. C.)

Four Years in British Columbia and Vancouver Island. Its Forests, Rivers, Coasts, and Gold Fields, and Resources for Colonisation. Illustrations. 8vo. 16*s*.

MELVILLE'S (Hermann)

Typee and Omoo; or, Adventures amongst the Marquesas and South Sea Islands. 2 Vols Post 8vo. 7*s*.

MENDELSSOHN'S

Life. By Jules Benedict. 8vo. 2*s*. 6*d*.

MEREDITH'S (Mrs. Charles)

Notes and Sketches of New South Wales. Post 8vo. 2*s*.

Tasmania, during a Residence of Nine Years. Illustrations. 2 Vols. Post 8vo. 18*s*.

MERRIFIELD (Mrs.)

on the Arts of Painting in Oil, Miniature Mosaic, and Glass; Gilding, Dyeing, and the Preparation of Colours and Artificial Gems. 2 Vols. 8vo. 30*s*.

MESSIAH (THE):

A Narrative of the Life, Travels, Death, Resurrection, and Ascension of our Blessed Lord. By A Layman. Author of the "Life of Bishop Ken." Map. 8vo. 18*s*.

MILLS' (Arthur)

India in 1858; A Summary of the Existing Administration--Political, Fiscal, and Judicial. *Second Edition*. Map. 8vo. 10*s*. 6*d*.

MILMAN'S (Dean)

History of Christianity, from the Birth of Christ to the Abolition of Paganism in the Roman Empire. *New Edition*. 3 Vols. 8vo. 36*s*.

Latin Christianity; including that of the Popes to the Pontificate of Nicholas V. *Second Edition*. 6 Vols. 8vo. 72*s*.

the Jews, from the Earliest Period, brought down to Modern Times. 3 Vols. 8vo. 36*s*.

Character and Conduct of the Apostles considered as an Evidence of Christianity. 8vo. 10*s*. 6*d*.

Life and Works of Horace. With 300 Woodcuts. 2 Vols. Crown 8vo. 30*s*.

Poetical Works. Plates. 3 Vols. Fcap. 8vo. 18*s*.

Fall of Jerusalem. Fcap. 8vo. 1*s*.

MILMAN'S (Capt. E. A.)

Wayside Cross. A Tale of the Carlist War. Post 8vo. 2*s*.

MILNES' (E. MONCKTON, LORD HOUGHTON)

Selections from Poetical Works. Fcap. 8vo.

MODERN DOMESTIC COOKERY.

Founded on Principles of Economy and Practical Knowledge, and adapted for Private Families. *New Edition*. Woodcuts. Fcap. 8vo. 5*s*.

MONASTERY AND THE MOUNTAIN CHURCH.

By Author of "Sunlight through the Mist." Woodcuts. 16mo. 4*s*.

MOORE'S (Thomas)

Life and Letters of Lord Byron. Plates. 6 Vols. Fcap. 8vo. 18*s*.

Life and Letters of Lord Byron. Portraits. Royal 8vo. 9*s*.

MOTLEY'S (J. L.)

History of the United Netherlands: from the Death of William the Silent to the Synod of Dort. Embracing the English-Dutch struggle against Spain; and a detailed Account of the Spanish Armada. Portraits. 2 Vols. 8vo. 30*s*.

MOUHOT'S (HENRI)

Siam Cambojia, and Lao; a Narrative of Travels and Discoveries. Illustrations. 8vo.

MOZLEY'S (Rev. J. B.)

Treatise on Predestination. 8vo. 14*s*.

Primitive Doctrine of Baptismal Regeneration. 8vo. 7*s*. 6*d*.

MUCK MANUAL (The) for Farmers.

A Practical Treatise on the Chemical Properties of Manures. By Frederick Falkner. *Second Edition*. Fcap. 8vo. 5*s*.

MUNDY'S (Gen.)

Pen and Pencil Sketches during a Tour in India. *Third Edition*. Plates. Post 8vo. 7*s*. 6*d*.

MUNDY'S (Admiral)

Account of the Italian Revolution, with Notices of Garibaldi, Francis II., and Victor Emmanuel. Post 8vo. 12*s*.

MUNRO'S (General Sir Thomas)

Life and Letters. By the Rev. G. R. Gleig. Post 8vo. 3*s*. 6*d*.

MURCHISON'S (Sir Roderick)

Russia in Europe and the Ural Mountains. With Coloured Maps, Plates, Sections, &c. 2 Vols. Royal 4to.

Siluria; or, a History of the Oldest Rocks containing Organic Remains. ***Third Edition***. Map and Plates. 8vo. 42*s*.

MURRAY'S RAILWAY READING.
For all classes of Readers.

[*The following are published*:]

WELLINGTON. BY LORD ELLEEMERE. 6*d*.

NIMROD ON THE CHASE, 1*s*.

ESSAYS FROM "THE TIMES." 2 Vols. 8*s*.

MUSIC AND DRESS. 1*s*.

LAYAND'S ACCOUNT OF NINHVEH. 5*s*.

MILMAN'S FALL OF JERUSALEM. 1*s*.

MAHON'S "FORTY-FIVE." 3*s*.

LIFE OF THEODORE HOOK. 1*s*.

DEEDS OF NAVAL DARING. 2 Vols. 5*s*.

THE HONEY BEE. 1*s*.

JAMES' AESOP'S FABLES. 2*s*. 6*d*.

NIMROD OF THE TURF. 1*s*. 6*d*.

OLIPHANT'S NEPAUL. 2*s*. 6*d*.

ART OF DINING. 1*s*. 6*d*.

BALLAM'S LITERARY ESSAYS. 2*s*.

MAHON'S JOAN OF ARC. 1*s*.

HEAD'S EMIGRANT. 2*s*. 6*d*.

NIMROD ON THE ROAD. 1*s*.

WILKINSON'S ANCIENT EGYPTIANS. 12*s*.

CROEEH ON THE GUILLOTINE. 1*s*

HOLLWAY'S NORWAY. 2*s*.

MAUREL'S WELLINGTON. 1*s*. 6*d*.

CAMPBELL'S LIFE OF BACON. 2*s*. 6*d*.

THE FLOWER GARDEN. 1*s*.

LOCKHART'S SPANISH BALLADS. 2*s*. 6*d*.

LUCAS ON HISTORY. 6*d*.

BEAUTIES OF BYRON. 3*s*.

TAYLOR'S NOTES FROM LIFE. 2*s*.

REJECTED ADDRESSES. 1s.
a PENN'S HINTS ON ANGLING. 1s.
    MUSIC AND DRESS.
    Reprinted from the "Quarterly Review." Fcap. 8vo.1s.
    NAPIER'S (Sir Wm.)
    English Battles and Sieges of the Peninsular War. **Third Edition**. Portrait. Post 8vo. 10s. 6d.

Life and Letters. Edited by H. A. Bruce, M.P. Portraits. 2 Vols. Crown 8vo.

Life of General Sir Charles Napier; chiefly derived from his Journals and Letters. **Second Edition**. Portraits, 4 Vols. Post 8vo. 48s.
    NAUTICAL ALMANACK.
    Royal 8vo. 2s. 6d (***Published by Authority***.)
    NAVY LIST (Quarterly).
    (***Published by Authority***.) Post 8vo. 2s. 6d.
    NELSON (Robert),
    Memoir of his Life and Times. By Rev. C. T. Secretan, M.A. Portrait. 8vo. 10s. 6d.
    NEWBOLD'S (Lieut.)
    Straits of Malacca, Penang, and Singapore. 2 Vols. 8vo. 26s.
    NEWDEGATE'S (C. N.)
    Customs' Tariffs of all Nations; collected and arranged up to the year 1855. 4to. 30s.
    NICHOLLS' (Sir George)
    History of the English Poor-Laws. 2 Vols. 8vo. 28s.

Irish and Scotch Poor-Laws. 2 Vols. 8vo. 26s.
    NICHOLLS' (Rev. H. G.)
    Historical Account of the Forest of Dean. Woodcuts, &c. Post 8vo. 10s. 6d.

Personalities of the Forest of Dean, its successive Officials, Gentry, and Commonalty. Post 8vo. 3s. 6d.
    NICOLAS' (Sir Harris)
    Historic Peerage of England. Exhibiting the Origin, Descent, and Present State of every Title of Peerage which has existed in this Country since the Conquest. By William Courthope. 8vo. 30s.
    NIMROD
    On the Chace--The Turf--and The Road. Reprinted from the "Quarterly Review." Woodcuts. Fcap. 8vo. 3s. 6d.
    O'CONNOR'S (R.)
    Field Sports of France; or, Hunting, Shooting, and Fishing on the Continent. Woodcuts. 12mo. 7s. 6d.
    OXENHAM'S (Rev. W.)
    English Notes for Latin Elegiacs; designed for early Proficients In the Art of Latin Versification, with Prefatory Rules of Composition in Elegiac Metre. **Fourth Edition**. 12mo. 3s. 6d.
    PAGET'S (John)
    Hungary and Transylvania. With Remarks on their Condition, Social, Political, and Economical. **Third Edition**. Woodcuts. 2 Vols. 8vo. 18s.
    PARIS' (Dr.)
    Philosophy in Sport made Science in Earnest; or, the First Principles of Natural Philosophy inculcated by aid of the Toys and Sports of Youth, **Ninth Edition**. Woodcuts. Post 8vo. 7s. 6d,
    PEEL'S (Sir Robert)
    Memoirs. Edited by Earl Stanhope and Mr. CARDWELL. 2 Vols. Post 8vo. 7s. 6d. each.
    PENN'S (Richard)
    Maxims and Hints for an Angler and Chess-player. **New Edition**. Woodcuts. Fcap. 8vo. 1s.
    PENROSE'S (F. C.)
    Principles of Athenian Architecture, and the Optical Refinements exhibited in the Construction of the Ancient Buildings at Athens, from a Survey. With 40 Plates. Folio. 5l. 5s.
    PERCY'S (John, M.D.)

Metallurgy; or, the Art of Extracting Metals from their Ores and adapting them to various purposes of Manufacture. **First Division**--Fuel, Fire-Clays, Copper, Zinc, and Brass. Illustrations. 8vo. 21*s*.

Iron and Steel, forming the **Second Division** of the above Work. Illustrations. 8vo.
    PHILLIPP (Charles Spencer March)
    On Jurisprudence. 8vo. 12*s*.
    PHILLIPS' (John)
    Memoirs of William Smith, the Geologist. Portrait. 8vo. 7*s*. 6*d*.

Geology of Yorkshire, The Coast, and Limestone District. Plates. 4to. Part I., 20*s*.--Part II., 30*s*.

Rivers, Mountains, and Sea Coast of Yorkshire. With Essays on the Climate, Scenery, and Ancient Inhabitants. **Second Edition**, Plates. 8vo. 15*s*.
    PHILPOTT'S (Bishop)
    Letters to the late Charles Butler, on the Theological parts of his "Book of the Roman Catholic Church;" with Remarks on certain Works of Dr. Milner and Dr. Lingard, and on some parts of the Evidence of Dr. Doyle. **Second Edition**. 8vo. 16*s*.
    POPE'S (Alexander)
    Life and Works. ***A New Edition***. Containing nearly 500 unpublished Letters. Edited with a New Life, Introductions and Notes. By Rev. Whitwell Elwin. Portraits, 8vo. (***In the Press***.)
    PORTER'S (Rev. J. L.)
    Five Years in Damascus. With Travels to Palmyra, Lebanon and other Scripture Sites. Map and Woodcuts. 2 Vols. Post 8vo. 21*s*.

Handbook for Syria and Palestine; including an Account of the Geography, History, Antiquities, and Inhabitants of these Countries, the Peninsula of Sinai, Edom, and the Syrian Desert. Maps. 2 Vols. Post 8vo. 24*s*.
    PRAYER-BOOK (The Illustrated),
    with 1000 Illustrations of Borders, Initials, Vignettes, &c. Medium 8vo.
    PRECEPTS FOR THE CONDUCT OF LIFE.
    Extracted from the Scriptures. **Second Edition**. Fcap. 8vo. 1*s*.
    PRINSEP'S (Jas.)
    Essays on Indian Antiquities, Historic, Numismatic, and Palaeographic, with Tables. Edited by Edward Thomas. Illustrations. 2 Vols. 8vo. 52*s*. 6*d*.
    PROGRESS OF RUSSIA IN THE EAST.
    An Historical Summary. Map. 8vo. 6*s*. 6*d*.
    PUSS IN BOOTS.
    With 12 Illustrations, By Otto Speckter. Coloured, 16mo. 2*s*. 6*d*.
    QUARTERLY REVIEW (The).
    8vo. 6*s*.
    RAWLINSON'S (Rev. George)
    Herodotus. A New English Version. Edited with Notes and Essays, Assisted by Sir. Henry Rawlinson and Sir J. G. Wilkinson. **Second Edition**. Maps and Woodcut. 4 Vols. 8vo. 48*s*.

Historical Evidences of the truth of the Scripture Records stated anew, the Bampton Lectures for 1839. **Second Edition**. 8vo. 14*s*.

History, Geography, and Antiquities of the Five Great Monarchies of the Ancient World. Illustrations. 8vo. Vol. I., Chaldaea and Assyria. 16*s*. Vols. II. and III., Babylon, Media, and Persia.
    REJECTED ADDRESSES (The).
    By James and Horace Smith. Fcap. 8vo. 1*s*., or **Fine Paper**, Portrait, fcap. 8vo. 5*s*.
    REYNOLDS' (Sir Joshua)
    His Life and Times. From Materials collected by the late C. R. Leslie, R.A.. Edited by Tom Taylor. Portraits and Illustrations. 2 Vols. 8vo.
    RICARDO'S (David)
    Political Works. With a Notice of his Life and Writings. By J. R. M'Culloch. ***New Edition***. 8vo. 16*s*.
    RIPA'S (Father)
    Memoirs during Thirteen Years' Residence at the Court of Peking. From the Italian. Post 8vo. 2*s*.

ROBERTSON'S (Canon)
History of the Christian Church, From the Apostolic Age to the Concordat of Worms, A.D. 1123. **Second Edition**. 3 Vols. 8vo. 38*s*.

Life of Becket. Illustrations. Post 8vo. 9*s*.
ROBINSON'S (Rev. Dr.)
Biblical Researches in the Holy Land. Being a Journal of Travels in 1838, and of Later Researches in 1852. Maps. 3 Vols. 8vo. 36*s*.
ROMILLY'S (Sir Samuel)
Memoirs and Political Diary. By his Sons. **Third Edition**. Portrait. 2 Vols. Fcap. 8vo. 12*s*.
ROSS'S (Sir James)
Voyage of Discovery and Research in the Southern and Antarctic Regions, 1839-43. Plates. 2 Vols. 8vo. 36*s*.
ROWLAND'S (David)
Manual of the English Constitution; Its Rise, Growth, and Present State. Post 8vo. 10*s*. 6*d*.

Laws of Nature the Foundation of Morals. Post 8vo.
RUNDELL'S (Mrs.)
Domestic Cookery, adapted for Private Families. **New Edition**. Woodcuts. Fcap. 8vo. 5*s*.
RUSSELL'S (J. RUTHERFURD, M.D.)
Art of Medicine--Its History and its Heroes. Portraits. 8vo. 14*s*.
RUSSIA;
A Memoir of the Remarkable Events which attended the Accession of the Emperor Nicholas. By Baron M. Korff. 8vo. 10*s*. 6*d*.
RUXTON'S (George F.)
Travels in Mexico; with Adventures among the Wild Tribes and Animals of the Prairies and Rocky Mountains. Post 8vo. 3*s*. 6*d*.
SALE'S (Lady)
Journal of the Disasters in Affghanistan. Post 8vo. 12*s*.
SALE'S (Sir Robert)
Brigade in Affghanistan. With an Account of the Defence of Jellalabad. By Rev. G. R. Gleig. Post 8vo. 2*s*.
SANDWITH'S (Humphry)
Siege of Kars. Post 8vo. 3*s*. 6*d*.
SCOTT'S (G. Gilbert)
Secular and Domestic Architecture, Present and Future. **Second Edition**. 8vo, 9*s*.

(Master of Baliol) Sermons Preached before the University of Oxford. Post 8vo. 8*s*. 6*d*.
SCROPE'S (G. P.)
Geology and Extinct Volcanoes of Central France. **Second Edition**. Illustrations. Medium 8vo. 30*s*.
SELF-HELP.
With Illustrations of Character and Conduct. By Samuel Smiles. 50*th* **Thousand**. Post 8vo. 6*s*.
SENIOR'S (N. W.)
Suggestions on Popular Education. 8vo. 9*s*.
SHAFTESBURY (Lord Chancellor);
Memoirs of his Early Life. With his Letters, &c. By W. D. Christie. Portrait. 8vo. 10*s*. 6*d*.
SHAW'S (T. B.)
Student's Manual of English Literature. Edited, with Notes and Illustrations, by Dr. Wm. Smith. Post 8vo. 7*s*. 6*d*.
SIERRA LEONE;
Described in Letters to Friends at Home. By A Lady. Post 8vo. 3*s*. 6*d*.
SIMMONS
on Courts-Martial, 5*th* **Edition**. 8vo. 14*s*.
SMILES' (Samuel)
Lives of British Engineers; from the Earliest Period to the Death of Robert Stephenson; with an account of their Principal Works, and a History of Inland Communication in Britain. Portraits and Illustrations. 3 Vols. 8vo. 63*s*.

Industrial Biography: Iron-Workers and Tool Makers. Post 8vo, 7*s*. 6*d*.

Story of George Stephenson's Life. Woodcuts. Post 8vo. 6*s*.

Self Help. With Illustrations of Character and Conduct. Post 8vo. 6*s*.

Workmen's Earnings, Savings, and Strikes. Fcap. 8vo. 1*s*. 6*d*.
SOMERVILLE'S (Mary)
Physical Geography. **Fifth Edition**. Portrait. Post 8vo. 9*s*.

Connexion of the Physical Sciences. **Ninth Edition**. Woodcuts. Post 8vo. 9*s*.
SOUTH'S (John F.)
Household Surgery; or, Hints on Emergencies. **Seventeenth Thousand**. Woodcuts. Fcp. 8vo. 4*s*. 6*d*.
SMITH'S (Dr. Wm.)
Dictionary of the Bible; its Antiquities, Biography, Geography, and Natural History. Illustrations. 3 Vols. 8vo. 105*s*.;

Greek and Roman Antiquities. **2nd Edition**. Woodcuts. 8vo. 42*s*.

Biography and Mythology. Woodcuts. 3 Vols. 8vo. 5*l*. 15*s*. 6*d*.

Geography. Woodcuts. 2 Vols. 8vo. 30*s*.

Latin-English Dictionary. 9*th Thousand*. 8vo. 21*s*.

Classical Dictionary. 10*th Thousand*. Woodcuts. 8vo. 18*s*.

Smaller Classical Dictionary. 20*th Thousand*. Woodcuts. Crown 8vo. 7*s*. 6*d*.

Dictionary of Antiquities. 20*th Thousand*. Woodcuts. Crown 8vo. 7*s*. 6*d*.

Latin-English Dictionary. 25*th Thousand*. 12mo. 7*s*. 6*d*.

Latin-English Vocabulary; for those reading Phaedrus, Cornelius Nepos, and Caesar. **Second Edition**. 12mo. 3*s*. 6*d*.

Principia Latina-- Part I. Containing a Grammar, Delectus, and Exercise Book, with Vocabularies, 3rd **Edition**. 12mo. 3*s*. 6*d*.

Part II. A Reading-book, containing Mythology, Geography, Roman Antiquities, and History. With Notes and Dictionary. Second Edition. 12mo. 3*s*. 6*d*.

Part III. A Latin Poetry Book. Containing:--Hexameters and Pentameters; Eclogae Ovidianae; Latin Prosody. 12mo. 3*s*. 6*d*.

Part IV. Latin Prose Composition. Containing Rules of Syntax, with copious Examples, Explanations of Synonyms, and a systematic course of Exercises on the Syntax. 12mo. 3*s*. 6*d*.

Graeca; a First Greek Course. A Grammar, Delectus, and Exercise-book, with Vocabularies. By H. E. Button, M.A. 3*rd Edition*. 12mo. 3*s*. 6*d*.

Student's Greek Grammar. By Professor Curtius. Post 8vo. 7*s*. 6*d*.

Latin Grammar. Post 8vo. 7*s*. 6*d*.

Smaller Greek Grammar. Abridged from the above. 12mo. 3*s*. 6*d*.

Latin Grammar. Abridged from the above. 12mo. 3*s*. 6*d*.
STANLEY'S (Canon)
History of the Eastern Church. **Second Edition**. Plans. 8vo. 16*s*.

Jewish Church. From Abraham to Samuel. **Second Edition**. Plans. 8vo. 16*s*.

Sermons on Evangelical and Apostolical Teaching. **Second Edition**. Post 8vo. 7s. 6d.

St. Paul's Epistles to the Corinthians. Second Edition. 8vo. 18s.

Historical Memorials of Canterbury. **Third Edition**. Woodcuts. Post 8vo. 7s. 6d.

Sinai and Palestine, in Connexion with their History. **Sixth Edition**. Map. 8vo. 16s.

Bible in the Holy Land. Being Extracts from the above work. **Second Edition**. Woodcuts. Fcp. 8vo. 2s. 6d.

Addresses and Charges of Bishop Stanley. With Memoir. **Second Edition**. 8vo. 10s. 6d.

Sermons Preached during the Tour of H.R.H. the Prince of Wales in the East, with Notices of some of the Places Visited. 8vo. 9s.
    SOUTHEY'S (Robert)
    Book of the Church. **Seventh Edition**. Post 8vo. 7s. 6d.

Lives of Bunyan and Cromwell. Post 8vo. 2s.
    SPECKTER'S (Otto)
    Puss in Boots. With 12 Woodcuts. Square 12mo. 1s. 6d, plain, or 2s. 6d. coloured.

Charmed Roe; or, the Story of the Little Brother and Sister. Illustrated. 16mo.
    ST. JOHN'S (Charles)
    Wild Sports and Natural History of the Highlands. Post 8vo. 3s. 6d.
    ST. JOHN'S (Bayle)
    Adventures in the Libyan Desert and the Oasis of Jupiter Ammon. Woodcuts. Post 8vo. 2s.
    STANHOPE'S (Earl)
    Life of William Pitt. With Extracts from his M.S. Papers. **Second Edition**. Portraits. 2 Vols. Post 8vo. 42s.

Miscellanies. **Second Edition**. Post 8vo. 6s. 6d.
    STEPHENSONS' (George and Robert)
    Lives. Forming the Third Volume of Smiles' "Lives of British Engineers." Portrait and Illustrations. 8vo. 21s.
    STOTHARD'S (Thos.)
    Life. With Personal Reminiscences. By Mrs. Bray. With Portrait and 60 Woodcuts. 4to. 21s.
    STREET'S (G. E.)
    Brick and Marble Architecture of Italy in the Middle Ages. Plates. 8vo. 21s.
    STUDENT'S HUME.
    A History of England from the Invasion of Julius Caesar to the Revolution of 1688. Based on the Work by David Hume. Continued to 1858. **Twenty-fifth Thousand**, Woodcuts. Post 8vo. 7s, 6d.

A Smaller History of England. 12mo. 3s. 6d.

HISTORY OF FRANCE; From the Earliest Times to the Establishment of the Second Empire, 1852. Edited by Dr. Wm. Smith. Woodcuts. Post 8vo. 7s. 6d.

HISTORY OF GREECE; from the Earliest Times to the Roman Conquest. With the History of Literature and Art. By Wm. Smith, LL.D. 25**th Thousand**. Woodcuts. Crown 8vo. 7s. 6d. (Questions. 2s.)

A Smaller History of Greece. 12mo. 3s. 6d.

HISTORY OF ROME; from the Earliest Times to the Establishment of the Empire. With the History of Literature and Art. By H. G. Liddell, D.D. 25**th Thousand**. Woodcuts. Crown 8vo. 7s. 6d.

A Smaller History of Rome. 12mo. 3s. 6d.

GIBBON; an Epitome of the History of the Decline and Fall of the Roman Empire. Incorporating the Researches of Recent Commentators. *9th Thousand*. Woodcuts. Post 8vo. 7s. 6d.

MANUAL OF ANCIENT GEOGRAPHY. By Rev. W. L. Bevan, M. A. Edited by Dr. Wm. Smith. Woodcuts. Post 8vo. 7s. 6d.

THE ENGLISH LANGUAGE. By George P. Marsh. Edited by Dr. Wm. Smith. Post 8vo. 7s. 6d.

ENGLISH LITERATURE. By T. B. Shaw. Edited by Dr. Wm. SMITH. Post 8vo. 7s. 6d.
 SWIFT'S (JONATHAN)
Life, Letters, Journals, and Works. By John Forster. 8vo. (*In Preparation*.)
 SYME'S (Professor)
Principles of Surgery, 5*th Edition*. 8vo. 14s.
 TAIT'S (Bishop)
Dangers and Safeguards of Modern Theology. 8vo. 9s.
 TAYLOR'S (Henry)
Notes from Life. Fcap. 8vo. 2s.
 THOMSON'S (Archbishop)
Lincoln's Inn Sermons. 8vo. 10s. 6d.
 THOMSON'S (Dr.)
New Zealand. Illustrations. 2 Vols. Post 8vo. 24s.
 THREE-LEAVED MANUAL OF FAMILY PRAYER;
arranged so as to save the trouble of turning the Pages backwards and forwards. Royal 8vo. 2s.
 TOCQUEVILLE'S (M. De)
State of France before the Revolution, 1789, and on the Causes of that Event. Translated by Henry Reeve, 8vo. 14s.
 TRANSACTIONS OF THE ETHNOLOGICAL SOCIETY OF LONDON.
New Series. Vols. I. and II. 8vo.
 TREMENHEERE'S (H. S.)
Political Experience of the Ancients, in its bearing on Modern Times. Fcap. 8vo. 2s. 6d.
 TRISTRAM'S (H. B.)
Great Sahara. Illustrations. Post 8vo. 15s.
 TWISS' (Horace)
Public and Private Life of Lord Chancellor Eldon, with Selections from his Correspondence. Portrait. *Third Edition*. 2 Vols. Post 8vo. 21s.
 TYNDALL'S (John)
Glaciers of the Alps. With an account of Three Years' Observations and Experiments on their General Phenomena. Woodcuts. Post 8vo. 14s.
 TYTLER'S (Patrick Fraser)
Memoirs. By Rev. J. W. Burgon, M.A. 8vo. 9s.
 VAUGHAN'S (Rev. Dr.)
Sermons preached in Harrow School. 8vo. 10s.
 VENABLES' (Rev. R. L.)
Domestic Scenes in Russia. Post 8vo. 5s.
 VOYAGE to the Mauritius.
By Author of "Paddiana." Post 8vo. 9s. 6d.
 WAAGEN'S (Dr.)
Treasures of Art in Great Britain. Being an Account of the Chief Collections of Paintings, Sculpture, Manuscripts, Miniatures, &c. &c., in this Country. Obtained from Personal Inspection during Visits to England. 4 Vols. 8vo.
 WALKS AND TALKS.
A Story-book for Young Children. By Aunt Ida. With Woodcuts. 16mo. 3s.
 WALSH'S (Sir John)
Practical Results of the Reform Bill of 1832. 8vo. 5s. 6d.
 WATT'S (James)
Life. With Selections from his Private and Public Correspondence. By James P. Muirhead, M.A. *Second Edition*. Portrait. 8vo. 10s.

Origin and Progress of his Mechanical Inventions. By J. P. Muirhead. Plates. 3 Vols. 8vo. 45*s*.
WELLINGTON'S (The Duke of)
Despatches during his various Campaigns. Compiled from Official and other Authentic Documents. By Col. Gurwood, C.B. 8 Vols. 8vo. 21*s*. each.

Supplementary Despatches, and other Papers. Edited by his Son. Vols. I. to IX. 8vo. 20*s*. each.

Selections from his Despatches and General Orders. By Colonel Gurwood. 8vo. 18*s*.

Speeches in Parliament. 2 Vols. 8vo. 42*s*.
WILKINSON'S (Sir J. G.)
Popular Account of the Private Life, Manners, and Customs of the Ancient Egyptians. **New Edition**. Revised and Condensed. With 500 Woodcuts. 2 Vols. Post 8vo. 12*s*.

Dalmatia and Montenegro; with a Journey to Mostar in Hertzegovina, and Remarks on the Slavonic Nations. Plates and Woodcuts. 2 Vols. 8vo. 42*s*.

Handbook for Egypt.--Thebes, the Nile, Alexandria, Cairo, the Pyramids, Mount Sinai, &c. Map. Post 8vo. 15*s*.

On Colour, and on the Necessity for a General Diffusion of Taste among all Classes; with Remarks on laying out Dressed or Geometrical Gardens. With Coloured Illustrations and Woodcuts. 8vo. 18*s*.
WILKINSON'S (G. B.)
Working Man's Handbook to South Australia; with Advice to the Farmer, and Detailed Information for the several Classes of Labourers and Artisans. Map. 18mo. 1*s*. 6*d*.
WILSON'S (Bishop Daniel,)
Life, with Extracts from his Letters and Journals. By Rev. Josiah Bateman. **Second Edition**. Illustrations. Post 8vo. 9*s*.
WILSON'S (General Sir Robert)
Secret History of the French Invasion of Russia, and Retreat of the French Army, 1812. **Second Edition**. 8vo. 15*s*.

Private Diary of Travels, Personal Services, and Public Events, during Missions and Employments in Spain, Sicily, Turkey, Russia, Poland, Germany, &c. 1812-14. 2 Vols. 8vo. 26*s*.

Autobiographical Memoirs. Containing an Account of his Early Life down to the Peace of Tilsit. Portrait. 2 Vols. 8vo. 26*s*.
WOOD'S (Lieut.)
Voyage up the Indus to the Source of the River Oxus, by Kabul and Badakhshan. Map. 8vo. 14*s*.
WORDSWORTH'S (Canon)
Journal of a Tour in Athens and Attica. **Third Edition**, Plates. Post 8vo. 8*s*. 6*d*.

Pictorial, Descriptive, and Historical Account of Greece, with a History of Greek Art, by G. Schaef, F.S.A. **New Edition**. With 600 Woodcuts. Royal 8vo. 28*s*.
WORNUM (Ralph).
A Biographical Dictionary of Italian Painters: with a Table of the Contemporary Schools of Italy. By a Lady. Post 8vo. 6*s*. 6*d*.
YOUNG'S (Dr. Thos.)
Life and Miscellaneous Works, edited by Dean Peacock and John Leitch. Portrait and Plates. 4 Vols. 8vo. 15*s*. each.

www.ingramcontent.com/pod-product-compliance
Lightning Source LLC
Chambersburg PA
CBHW050656300725
30342CB00028B/469